CRICKET

A History of its growth and development throughout the world

Rowland Bowen

CRICKET

Introduction by C. L. R. James

A history of its growth and development throughout the world

Eyre & Spottiswoode · London

First published 1970
by Eyre & Spottiswoode (Publishers) Ltd
11 New Fetter Lane, London EC4
© 1970 Rowland Bowen
Printed in Great Britain
by Cox & Wyman Ltd
Fakenham, Norfolk

SBN 413 27860 3

To W.H.J.R.

Who, having very much the same kind of mind, intolerant of stupidity, incompetence and knavishness, has nevertheless influenced me at least to modify my own intolerance in writing and compiling this account.

Contents

CONTENTS

Illustrations

A★   9

The drawing of Lord's on the title page is based on plate 28

Author's Preface

Several books have given a history of the game as their purpose but of all these only three have actually been so entitled. The first, and easily the best, was that by H. S. Altham; and it was followed many years later by two more, by Eric Parker and by Roy Webber.

Altham's work started as a series of articles on the history of the game in the early years of *The Cricketer*: later he pulled them together, revised them in the light of much fresh knowledge then becoming available, and published them in book form in 1926. As a work, that first edition has not been surpassed either by later editions or by histories from other hands.

There is, however, a criticism which can be made of Altham's book, that it is less a history of cricket than an account of cricket's rise in stature to its modern international level, on the one hand, and, on the other, of cricket played by a certain, comparatively narrow section of the population of these islands and even then indeed of only one part of these islands. In some ways its concentration on public school, Varsity and Test cricket, is similar to those histories of England which tell a great deal about the kings and queens, much about the barons, something about parliament but hardly anything of England itself. (Such histories of Scotland that exist have rarely been so confined.)

It is my purpose with this volume to try and tell the full history of the game, and without confining the survey to one class, or one section or, indeed, one country. In order to achieve this much has to be said which will be found in no previous history of the game; at the same time, I have not devoted any, or much, space to commentaries, on, for example, Test matches, so that there remains much in other histories which will not be found here.

However, at the end of the book is an extensive series of synoptic chronological charts showing what was going on and where, from the earliest days until our own. For the last century and a little further the chronology by areas is shown in different columns, so that, for example, one may at once compare what was happening in the West Indies with what was happening in South Africa. These charts contain many progressive records occurring in each country, and much administrative detail too. Bibliography also features, in terms of the earliest, and also the most noteworthy publications in each area. Annual results of various competitions are not shown: they are summarized when each current competition began. Nor are the results of Test and other international matches which can be readily found in a variety of reference books. But much *is* given which would only be found with great difficulty otherwise: acknowledgement is due to *Wisden*, to *The Cricket Quarterly*, and to the *New Zealand Cricketer* for the original versions of these chronological tables.

It is the provision of these tables which has made it possible not to overload the text with figures of various kinds, though some are unavoidable.

Finally, if one thing is certain, it is that this book will not achieve the literary merit of Altham's work.

Eastbourne, Spring 1969   ROWLAND BOWEN

Apart from additions to the Appendices and amplification to the text on some important matters of detail, it has only been found necessary to modify the text in the light of the events involving South Africa in 1969 and 1970 by adding the last four lines on page 235.

Mullion, Autumn 1970   R.B.

Author's Acknowledgements

I wish to acknowledge the great help derived from the wise and useful comments made by R. L. Arrowsmith, John Goulstone, and C. L. R. James who read this book in manuscript. But for them it would have been a much worse book. If it nevertheless exhibits some opinions that appear to be contrary to those held by them, it is not that they made no comment but that in some instances I preferred my own opinion. On the whole, where contrary opinions were offered I have heeded them.

My thanks must also go to very many others and, apart from those already mentioned, to the following for significant or general assistance over a long period of time: Kenneth Bridger, Gerald Brodribb, Arthur Carman, J. Carter, John Ferguson, P. W. Filby, Ernest K. Gross, L. E. S. Gutteridge, H. R. Holmes, R. G. Ingelse, E. H. Jackson, David Kelly, Diana Rait-Kerr, Donald King, Edward Knight, John Melluish, Patrick Morrah, Roger Page, V. Pattabhiraman, S. S. Perera, S. J. Reddy, David Roylance, Norman Stanley, Douglas Steptoe, A. M. C. Thorburn, A. H. Wagg and Keith Warsop. There are many others, alas no longer with us, and if they are not referred to in the book, they already have their full reward anyway. These and others have provided me with information and views which have all gone to support the text or the many details in the Appendices of this book. Most of them in their modesty, will not realize what help they have been.

Next I must thank J. H. St J. McIlwaine and L. E. S. Gutteridge for their help in locating in British, French and North American libraries, lexicographical and other books, sometimes of a very rare nature, which have contributed materially to what I have had to say not only about the early origins of the game but even up to the end of the eighteenth century. John McIlwaine has also been responsible for the detailed Index which is not only a guide to the entire volume but a handy reference tool to the Appendices. Special thanks are also due to Bernard Hollowood for his decorations in the appendices done in the restricted time which was all that could be given him between receiving the page proofs from the printer and returning them.

I would also like to express my thanks to those, dead or alive, between whom and myself there is a measure of disagreement: but for them it is certain that I would never have started writing about the game, probable that I would never have started *The Cricket Quarterly*, and more than possible that this book would never have been written. My first impulse to writing anything about the game was solely to correct error: that led me on, and on. In ten years or so of research and writing I have been astonished at the way long-accepted facts have proved on investigation to have been no facts at all, and much-cherished opinion quite legendary: in establishing many fresh new facts, I hope I have not also laid the foundation for other myths! My sole concern, in writing, in researching, in reviewing and in publishing has been the propagation of truth: with one exception – about South Africa I have also been concerned with maintaining principles, on which people may differ though not, in my view, without sinning for, in words widely believed to have been due to Citizen Tom Paine who occurs early in this book, 'we hold these Truths to be self-evident, that all Men are created equal, that they are endowed by their Creator with certain unalienable Rights, that among these are Life, Liberty, and the Pursuit of Happiness'. Sir Pelham Warner used often to say that cricket knows no bounds of race, creed or colour. It is more than a pity that irritation is to be found on some faces when these words are repeated to them.

Note
Throughout this book the symbol ⋆ is used with its normal cricket signification of 'not out' when attached to an individual innings, and of an unbroken partnership when attached to a partnership

Introduction

This history of cricket by Rowland Bowen is a type of cricket history which I have never read before and whose forebears, either in method or material, as far as I know, do not exist. Let me add that I do not expect within the next generation to see any book of this kind and this quality again. Now I have committed myself. I have broken all the rules. I have *not* eschewed superlatives, I have indulged myself superlatively, not only in retrospect but in prospect. All I can say is what Luther said when faced with a fundamental crisis: 'I can do no other'.

The best thing that I can do is to try to show by example what the author is doing. Everybody knows more or less what is meant by the Golden Age of cricket. Ask anyone who has the faintest knowledge and he will tell you it is the age which began towards the end of the nineteenth century and continued at least to 1914. It was the age of a new style of batsman who took batting into reaches undreamed of by their ancestors; Ranjitsinhji, Fry, A. C. MacLaren, R. E. Foster, Johnny Tyldesley, J. B. Hobbs, R. H. Spooner. The same phenomenon appeared in Australia, Victor Trumper, R. A. Duff and Clem Hill: this revolution in batting caused a revolution in bowling and the strategy of captaincy and field-placing. Batsmen (and bowlers too) were great individualists; matches were dramatic contests, great crowds poured out to see not only Tests but lesser games as never before and never since. When Rowland Bowen writes on this period, we see what, quite uniquely, for him makes the age Golden:

'In this country it was the period when a Board of Control was set up: when Test match selection became a central responsibility: when overseas tour selection became, in a slightly different form, also a central responsibility; when the control of county cricket was also centralized; and when minor county cricket was first organized. It was a period which spanned the first South African tour to this country and the Triangular Tournament of 1912: at the beginning it almost took in the start of the Currie Cup in South Africa, and even more closely almost took in the start of the Sheffield Shield in Australia, while the start of the Plunket Shield in New Zealand came later on in the period. The New Zealand Cricket Council was established in 1895: the South African Cricket Association a shade earlier: the Australian Cricket Council just before, but ended not long after the start and was replaced after a few years by the Australian Board of Control. Its commencement very nearly saw the start of the Bombay Tournament in India: shortly after that it only just failed to see the first All-India tour to England but did succeed in seeing it just before its close, while almost throughout it saw that great Imperial symbol, Ranji. Its start just missed the rise of international touring in South America, and almost completely took in the rise of West Indian cricket. It saw the greatest age of Philadelphian cricket.'

He is not as yet near the end. He continues:

'And at home, it saw the formation of the Scottish Cricket Union, the formation of county competitions in Scotland and North Wales, and the very early beginnings of what was to become the Club Cricket Conference. The serious development of League Cricket came about during the period and the start had preceded it by only a few years. In legislation, the last modernizing change in the Laws took place: the six-ball over, the optional follow-on, the raising of the limit of the follow-on, the first new ball rule, and the steady extension of the period within which one could declare (not finally consummated till after the Second War), and facts were faced, however unpalatable, in recognizing that drawn matches were inevitable when points were awarded for a first innings lead towards the end of the period. Some attempt also was made to make the first-class game more popular by tentative experiments with a Saturday start. (Great matches had generally started on Mondays and Thursdays for very many years.) Finally, Yorkshire, to its praise, in this period became the first county to ensure all the year round payment for its players as well as to establish a provident fund for them when retired: a very significant social change, and not hitherto attempted or even thought of by any other county and by no means fully emulated by all counties up to the present time. It is difficult to think of any other period of the game's history when so many important things happened.'

That is how Rowland Bowen sees the game. That is his History, from the earliest times to the present day.

We go on to full details of the game as played from 1894 till 1914. We learn that, in 1896, Ranji beat a record that W. G. had set up in 1871. In 1899 Ranji was the first batsman to pass 3,000 runs in a first-class season and in 1900 he made another 3,000 runs. Our historian does not omit these stand-bys. We have an original glimpse of Hobbs, 'perhaps the most successful opening batsman who ever lived', who was so successful, we are told, because he had 'an instinctive understanding of his partner, whether it was Tom Hayward, Andy Sandham, Wilfred Rhodes or Herbert Sutcliffe'. 'In 1888, league cricket had commenced in the Birmingham area. Within a few years leagues had become the normal way to play club cricket in much of the Midlands and all the North of England, later spreading into Scotland and Wales. This kind of cricket was played "harder" '. This we are told was not in accordance with southern tastes, nor was it to be for nearly three generations. Those who played country-house cricket (which is fully analysed) adopted a hostile attitude towards the game as played in the leagues. We take up school cricket in that period, and club cricket. Then, and on the same scale, the author deals with 1894–1914 abroad, and abroad includes the Fiji Islands, Brazil, in fact wherever a ball was bowled. Part three of the chapter 'The Golden Age' deals with 'Conduct of the game and administration'. But we are not nearly finished with the Golden Age despite the fact that the three sections together comprise 33 pages.

To keep our eye steadily on one period (the only way we can visualize the whole) let us stick to the Golden Age. In the Appendices under Other Countries between 1894 and 1914, there are 33 entries; under Canada and the United States, there are 63; under India, 25; under New Zealand, 77 entries. For what I hope I can call without offence the big cricketing countries: under West Indies there are 57 entries; under Southern Africa there are 99 entries; under England there are 109 entries and under Australia there are 133. The first entry of the appendix for Pakistan begins in 1947, so it is obvious that there can be no comparison with other periods of the Golden Age.

I will not dare to select what interests me specially in the appendices in the Golden Age. I only point to their comprehensive and detailed character. It so happens that I find myself interested in the statistics I read there about one famous cricketer, Spofforth, the great Australian bowler. In such a plethora of detail about every country, the reader is certain to see statistics and events which interest him particularly. Spofforth interests me: for example I note that in 1878 at Lord's, Spofforth performed the hat-trick against the MCC, the first time that this had been done by an Australian in English first-class cricket. Again in 1878–9 Spofforth performed the hat-trick in the English first innings of the Melbourne Test, the first occasion in a Test match. In 1881–2 in a minor match in Australia, Spofforth took all 20 wickets for 48 runs, all bowled. In 1882 in a Test match in England, Spofforth took 14 wickets for 90. We learn that no Australian has bettered this in Test matches and it has been equalled only by C. V. Grimmett against South Africa in 1931-2. In first-class matches in 1884, Spofforth took 207 wickets at an average of 13·25 runs per wicket. He is the first of only two touring Australians to take over 200 wickets in an English touring season. Against an English eleven at Birmingham, he took seven wickets for three runs. What strikes me is that he is not only a famous man historically, but like W. G. in his great years, what he did after all these years still remains unparalleled.

I shall select, to give some idea of what they are; entries for two years in the Appendices covering England and the West Indies:

England 1902	First Tests played at Edgbaston and at Bramall Lane, the latter being the only Test ever played in Sheffield. A new match aggregate of 1427 runs for 34 wickets set up in the game between Sussex and Surrey at Hastings. The first MCC tour to Holland, captain A. H. Hornby. *Ayres' Cricket Companion* first appeared, annually until 1932. W. H. Hyman scored the then record number of sixes – 32, in his innings of 359* for Bath Association *v.* Thornbury at Thornbury; the record for many years. The record six-wicket partnership in England of 428 made by W. W. Armstrong (172*) and M. A. Noble (284) for Australians *v.* Sussex at Hove. K. S. Ranjitsinjhi (230) and W. Newham (153) made 344 for the seventh wicket, the English first-class record, for Sussex *v.* Essex at Leyton. Sussex made their record score of 705 for eight wickets declared *v.* Surrey at Hastings. Scottish County Championship inaugurated.
West Indies 1913	Second tour by MCC (captain, A. W. F. Somerset): won two and lost one of the representative matches. In the match *v.* Barbados, A. W. F. Somerset (55) and W. C. Smith (126) added 167 for MCC's last wicket (the West Indian record for that wicket), the Barbados pair, P. H. Tarilton (157) and H. W. Ince (57*) having already made 100 for the Barbados last wicket in the same match, a most unusual occurrence in any class of cricket. P. H. Tarilton made 1,084 runs, average 83·38, in all matches in the Barbados season, the first time it had been done in that island. Sir Hesketh Bell presented a cup for competition on a knock-out basis amongst the Leeward Islands, of which he was then Governor. The first winners were Antigua. E. R. D. Moulder carried his bat for 104* for West Indies *v.* MCC at Bourda, the first time anyone had carried his bat for a century in first-class cricket.

Doubtless, readers in Australia, South Africa, New Zealand, India and Other Countries will turn eagerly to those special sections which deal with them.

I read the West Indies appendix recognizing much, but I read them all, and members of Other Countries would recognize me as a brother.

There is such a mass of material in this book on the game and relevant matters that I can allow myself references here to only two. The first because there is not much available about it for the ordinary reader of cricket history and, also because it is the kind of information that will startle anybody. 'In the United States,' Rowland Bowen writes, 'this was the hey-day of cricket in and around Philadelphia – cricket which sustained the game in Boston and Baltimore, in New York and even in an almost typically English country-house form in Virginia. Cricket in America is so much regarded now as a joke or a curiosity that it is difficult to realize that it was in this period that the prospect of Philadelphia actually playing Test matches one day was not to be laughed at. Let us consider a few of the events of the Golden Age of cricket as they affected Philadelphia: for four years around the turn of the century, there were two competing monthly cricket magazines in that *city* – two! Few countries are able to support one nowadays. . . . Look at the tours: from 1896 to 1914 Haverford College undertook five tours to England to play other schools, and clubs. It was many years before any English school toured abroad. The Gentlemen of Philadelphia came here three times, and each time their record was good and some of the play remarkable. Three of the constituent clubs each made tours here to play clubs and country teams and ground teams. There were six trips to Bermuda and to Jamaica. Twelve teams from these islands made tours to North America and chiefly to Philadelphia, and these included Kent, the first county to tour abroad, the MCC, and many of the leading players of the time, Ranji among them. It was an extremely pleasant ending to a cricket season to cross the Atlantic in early or mid-September and play on till October in the marvellous surroundings to be found there. There were three Australian tours, official in 1896 (when again they managed to lose to Philadelphia in one of their matches by an innings) and 1912, and unofficial but hardly less powerful in 1913. And never was Philadelphia found to be playing above its class.'

Rowland Bowen goes on to say, 'Philadelphia had one very great player, of world class – John Barton King', but I am not going to say a word about John Barton King because anybody who knows anything about cricket knows that this American from Philadelphia proved himself to be one of the finest fast bowlers the game has ever known.

The second point I select is the concern of the founder and editor of *The Cricket Quarterly* with cricket periodicals. Here I would only mention one instance, taken from the appendices which I find myself reading as much as the text. I see that in 1877 the *American Cricketer* was founded, weekly till the end of the century, monthly until its demise (though very irregular towards the end) in 1929, and thus the longest lasting of any cricket magazine.

Who in the name of Heaven would have guessed that of a publication on cricket in America?

As much for the information as to insist upon the value of the appendices, we read that in the United Provinces (of India) instructional books on the game appeared in Urdu and Hindi; 'probably elsewhere and in other languages, judging by the success of the game in the Bombay area'.

Some words now, few but necessary, as to the method which the author uses. The reader of this introduction will already have felt the impact of the kind of passionate research and investigation which went into this book. We can note that cricket was recorded in France in 1478 but that, doubt having been cast on the correct reading of the document, Rowland Bowen took the matter up directly with the Directeur-General of the *Archives de France* and received the reply that, after looking at the original and consulting several specialists on handwriting of the fifteenth century, the reading 'criquet' was unassailable. What I personally like, however, is the reference to one William Bedle, born 22 February 1679. He is the first man known to have achieved great prominence in the game, for when he died in June 1768, nearly ninety years of age, he was 'formally accounted the most expert cricket player in England'. The conclusions drawn are those of a genuine historian. The fact is unquestionable and it can mean three things: first that he was indeed a great player. Secondly, that there were means *then* of judging comparative prowess, and thirdly that his fame lasted at least a generation after he last played. The material is slight, the implications are enormous and justifiable: already the game was national.

This book means a great deal to me not merely as a history of cricket but as history. Over the last years I have been noting a new type of historical writing. In English there is *The Making of the British Working Class* by E. P. Thompson. In French there are two books, *The History of the Sans-Culotte* by A. Soboul, which deals with the ordinary people whom historians at last recognize today as primary in any consideration of the French Revolution. An Englishman, Mr R. Cobb, has written in French a history of the French Revolutionary armies of the period 1793-4, an army essentially of the *sans-culottes* and the ordinary people. A friend of mine in the United States will soon have published material which deals with the life of the slave before the Civil War, what he did as a human being, what he thought and how he adjusted himself to his difficult situation. These and other books are breaking new ground in a manner that treats their material as fundamental and not subsidiary to what we usually know as history. This history of cricket obviously does not treat the subject as if the ordinary cricketer was a *sans-culotte* but the method, the tone, the tempo, the range, show that we have here something new, not only in the history of cricket but in the writing of history. Hegel says that the owl of Minerva flies only at dusk. That is to say, one seriously examines and explores a situation, a totality, only when it is in the stage of its decline. Rowland Bowen, I would suspect from this book, even if he did not agree with this, would not disagree. It seems to me that a book like this which delves so deep and shows cricket to have been a part of every period of the history of England and the colonial territories makes one thing clear, that cricket is an integral part of the British civilization. I believe that whatever road that civilization takes, it will take cricket with it.

London, January 1970   C. L. R. JAMES

Cricket

A HISTORY OF ITS GROWTH AND
DEVELOPMENT THROUGHOUT
THE WORLD

1

PREHISTORY

History begins, and can only begin, when you have some kind of a written record. Before that all is prehistory, no matter what other evidences you can adduce, from coins, pottery, living habits, and so on. This does not mean that it is impossible to make a reconstruction of what was going on before history begins: indeed much has to be added to historical written records themselves before true history can be narrated. But, whereas the speculation that any historian has to make has to be complementary to the written record which survives, *before* the written record begins speculation is on its own.

It is on its own in a relative way: suppose the written record of a town starts many years after the foundation of that town – we do not start thinking that nothing can be said about what happened the day before the first written record. People must have been writing, reading, eating, sleeping, buying, selling, praying, as much before the first surviving written record as after. We can extend back: we can bring in all the other evidences: we can point to ruins discovered far below the present foundations which show that the town existed hundreds of years before the first written record: we can judge from the town's situation how and why the town might have been founded, and with luck, we may find somewhere else another written record which does not, at first sight, refer to this town, but which, by a process of elimination can only refer to the town we are studying. There is an element of doubt: there must always be this element in prehistory. Nevertheless, a careful and imaginative historian may be able to build such an edifice that only a quite fundamental later discovery could overturn it. That happened with the decipherment of Linear B.

It is doubtful if any such solid edifice can be built about the prehistory of cricket, or even a framework erected on proven foundations. But there is a good deal more evidence available nowadays than even in the recent past, and a wholly plausible and coherent theory can be put forward even if there are large gaps in it. The soundness of the theory will only be apparent as and when new discoveries are found to tend to confirm it: if they do not, something else will have to be thought up.

It is possible to start the history of cricket, that is to say, from written records, from around the first quarter of the seventeenth century. There are, it is true, some earlier records but they are so scattered that they have to be taken with 'archaeological' and other evidence rather than relied on by themselves.

So one cannot tell prehistory as a story: one has to exhibit the various pieces of evidence, and speculative ideas, and see what they amount to. There are a great many of these, and some of them overlap into the historical period, being indeed written records.

When the first certain references to cricket in England are encountered, it is apparent that, very few years later, the game was widespread and popular amongst all sections of the community in southern, or rather, south-eastern England. Why this was so, will be discussed in the next chapter: meanwhile it is enough to note the fact.

By the middle of that same seventeenth century, the game evidently enjoyed an enormous popularity in Ireland, for Cromwell ordered the destruction of all bats and balls in Dublin, and large numbers were given up for burning in 1656. Two hundred years later, the Irish were again found to have a strong love for the game: there seems to have been some kind of affinity for it amongst parts of what are loosely called the Celtic populations of the British islands.

These Celtic populations are far larger than is generally realized: recent mapping of blood-groups shows that large parts of England have a population of a predominantly Celtic-type blood-group and, most significantly, that there are even to this day large 'islands' of this blood-group in Surrey and Hampshire. If the probable 'racial' composition of these islands historically is examined, it can be seen that the 'invasions' by Saxons, and Norse, and Normans, can only have had a marginal effect on the general population (as distinct from the political and legal effect). The population of the Roman province of Britain in the early fifth century can be put at around two million: logistics alone would have prevented such a population from being submerged by invaders since there could never have been enough of them. Doubtless there were local massacres, and certainly there were large-scale migrations of British from some areas to, amongst others, the empty land that was to become Brittany, but it is difficult to see that the end-result could ever have been a Saxon-populated England, and the blood-group maps of the mid-twentieth century show that it was not. What a pity this technique was not in existence some 120 years ago before the railway age made the population so mobile and mixed!

These Celtic peoples are important because cricket, when it first reached English history, is located in and around what had been a very isolated part of the country, the Weald of Kent, Sussex, Surrey and Hampshire. It was at Newenden, on the Kentish border with Sussex and in this heartland of its growth, that the first probable reference to cricket occurs: it is not possible to be certain about it though it is difficult to think of any other explanation to account for it, so it is legitimate to put it into prehistory. The reference is to the word 'creag' which appears in the Wardrobe accounts for the twenty-eighth regnal year of Edward I, that is, 1299–1300: *Domino Johanni de Leek capellano Domini Edwardi fil' Regis pro den' per ipsum liberat' eidem Domino suo ad ludendum ad Creag' et alios ludos per vices per manus proprias apud Westm' 10 die Martii 100s. Et per manus Hugonis camerarii sui apud Newenton mense Martii 20s. – Summa 6.0.0.'*

Expenditure therefore for Prince Edward to play at 'creag' and other games with his friends. The word was probably pronounced something like 'craig' and so we would have 'craiget' – compare with the spelling in the Guildford court case, mentioned later, some three hundred years after this, of 'kreckett'.

No one, scholar or other, has ever come up with any other explanation than that 'creag' was cricket and its occurrence on the edge of the wild Wealden area makes any other possibility unlikely. For it was a wild area, and even dangerous, and remained so in parts well on into the eighteenth century: the Brighton Road was not a safe one to travel (nor indeed were roads elsewhere, for other reasons). The Romans went round the Weald, and so, a thousand years later, did the Normans: troops do not march through jungles now and they did not then. It seems most likely that the population of this area remained to a great extent untouched, although this cannot be proved save only from what remains in the western part of it of a predominating Celtic blood-group.

One of the peculiarities of cricket is its numbering system, all based on eleven or sub-divisions or multiples of eleven.[1] There is no apparent reason why it should play such a prominent part, to such an extent that when we talk of an 'eleven' (though the number has been borrowed by soccer and hockey and no doubt other games), we are at once known to be talking about a cricket team.

---

[1] First brought to notice by 'H.P.-T.' (P. F. Thomas) in *Old English Cricket*, a collection of five pamphlets issued between 1923 and 1929.

The only possible reason seems to be that there must once have been a numbering system in and about the area where cricket arose, itself based on eleven. It is noteworthy, therefore, that in an area of Northern France extending roughly from the Seine and on into Flanders, there was just such a numbering system which went beyond anything known in England, in that it gave eleven inches to a foot, and sub-divided the inch itself into eleven parts (known as 'lines' or 'lignes')[1]

And the first *certain* reference to cricket anywhere is precisely in north-eastern France, in Flanders, near St Omer, in 1478. This is to be found in a document in the *Archives de France* (see plate 1) which reads as follows:

'Le XIème jour d'octobre darrenier passé, environ une heure ou deux après disner, le dit suppliant se partit du chasteau de Liettes [now known as Liettres] près de la ville de Therouenne [in the arrondissement of St Omer, Pas-de-Calais] duquel il estoit canonnier pour venir jouer et passer le temps en la ville dudit Liettes et arriva en ung lieu on en jouoit à la boulle près d'une atache ou criquet. . . .' (The document is dated at Thouars in December 1478).[2]

At that time, of course, the area in question was part of the domains of the House of Burgundy, and did not become part of the kingdom of France till nearly two hundred more years had passed, in the meantime becoming part of the Spanish Netherlands.

If the eleven-based system here was found in the area where cricket arose, as indeed it was, and if that area was also an area unlikely to have been disturbed by invasions from elsewhere, it follows that any connection between south-east English numerology and northern French and Flemish numerology must have existed at least before Norsemen or Normans came on the scene. It is therefore even more interesting to note that in Roman times, there were Belgic tribes in both areas, with the same name in each, being but two portions of the same tribe, the Atrebates.

Though cricket was not involved, a Gallo-Roman noble was playing an organ-

---

[1] See H. Doursther, *Dictionnaire Universel des Poids et Mesures Anciens et Modernes* (1840; photo-reprint, Amsterdam, 1965).

[2] Some doubt has been cast by authorities in this country on the reading of the text in question (*Archives de France*, Trésor de chartes, côté JJ 205, folio 103 v°. acte no. 189). Accordingly I wrote to the Directeur-Général des Archives de France, putting this to him, and offering him more than one escape route if a scrutiny of the original happened to confirm that there had been a misreading. He replied: 'Vérification faite sur l'original et après consultation de plusieurs spécialistes des écritures du XVème siècle, il ne semble pas que la lecture du mot CRIQUET puisse prêter à la moindre contestation.'

ized ball-game, necessitating its own layout, towards the end of the fifth century, as power was passing out of the hands of the Roman Emperors in the west into that of their nominal viceroys, the Visigothic kings. He was Apollinaris Sidonius (who later became a bishop and some say that he was the original of St Apollinaris). He was a man of culture as well as of property, holding an important social position: quite remarkably like the English landed aristocracy of the eighteenth century. It is just the kind of environment where cricket could have had much encouragement: yet his letters do not show any sign of cricket being the game concerned.

From all this it seems that cricket was an old Celtic game in a form more primitive than is known now, except in back gardens or on beaches where what is played may well reflect what was played fifteen hundred or two thousand years ago. The game would not have been confined to any one Celtic tribe, even if it was not played by all of them: it would not have been played except in areas much favoured by the weather, where hot summers allowed early harvests and enabled the people to play instead of work: such areas can never have been many in the past, and are not now. Not that the playing area would have been narrowly confined and this accounts for it being played in France itself, probably from the thirteenth century, certainly from the fifteenth, onwards, as well as in overseas territories settled by France (such as what is now Canada, where French Canadians played it after Mass on Sunday in 1785, or in former French West Indian Islands, such as St Lucia), in Germany where it is known before the end of the eighteenth century, and in Denmark a little later. The game took various forms in different localities and the German version has differences not to be accounted for by the lack of understanding of the onlooker and, much more to the point, so has the primitive form of the game played in the old British North American colonies.

There is another attractive hypothesis which fits nearly, but not quite all, the same facts as the Celtic one, and maybe some of them rather better. It involves the Jutes who did not come, as their name suggests, from Jutland: they were, culturally at any rate, closely linked with the Franks of the lower Rhine, and were a branch of the Anglo-Saxons who came into Kent, who settled also just beyond Kent in the Hastings area of Sussex and in the Isle of Wight and on both sides of the Solent (just where one of the Celtic blood-group 'islands' survives). They had cross-channel links into the 'eleven-based' area, and etymology, which will be mentioned a little later, certainly is no hindrance to this possible Jutish origin. If the origin was not Celtic, but Jutish, it can hardly be much later than the second wave of Teutonic invasions of Britain and Gaul about the fifth century.

There was, at any rate, a game which can safely be taken as being the 'Creag' ', called by various different names, some generic, as 'crosse' and 'stool-ball', some local as 'cricket' or 'wicket'[1] (and possibly even 'picket' as that meant wicket) or when translated, 'gate-ball' or 'hit-ball' and which consisted of a simple game where one player bowled a ball to another, and the other hit it, and if he hit it far enough (and sometimes if not) he ran to a goal and scored a point. In another version, or perhaps an earlier one, that goal was a point on a circle, and hence rounders. The goal was where the bowler bowled from, or somewhere near. There is nothing special about this game: give a couple of boys a ball and a stick to hit it with, one stick only, and primitive cricket will almost certainly be evolved within the hour. If not cricket, then primitive golf, taking the stick in turn: and if two sticks, then primitive hockey. It is obviously a very old game and we do not need to attach any special laws to it to say that it is cricket, nor, through the absence of those laws, to say that it is not.

Crosse[2] is a generic French word: much much later in its life, it gave its name, as lacrosse, to a French-Canadian game derived in part from the play of North American Indians, and for convenience it is referred to here only as 'crosse' otherwise there is confusion. It is known in the thirteenth century, and it is also known that it covered the three different games played with clubbed staff and ball, golf, hockey and cricket, to use their modern names. In 1611 it was defined in the first French-English dictionary ever made, by Randle Cotgrave, as cricket, so that is how Cotgrave, or his informant, regarded it. In the following century, a depiction of the game by H. F. d'Anville Bourguignon dit Gravelot (1699–1773) was done during a few years' visit to England, showing children playing, as an illustration to a small collection of children's games. He called it 'the game of cricket' – twenty years later, he used the same illustration in a book of the same type in France, and called it '*le jeu de la crosse*'. This of course is proof that *crosse* still comprised cricket, and was by then often used for cricket in France (or Gravelot would have called it in his French edition if not cricket, then criquet).

The word cricket is generally derived from the Anglo-Saxon cricce, a crooked staff: that is to say, a staff with a crook, or, it is thought, clubbed at one end. This derivation is strengthened in the minds of some by reference to the supposed origin of the game on short-cropped downland with shepherds taking part. It may well not be correct at all, but rather a kind of 'jobbing back'. For the French

---

[1] See Joseph Wright, *English Dialect Dictionary* (London, 1898).
[2] For more on crosse and cricket, see J. J. Jusserand, *Les Sports et jeux d'exercice dans l'ancienne France* (Paris, 1901). Crosse, of course, occurs in Rabelais.

criquet[1] had another derivation and it seems far more likely that the word is not derived from the implement with which the game was played (if anyone did ever play it with a crooked, as distinct from a clubbed, staff) but from the goal which was defended.

For criquet comes from the Flemish or Dutch '*krickstoel*'[2] and that piece of furniture is a low stool, from eighteen inches to two feet long, on which one kneels in church.[3] Its profile is very similar to that of the early long low wicket in cricket, or indeed of the early stool in stool-ball. There is, in fact, a 1643 reference to cricket meaning a low stool.

Dr H. F. Squire, in his erudite study of the possible origins of cricket in *Henfield Cricket*, thought that stool-ball and cricket were allied in some way, but he did not appear to know that the word 'stool'[4] is old Sussex dialect for the stump of a tree. And the profile of that stump would, in turn, closely resemble the long low wicket of early cricket and the Dutch krickstoel. Stool-ball itself was until relatively modern times, when it was formalized as its own distinct game, a generic word covering both rounders and cricket: illustrations exist showing what are quite obviously both games, and in them, the stool is of this long low variety. It is not usually possible to know which of the two games was involved (or indeed any other) when stool-ball was referred to.

It has been the fashion to think of cricket as in some way originating on short-cropped downland, where the grass is much nibbled by the sheep, and the bat derived from the shepherd's crook, thus producing an unsatisfactory etymology for the name of the game. It is not possible to reconcile the basic etymology involving *cricket* = *stool* with this, and for a number of reasons. The meaning of *stool* = *stump of a tree* is quite inapt for downland: there were no trees *on* the downs until the mid-eighteenth century, and most of those which are nowadays familiar date from much later even (there were of course always trees on these sheltered flanks of downland but no cricket would ever have been played there). Thus if that stool be connected with cricket, it could only have done so in the Weald and the Weald quite specifically excludes all downland. Moreover, cricket did not need short-cropped downland to originate or grow: any level space with

[1] See F. Godefroy, *Dictionnaire de l'ancienne langue française et de tous ses dialectes du IXe au XVe siècle*. Godefroy seems to have relied for criquet to some extent on La Curne de Sainte Palaye, *Dictionnaire Historique de l'ancien langage français*, which, though not published until 1877, was compiled by La Corne between 1740 and 1760.
[2] See J. F. Bense, *Dictionary of the Low-Dutch Element in the English Vocabulary* (The Hague, 1926–38).
[3] Indeed that type of stool was once generally called a 'cricket' in England, and still is occasionally locally.
[4] See W. D. Parish, *A Dictionary of the Sussex Dialect* (Lewes, 1875); expanded edn by H. Hall (Chichester, 1957).

B

reasonably close grass would have sufficed, and there are many indications connecting churchyards with cricket. Churchyards, until at least the early seventeenth century, were not graveyards: they were enclosed level spaces, and they were much used for all manner of games, some of them needing many players. Sunday was the only free day for much of the population: Mass over, they went and played in the churchyard. It was by no means always cricket that was played: most of the evidence of games in churchyards is indeed not of cricket. But in the early seventeenth century there is a number of references to cricket being played in churchyards and of being connected in some way with the church – the old pre-Reformation custom had not yet been killed. (And of course where there was no Reformation, it continued and so, as will be seen, the French-Canadians played cricket after Mass on a Sunday in 1785 in Montreal: and to this day the French version of the game which has survived in St Lucia is played on Sundays and other festivals which, in this context, means religious festivals). John Arlott has an amusing recollection of an old cricket notice dating from a great many years ago of the village team being set down on a notice on the church door with the remark, 'them as don't attend service, shan't play cricket': it is an interesting survival of a very old tradition.

If, however, there were any question of cricket originating on short-cropped downland (whatever happened at a much later stage when advantage was taken of the natural mowing machine which is a sheep), it only just survives a scrutiny of the facts. The great sheep farming monasteries were for the most part situated in Yorkshire (Jervaux, Rievaulx, Fountains) yet there has never been any suggestion that cricket originated or had much development in the early stages in that large shire. Other than Canterbury (which drew from Romney Marsh) there was no monastic establishment in Sussex or Kent which was deeply involved with the wool trade. Not far removed from downland, there were large monastic establishments in the upper Thames valley but there is neither record nor suggestion of cricket being played or being developed in the Chilterns, or on the Berkshire Downs or even on the chalkland of Wiltshire and Dorset, all within the commercial orbit of those upper Thames monasteries. (The place names which incorporate 'crick' or 'cricket' are irrelevant: they do not commemorate the game but serve to show only that the game's name could have been associated with the crook.)

There were indeed sheep on the South Downs too but for every one on the uplands there seems to have been at least one in the valleys or in the Weald behind. It is noteworthy that, of the place names associated with early references to cricket, approximately half are Wealden names – and the earliest probable reference to cricket in this country is on the edge of the sheep-bearing area of Romney Marsh.

The idea of shepherds playing cricket on ground prepared for them by their flocks' nibblings seems to be one more of those late eighteenth- and early nineteenth-century fantasies of the romantic imagination, fed by the fact that, in that late eighteenth century, just those conditions seem to have existed and furnished the occasion for Hambledon to arise (as later the use of sheep at Lord's maintained the fantasy). But it is needless to look for shepherds and a more tortuous etymology for the name when the name is so readily taken from the object which one had to defend, in an enclosure both flat and large enough for under-arm bowling, an enclosure, moreover, habituated to games: the church-yard. Evidently, but not certainly, country churchyards are likely to have seen early developments but the game may well have made its way to town quite early too. Single-wicket is a town game *par excellence.* with a mark on a wall for wicket: it is for that reason, except in the more spacious version when more than five players took part on each side, that no shots could be scored behind the wicket.

There is etymological support for the idea that the game refers to the thing defended from two widely different parts of the country. It was for long the custom in Kent, certainly to the end of the eighteenth century, to talk about playing 'at crickets': this is clearly a likely usage if 'crickets' meant the objects defended, and relatively unlikely if it referred to the weapon. But in Yorkshire, where the old word for the game was wicket, the term 'crock' or 'cruck' is used to designate a length of curved timber used in farm building, and very much of the shape, though much larger, of an old-fashioned cricket bat. However, tempting though it is to assimilate 'cruck' to the shepherd's crook (whose shape it did not in fact resemble), it is clear that the word used to define the game was, as in the south, the object defended. If in fact the word 'cricket' derived from the imple-ment, it is strange that in the north where a very similar word existed to describe an object of very much the same shape as the implement, that word was not used.

Mention has been made of picket: this word had the same meaning as what we would now call a stump or wicket, though it is not found in connection with the game. Wicket, however, is used not only for a stump, but also for the game itself: and it also means a wicket-gate of the type used for sheep-pens. In the Celtic context, remembering the p/q transition in the Celtic languages,[1] the

---

[1] This refers to the development in the Celtic language (paralleled in some of the Italic dialects) in which Gaulish and Brythonic (including Welsh, Breton and Cornish) change the 'qu' sound to 'p' whereas the Goidelic dialects (including Irish, Gaelic and Manx) retained it, later modifying it to 'k'. A further mutation from 'p' to consonantal 'w' is not impossible.

cricket/picket possibility is interesting, and may account for cricket/wicket too. Gate-ball ('Thorball'), as found in the early German and Danish accounts is obviously but wicket, again.

There is thus a good deal of interesting and suggestive etymology and one day it may be possible to reconcile it all fully, though there is little real confusion even now. Florio's dictionary referred to the game in 1598 – he did not say much: *sgrillare*, to play cricket-a-wicket, to make merry.[1] Florio was living in England and was to do so for several more years: it can be taken that he knew of cricket accordingly, although his own entry obviously has some confusion with the insect. But he does say 'cricket-a-wicket': this could be mere alliteration, but if so what a strange chance that he should have used both words under which the game has been known down into this century. There is no suggestion that cricket was at that time being played in Italy, as a result of what Florio says: there is equally no reason why it should not have been.

A few months earlier John Derrick, aged fifty-nine, deposed in a court case in Guildford that he had played at 'kreckett' and other 'plaies' on a certain plot of ground when he was a boy. So the game is known in England some time in the 1550s: and from now on other references start coming in thick and fast. The prehistory of cricket is at an end.

---

[1] It has often been alleged that Giovanni Florio was an uninstructed Italian who muddled things up, and that his reference is not worth much. But Florio had been publishing lexicographical works for some years before his dictionary in 1598, and he had not been in Italy for years. Moreover, he remained in England for many more years, issuing further editions of the dictionary but which made no alteration to this definition. It has also been stated that an earlier edition of his dictionary had been published in Italy in 1595 but no trace of such a thing has ever been found and the best opinion on the subject, at the British Museum, is that such a publication was most unlikely.

The first known depiction of cricket, by Gravelot, issued in England in 1739 as 'the game of cricket' and in France twenty years later as 'le jeu de la crosse'. See page 32.

2

FIRST LIGHT

It would be wrong to call it strictly dawn: the dawn must have been hundreds, perhaps even thousands of years earlier. First light on the subject it is, however, as we come across an increasing number of references to the game in south-eastern England during the first part of the seventeenth century.

The great puzzle is: why do we then, and only then, start getting these references? A century later we are inundated with newspaper references, and there is no need to ask why: the flood exists because newspapers were themselves relatively new and the medium for reporting on the game has only just come into existence. But in the early seventeenth century, this is not at all the position: there is no difference between the sixteenth century (or even the fifteenth) and the seventeenth so far as diarists are concerned. Yet references have not been found in diaries or documents earlier: and they multiply now. There must be some very good reason, and there may well be more than one.

There is another puzzle too. Why did the game suddenly experience this great spread of popularity in these islands but not, apparently, in Europe, nor indeed ever in Europe until much later under an anglicizing influence in Holland and Denmark? Any answer to the first puzzle must also, in some sense, be an answer to the second.

A possible answer to its spread in this country may have been English troops in Ireland in Elizabeth I's reign encountering the game there, perhaps in a more developed form, who said words to the effect, 'why that's cricket', and having learnt the local variations came back with them, since they made for a better game. Although this is pure speculation, it does provide some kind of a link between the scattered Celtic populations, and it also takes into account the popularity of the game in Ireland not many years later when Cromwell tried to exterminate it. That popularity has to be taken into account since it is difficult to see what factor could have made a game imported from England popular at that period amongst the Irish people and not merely amongst their overlords.

However, there are at least two other possibilities which do not conflict with each other, nor with the last proposition. Games, as such, were banned by the Tudors, part of a reactionary attempt to preserve and encourage archery. That archery was obsolete as a mode of war no more occurred to the early Tudors than it seemed to occur to the British General Staff after Cambrai that cavalry had no further place in warfare: the military mind is ever retrogressive, into something that it thinks it understands and is therefore 'safe'. The Tudor prohibitions on games lacked effect, for people started inventing new games which were not covered by the statute, and that in due course led to a blanket prohibition of any games which might be invented from then on. Still, if one thing is certain from its prehistory, cricket was not an invented game, certainly not invented in the Tudor period. It is a fair supposition, though it cannot be more than that, that cricket, being until then a game for children and young men (as most probably the great majority of games ever were in unsophisticated societies) and being not under any legal ban, came to be played by somewhat older men; just as, for example, some well-known older men played bowls in that period. And as the legal ban became more pervasive, more people will have started, or rather continued, to play cricket: then, no doubt, someone asked the players in language appropriate to the age, 'what were they a-doing of there?' and got the reply 'mind thy own business, G'arge, no one ever said we wasn't to play cricket'. And authority scratched its head and wondered what to do about it, and decided to do nothing because authority had at least come round to the view that archery could no longer be rescued, and was not even worth rescuing: it was not yet, perhaps, ready to admit that to the people at large, but it thought it was probably better to let sleeping dogs lie locally. So, by a kind of legal accident, cricket was tacitly encouraged by the freedom which it enjoyed in contrast to the penalties attaching to playing other games.

Not of course that other games were entirely banned: tennis, what is called real, or royal, tennis was a highly aristocratic game played all over Europe, and which no one had ever thought to ban, or could have banned. Played by princes and prelates, and lesser gentry and monks, it could have no popular appeal both because by the standards of any age it was costly to play (in terms of buildings and apparatus), because only a handful of people could play at any one time, and because there was no space for more than a few onlookers.

A further point has to be remembered: there was, at this time, an old-established hereditary aristocratic class, ex-feudal, or still feudal, in almost every country in Europe. There was hardly any such thing in England: the baronial wars and the Tudor extirpations had eliminated almost all the traces of such a class in England. In addition, the seizures of Church property and their redistribution amongst a vast crowd of *novi homines* had just brought out of the urban middle-class traders and lesser rural gentry a brand new English upper-class: half a century before it had simply not existed, but now it was beginning to sit firmly in the saddle, in a literal as well as a metaphorical sense. These people were not tennis players: they may well have been cricket players but were anyway in close touch with the people, who were.

So we can see a comprehensive answer to the puzzles of why the game suddenly became popular in England, and why it did not on the Continent. It did not on the Continent because the social and legal reasons did not exist there to give it tacit or overt encouragement: boys and young men went on playing, but in an unorganized way. If they were socially aspiring, they may have played tennis, and they may have played other games, but there was no need for them to continue with the child's game of cricket as, for good legal reasons, there was in England. Moreover, and probably more important: whereas here our *novi homines* found nothing incongruous in playing the game of the people, those people of whom they had so recently formed a part and very often within their own lifetime, the European aristocracy had neither incentive nor desire, more likely a revulsion, to play a game of the people as earthy as was cricket.

J. J. Jusserand in his *Les sports et jeux d'exercice dans l'ancienne France* suggested that there appeared to be little difference between the development of cricket in France from what it underwent in England, until the eighteenth century. He was writing in 1901 and his view was then tenable on the somewhat scanty information about seventeenth-century cricket in England then available: it needs some modification now, but he may well have had a clue to the problem when he talked about the decadence of sporting activity in France in that century as compared with England. In France, he pointed out, sport remained provincial but in England it went to town and captured society. From about the time of Louis XIII the nobility in France were more or less compelled to attend the King's Court: they were endowed with privilege but without power, and became absentee landlords for many generations. In England no such thing happened: the nobility and landed gentry were country folk *par excellence* (only much later was the phenomenon to be seen of urban unlanded nobility). This essential difference in the socio-political life of the two countries may well be some part of the explanation of why cricket developed in England and not in France: but what about elsewhere in Europe? It is possible that the more positive example provided by French society in the artistic and musical sphere had its own influence too on the general attitude towards sport and games in Europe: a greater influence than the, in the eyes of the European aristocrat, somewhat lumpish English would have had. But, as will be seen, the game did not die out on the Continent: it continued to exist, and evidently, in some degree, to develop and there are two striking examples of this at the end of the eighteenth century which only make sense on the basis that some people, to put it no higher, were playing cricket at an acceptable standard. One thing, however, is true: we will all know a great deal more about the development (if not also the origin) of cricket in England when, in due course, more is known about it in France in the three centuries after that first mention of *criquet*: there can be little doubt that the information is there, somewhere, buried away in old archives and journals, some of them perhaps even published but never consulted, for any possible light they may throw on cricket, by English people.

Fashions spread with remarkable ease to other countries, across frontiers and iron curtains, and even bamboo ones: though, it may be objected, we can see why, at that time, as the sixteenth century merged into the seventeenth, the game did not become popular in Europe, how is it that it did not do so later on? The answer lies in the later history of the game.

There is a curious point about the increase in the number of references to the game in the early and mid-seventeenth century and that is that many of them are due to hostility to the game: a reaction against it, in fact, by Puritans. A good example is the description by Thomas Wilson, a leading Puritan of Maidstone, who told how Maidstone had formerly been a very 'prophane' town with people playing cricket. Puritan pressure was probably behind some of the prosecutions for playing the game. Another source of references is to be found buried away in the proceedings of coroner's courts when inquiring into the causes of death of people injured while playing cricket.

What sort of a game was it that was being played in the first half of the seventeenth century? I infer that it provided for two innings a side from the earliest indication of any number, two, in 1721, the rule during the next 150 years. The Laws take the matter for granted and do not even imply anything until 1835 although, some sixty years earlier, provisions regarding bets made it clear that two innings a side was the custom. But precise descriptions of actual games are, so far, lacking, and we know for certain of only two 'laws': that a man could be out 'caught' and that if he was in danger of being out 'caught' he could charge down his opponent trying to catch the ball. It is not possible to say what limitations

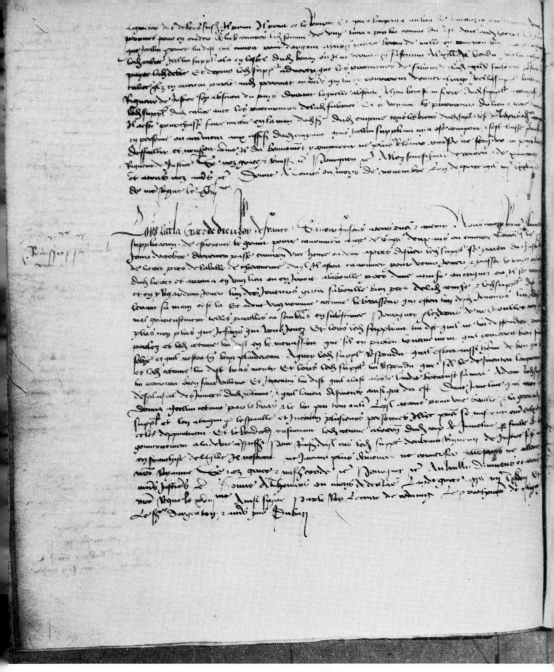

1. Document from the Archives de France, Trésor de chartes, giving the first evidence for the existence of 'criquet' in Northern France in 1478, near St Omer. For elucidation of the text, see page 30. 'Criquet' occurs near the end of the fifth line after the gap

2. A facsimile reproduction of the records of the court case in 1598 (NS) in which John Derrick testified to having played cricket on a plot of ground in Guildford when he was a boy

there were on his charging down his opponent, but the right to do so existed until about 1787. That is to say, we know that in the early seventeenth century charging down the opponent was allowed, we know that the 1744 laws, only changed in this respect about 1787, allowed the opponent to be hindered but without using bat or arm to do so, and only within the batsmen's running ground, and we know, an interesting overseas survival, that charging down occurred in the 1846 International match between the U.S.A. and Canada, and was disallowed. But the batsman thought he was in his rights in doing so, and that is why it is an interesting survival; over and over again in human affairs we find that those who have gone overseas from their home country perpetuate ways and habits long since forgotten or changed at home. If you want to know what was happening in a country, find out what its colonists were doing fifty years later.

Little is known, from direct evidence, about the game as it was played. But we can make large inferences by using more information derived from exiles. If exiles (or emigrants or colonists) are one group of highly conservative people trying to maintain in their new home what they believed to be the circumstances of their old home, another highly conservative group is made up of school children. Students of folklore know this very well but it is less well-known or appreciated in other walks of life. Happily for cricket's history, there are not only records of exiles playing cricket in North America, there are records of child exiles playing cricket at school on the continent of Europe.

These records are intriguing, for they come from the modern Catholic public school of Stonyhurst, which had been founded as a Jesuit school for the children of English Catholics at St Omer in 1593. The school moved to England when the French Revolution threatened it nearly two hundred years later, and when it moved it brought with it its own version of cricket. Although it is dead now, it was played down into the latter part of the last century, and it was played long enough for people to make a record of just what sort of game it was, and what its rules were, and even to photograph it. St Omer is where, 115 years before, the first known certain reference to the game was recorded. There is no suggestion that the English boys learnt cricket in Flanders – we *know* that boys had been playing cricket in England long before the school was founded at St Omer – but what we can never know is the extent to which the game they played was the English version, adapted to confined surroundings, or that same version, however adapted but further modified by being in contact with the Flemish version. Thus, while it can be said with certainty, from knowing how traditional children's games are, that the Stonyhurst game reflected at least cricket as known in England at the end of the sixteenth century, what it is not possible to say is the

B*

extent to which it may also have reflected not merely the version in Flanders but the method of playing that version over a hundred years earlier. It is far from impossible that what died out towards the end of the last century included customs unchanged for four hundred years, or more. (See plates 6 and 7.)

Cricket, as far back as it can be taken, was what is now called a double-wicket game, and not, as Dr Squire and others have thought, originally a single-wicket game. My main reason for this assertion is that it is psychologically difficult to imagine the creation of the double-wicket game from out of the old single-wicket game[1] but it is easy to imagine a simplification from double to single wicket for *ad hoc* reasons. A small piece of supporting evidence is to be found in the provisions for making a run in single-wicket: there *and* back. Such a provision could hardly have existed had single-wicket come first.

In an old description[2] of a primitive version of cricket in North America (under the name of Wicket, a good old north country name for it still), it appears that the ball was bowled alternately, from one end to the other, and then back again from the other. This also appears in an early German account[3] of the game. But Stonyhurst cricket was always played as a single wicket game, yet so far from this being any contradiction about which came first, it is a vindication of that assertion: for, in Stonyhurst cricket, the boy who stood in the position of wicket-keeper was known as 'second bowler' *though he never bowled.*

So it is possible to tell confidently from these good historical sources that the original game was double-wicket, and that bowling was from each end in alternate balls, and not by overs as it has since come to be. Even when overs were instituted, it was for long the custom for the bowler not then bowling to act as wicket-keeper, the more responsible position in those days being long-stop. However, this is to go too far ahead of the story.

There are other facts that can be stated about the game in those far-off days some three hundred and fifty years ago: the wicket was wide and low, up to six feet wide, and a few inches high, and it remained broad (though not so broad)

---

[1] This, of course, does not refer to the present so-called revival of single-wicket under invented laws, but to the old game which was played in various places right up to the last war, and the laws of which will be found appended at the end of the pre-1946 Code.

[2] From G. D. Seymour, 'The Old-Time Game of Wicket and Some Old-Time Wicket Players', in vol. 2, *Proceedings of the Society of Colonial Wars in the State of Connecticut* (paper dated 1909). See also plate 4.

[3] Herr Gutsmuth, *Spiele zur Übung und Erholung des Körpers und Geistes für die Jugend* (Hamburg, 1796). Gutsmuth's book gives a lengthy description of cricket which he says was not then known in Germany but, what is more valuable, he describes a German game called German Handball which is clearly one of the games which produced cricket and rounders, and, from what he says, lies somewhere between these two games in its methods of play.

and low in this country until after half-way through the following century, and in its more primitive form in America until almost our own time. The bat, to meet the shape of the wicket, was curved in a similar manner to that of a modern hockey stick, but more clubbed. The bowling was true bowling, all along the ground: and it too, together with the bat, remained like that till the next century. Yet the batsman could undoubtedly sweep the ball up into the air, or he could never have offered a catch: that this is likely anyway may be surmised from the rough nature of the pitch in those days: however one may have tried to bowl the ball *along* the ground, the ground itself must often have caused it to pop up.

The first known measurement for the length of the pitch is the twenty-three yards wicket-to-wicket of the 1727 Articles of Agreement between the Duke of Richmond and Mr Brodrick (this has another interesting feature, that they expressly provide for a run not to be scored if a batsman is caught whilst running, thus implying that it was sometimes the custom for such runs to be added to the score – not illogical if the batsmen are running their second run). The 1744 Laws, however, expressly refer to twenty-two yards. A Danish account of 1801 refers to 25–30 paces; if we take this as being the average thirty inches from left to right heel, this would be from just over twenty-two yards to some seventy-five feet (but if we take the other meaning of pace – the Roman one – from left heel to left heel again, we get something altogether too long and improbable). Seventy-five feet crops up again: in the game of 'wicket' in North America, seventy-five feet was laid down between the two wickets but the bowler could bowl up to ten feet in front of the wicket at his end, which would make the effective distance just under twenty-two yards. In Stonyhurst cricket, the overall length was thirty yards, but the bowler bowled from about twenty-seven yards (note the similarity with 'wicket'). In the game of *roulez là-bas* in St Lucia the distance between wickets is from twenty-five to twenty-seven yards but some of this length could be accounted for by an extension to allow for the four-foot long rods with which the runners touched in.

From all this it is possible to argue convincingly in different ways:

(a) that all these measurements are chance variations for different local reasons from one standard;

(b) that all these measurements indicate actual local differences and were not chance variations, with twenty-two yards being but one of them and coming from the most influential area;

(c) that the one standard was twenty-two units whatever those units happened to be locally (and differences between various kinds of yards, paces, ells

43

and so on could be quite enough to account for resulting differences in modern equivalent lengths);

(*d*) that the twenty-two yard length is relatively modern arising from Gunter inventing his chain of that length in the early seventeenth century (which itself derived from four rods, poles or perches each of five and a half yards).

The matter is open but I am inclined to favour (*c*) bearing in mind (*d*).

It must be admitted there is no lawyer's proof of these assertions; merely good inference from later evidence, of the type which any trained intelligence officer would make. One other assertion, itself by way of inference, can, however, be made concerning leg-before-wicket. It did not exist in its present form; but both the account of the old American game of wicket, as well as of what could, or can still, be found in backyard boy's cricket here, say 'if you obstruct the wicket with your leg three times, you are out'. But 'l.b.w.' as we know it was to wait till 1774 before it appeared. (Colonel R. S. Rait-Kerr appears to have been in error in his book on the Laws when he implies that the 1744 Laws had 'l.b.w.' in mind when they referred to players 'standing unfair to strike'; in the context of what amounts to an instruction to umpires, the reference seems to be to batsmen hindering the opponent making a catch by other than the means allowed.)

This then was the game which caught such a fast hold on almost all but the very highest social levels of the community before the Interregnum in England appeared to call a temporary halt to 'merrie England'. That halt was, however, rather the drawing of a curtain over the scene whilst much stage preparation went on behind: attempts were made to prosecute cricket players during the Commonwealth period, but they were unsuccessful, no doubt because no law existed to support such a prosecution, and all the while the game went on being played, though the suppression of the game in Ireland must not be forgotten. Added to those who would normally have played anyway, may well have been a number of gentlemen formerly prominent about the Court, now back in their country homes with little or nothing to do: they could hardly lead the life of Harold Nicolson's typical 'country gentleman' (George V) who did little but shoot game and stick stamps in albums, because the former was not organized along efficient lines, and the latter did not exist. But cricket did, and cricket is seen to be important in Court circles[1] after the Restoration: we can only conclude that those who before 1649 had not played, or had no time to play, had since learnt, and took their learning back with them. It did not only extend to the Court now: knowledge of the game had spread far beyond the Weald and its

[1] Lord Dacre, later Earl of Sussex, who married Charles II's daughter by the Duchess of Cleveland, was one such courtier who liked the game.

surroundings,[1] and was up into East Anglia and its neighbouring territory. Once again, this is not known from evidence of the game being played there: it is inferred from the knowledge of players of it, who came from those parts. They were to be found amongst the members of the Levant Company who were playing cricket on holidays in Aleppo in 1676: they were presumably playing the game before, or at the latest, shortly after the Restoration, and therefore knowledge of the game was likely to have been available in their counties even earlier.

There is interesting evidence of the formalization of the game before the Restoration. In 1629 a curate, criticized for playing cricket, retorted that there was nothing wrong in that, it was a game played by persons of repute and fashion.[2] This is the first known step in cricket's climb up the social ladder.[3] Getting on for a generation later in 1658 Edward Phillips, a nephew of John Milton, referred to cricket balls as such in a poem *The Mysteries of Love*: 'Would my eyes had been best out of my head with a cricket ball the day before I saw thee.' If special balls were being made, if special grounds were being prepared, it is very likely too that a code of Laws already existed also, though nothing is known of one from this time. (It was, incidentally, nearly another hundred years before the ball is referred to by its colour – 'the crimson ball' – in 'Seven-oke: A poem', describing a match on the Vine in 1753.) Probably the colour arose from an intensification by some natural dye of the natural hue of the leather colour itself. What is interesting is that the most perfect colour possible was adopted: red is at the opposite end of the spectrum from green, and it is as a matter of optical fact impossible for the human eye to focus the two colours together simultaneously (though the illusion often exists that one is doing so).

---

[1] John Derrick had said at Guildford in 1598 (N.S.) that he played cricket on a certain plot of land in the town when he was a boy, and as he was fifty-nine when he said this, this puts the date of his playing into the 1550s. Incidentally, it does not follow that his evidence in this particular court case implied that cricket was only a game for boys: he was simply stating what the use of this land by ordinary people had been when he was a boy.

[2] Henry Cuffen at Ruckinge on the edge of Romney Marsh, some sixty-three miles from Guildford: if you take either place as centre and draw circles with this distance as radius, you will enclose all London and the Home Counties as we know them. Supposing that the game had merely spread from Guildford to Ruckinge, it must have spread in other directions too: this then is the minimum area we can allow to cricket in the first part of the seventeenth century. In fact there was no such spread *in that* area: the game was already widespread in that area and spread *from* it.

[3] A statement that a ground at East Horsley had been sown with grass for cricket in about 1636 is not borne out by the actual facts. The ground had been rough and was ploughed up, and sown with grass, no doubt for grazing. While thus lying fallow, cricket was from time to time played on it. No more can be said and it is likely to have been another century or even more before a cricket ground as such was specifically made. Thomas Lord's might even have been among the first.

In all the game's history, the only known exception to the red ball is the unsatisfactory experiment with a blue ball in women's cricket in the 1890s.

Not only had knowledge of the game spread, it had enormously increased in popularity so that great matches were attended by crowds comparable with those who attended race-meetings: so much so that it was worth while specially brewing beer for crowds at either sport by 1668, so few years after the Restoration. Much had clearly been going on behind the scenes; yet from the beginning of the century, when hardly anything had burst on the scene, till Aleppo in 1676, was merely a long lifetime. This then is our First Light on the history of cricket.

There is, however, one speculation which can be made about this period. It may have been then that the separation between cricket and rounders began. It was noted, in discussing single-wicket, that the batsman had to get 'there and back' to make a run. Even now, in the ordinary game, one often sees batsmen running very wide and in single wicket, a somewhat circular, or oval, course can well have been followed instead of a dash and a sharp turn with the possibility of slipping. It is easy to imagine a development which would involve the batsman in running even wider, deliberately, round various objects such as stools, pickets (wickets) – or bases. Once that had occurred, 'rounders' has arrived and, therefore, baseball. There is no mention of rounders known before the eighteenth century and the single wicket game can scarcely have begun before the seventeenth century. Thus references before about the mid-seventeenth century to stoolball must almost certainly, on this basis, connote cricket. It follows that the first English reference to cricket would then be the 1523 reference to 'stoball', and similarly the first American reference, that 1621 mention of stoolball on the first Thanksgiving in the New World. Unhappily, these matters cannot yet be asserted as facts: they are so far but the product of logical reasoning based on a by no means improbable assumption.

3

THE FIRST GREAT PATRONS

By 1676 the first certain reference to the game being played overseas has appeared: it has also been possible to infer that cricket was being played by English people in at least two other areas, in Flanders and in North America.

It is even possible to put a name to one of the probable very early players of the game in North America. In 1646 there had been the first recorded cricket match, at Coxheath in Kent. One of those taking part was Samuel Filmer, who not many years later was found in Virginia where he had relations, one of whom indeed had been a governor of the colony. Several of them were important landowners there, and it is, incidentally, believed that President Fillmore (the thirteenth president) was connected with the family, Fillmore being a variant of the name. Samuel Filmer did not spend long in Virginia (probably during the Commonwealth only – he was back by 1663) but he was certainly young enough to have played when he was there.

There is a tantalizing reference to a game, once inferred to be cricket, having been forbidden on Sundays in New Amsterdam, eight years before it became New York.[1] But the original Dutch reads '*balslaen*' and it is impossible to be certain that cricket was intended: if it was, it would not be surprising, for stool-ball (and almost certainly at that time it was cricket that was intended) was noted in America in 1621, and it is as certain as anything can be that the colonists brought their games with them. All the same, we do not *know* of cricket in North America until 1709 when William Byrd, who was educated at Felsted, played many games of cricket with his friends on estates along the James River in Virginia. We can take it for granted that it is the earliest known set of instances amongst hundreds of others now lost, or at least buried beyond our sight: we can

[1] See plate 3.

47

also take it for granted that it cannot be a question of Byrd having learnt it while at school in England and of having brought it home with him, but of the game already existing and being played in America. How much more then, in England itself. Only a year after the Aleppo reference a high member of the Court habitually attended local cricket in Sussex, and he was connected by marriage with the Stuart blood: there are not so many more references during the later part of the century, but they all by their manner reinforce the idea of habitude and of popularity.

And well before the century was out, on February 22, 1679 (O.S.) was born one William Bedle. He is the first man known to us who achieved great prominence in the game, for, it was said of him when he died on June 3, 1768, 'aged near 90', that he was 'formerly accounted the most expert cricket player in England'. And that is all we know of his cricket activities. It is enough: he is the first of a long line which must include Fuller Pilch, W. G. Grace, Jack Hobbs and Walter Hammond – 'The most expert cricket player in England'.[1] It is worth pondering these words: they mean three things, that he was indeed very great, that there were means *then* available of judging comparative prowess, and that his fame lasted at least a generation after he last played.

All this is simple stuff to us with our daily newspapers, our magazines, our wireless commentaries, and our annuals: none of those things existed in Bedle's day, except only the first rudimentary beginning of newspapers, so rudimentary that it must have been late in his own playing career that it became at all usual to refer to cricket, though not yet to mention individuals. But the knowledge was there, and was shared, and remembered: and if this tells us nothing else at all, it tells us how very deeply dug-in cricket must have become in the national consciousness. It is tantalizing in the extreme to know no more about this giant than those words of praise in a short news item announcing his death. But there are other things just as tantalizing.

As the newspapers proliferate in the eighteenth century, so cricket references multiply, but with a sort of stutter early on. There were several matches from 1705 to 1709, all of them fairly 'big': that is, they were not just games between villages, but representative of wide areas – London v. Croydon, West Kent v. Chatham: little more than the fact of their existence is known, however, and then for eight more years there is nothing. But after that, from 1717, there is no year which passes without at least one reference to a cricket match being found.

---

[1] It is a commentary on the decline of English cricketers that following over a hundred years during almost all of which that wonderful phrase could be used of someone, it is not possible to add any name to follow Hammond's.

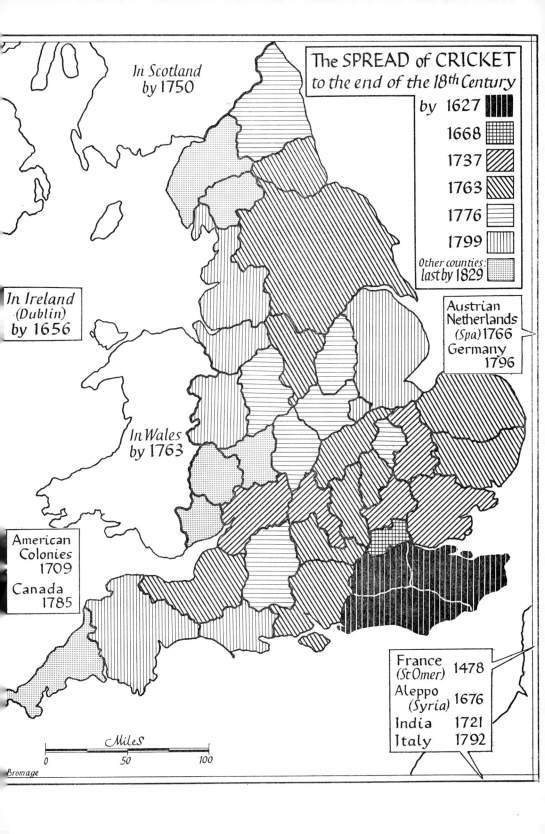

The SPREAD of CRICKET
to the end of the 18th Century

by 1627
1668
1737
1763
1776
1799

Other counties:
last by 1829

In Scotland
by 1750

In Ireland
(Dublin)
by 1656

In Wales
by 1763

American
Colonies
1709

Canada
1785

Austrian
Netherlands
(Spa) 1766
Germany
1796

France
(St Omer) 1478
Aleppo
(Syria) 1676
India 1721
Italy 1792

Miles
0   50   100

Bromage

Of course, references to cricket matches do not exhaust references to cricket; in plays, in poems, and in semi-political tracts they run parallel with the references to actual play and, for the most part, add nothing to the story.

We watch the build-up in those early years of the eighteenth century and witness grounds and places subsequently famous in the game coming to notice: Malling in 1705; White Conduit Fields, Islington, in 1718 (two generations before the forerunner of the Marylebone Cricket Club made it more famous); Broadwater Green in 1722; Kennington Common in 1724; and in the following year there is the first mention of cricket on the first really celebrated ground of all, the Artillery Ground in Finsbury just outside the City of London (the home of the H.A.C.). Then we find the game at Moulsey Hurst in 1726, Henfield in 1727, and even as relatively far afield as Gloucester in 1729, whilst 1730 saw no fewer than twenty matches recorded. From then on, we are 'away'.

Yet there is an enormous amount missing. We know, for instance, that seamen of the East India Company were playing cricket at Cambay in 1721: only the second certain reference to our people playing the game in non-British territory. Yet just as the merchants of Aleppo can have suffered from no isolated case of cricket fever, nor can the seamen of the East India Company.

Most remarkable of all is the clear and unequivocal reference by César de Saussure in June 1728. He talks of county matches as being a commonplace: of the newspapers giving advance notice of them, and later of the result being known as one of the more important pieces of news, and of such matches attracting large crowds. What is important is that by that date, *we only now know of one* county match, and that doubtfully entitled, and of two others in which a county took part: at least if the nomenclature which has come down to us is correct. Yet de Saussure talks about county matches 'often' being played.

One can only ask, with bewilderment, and with anxiety: What have we lost? Was William Bedle one of those who played in de Saussure's matches? The possible sources of information have been combed and re-combed yet nothing on these games has been found. And all the time something was being established which, 250 years ago, was the ancestor of something that is dying now: county cricket.

This is another of the great puzzles about the game: *why* county cricket? Why did great cricket become centred on the counties in a period when the counties certainly meant a great deal socially, but when travelling conditions must have made county cricket an extremely difficult enterprise to organize?

The answer appears to lie in the rise of the great patrons of the game. Having arisen, having established county cricket as the means *par excellence* of playing a great match, even if only a few counties were, or could be, involved at that time, later comers had to take it for granted that the county was the true basis for the game's organization and so they have remained into a period when most people in England are not normally conscious of what county they live in and back their county team as they might back a football team: not because the team in any way represents where they live, still less the people generally of their area, but because county cricket has acquired an independent existence of its own. These great patrons included some of the 'principal noblemen and gentlemen of quality' as the hallowed phrase has it: the Duke of Richmond (so misleadingly described as 'The Duke who was cricket': a term which must surely belong to the 3rd Duke of Dorset much later in the century), Sir William Gage, Mr Edwin Stead, and others. They sought out the best players in their locality, and formed them into powerful teams, and it then needed little subsequent change for the teams to be hailed as representative of all Kent, or all Surrey, or all Sussex: at first, no doubt, they made themselves financially responsible for the teams, whether playing under their own name or not, later they may have contributed towards the expenses, which were heavy. (A hundred years later, on the eve of the railway era, it could cost £100 of the money of that time just to take a team to London and back from Kent and from £200 to £300 to stage a match in Kent: that, at sixpence a head admission, meant anything up to 12,000 spectators before there was any return at all to the players. Yet larger crowds than these were attained, so a two-day and even more a three-day match between great teams may well have been profitable, and even highly rewarding.)[1]

Big landlords were not the only patrons of the game. As early as 1668 the brewing interest was involved in the game. Mine host of the Ram Inn in Smithfield was rated for a cricket ground: in the same year magistrates had decided that those who brewed beer on special occasions, such as race-meetings and cricket matches, need not pay excise duty. Clearly, quenching the thirst of those who watched – and played – cricket on a hot day was as profitable an industry three hundred years ago as now. Advertisements of matches (as opposed to announcements) in the Press were virtually all inserted by innkeepers. Nor did the connection ever cease: in the mid-eighteenth century John Pettit, at Dartford, had three cricketers on his staff, one of whom (Frame) he had enticed away from Surrey, and later on Porter in Chertsey imported Lumpy Stevens to strengthen

---

[1] In 1745 players were paid one and a half guineas each for an away match, one guinea for a home match and backers of the home side paid the scorer half a guinea. Twelfth man was paid as players. Umpires were not paid, which may or may not suggest that these posts were filled by 'gentlemen' (John Goulstone, in *The Cricketer Spring Annual 1960*, p. 76, and personal communication).

the local team – and, of course, there was the Bat and Ball Inn on Broad Ha'penny Down at Hambledon, though there is no evidence that that hostelry, of itself, was responsible for the procurement of players as was the case at Dartford and Chertsey. Our modern brewers have not, so far as is known, yet got round to the direct hiring of players for particular teams as did their forebears, but they would clearly be able to quote ancient precedent if they did.

Once the habit of making up representative county teams had been established, they will have continued of their own volition, just as they have to this day when they have long since ceased to be representative and when all *raison d'être* for them has largely vanished. But matches by such teams were not then the only great matches. From time to time, great local teams would arise, and the great Dartford team of the 1750s and 1760s was probably the first of these, certainly the first we can mention; others may have existed but we do not know enough about them. Big cricket had been played at Dartford from the start of the century, and by Dartford too but it was just after the turn of the half-century, when Dartford were so strong that London had to have as given men four of the best players in England: three years later, with two given men, Dartford could beat England twice. The England eleven was remarkably representative, no fewer than six counties providing players in it. But by that date no fewer than nineteen counties were known to have seen cricket played within their borders, as far afield as Somerset in the west, and Durham in the north. The game had clearly spread far indeed, even if East Anglia and the south-east continued to be the most popular – or, what is obviously not necessarily the same thing, the best reported areas.

Much had been happening: in 1744 the first two matches whose full scores have come down to us were played, and the second of these gave rise to James Dance (alias Love)'s heroic poem, so well known to so many lovers of the game, from quotation if not indeed from the complete text (put out in an admirable edition some forty years ago by F. S. Ashley-Cooper). Here are a few less-often quoted lines from it:

> When the retiring Sun begins to smile,
> And sheds its Glories round this sea-gurt Isle;
> When new-born Nature deck'd in vivid green,
> Chaces dull Winter from the charming Scene:
> High panting with Delight, the jovial Swain
> Trips it exulting o'er the Flow'r-strew'd Plain;
> Thy pleasures, CRICKET! all his Heart controul;

Thy eager Transports dwell upon his Soul:
He weighs the well-turn'd Bat's experienced Force,
And guides the rapid Ball's impetuous Course,
His supple Limbs with nimble Labour plies,
Nor bends the Grass beneath him as he flies.
The joyous Conquests of the late flown Year,
In Fancy's Paint, with all their Charms appear,
And now again he views the long wish'd Season near,
O thou, sublime Inspirer of my song!
What matchless Trophies to thy Worth belong!
Look round the Globe, inclin'd to Mirth, and see
What daring Sport can claim the Prize from Thee!
Not puny Billiards, where, with sluggish Pace,
The dull Ball trails before the feeble Mace.
Where no triumphant Shouts, no clamours dare
Pierce thro' the vaulted Roof and wound the Air;
But stiff Spectators quite inactive stand
Speechless, attending to the Striker's Hand:
Where nothing can your languid Spirits move,
Save when the Marker bellows out Six love!
Or when the Ball, close cushion'd, slides askew,
And to the op'ning Pocket runs, a Cou.
Nor yet that happier Game, where the smooth Bowl,
In circling Mazes, wanders to the Goal;
Where, much divided between Fear and Glee,
The Youth cries Rub; O Flee, you Ling'rer, Flee!
Not Tennis self, thy sister sport, can charm,
Or with thy fierce Delights our Bosoms warm.
Tho' full of Life, at Ease alone dismay'd,
She calls each swelling Sinew to her Aid;
Her echoing Courts confess the sprightly Sound,
While from the Racket the brisk balls rebound.
Yet, to small Space confin'd, ev'n she must yield
To nobler CRICKET, the disputed Field.

Evidently, the heroic style of the Augustan age of English poetry is well suited to writing about the game. The match was Kent *v.* All England on the Artillery ground, on June 18, 1744, and was quite important for historical reasons since it is clear that the ball was still bowled and not yet pitched although the wicket was now upright: and it is clear from illustrations of that and somewhat later periods, and from old bats, that true bowling must have continued for a little while yet. The game cannot have been very different in its essentials from that depicted in the last chapter.

The game had seen thirty matches recorded in 1730: in the next decade, 150 matches are known, and in the following one nearly 260. Some 230 matches are known in the 1750s when Dartford came to the fore, and about as many in the following decade. The first known full Laws date from 1744, and are clearly the Laws under which Kent played All England that year: they are not the earliest expressions of what was right and proper, however, for these may be found in a copy of 'Articles of Agreement' for the matches between the Duke of Richmond's team, and Mr Brodrick's team in 1727. These articles are in no sense laws: they are rather of the nature of 'instructions to umpires and team managers' amplifying and explaining certain points. They are valuable in so far as they touch on what were apparently points of dispute in those days, and in so far as they clearly presume the existence of a full code. Such a code has never been discovered, but 'H.P-T.' showed in masterly fashion[1] that an earlier code may be disinterred from the more sophisticated language of the 1744 code, by a close study of language. That code must have been ancient indeed, and smells rural in its wording. The growth of the game, however, had made it necessary for some authoritative body of people to pronounce on the Laws by the middle of the century, and hence the 1744 code. This code derives from a meeting of 'the London club': little else is known about such a club, and the code was revised in 1755 at the Star and Garter in Pall Mall but with the assistance of other clubs. There was need for a more or less permanent cricket body to supervise the Laws, but such a body was still over the horizon.

---

[1] In *Old Time Cricket* (1924), one of the six pamphlets already cited, see page 29.

4

THE RISE OF THE GREAT CLUBS

The game had certainly become a major sport by the middle of the century, but the loss in the early 1750s of three of its patrons (Frederick Prince of Wales and the Duke of Richmond, through their deaths, and Lord John Sackville through his insanity) led to a contraction in the number of 'great' games, if the surviving evidence can be believed. Certainly there was little mention of the game having any great backers and it seems to have reverted very much to the position it had held about 1720 before the great patrons. Such important games as took place were often between parish sides, and someone living in the 1760s might have been excused for thinking that the game as a major public spectacle was very much a thing of the past. In 1767 it was reported that the game was going out of fashion and being replaced by golf, and in 1771 a report spoke of the 'expiring fame of cricket'. Yet there was something new on the horizon by 1771.

It was not before 1749 that there is any reference known to the game in Hampshire (although, of course, this does not imply that the game was not being played there). Seven years later comes the first mention of Hambledon – one of these mid-eighteenth century parish games. Some time in the late 1760s the Hambledon Club was formed: it has a clear London origin, in that a majority of its founders were former pupils of Westminster School (just as later they were influential in the early Marylebone Club also). No one has been able to explain exactly why a rather out-of-the-way Hampshire village should have become the centre for some London gentlemen to get together themselves and to gather in several of the finest players of the game that had ever been collected together in one club. The club arose with the appearance of a new generation of wealthy patrons, Sir Horace Mann, Mr Rowed of Caterham (whose place was taken for Surrey by the Earl of Tankerville), the Duke of Dorset and others, and they, with the Hambledon Club's own members and backers, were responsible for the rise of the game again in the early 1770s (how important the patrons were may be judged by the way in which 'first-class' cricket fell away in 1784–5 when Sir Horace Mann and the Duke of Dorset[1] had little time to sponsor matches). It is easy to see how, in the eyes of those who came after, there seemed to have been nothing which had gone before, with the brilliance of the Hambledon players eclipsing those already obscured by the mid-century darkness. They were not all Hampshire men, of course: many were from Sussex and Surrey and even farther.

It was not long before the Hambledon club's sides were becoming famous for their deeds: it was formed somewhere around 1767. In 1769 occurred the first known century opening partnership: the same year, the first record of a century scored in the game, by John Minshull, for the Duke of Dorset's XI against Wrotham.

Here is this score:

31 August 1769   Duke of Dorset's XI v. Wrotham

HIS GRACE'S FIRST HANDS				HIS GRACE'S SECOND HANDS		
Duke of Dorset	111113IIII	r.o	12	IIIIIII2II2I	b	14
Esq. Bishop	III	b	3	31	ct	4
Minchin						
(John Minshull)	312II3IIIIIII	ct	18	121312232311142323111131121		
				IIII2IIIII3II3II4II24221I2II		
				1224123	b	107
Pattenden	IIII22IIIII	b	12	121IIII2IIII311213	ct	24
Fish	II	b	2	2III312	ct	11
Bartram	IIII3	r.o	7	31231162211	r.o	23
Wood		b	0	21312	ct	9
Bowra	21221	b	8	1213121		11
Whitting	2	ct	2	3	b	3
Oliver	1	b	1	13	ct	4
Shearcy	1		1	2121312	r.o	12
Byes	2		2	111211133		14
	TOTAL		68			236

The Wrotham score does not survive. A few weeks after this match, the Duke of Dorset engaged Minshull as gardener, at 8s per week.

It is not possible to say if it *was* the first century – it is nowhere remarked on in

---

[1] In 1783 the *Whitehall Evening Post* for July 8 quotes the Duke of Dorset's cricketing expenses at over £1,000 a year, exclusive of betting and incidental costs of entertainment.

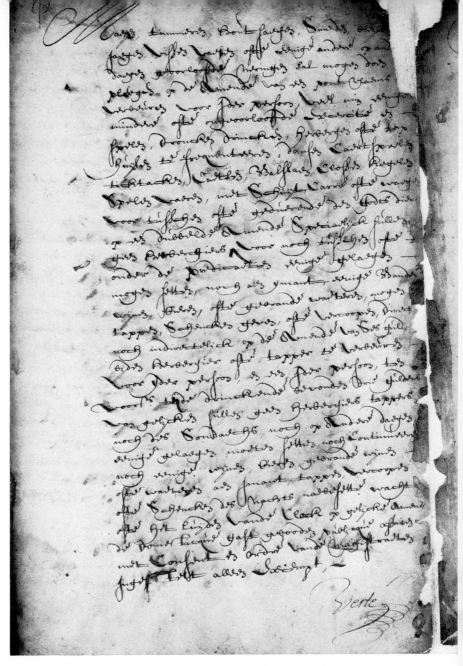

3. An ordinance of New Netherland, 26 October, 1656, provided penalties for
performing a number of actions on Sundays. There is no reason why the Dutch
of New Amsterdam, or English colonists coming in from New England, should
not have been playing cricket there eight years before the town became New
York, but the original document (line 9) refers to *balslaen*. This is too general
a word to be necessarily confined to cricket, but the possibility cannot be
excluded

REWARD OF MERIT.

4. A depiction of the game of 'wicket' – it was cricket in an antique form but still played in this form in America, even into this century

First Cricket Match in Scotland

5. A glass goblet, presented by Sir Ronald Campbell to Haddington CC, showing the first recorded cricket match in Scotland, in 1785 on the estate of the Earl of Cathcart, from a contemporary painting by David Allen. In the foreground are members of the Earl's family. The engraving on the other side, taken from Richard Daft's *Kings of Cricket*, portrays Fuller Pilch, William Clarke and Tom Lockyer

contemporary newspapers, and it is impossible to say whether that means it was a quite ordinary occurrence or whether the feat was simply not heard about. The score was to lie unknown in the Sackville papers until 1959 when it was unearthed by a young man, not then yet out of his teens – John Goulstone.

There is another important matter about this match – the full stroke-by-stroke score was kept of the Duke of Dorset's team, and was obviously being kept long before it looked as if Minshull was going to establish any kind of record. What then can be the meaning of those old paintings of men sitting half-way to the wicket cutting notches into staves, found for many years after 1769 if, by that date and by inference therefore much earlier, 'scoring' as notch-cutting was called, had been reduced to pen and paper? It cannot merely have been artistic licence because the Kent *v.* Hampshire match of July 8–9 1783 was first reckoned to have been a tie because the scorers had made an error – one of them, Pratt, produced his stick as evidence that he had made a mistake in once cutting the eleventh, instead of the tenth, notch longer than the others.

It seems that the old method of 'scoring' continued in existence, perhaps to provide the 'official' tally of the final totals, though the details had for many years been committed, perhaps less accurately, to paper. If so, it is another example of the way 'scoring' in cricket has remained officially well behind unofficial scoring: even now, the official scorers keep an inadequate detail of what goes on in a match and it has to be contrasted with the wealth of data maintained by Press or wireless statisticians, where one may find out how many balls were bowled by each bowler to each batsman and many other far from negligible items.

The game was becoming highly organized, and the thirst for statistical information was about to be met: from the time of the formation of the Hambledon Club to the end of the century, such changes were to be made to the game as were to transform it almost to what it is now, by comparison with what had gone before.

Nevertheless, despite its short-lived eminence, some sixteen years at most, the Hambledon Club has achieved an importance in the minds of cricket lovers far beyond its merits.[1] The reason is that well over a generation after it had lost its

[1] It is commonly stated for example, and so frequently as to have become accepted truth, that the Hambledon Club was for a period a law-giving authority. There is no evidence for this, indeed, the evidence all points the other way. There were three changes in the Laws in the Hambledon period other than major revisions. The first of these was in 1771 when, in September, a committee of Hambledon players decided to limit the width of the bat: that, although it was to be accepted generally, can have been no more than a local decision. It was adopted by the revisers of 1774 at the Star and Garter tavern: proof, if any were needed, that the *ipse dixit* of some paid cricketers in a country district was not sufficient authority to issue a new Law or a change to an old one. The

importance, a book appeared which, by its sheer literary worth, struck a chord which has gone echoing down time. The book was by Charles Cowden Clarke, and he wrote it from reminiscences by John Nyren[1] about the players of his father's time: Nyren must have been speaking from largely first-hand knowledge and what he said must be largely accurate but it is not as a chronicle that it evokes a response, it is the way, the almost unaffected way in which it was written, so that Clarke makes us hear the very sound of the old man himself talking. The book set up a permanent memorial to the Hambledon Club of a kind which is utterly lacking for almost any other cricket club in the world, at any time. It did very much more: it established cricket as a game to which there attached a literature and made it, for that reason alone, outstanding as a game. There had been books written, good books indeed, about tennis, and about racing, about hawking, and about chess, but there had been nothing which idolized its players, nothing which made an appeal even to the non-lover of the game, as did Clarke's book. It set cricket up on a pedestal: how far that pedestal may have been justified we shall consider later on.

[1] Amongst the myths which surround Hambledon is the one that the Nyrens were originally Nairnes, and Jacobites. This particular myth was exploded by the researches of Edmund Esdaile, an epitome of which appeared in *The Cricket Quarterly* III, pp. 94–95, and which show conclusively that the Nyrens had no Nairne connection, being, until about the mid-eighteenth century, Nierens or Nierings, stemming from one Gaspar Nieren born about 1600 of a father who originated in Kent. The family were always located in Sussex from then on. The myth was first given some currency by E. V. Lucas from remarks by a grand-daughter of John Nyren: he was evidently unable to reconcile it with biographical facts known to him, but it was another sixty years before the truth was established.

---

second was the addition of a third stump which is said to have occurred after a match in London where Hambledon players were involved in 1775: but it was many years before this became general, and it was not found in the Laws until 1785, and those Laws did not emanate from Hambledon. Had Hambledon been any kind of law-giving authority, there would have been editions of the Laws issued with this particular change long before then: no editions of the Laws were ever issued which in any way convey the authority of the Hambledon Club, however indirectly. The third was the mention, for the first time, of two bails for each wicket in what has been described as an 'unofficial' edition of the Laws issued in 1786 in Maidstone: Hambledon did not come into the matter at any time. In 1791 the Hambledon Club deferred to those of its members who were members of the Marylebone club for a decision on a point of interpretation – showing clearly enough where the law-giving authority lay then; in the whole twenty-four years covered by the extant Minute-Book of the Hambledon Club, this is the only reference to the Laws, and then only indirectly. It is not credible that, had Hambledon been a law-giving authority, some reference to its discussions would not have appeared in its Minutes. None does: and in all its history, the September 1771 decision is the only one which touches on law-making – and even that, objectively speaking, amounts to no more than a statement that Hambledon players were not ready to play with a bat of unlimited dimensions. There was no one complete comprehensive and detailed code of Laws and 'playing regulations' in the eighteenth century: Hambledon's decision about the bat is but one of many local variations. Others will have come into the Laws for other reasons and from other sources: Hambledon may have been fruitful in such suggestions, but that is a far cry from making it a law-giving authority.

The book did more: it made people talk, as they still talk, about Hambledon being the birthplace of cricket, and then when that idea ceased to be tenable, about it being the cradle and, if not that, then the first club – all untrue. There is no need to argue this point – one does not put a lusty young man into a cradle. But the myth dies hard. Ashley-Cooper tried to explode it over seventy years ago by referring to much London cricket well before Hambledon and to cricketers as famous in their times as the Hambledon players were to be. Still, however, people say that cricket began at Hambledon. Yet, the Hambledon Club never played an eleven-a-side game in all its existence, and may well never have played any other kind of game. This is, indeed, almost certainly the truth: the closer one can get to the original source describing the correct titles of the teams taking part in these Hambledon matches, the more difficult it is to find Hambledon at all. There is an occasional Hambledon Town match – there is an occasional Hambledon parish match (the first mention of Hambledon in 1756 was in such a match). There are very few Hambledon Club matches which survive a scrutiny of this type, and those that do survive probably do so because the original source is lacking: amongst those very few there may be an even smaller number of matches which were 'Gentlemen of the Hambledon Club' (a title which should exclude the paid players, but which did not always do so in the next century). But hardly any of the games in which the famous paid players took part were Hambledon matches: for the Hambledon Club organized Hampshire county matches, and it organized very many other matches got up by its leading members. It resembles the present-day symbiosis between the Marylebone Club and the Middlesex county team – but of course the Marylebone Club does play a large number of matches under its own name, whereas Hambledon may well have played none at all.

The Hambledon Club did not indeed *have* to play matches under its own name to become famous: it collected together the greatest players of the time, it sent teams (that is, teams got up by members) to other centres, where they were an immediate focus of attraction to people for miles around (travelling by coach and by horse from Dorking to Sevenoaks, for instance), and the playing ability of the teams, as well as its own organization made it a real director of the game, and it was under Hambledon that the transformation was taken so far, though it was probably not started by it.

That transformation started before Hambledon, when bowling ceased to be the method of delivery, and pitching the ball took its place. We do not know precisely when the change-over started, nor when it was concluded, but so far as great games were concerned, it had not started by 1744 and it had finished before

59

1773; roughly a generation, and comparable in time to the change-over in the nineteenth century from under-arm to over-arm via round-arm (from about 1830 to 1860). We know nothing about the controversy that this must have aroused and it must have been aroused because a pitched ball cannot be dealt with satisfactorily with the old bat, and it is not much use bowling it against a long low wicket. Nothing defined the bat at this time, but the upright wicket was defined by 1744, yet we do not know when the change had occurred. An analysis of the duration of matches suggests the change began in the late 1730s and was completed in the 1760s, probably early in that decade. It is just possible that a very careful statistical investigation into scoring might pin it down, since scoring must have been very much easier against the pitched ball, than against the bowled ball. Conversely, it must also have been easier to some extent to get a batsman out with a pitched ball, if you were a good 'bowler'. A study of the scoring of the period does show that the run rate rose fairly sharply during and after the Hambledon period, and confirms that the change-over had been consummated before Hambledon arose. Buckley suggested, not improbably, in his unpublished 'More Historical Gleanings', that the ball in the 1744 game between Kent and England was not actually bowled but 'thrown' so that it skimmed in the air just above the surface of the ground, and that this match was at the very inception of what was to be called length bowling. His suggestion fits the statistical analysis of the duration of games at this time very well.[1]

---

[1] Bowling has two meanings: one is its original meaning of *rolling* a ball along the ground, and the other is its special cricket meaning of the bowler delivering a ball to the batsman within the definition of current laws. Throwing has also two meanings: one is the normal straightforward meaning of propelling a ball *other than* by rolling it and the other is its special cricket meaning, which has altered with the years, of a bowler's delivery which is not in accordance with the current laws.

Until the mid-eighteenth century all cricket bowling was true bowling. Then we had what is called under-arm and this may be 'cricket' bowling but it is not true bowling – it is true throwing. If anyone doubts this, let him 'bowl' under-arm and 'throw' under-arm and he will be hard put to it to find any difference for there is none.

Round-arm when it first appeared before the eighteenth century was out and until it was legalized was at first called 'cricket' throwing: as its delivery did not differ from the under-arm delivery which was true throwing, save only in that the arm was raised outwards from a vertical plane, or near-vertical plane in which under-arm had been delivered, it followed that it was not only 'cricket' throwing, it was also true throwing, like under-arm. But under-arm was not regarded as throwing by cricketers: nor, when round-arm was legalized was it regarded as throwing by cricketers. We thus reach a stage where round-arm was 'cricket' bowling but also throwing! It is fascinating that it was originally condemned as 'straight-armed bowling'!!

In due course, round-arm became over-arm: and, as with round-arm, over-arm was at first regarded by cricketers as throwing. Insofar as the delivery was no more than a more vertical round-arm it was indeed true throwing. At some unknown stage, the idea took root that 'cricket' bowling involved a straight arm. In due course over-arm was legalized as 'cricket' bowling but it was not true bowling: having become legalized, after a period of time cricketers began to discern two types of over-arm bowling, one, which was not to be distinguished from round-arm,

It is extraordinarily tempting to quote at length from Charles Cowden Clarke's book on these old cricketers; there is a flavour about how he reproduced Nyren's words that cannot be captured by one's own writing:

There was high feasting held on Broad-Halfpenny during the solemnity of one of our grand matches. Oh! it was a heart-stirring sight to witness the multitude forming a complete and dense circle round that noble green. Half the county would be present, and all their hearts with us – Little Hambledon, pitted against all England, was a proud thought for the Hampshire men. Defeat was glory in such a struggle – Victory, indeed, made us only 'a little lower than the angels'. How those fine brawn-faced fellows of farmers would drink to our success! And then what stuff they had to drink! – Punch! – not your new *Ponche à la Romaine,* or *Ponche à la Groseille,* or your modern cat-lap milk punch – punch be-deviled; but good, unsophisticated, John Bull stuff – stark! – that would stand on end – punch that would make a cat speak! Sixpence a bottle! We had not sixty millions of interest to pay in those days. The ale, too! – not the modern horror under the same name, that drives as many men melancholy-mad as the hypocrites do; not the beastliness of these days, that will make a fellow's inside like a shaking bog, and as rotten; but barleycorn, such as would put the souls of three butchers into one weaver. Ale that would flare like turpentine – genuine Boniface! – This immortal viand (for it was more than liquor) was vended at twopence per pint. The immeasurable villainy of our vintners would, with their march of intellect (if ever they could get such a brewing), drive a pint of it out into a gallon. Then the quantity the fellows would eat! Two or three of them would strike dismay into a round of beef. They could no more have pecked in that style than they could have flown, had the infernal black stream (that type of Acheron!) which soddens the carcass of a Londoner, been the fertilizer of their clay. There would this company, consisting most likely of some thousands, remain patiently and anxiously watching every turn of fate in the game, as if the event had been the meeting of two armies to decide their liberty. And whenever a Hambledon man made a good hit, worth four or five runs, you would hear the deep mouths of the

---

and which was a throw, a true throw, and one which became what cricketers regard as legitimate bowling, but which is all the same still truly a throw. The former came to be penalized as a 'cricket' throw: the latter is accepted as correct. Note that all the way from the beginning of under-arm, all 'cricket' bowling has in fact been true throwing. The distinction that cricketers make is an artificial one, and if, for example, over-arm were suddenly made illegal, what they call throwing would prevail in almost every delivery, and in fact every delivery would be a true throw, as it is now.

But a true throw is not a 'cricket' throw and a 'cricket' bowl is not a true bowl.

whole multitude baying away in pure Hampshire – 'Go hard! – go hard! – *Tich* and turn! – *tich* and turn!'[1] To the honour of my countrymen, let me bear testimony upon this occasion also, as I have already done upon others. Although their provinciality in general, and personal partialities individually, were naturally interested in behalf of the Hambledon men, I cannot call to recollection an instance of their wilfully stopping a ball that had been hit out among them by one of our opponents.[2] Like *true* Englishmen, they would give an enemy fair play. How strongly are all those scenes, of fifty years by-gone, painted in my memory! – and the smell of that ale comes upon me freshly as the new May flowers. (*The Cricketers of My Time*)

It is difficult also to select the names which should appear in a history of the game when all are noteworthy; and at a period when the very prowess of what often amounted to and was sometimes called an England XI brought into the limelight notable players amongst their opponents. So mention is now made of four only of all that period.

The first is James Aylward, since for very many years he appears to have held the record for the highest score made by a batsman. This was when he made 167 for what should correctly be entitled Hampshire, against England. He started his innings, according to a printed bill of the match, at five o'clock on Wednesday, June 18, 1777 and was not out till after three o'clock on Friday, and he made it going in first out of a total of 403, at that time quite the largest score by one team, and for many years after. Hampshire won by an innings against a team which contained two more of these four players. The second of these was 'Shock' White: he was notable because one day in 1776 he had turned up with an enormous bat, and the result was a limitation henceforth on the width of a bat. Shock White[3] belonged to Reigate, a notable home of early cricketers. On the loser's side also incidentally was John Minshull who had scored that first recorded century eight years earlier, but which had aroused nothing like the interest of Aylward's feat. The third of these players is Edward Stevens, more usually referred to as 'Lumpy'. He it was who, in a five-a-side game in 1775 on the Artillery ground, several times passed the ball through the two-stump wicket, and this led to the gradual introduction over the next five years of a third stump in all important matches. He, like Aylward (who died at ninety-one in 1831) and so

[1] Rule 15 of the Game of Wicket ('The Old-Time Game of Wicket') says that 'in crossing, the striker shall tick his bat down or over the tick marks to have a cross count, except when caught or ticked out'. A *cross* is a *run*, *ticked out* was *run out*, and *tick* is the same word as *tich* or *touch*.
[2] There were no boundaries, of course, in those days or for a century to come.
[3] There was another much less known cricketer called White, with the same nickname as his contemporary – time may have confused the two.

many other old-time cricketers, lived to a great age, dying in 1819 aged eighty-four. His portrait (plate 8) is one of the only two portraits of cricketers who played in the eighteenth century which are known (always omitting great men of affairs whose portraits are known to us for other reasons than cricket).

The fourth player is William Beldham, known as 'Silver Billy', a fine all-round player of whose batting deeds we know far more than of his bowling, there being no analyses at that time, nor, often, any crediting to bowlers unless they took wickets without the interposition of other players. Beldham played hardly at all at Hambledon, though fairly frequently in games got up by the club elsewhere – he started, of course, in the latter days of the club as a great cricketing organization, for his first match was in 1787 for England against the White Conduit Club (as it was still called) at Thomas Lord's first ground, and he played from then until 1821, carrying his bat for 23 in his last match for Players against Gentlemen at Lord's (present) third ground, and by then aged fifty-five. He lived many years more, dying at the age of ninety-six in 1862 at Tilford in Surrey (where for a time the cricket statistician and historian F. S. Ashley-Cooper lived). Beldham's portrait too is noteworthy, being the only known photograph (plate 12) of a player who played on the old Hambledon ground in that club's heyday.

There was a great *esprit de corps* amongst the Hambledon players, and in the *Hambledon Cricket Chronicle* (edited by E. V. Lucas and F. S. Ashley-Cooper) there are references to their love of singing: here is another, less well known, from a diary kept by John Baker of Horsham who rode over to Sevenoaks to watch the match between Hampshire and All England on the Vine in June 1773:

The Hants cricketers had one large room to themselves at the Crown Inn which is the Post Office, and after each day, though so shamefully beat on each, spent the evening very merrily, singing catches (and very well too) and some other songs with great joviality which made me a little doubt their being at all concerned.

Cricket is, and always had been, an earthy game and any attempt to pretend to the contrary leads to hypocrisy. A fascinating example of both assertions will be found in Ashley-Cooper's *The Hambledon Cricket Chronicle* where he notes that the fifth of the toasts always to be drunk at a Hambledon Club dinner, from 1781 onwards, was 'To the immortal memory of Madge'. E. V. Lucas, in his Introduction, spends almost a page speculating who Madge may have been, and he goes very wide of the mark indeed, especially when, almost at the start of what he says, he says it cannot have been any fair lady as cricketers gathered together did not normally talk about women. Maybe they did not in his time, nor were the

Hambledon members quite doing that either: they were toasting an eighteenth-century word for the female reproductive organs! Yes, cricket is an earthy game.

The Hambledon Club was at the peak of its fame from 1772 until 1787, just fifteen years: there had evidently been a decline in the last two or three years, and then with the rise of the Marylebone Club Hambledon quickly dimmed. It did so, however, in very curious circumstances which, however, have nothing to do with cricket. On August 29, 1796 fifteen people attended a meeting of the club, of whom only three were members (a pattern which had been followed for some little time previously). One of these was the Honorary Secretary, Thomas Bonham (a forerunner of the Bonham-Carter family, and brother of the High Sheriff of Hampshire, himself a steward of the club the previous year). Amongst those present, as noted by Bonham in his own hand, was 'Mr Thos Pain, Authour of the rights of Man'. 'Mr Thos Pain' – Citizen Tom Paine – was under sentence of death *in absentio* on a charge of treason; he was at this time residing in Paris, but his known movements do permit him to have been in Hampshire on this date. He was a lover of cricket and had once been collector of Customs at Lewes, a noted cricketing centre, before he went to advise the Americans on their independence, and to draft the celebrated 'Declaration of Independence' (eventually issued without including that one important clause of his forbidding slavery). What on earth was he doing in the Hambledon Club at this time? There can be almost endless speculation about this, but it would be for an altogether different kind of history.

Although the club is generally stated to have come to an end in the 1790s and though indeed as an important cricket club it had ceased somewhat earlier, it went on playing cricket in a minor way for another generation, and there are occasional references to such matches.

Unlike the Hambledon Club (with whom it shared a number of founding members, as well as others) the Marylebone Club was a cricket club. It played under its own name, and those players (amateur players we would call them) were often of some considerable ability, and did play occasionally against teams not quite of the highest order, without added assistance in the way of 'given' men, who, one suspects, very often became part of what would now be called the permanent ground staff. The club was, moreover, situated, despite its three moves to each of Thomas Lord's grounds, just beyond the expensive, residential development north and south of Oxford Street, and west of the Prince Regent's Park. It was ideally sited to attract the nobility and gentry from 'clubland' in St James's and nearby, and it very rapidly indeed achieved an eminence for both social and cricket reasons never attained by any other club in the country, or

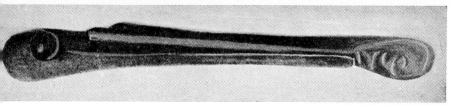

6–7. A boy at Stonyhurst in the last century with the typical bat used in a very early version of cricket preserved by these Catholic schoolboys in exile in the low Countries for two hundred years: the other photograph shows more clearly the bat and ball

8. The earliest known portrait (at Knole) of a man famous only for his cricket – 'Lumpy' Stevens

An early announcement about cricket a New York paper of 1789: it is by means the earliest, but is not without terest with its appearance so few years ter New York had been evacuated by e British

10. The well-known painting of Mr Hope of Amsterdam, now owned by the MCC, playing cricket with his friends in Rome in the early 1790s, before the French Revolution had yet swept down into Italy. Hope, despite his name, though of ultimate English origin was a member of a well-known firm of merchants in Amsterdam which still exists, and this portrait gives some indication of the spread of the game at that time in Europe

even in the world – although in their own smaller spheres, the Calcutta Club, founded only a few years after the Marylebone Club, and the Melbourne Club some two generations later, achieved a similar local eminence.

Lord's and the MCC – the two institutions are so often coupled together in this phrase and their history is inevitably bound up together. It has, certainly till very recently, been something of an advantage to cricket and to the MCC that the ground was named Lord's, with the suggestion of aristocratic influence inherent in such a name. Thomas Lord, however, was the son of a Yorkshire landowner dispossessed through his support of Prince Charles during the '45. He came to London and was able to make his way and to some extent retrieve the family fortunes: became a supplier of wine to the King and other notables, and through this came to know the Earl of Winchilsea, one of the great patrons of cricket of the day, and a member of the White Conduit Club. He it was who suggested to Lord, in 1786, that if the latter were to establish a private ground where the White Conduit Club could play (thus differing from the ground at Islington where anyone could play for a nominal sum), he would be well supported. So Lord obtained the lease of his first ground from the Portman family; in May 1787 it was ready for use, and the White Conduit Club moved there. By July that year it had started to become known as the Marylebone Cricket Club.[1] The ground was later resumed by the Portman estate for building development, and the modern Dorset Square occupies the site. (The name has nothing to do with the 3rd Duke of Dorset, possibly the greatest patron of the game in the eighteenth century, and the Sackville family were in no way involved: the name comes from the family connection the Portman family had with the county of

---

[1] The clubs are called the White Conduit Cricket Club and the Marylebone Cricket Club, because that is what they were often called at the time, and of course the second is still properly so-called. But both 'White Conduit' and 'Marylebone' were topographical terms and they may well have been merely descriptive and not formal names. There is no evidence in fact of a formal White Conduit Cricket Club: what is known is of gentlemen from the Star and Garter Club (see page 66) who frequented, with others, the White Conduit Fields to play cricket and who, without others, moved to Marylebone. Any formal organization called the Marylebone Cricket Club may well not have come into existence at that time or indeed for another three or four years. It may, however, have had a formal organization of a much smaller scope rather before, just as those dining clubs which still exist, and which have regular dinners usually at one favourite restaurant and which usually need some kind of rules to ensure cohesion. The Rules of the Marylebone Cricket Club suggest strongly that it began in that sort of way, for how otherwise could its first rule be to state when the Anniversary Dinner should be held? That is exactly what one would expect for a group of gentlemen who associated for their convivial purposes at the Star and Garter tavern, and played cricket together in north London. All early records of the club were lost in the fire in 1825 – had they not been it is reasonably certain that they would have disclosed a date for the club either much before 1787 (which is no more than a date for Lord's first ground) when members first went out to Islington, or a few years later – but not 1787 which has no significance in terms of the history of the club.

c

Dorset.) It was in 1808 that Lord established his second ground, in Lisson Grove, but was able to continue in occupancy of his first ground for another two years: the MCC stayed on the first ground, but another club, the St John's Wood Club, played on the second ground (it was later, when the MCC moved, absorbed into the MCC). The second ground too had to be given up as the Regent Canal was taken right through it. Lord had moved the turf he had fostered at Dorset Square to Lisson Grove in the winter of 1809–10, and now it had to be removed once more to its present resting-place: this occurred in 1813. His name has stuck to his ground ever since. Lord himself was something of a cricketer, and his name will often be found in *Scores & Biographies*:[1] he was primarily a bowler, slow according to Haygarth, but a Nottinghamshire account says he was fast: perhaps he varied them!

The most important thing about the MCC is that from its early days, it seems to have assumed, and was conceded, law-making powers. How did this come about? It was not simply because its founders and early members were both prominent noble and gentleman cricketers, as well as notable men of affairs: there were real historical reasons.

There had been revisions of the Laws in 1755 and 1774 which had been made by the so-called Star and Garter Club.[2] The club was so-called because it generally met at the Star and Garter tavern in Pall Mall and most probably had no coherent organization at all, but was simply a group of people who enjoyed

---

[1] *Scores and Biographies* is the short title by which is known the monumental collection of old matches and biographies of old cricketers by Arthur Haygarth the publication of which began in 1861. For more on this see below, pages 88–90.

[2] There were several inns by the same name of Star and Garter but the one in question is almost certainly the same one at Nos. 94–96 Pall Mall that also saw meetings from time to time of the Jockey Club, as well as of other convivial clubs. Volume XXIX of the *Survey of London* makes it clear, however, that this is a strong probability rather than a certainty as there was during most of the eighteenth century another inn of the same name at No. 44 Pall Mall and during part of the time, yet a third at No. 21. Contemporary writers do not identify which of the two, or three, they are referring to. But the other two hostelries were not of the same fame as that at Nos. 94–96: its buildings have long since vanished and the Carlton Club once stood upon the site: it is now occupied by an office block, numbered 100. In this connection the book by Lord Harris and F. S. Ashley-Cooper, *Lord's and the MCC*, refers to the origins of the MCC as being found in a convivial club which met at the Star and Garter and which was known as the *Je ne sçai quoi* [sic] club. This can hardly be: the contemporary evidence, contained in an article on this club in *The Attic Miscellany* for 1790 is that the *Je ne sçai quoi* club was not formed before 1786 (which is too late for it to have anything to do with those habitués of the Star and Garter who were already cricketing at Islington) and amongst a number of names of members given, only the Duke of Dorset was connected with cricket. A publication of the Rowfant Club of Cleveland, Ohio, in 1923 on Captain Charles Morris, who according to Ashley-Cooper was secretary of the *Je ne sçai quoi* club, makes no mention in some 170 pages either of that club or of cricket. The book, in a small limited edition, was well researched and could have been expected to contain such references had they been ascertainable.

their own company and met regularly together, even to arranging formal dinners of which some record is known. About 1782 (it is not possible to be more precise) some of these habitués who were keen on cricket became known as the White Conduit Club from the area where they were wont to play in Islington, though they were also sometimes referred to as the Star and Garter Club. Those habitués in due course removed themselves to St Marylebone and it is in this way that the accepted custom of law-giving was handed through to the MCC.

Of course the membership itself at that time would have been enough to ensure that any laws made would be generally regarded and in this connection reference has already been made to the Duke of Dorset. He it was who had John Minshull in his employ, he it was who made many matches at Hambledon, and elsewhere, with or against the Earl of Tankerville (who employed Lumpy Stevens) and Sir Horatio Mann (nephew of Horace Walpole's friend: Walpole himself hated cricket, but even so he was once found watching it near Paris), yet another great patron of the game. The Duke of Dorset was Ambassador in Paris at the time of the outbreak of the French Revolution. In the summer of 1789 he asked the Duke of Leeds, then Foreign Secretary, for an assurance of goodwill from the British Government to France. The Duke of Leeds was himself a keen cricket lover and it appears that it was he who arranged for a tour of English cricketers to Paris by way of a 'goodwill' visit. It is commonly said that the tour had been arranged by the Duke of Dorset but though he was most probably the originator of the idea, he was in no position to make detailed arrangements at that particular time. At all events, the first encounter the Duke of Dorset had with the team was when he met it in Dover, himself fleeing from the Revolution. It was probably the first cricket tour to have been arranged for political reasons – it was certainly the first, but by no means the last, to be cancelled for such reasons.

The great unanswered question – unanswered because never apparently asked – is who were the team going to play? Were they to act as a 'circus', like Spalding's two baseball 'nines' who toured England in 1874, to split into two teams playing five-a-side? Surely it was not to play as a team the English residents in Paris for no more then than now could they have met the full English strength? What then of the French? Were there French players good enough to take on the team, or even good enough to make up two mixed elevens? If so, their names are not known to us, nor what happened to them: if these questions could be answered, a whole new vista of old cricket would open up.

5

THE SPREAD AND SOPHISTICATION OF THE GAME

The English, more than any other nation in these islands or perhaps the world, are sport mad. It is difficult to imagine any other country where a leading and serious daily newspaper could publish a letter from an educated man complaining that once 'we used to turn from the front pages with their politics and wars to the back pages with their restful sport, but now we can no longer do so': it is not a comment that would ever be made in *Le Monde* or the *Neue Zürcher Zeitung* and the letter at once shows one of the reasons for the popularity of sport in England – to enable people to bury their heads in the sands ostrich-wise.

By the end of the eighteenth century, there were three sports which commanded the attention of the greater part of the population: racing, boxing and cricket. They each had their different appeals: cricket was the only team game then, and for another sixty years, which had anything like mass support (only in the 1890s did football – soccer – seriously rival and even overtake cricket as a game to play and watch), and it had, moreover, a certain hieratic quality. This combined with its special code of Laws the basis of which was fair play and sportsmanship (quite unlike either racing or boxing at that time) set it apart and made it something which could appeal to those members of the public at all levels who disdained some aspects of the other two sports. It had also more positive attractions: it possessed a fascinatingly complicated method of scoring – perhaps more complicated than any other team game known even now. It provided the opportunity for displaying a great variety of different physical skills during actual play, and it was and is (outside the present new-fangled single-innings matches) the only game where you could 'come again': you could have a disastrous first innings but you could (if you could!) recover and even win in the second innings. This is surely one of its most important features and why those who advocate single-innings cricket are in danger of ridding the game of the keystone of its attraction.

Those are some of the reasons why the game became so popular and has retained the popularity it still possesses. It was helped to popularity by its 'sophistication'. This took place to an enormous extent in the last part of the eighteenth century so that when the new century dawned virtually only two great changes had still to happen, and one of them comparatively minor (over-arm bowling, and declarations). From a rural game with Laws only just emerging from the rural, it had been pulled to, virtually, the modern game, in some fifty years.

Consider what had been done: the wicket had become upright, and contained three stumps, charging down an opponent had been prohibited and laws prescribed against obstruction, leg-before-wicket had been brought in, the width of the bat had been limited, short runs had been legislated for, as also had been rolling, watering, mowing and covering the wicket; a new ball at the start of each innings had been allowed for: the first cricket annual had appeared, as also had the first collections of scores, the first batting averages had been compiled (though not, so far as is known, published). It may be speculated that the first averages and first annuals[1] had been compiled to meet a requirement for positive information on 'form' for gambling: but this can hardly have been the reason for the publication of collections of old scores, however, and it seems likely that, already by the 1790s, the desire to relive old matches by seeing their details set out in print, and the desire to compare one cricketer with another, which is the basis for all cricket statistics, had already been aroused: and was being met. The Laws left only quite minor details to be altered and argued about with the two exceptions mentioned. Anyone watching a game in 1800 could understand our modern game and could appreciate its appurtenances: anyone from now transported back would find it as easy to appreciate the game then played as he would the modern game, and arguably more so, since there seems to have been in 'great' games more skill maintained throughout the game than one often finds even in a Test match.

Almost in parenthesis, these changes had the effect of crippling the game in America: for many of them had taken place during a period when there was virtually no intercourse with Europe, let alone intercourse on the scale enjoyed before 1774. Even some twenty years earlier, it had been possible to distinguish in New York between the London game and the game played in the colonies:

---

[1] Samuel Butcher, *List of all the Principal matches of Cricket that have been played in the year* (1790–1805), first issue 1791, last in 1806.

now they had become almost two distinct games. Wicket, or cricket, in North America would never be brought up-to-date but would linger on to die a long death in our own century: cricket as played in England had to be introduced as, to all intents and purposes, a new game.

In England the picture was of course quite different. By the end of the eighteenth century cricket had been recorded in thirty-one of the English counties, and those not mentioned lying very much to the north and west of the country. Beyond England it was being played in Scotland (and far enough north too, in Elgin), in Wales, and, not surprisingly, in Ireland. (The opening few years of the next century would see many additions to the counties where cricket was known.) It is indeed safe to say that even if there was a county in England where it had not yet been played (and it is far more likely that there was not but simply that no record was made) then there can have been none where some people did not know of the game and had indeed probably played it. The case in Scotland may well have been similar: James Hogg in his book *The Confessions of a Justified Sinner* places the scene in Edinburgh of the *early* eighteenth century and makes the young gentlemen about town play cricket: what is significant is that when he first came to Edinburgh in the 1790s, he found the game so frequently played as to take it for granted it must have been played at the earlier period set in his novel. Even stronger evidence for cricket in Scotland is the playing of the game in Savannah, Georgia, by Highland Scots in the 1730s on the occasion of St Andrew's Day: presumably they knew the game before they sailed for America.

The game was becoming popular, even fashionable, throughout town and country and at all levels of society. It always had been, in what surely was its nurturing ground in south-eastern England, and without distinction of class or position socially. Later the Victorians were rather consciously to make a boast of something the eighteenth century took for granted (and much later in our own time, village clubs in the London commuter belt would be taken over by people working in the City who would prefer to form teams different from the local teams and so, at a time when social divisions were coming to an end in the country at large, they were being deliberately created in the realm of cricket – not to its advantage).

In the south-east there can hardly have been a village of any size which did not field a team at least once during the summer. Nor was cricket confined to the countryside: it was being played in some of the public and grammar schools, in its adult form, and had for long been played at the Universities. But it was being played in the towns too, and not just by aristocratic clubs. The leading cases are

Sheffield, Nottingham and Leicester where, in each case, well before the century was out, cricket was not only thriving but becoming a cause of riots too: riots on a scale not seen since at Calcutta, Kingston (Jamaica) (or elsewhere in the other West Indies), or Sydney. The game had caught on in a very big way amongst the ordinary townsmen: it does not appear to have commanded such support in any other sizeable town in the country, and there is an interesting reason for it. In each town there was a trade which could be performed at home in a craftsman's own time, and for which he was paid by the piece: cutlery, lace, and hose. So the custom had grown of men working at night or in the early morning, and playing cricket all the day: hence the early pre-eminence of Nottingham and Sheffield cricketers, and the reason for the first formation of the Yorkshire County Cricket Club taking place in 1863 in Sheffield rather than any other town in the county. Of course, as factories took the place of home work in these three towns, the availability of men for cricket and the popularity of the game became, as time passed, little more than in any other town.

The Laws that were generally accepted were by then being laid down by the Marylebone Club. There is clear evidence that these Laws were not the only laws in existence: unofficial laws circulated in the following century which enshrined local variations of long standing, and it seems more than likely that different versions of the game were played in different parts of England during most of the eighteenth century, and that it was only as the nineteenth century approached that there was something near uniformity. Even then it was not, and is not now complete: it would be interesting to compute precisely how many matches each season nowadays over the whole country are played strictly according to all the official Laws. A glance at any Sunday paper with its coverage of cricket in a particular region (not merely where the northern Leagues are playing) will demonstrate this: how many matches are finished on one innings each, obviously with a great deal of time still to play, though the Laws clearly say that a match shall be played out if there is time?

It seems most likely that the versions of the game being found on the Continent around the turn of the century, and earlier, in France, in Germany, in Denmark, and in the Kingdom of Naples were not due to any English importation but to the existence of the old game of cricket which seems likely to have been played in some form or other over most of Europe: for instance would Murat's Naples (Napoleon's Naples, to make the point clearer) have encouraged its army officers to play a game known to be specifically English? And how far for instance can one explain the otherwise baffling portrait (plate 10) of Mr Hope of Amsterdam playing cricket in Rome in 1793? (Despite his name which no doubt shows his ultimate English origin, he was in fact a member of a well-known Dutch merchant firm which survives to this day.) Moreover, descriptions of the game from Hamburg in the 1790s show significant variations often quite similar to outdated provisions of American 'Wicket', which may well not be due to error on the part of the author, but rather to acute observation. For example, the ball was bowled alternately from each end of the pitch (i.e. not in 'overs'). Moreover, the ball has to be 'rolled' not 'thrown' (i.e. bowled in the true sense, not the pitched ball). And the striker is out if he stops the ball from hitting his wicket with his foot or his body generally. There is no more reason to believe that there was uniformity in the Laws governing cricket in England, the British Isles, or in Europe than there was in weights and measures.

The game was of course spreading its wings far outside the British Isles by now and that is to be expected. When people go in large numbers to other countries, and establish colonies there, so far from abandoning their social habits and customs, they do their best to maintain them; and not only that, to maintain them in the state that they knew when the first substantial number of them arrived in their new homeland. Thus not only is much of the accent and pronunciation of English to be found, at all events until quite recently, amongst the generality of people in the United States similar to that spoken in England in the first part of the seventeenth century, so also had they taken that very old version of cricket with them, and were playing it right into the twentieth century in isolated parts of New England.[1] So it was everywhere else, where circumstances permitted it: there were already the traders (hardly colonists) in Aleppo in 1676 regularly playing on their holidays: the seamen of the East India Company playing not many years later: and cricket was being played in Calcutta and in Bombay and outside Seringapatam well before the eighteenth century closed. We must also infer that the game was being played in all the British West Indian islands from a quite early time, though we do not know of it for certain until early in the following century and we can note that the French even appear to have introduced their version of cricket into St Lucia[2] before it became British (just as they undoubtedly

[1] Litchfield and Hartford counties in Connecticut and Berkshire county in Massachusetts.
[2] Details available of this version (obtained by oral inquiry from several St Lucians) show that it is an ancient form of the game indeed, and with many similarities with other early versions. The length of the pitch is longer than that of the present cricket pitch at about twenty-six or twenty-seven yards (about the effective length of the pitch in both Stonyhurst cricket and the American 'wicket'): there are no overs but the ball is bowled from whichever end it finishes up at (much as in 'wicket'): the game is double-wicket *but* the batsmen do not run, they have runners with rods about four feet long to touch down at the end of the run (a quite original feature): there is no obstruction or 'l.b.w.' as such but if the batsman prevents the ball from hitting his wicket three times by interposing his leg, he is out (cf. again 'wicket' and the version of the English children's game in which 'three times on the leg and it's out'): all bowling is true along the ground under-

introduced it to Canada for their settlers to be found playing cricket in 1785). So early in the next century is cricket being played as a matter of course in Australia that we can be certain it was being played much earlier still, as soon after the arrival of the First Fleet as other pressing tasks made a game of leisure feasible. Within a few years more it was being played in New Zealand, long years before it was officially proclaimed a colony. Again, early in the century, it is to be found being played in Cape Town, on a ground still in popular use, and there have long been reasons for believing it was played in the Cape during the first British occupation at the end of the eighteenth century.

The game, in fact, went with the people, and if the people did not go, then it went with the Army or the Navy. Recreation had to be found for troops and sailors: cricket was an ideal source of it, and the very activity it demanded must often have been welcome to shipbound mariners. So far as the Army was concerned, with some exceptions such as the Guards, recruiting in Britain was done locally where the regiment was stationed: the many battalions stationed in the south of the country during the Napoleonic wars must have been well filled with cricket players, and often keen and good ones, before they were moved: it would be fascinating to trace out some of these movements and see what could be inferred about some local spurt in the interest of cricket in some out of the way corner.

Though it is going a little ahead of the story, there is one interesting question which arises in connection with the spread of cricket overseas. It concerns the length of the over. Arthur Haygarth said, and said repeatedly, in his *Scores &*

---

arm, and fast (said to be as fast as Hall and Griffith!): the bat is curved like the old-fashioned cricket bat: and the wicket is broad and relatively low, about fifteen inches high and twenty inches wide, and generally without any centre stump, though there is a crosspiece. The game is played for fun and is played on Sundays and festivals, but there is some distinction between important matches and less important ones in that a hard ball is used for important games and a softer one for others.

The bowler may pitch the wicket where he likes (another old survival) but if the ball goes through the wicket, the batsman is not out. Apart from the leg obstruction rule, the batsman may only be out bowled, caught or run-out. The game is called '*roulez-la-bas*' and is not thought of as cricket at all, though its similarities are recognized. In other words it is not derived from our modern game (using 'modern' to mean anything since St Lucia finally became British, in 1815) but is an historical fossil. Some sophisticated St Lucians, aware of the French phrase at bowls '*roulez le bois*', wonder if their own game's name is not perhaps a corruption of the bowls phrase: if so, this is the first substantial connection with bowls to have been unearthed. It is necessary to caution readers that the above information has been derived from St Lucians in England, care being taken when questioning them not to suggest any particular answer. Inquiry in St Lucia suggests that the game has in recent years been much more assimilated to cricket's normal customs and it may well be that this old version of the game will disappear before long, being turned into one of the many informal kinds of cricket played, and especially by children, in so many parts of the world.

Biographies that the over had once been of six-balls length: yet none of the official Laws shows a suspicion of this. The unofficial laws that start to appear in the early part of the nineteenth century make it clear sometimes that six-ball overs were the custom in country districts, sometimes in one-day matches. This clearly means the great majority of matches ever played! The earliest length of an over known in Australia, New Zealand, and the West Indies (or, if not quite the earliest, then not far from it) was one of six-balls length. Once again the custom of the people was carried with them overseas and an interesting question arises: when and where did the six-ball over originate? It was, it seems, one of the many eighteenth-century variants of the game: how was it that, so widespread though it became, it nevertheless did not reach the official laws until the 1880s, and then only in one-day matches (which, again, meant the great majority)?

The playing conditions, and duration, of matches are of interest but it is not only very difficult to find out just what these were, it is virtually impossible to give more than general indications. Even now, when playing conditions of competitive first-class matches are supposed to be standardized, there is very considerable actual variation, and not only in England. In the eighteenth century matches were often begun at noon, though earlier starts are also found, 11.0 and even 10.0 (the equivalents of 1.0 p.m., 12 noon and 11.0 a.m. B.S.T.). Dinner was taken between 2.0 and 3.0 – such comparatively late meals were found in important matches almost to the end of the nineteenth century: only later did they become 'luncheon' and, by now, cricket's meal-times are out of line with those of the populace generally. Tea was sometimes taken out on to the ground in the jollier games towards the end of the last century, but became an interval in its own right (much deplored by some) not long before the First World War. Play went on in the eighteenth century often till 7.30 – which was very late in southern England before B.S.T., but this time drew back to 6.30 well before the end of the nineteenth century. In one-day matches both start and finish were, and are, likely to have been earlier and later respectively. Yet there were several two-day and longer matches in the eighteenth century where play seems to have gone on for some eight and a half hours (excluding intervals) each day, giving in two days just about the same playing time as in a modern three-day county match. It is important also to remember that the interval between innings was often very much longer than the modern ten minutes, nearly half an hour on occasions, and very frequently, twenty minutes in late nineteenth-century county and Test matches (before the tea interval had obtruded into the game).

As to duration, matches were to be played out. 'Unfinished' matches, as they were once called, started becoming frequent in the middle of the last century but not till 1882 could one-day matches be decided on one innings. Towards the end of the eighteenth century, however, three-, four-, and even five-day fixtures in top-class cricket were frequent.

In the early days, cricket was played during as much of the year as was possible. Once winter had really set in, of course, the game was not played until signs of spring showed again: thus even into the present century, the season began at Trent Bridge on Easter Monday no matter how early that occurred, and even this century too has seen cricket played well on into October. But it had lasted later, even into November in the days before football was organized, and it was often resurrected, on ice, in years of hard frost: matches in late February have not been unknown in the past. Once organized winter games came into fashion, the cricket season both at the top level and to a lesser extent at the club level, contracted.

Overseas, cricket seasons have not been defined: conventionally there are periods in each of the West Indian islands when cricket is played, but the exigencies of tours from overseas countries often compel first-class and Test cricket in what might be 'out of season' for some of the islands: basically, the game can be played there all the year round, and this is also the case in Ceylon where it is not possible to talk of the cricket season. Similarly, in India and Pakistan, what dictates when cricket is played is the monsoon, and the really hot weather which makes the game no joy but a penance. South Africa and South America play in our winter which is their summer, but, farther north in Africa, there is a well-organized competition at club level in Southern Rhodesia in their winter (if it can be called that). New Zealand plays as does South Africa, and so now does Australia: but there was a time when cricket was played during a much more extensive part of the year than now, and in Queensland it was played during their winter until well after the turn of the last century. It could still be played at that time if it were not for the competing interest of football: again it is the winter games which dictate the term of the summer game now. In North America, cricket used to be played during much of the year: that St Andrew's Day should have been celebrated by playing cricket in Georgia is not unusual for such a climate, but good-class cricket, and indeed international cricket, farther north, in and around Philadelphia used to go well on into October. There was something of an intermission, by no means absolute, in July and August, owing to the heat, with a resumption in the relative cool of September. It could hardly ever begin much earlier than May, however, owing to the climate.

One other amusing comment can be made: before 'daylight saving' was made the law of the land in Britain, there was more than one club of early risers who would play for two or three hours before breakfast and going off to work: and since 'daylight saving' came in, it has been possible to see cricket being played in Scotland (and no farther north than the central Lowlands) nearer ten o'clock of an evening than nine. It is probable that there is no time of the day at which cricket has not been played, nor any day of the year (even in one hemisphere).

This is a good point at which to consider the early technique of the game. So long as the ball was truly bowled, so long as the bat was curved so as to make sure of contact with the ball, there was hardly any place for technique in play. Stratagems of field placing – and of wicket-pitching too – there might be, but no technique, or so little as not to be worth the name. What after all could the bowler do? He could bowl fast, or he could bowl slow: if he bowled slow, he was likely to have been murdered. If he bowled fast, he had some chance of penetrating the defence of the curved bat before the long low wicket: but if he were hit, the chances were that the hit would go a long way, for the old-fashioned bat had plenty of weight behind it in the hands of those strong enough to wield it. Such chance of deliberate mystification as the bowler may have possessed was if he could have bowled the ball with sufficient spin to make its course a curved one: if this ever happened, no record of it has survived. Any other chance the bowler had arose by accident of delivery (if also from shrewd pitching of the wicket), if the ball should be deflected upwards or sideways in its course by unevenness of turf. But he could not depend on this, and its occurrence would have been so infrequent as to preclude the batsman from developing any special kind of stroke to meet such a situation.

As the ball came to be pitched, and no longer bowled in a true sense, this changed. The bowler no longer had one weapon – pace: he could add two more, length and direction, and he could develop another two, spin and 'pace off the wicket'.[1] David Harris of the Hambledon Club was the first who was reported to have achieved this pace off the wicket, for it seems to have been a little more than 'lift'. Lumpy Stevens perhaps had been one of the first celebrated bowlers to achieve accuracy of length and direction: Harris added to it. His delivery seems to have been very extraordinary. This is how Nyren described it:

[1] Pace off the wicket exists. It is sometimes asserted that it is impossible in theory and that therefore it never occurs. There is no doubt that it is often an illusion, but illusions shared can be said to have a degree of reality and batsmen who pretend that there is but an illusion are likely to lose their wickets! But equally often it is no illusion at all and the explanation is simple: a spinning ball has two components of motion, one in the direction the ball is moving and the other circular. When the ball pitches, the forward motion is hindered by its friction with the ground; the circular motion is stopped abruptly (or nearly so) and this cessation must yield, apart from some rise in temperature, further force in the direction the ball is moving. Hence therefore pace off the wicket: the explanation is simplified, but physicists will recognize the basic truth.

His attitude when preparing for his run previously to delivering the ball, would have made a beautiful study for the sculptor. First of all he stood erect like a soldier at drill; then, with a graceful curve of the arm, he raised the ball to his forehead, and drawing back his right foot, started off with the left. His mode of delivering the ball was very singular. He would bring it from under the arm by a twist, and nearly as high as his arm-pit, and with this action *push* it, as it were, from him. How it was that the balls acquired the velocity they did by this mode of delivery, I never could comprehend. To Harris's fine bowling I attribute the great improvement that was made in hitting for it was utterly impossible to remain at the crease, when the ball was tossed to a fine length: you were obliged to get in, or it would be about your hands, or the handle of your bat: and every player knows where its next place would be.

One comment must be permitted: Harris's 'push' sounds very like a 'throw' but then, of course, neither earlier, nor then, nor later did anyone think to penalize an under-arm delivery as a 'throw'.

It is unfortunate that we do not know anything of the developments of the game which brought about the pitched ball and the straight bat except the one clear inference that the transition in the best grades of cricket may have taken a quarter of a century. That long transition no doubt explains why it took time for the importance of 'length' to be appreciated. Extracting the fullest potential from the pitched ball must have been rather like opening Pandora's box; it was the best part of twenty years more before it was appreciated that one no longer needed to bowl fast. The man who has gone down to history as realizing this was Tom Walker, also of the Hambledon Club, who started bowling slow about 1792 (the year when he also started what was quaintly called the 'straight-arm' bowling and was later identified with round-arm). Walker's new-fangled style, in which he did not persist, was called 'throwing': nowadays, the view is that a straight arm precludes a throw. (To such confusion is the whole matter reduced once the word 'bowl' ceased to be used in its original sense.) William ('Silver Billy') Beldham, who encountered Walker's slow style as a young man, thought it was childish stuff but learnt soon enough that it was not.

It was not only bowlers who took a long time to realize what a revolution had occurred. Batsmen too had to revise their outlook. With the old bowled, or rolled, ball, it had certainly been the custom not to move out to meet the ball: it is difficult to judge whether there would have been any point in doing so. Whatever the case, Tom Sueter seems to have been the first of the great players to move out to the ball, in great contrast, as Nyren says, to the old stagers who never moved

77

from the crease (it might be worth resurrecting Sueter for a modern Test series!). He would jump in and hit the ball hard like a cannon-shot. Yet he did not master forward play: William Fennex, born 1759, seems to have been the first to do that and it was Beldham who may have been the first to 'cut the ball at the point of the bat'. It was remarked of Beldham that he would cut with the bat held horizontal (and so 'at the point') but others, and notably William Lambert early in the nineteenth century, cut with the bat held vertical. It is difficult to imagine just what kind of a stroke that may have been, or indeed whether it was proper to call it a cut, in modern terms. W. J. Lewis in his lexicography *The Language of Cricket*[1] did not pick out this usage, so it is difficult to say more about a stroke which seems to have been a kind of 'off-glance', to create a term. The true cut is an arm stroke, but implicit in it is the use of the wrists and the late cut which depends entirely on the wrists: it is an example of how batting would cease to be a matter of strength and force, but of subtle and graceful movements, as more use was made of the wrists. Batting and bowling underwent enormous development at this time and mutual discoveries of what each could do continued well into the next century. It is likely that batting had by no means exhausted its potential when bowling started moving into round-arm: and it is certain that bowling had not, for Fennex in his old age said that people (in the round-arm period) had no idea of what under-arm bowlers could do. He seems to have been right, for long after round-arm had begun to hold sway, William Clarke was to model himself on the old under-arm bowlers and he delivered the ball rather as Harris seems to have done fifty years and more before: and he was a highly successful bowler.

[1] Oxford University Press, 1934.

6

THE EARLY NINETEENTH CENTURY TO THE LEGALISING OF ROUND-ARM 1801-1834

In 1795 Habeas Corpus had been suspended and there was much fear of ideas emanating from the French Revolution penetrating into the country; in 1832 the first of the two great Reform Bills became law, and the first steps were taken to emancipate electorally the population of this country, as well as to remove the obviously fraudulent packing of the House of Commons by means of the system of Rotten Boroughs. The English in the greater part of North America had had the vote for fifty years by then: it was to be another eighty years before all the English at home were to obtain it, and still another ten years before all women got it.

It was a period, then, when aristocracy was only just starting to loosen the reins of Government: yet all the time it was willing and happy to play cricket with all and sundry, and did so. England was the only country, apart from its former colonies now the United States, where a team game held sway – where it was indeed extremely popular. It is fascinating to speculate what European history might have been had circumstances permitted a similar popularity for cricket, or for any other team game, in France or what was to become Germany, or in the Austro-Hungarian Empire and Russian Empire.

The period began with cricket lifted on to a fairly high plane of endeavour and success, with the under-arm action established but gradually being mastered by the batsmen: it ended with under-arm cast aside in favour of round-arm and with over-arm itself prefigured. But for many years little is known of what was going on, as the following figures show: taking every fifth year from 1799 to 1834, it is possible to locate in 1799 a total of 66 matches up and down the country (somewhat less than during most of the twenty or thirty years before) of which the full scores are known of 27. In 1804, there are more than 31 matches, and only 12 full scores: in 1809, only 34, with only 15 full scores: in 1814 the figures increase with some 73 matches (but many of them minor to those in 1799) but only 21 full scores. After that the picture improves: in 1819, 51 full scores are known and over 100 matches – a similar figure exists for 1824, 52 full, and 113 matches in all. By 1834, 94 full scores are known, there having been a steady upward progress from 1824.

Much of the later increase is likely to have been due to fuller reporting: just as much of the apparent earlier decrease as we go into the century will have been caused by a lack of it. But why were fewer matches reported? There is some contemporary evidence that it was due to the wars, and it is therefore a little surprising that there was not a much earlier fall. (The raising and training of the local militia will have had an increasing effect on games.) There do seem to be grounds for thinking that fewer matches were played, and certainly fewer of a good quality: and that it was not till the wars were over that the game gets back into its old stride. A Nottingham newspaper noted in 1813 that it thought the game had died there as it had not been played for some time: this was its first cricket notice for more than three years.

Some may wish to cast doubt on these figures. For instance, had we only been concerned with what is shown in *Scores & Biographies* we could have said with certainty that big matches had been omitted: a number of MCC matches for instance. But what is involved is a tally of all ascertainable references in all newspapers and periodicals whether or not the match was recorded in *Scores & Biographies*.[1] There can be little doubt both about the diminution, and about the later increase, an increase which continued well into the next period.

Was there no regimental cricket? Were the gentry so wholly occupied with the wars which were in any case not exactly continuous and had differing effects at different times? Or was it simply a failure to report, or a shortage of newspapers? Whatever the case, good cricket in the first part of the period was rare, and little difference is shown in the manner of play from what had just gone before; nor was any difference noticeable until just after the end of the wars.

[1] G. B. Buckley, a retired surgeon, extracted all important (measured generously) cricket references from London and provincial newspapers in the British Museum, completing his task before the last war when many of these old papers were destroyed by bombing. His results were published in two books, *Fresh Light on 18th-Century Cricket* and *Fresh Light on Pre-Victorian Cricket* – others remain in MSS, but of these the pre-nineteenth-century references were published in the *Cricket Quarterly*, vol. I. Dr H. F. Squire and his wife did the same work for Sussex cricket from holdings of Sussex newspapers (by no means all of which were in the British Museum) – their work was published in *Pre-Victorian Sussex Cricket* (1837–1850 remain in MSS). John Goulstone has been doing the same work for Kent cricket (again the British Museum holdings are not complete, but there are many holdings in Kentish libraries) – they have been published to the end of the eighteenth century in various issues of the *Cricket Quarterly*.

Yet round-arm had already begun to creep in; Tom Walker had tried it, or something like it, before the 1780s were out, playing Hambledon Club matches and he had specifically been warned against it. Despite all kinds of admonitions, once it had been reintroduced it made steady progress: to such an extent that in 1816 the more conservative elements in the game tried to prohibit it in a new Law so cumbrously worded[1] as rather to have the opposite effect. The opposers of round-arm declared it would limit scoring; its supporters denied this but they were wrong. For when in 1827 three experimental matches using round-arm were held (the clear prelude to its eventual legalizing which finally occurred after 1834) that season also saw the last seasonal batting average of over 35 runs per innings until 1862 (but for Fuller Pilch's in 1834 and 1835). Indeed from after 1828 until 1861 there were only five seasonal averages over 30. (From 1796 to 1828, there had been only seven seasons without such an average.)

It is interesting to find that the scoring rate, which had been tending to decline from early in the century, recovered itself sharply from 1816 on, when the first serious attempt to suppress round-arm was made, until 1827 when, for all intents and purposes, the opponents of round-arm capitulated, or at least foresaw their capitulation.

Cricket tended not to be very interesting during much of the period because of the extent to which it was subjected to gambling. There have always been different kinds of gambling in the game: it is gambling to play for a sum of money jointly subscribed, or even for a trophy similarly paid for. But it is not gambling of a kind which could do any harm to the game: the harm came when individuals started backing themselves or their teams, and when others started 'selling' matches. Some attempt was made to suppress the evil, at Lord's, in the early 1820s but it cannot have been successful or permanent, for bookmakers were still at Lord's fifty and sixty years later, and of course almost to the end of that time players were being accused of selling matches.

There was one man who made his mark on all the earlier part of the period both through his cricket and through his gambling. This was Lord Frederick Beauclerk. He was a clergyman, and from 1828 till his death in 1850 vicar of St Albans. He was a very fine batsman and a very fine bowler, and he also possessed a sharp tongue and a bad temper. He often seems a kind of equivalent to the former Bishop of Autun, the eventual Duc de Talleyrand-Périgord: a cleric without, it would seem, the faintest interest in being a clergyman, or any kind of

---

[1] 'The ball must be bowled (not thrown or jerked), and be delivered underhand, with the hand below the elbow. But if the ball be jerked, or the arm extended from the body horizontally, and any part of the hand be uppermost, or the hand horizontally extended when the ball is delivered, the Umpire shall call "No Ball".'

Christian, and one can well imagine a man like Beauclerk, once he had survived the initial terror of a revolution, becoming in the end one of its most distinguished servants.

Even amongst all the hagiography that exists about cricketers, an unqualified eulogy of Beauclerk has never been seen, and that is significant. But he was a fine cricketer, and Haygarth wrote in his *Scores & Biographies* that no one had a better average than him (Haygarth later qualified it to read 'one of the best averages'). Haygarth was right: Beauclerk heads the career averages of all those who played from Hambledon days to the legalizing of over-arm – his career aggregate is second only to Fuller Pilch (whose average would have been far higher had he played in the under-arm period): he scored more centuries than anyone except William Ward (who hit nine) and Pilch with ten: and he hit more fifties than anyone. If it had not been that he played before anyone thought to take a note of the bowling or even to give the bowler's name for batsmen caught or stumped, it is likely that Beauclerk would have shown similar eminence as a bowler. As it was he was many times amongst the season's three biggest wicket-takers, and several times first: in 1797 he took 66 wickets, the record seasonal total until 1831 when F. W. Lillywhite, with his round-arm, exceeded it. It is by no means improbable that Beauclerk was thus the first man to take 100 wickets in a season, but we shall never know this.

There was a lot that happened for the first time in the period: William Lambert[1] became the first to make two centuries in a match, in 1817. This was not done again for fifty years. The same match in which he did this saw over 1,000 runs scored, and that did not happen again for forty-six years. And his seasonal average was over 63 and that was not beaten for fifty-four years. Three years later William Ward scored 278, an innings not exceeded in an important match for fifty-six years.

If all this speaks something for the performers of these years it also adds volumes to the evidence that round-arm imposed a far lower rate of scoring.

But what was happening in other grades of cricket? In the leading 'public schools' cricket was becoming, despite some displeasure, something of a cult: a cult that would be fully sanctioned and encouraged later, from the 1830s onwards. The scores of games between Eton, Harrow and Winchester all saw their inception, though of course Eton had been beaten by Westminster many

---

[1] He did not play again in good-class matches after 1817 when he was accused of selling a match between England and Nottinghamshire. But he played a lot for Reigate after that and in other club cricket, and his last game was for Wilfred Blunt's team at Crabbet Park in 1839. This was the father of the poet and Radical Wilfred Scawen Blunt into whose hands came John Baker's *Diary*, quoted in connection with Hambledon on page 63. See plate 32 for illustration of Crabbet Park.

years before. So also was the first school century made, in 1825. Two years later saw the first University match, itself a good indication of the growing strength of cricket as something more than a game in the greater schools.

In the country as a whole, once peace had set in, there began a great outburst of club formation and this too was by no means confined to England but was to be found in Wales, Scotland and Ireland. It was also the period when the first great wave of county cricket clubs began to be formed: most of them not destined to last more than a few years, and only two to last into our own time, Northamptonshire and Perthshire. It was stated that without a proper county cricket club it was not possible to select a county team: not entirely true but the sentiment is interesting, and shows what a hold county cricket had in the minds of cricketers. It is not surprising after all, since we have seen how a French-Swiss traveller had discovered this a hundred years earlier, but now we are into a period where the single patron could no longer be relied on to find a county team, and a club was necessary, where many principal landowners in the county could join together.

In the mid-1830s the game was growing fast again, and this growth was to continue well into and beyond the following period. It is especially interesting that the signs of its growth were showing even before the railways had started to make travel both easy and cheap. It was a period when the country's production enormously increased and far beyond the fifty per cent increase in the population; there must have been many who had more money in their pockets than had ever been known before. Real wages achieved by the end of the first quarter of the century a peak not known since a hundred years earlier (but lest anyone should be too impressed by these figures, real wages as measured by a composite physical unit of consumables were not for another fifty years to achieve the level attained *four hundred years* before and even in *this* century real wages have been down below that medieval level, though now they are far above). As the railways started to spread, the impetus was taken up and continued.

This was the period when the game spread widely abroad. Brussels had known a game a few days before Waterloo: on the other side of Europe, Colonel Maceroni, under Joachim Murat, King of Naples, had formed a club in 1811 with many French and Neapolitan officers. The Ionian Islands, after being freed from the Turks were to be occupied by British forces for many years, who sowed the seeds of a love for cricket in Corfu which persists to this day. In northern France there were many lace-makers from Nottingham who settled and played cricket in such places as Dieppe, Calais, Boulogne, St Omer and elsewhere and met the occasional English team from across the Channel.

83

But the game did not spread on the Continent, and here, perhaps, is another reason why. The student of old newspapers will find, time and time again, references to 'this manly game': they occur during the last part of the previous century and during much of the first half of the new one. They occur in other writings too. It is a curious phrase, made more curious when combined as it often was to give 'this manly and athletic game'. 'Manly' is, of course, often found with reference to boxing and this gives us a clue: it was 'manly' to stand up and receive physical punishment, and nobody needs to be told that if he wishes to play top-class cricket nowadays, he must be ready to do just that. There had always been a degree of physical danger in the game: many of our seventeenth-century references exist because someone was killed or injured. That was because the batsman could hinder a fielder trying to catch him out[1] – something not entirely forbidden till late in the eighteenth century. What else could cause physical danger? Surely bowling itself, whether the true bowled ball along the ground that was never smooth and which could pop up and hit a batsman, or be pulled up as it tipped the edge of the clubbed part of the bat, or the pitched ball (and recall that William Fennex said none of the over-arm bowlers sent down a ball as fast as the under-arm bowlers did). We do not need 'bouncers' hurled, or thrown down, to intimidate and injure a batsman. This must have been the major reason for calling the game manly – not the very occasional possible injury to a rash fielder, still less his holding a fast return (for properly done, such a return barely even stings).

It has sometimes been thought humorous in cricket, and in boys' magazines, to quote real or hypothetical French, or German, nobility or Indian princes even, as seeing no point in being hit by the bowler: but in logic they each had something. Playing *jeu-de-paume* for example, one is rarely in any physical danger; doubtless children played dangerous games as children do, but on the Continent (and this is a theme that returns later on) people grew up and no longer played children's games: what *was* the point of a grown man putting himself into physical danger? The English – and not only the English in these islands (there are few games with so much physical danger as shinty) – thought differently, and here we can see Dr Arnold prefigured. It was a *manly* game, and manliness was a quality greatly to be encouraged, as it was so strangely understood: for, oddly enough, real manliness (which is surely sexual prowess) was thought distasteful and even in an odd way womanish. To such an extent were the characters of a century and more of this country's youth perverted! Confusion of a very basic

---

[1] Jasper Vinall in 1624 was one such at West Hoathly in Sussex, killed accidentally by Edward Tye with his bat, while Vinall was going for the catch.

kind of what was and was not true manliness seems likely to be the dominating reason why Europe generally did not play cricket in adult life: and still does not. (Indeed outside English-influenced countries, adults do not ordinarily play out-door games except as professional entertainers.)

Farther afield, there had been a British expedition to the River Plate in 1806 which had been interned: but soldiers and men played cricket in their captivity and may have been responsible for the hold the game has in the Argentine. In the West Indies, cricket clubs were known to be in existence in 1806 (and probably very much earlier) and in the United States the game still lingered on – in places, the more modern version, but more often the older colonial game. Benjamin Silliman, an American traveller to London in 1810, noted in his diary the differences between the game here and what he called 'our cricket'. But in the 1820s with the influx of mill-workers from Sheffield and Nottingham there came to be a real revival of the modern game, and especially in Philadelphia, where before the end of the period Haverford College had been founded, the nursery of many great cricketers later. Philadelphia was not the only area where cricket was played: it continued to thrive in New York and New England generally, and it was to be found in the 'Deep South' too. In Canada too the game was being played, both by the British garrisons there, and by local people, and in leading schools.

In South Africa, cricket was being played in 1808, and again two years later, on Green Point Common, still used for the game: probably the oldest surviving cricket ground but one outside the British Isles. And after that, nothing seems to have survived for some thirty years though there can be no doubt that the game was being played and indeed slowly growing.

In India the first century recorded was made in Calcutta in 1804 (this probably the oldest ground outside the British Isles) and there can be little doubt that in the three Presidency Cities of Bombay, Calcutta and Madras as well as in larger garrisons elsewhere, the game was being played. It is often referred to later on in the *Bengal Sporting Magazine*. It was, after all, a century old in India during this period. And beyond India cricket had been played in Singapore by the mid-1834.

In Australia, the game was being regularly played by the end of 1803, and after that it expanded just as the colonies did. The game was being played in the country districts of New South Wales before the 1820s were out: none of this being in any way surprising. It is possible that it was being played in New Zealand nearly thirty years before the colony was proclaimed.

Cricket was first heard of in Ceylon in this period – moreover, school cricket, almost as though pre-figuring the Victorian outlook. From this the game steadily grew in popularity amongst all sections of the population in Ceylon.

Thus, if not already established before the period began, it was at this time that the game is found established in all the leading areas where it is played to this day – all the areas which were to provide Test-match or other first-class international cricket.

But the game had still a lot of detailed development to undergo. By 1811 the choice of pitch, vested in the visiting team, devolved upon the umpires (but in country and minor games, the old rule persisted till late in the 1820s): wides also were provided for, for the first time. By 1821 the height of the wicket was increased by two inches, and the distance from the wicket of the popping crease was correspondingly increased. By 1825 the wicket was widened and the bowling crease lengthened. There was much change in the Laws about no-balls and about under-arm and round-arm, and also about l.b.w. An interesting but minor change in the Laws was the introduction of the word 'run' in place of 'notch'; it followed forty years after 'notching' had ceased generally to be the method of 'scoring'. There was still more to come. At the end of the period, besides the decision to legalize round-arm, it was also decided to revise the Laws thoroughly. The 1835 code was the first overall revision of the Laws since 1774, and arguably the most thorough undertaken by that time. Yet it did not send cricket into the modern age: that fell to the next period.

7

THE ROUND-ARM PERIOD 1835-1863

From the time that round-arm was legalized to that of over-arm covers just under thirty years and a period when the game seems to have increased in popularity enormously. In a typical five-week period in midsummer from 1838, taken every five years or so, *Bell's Life*, the sporting newspaper of the time with a very wide coverage of the game, lists about 130 cricket matches in 1838, but five years later the figure nearly doubles to 230, and five years later again, has trebled to 400. From then on it makes a slow progress to the 500 mark by the 1860s.

Penny postage came in in 1840: this meant not only a cheap postage (based on the fact that the cost of handling mail is not its transportation costs but its sorting and delivery costs) but also a novel one in that, for the first time letters could be, and had to be, prepaid instead of being paid for by the recipient. This alone must have encouraged the sending in of reports, and encouraged *Bell's Life* to ask for them. In 1841 came an oft-quoted War Office decision (but nothing at all to do with the Duke of Wellington, as has long been supposed) to provide, specifically, cricket grounds for every barracks in the country. Since there were few towns of any size at that time without a garrison (battalions in those days were approximately half the modern peace-time strength) many new cricket grounds must have been established and the troops presumably did not only play amongst themselves. The great railway network was largely built in the late 1830s and in the 1840s making transport both easy and cheap, as compared with the fantastic costs of transporting a team by coach. All these factors must have helped to increase the number of games played, and also the numbers of matches reported. What we do not know is to what extent the increase in these numbers reflects an actual increase in matches played or merely increased coverage by *Bell*. It could be something of both but, even so, the indications are that cricket did increase

87

enormously in popularity at that time, or rather in the first half of the period, for there seems to have been no similar increase in the later half. What does appear, however, is an increase in good-class matches reported, and this is just as significant both in itself and as possibly reflecting a further increase in the game's popularity.

There is another way of estimating the increase in the game's popularity, and that is by referring to *Scores & Biographies*. Haygarth had been trying to get it published for some years, using Fred Lillywhite[1] as his publisher. The fact that publication had been mooted for ten years or so before it matured is itself enough to indicate the growth of interest in the game even if that growth was not, as Haygarth unfortunately supposed it would be, enough to make his work a financial success (or perhaps we should say fortunately or we would never have had it). But it is also of interest to see how Haygarth accounts for the seasons at five-yearly intervals. To 1838 he gives 53 pages, and he increases this by 50 per cent for 1843 to 76 pages: he doubles the 1838 figure in 1848 when he gives 109 pages. He follows somewhat behind *Bell*, and in 1853 he only gives 118 pages. These seasons are all comprised in his first four volumes, which appeared from 1861 to 1863: they also comprise a period when he himself was actively collecting, and not just past history. His critical evaluation of a match worth recording probably remained fairly constant in this time, and especially during the period of publication. The game's popularity therefore was on the increase if important matches could more than double in ten years. We would not expect an increase in the total of minor matches to be in the same proportion but in a much greater proportion, and this would account for Haygarth lagging behind *Bell*.

It is also of some interest that Haygarth gives a very great increase, to 171 pages for 1858, and to 236 pages for the last five-year period, in 1863. In other words Haygarth quadruples the number of matches he records in the period, just as *Bell* very nearly does. *But*, and this is all-important, these seasons were not published till 1876 and 1877: by then Haygarth had become much less critical of what he should and should not include, a relaxation he was in later years again very much to regret. His account from 1838 to 1853 more nearly evaluates the increase in big cricket than from 1853 to 1863.

There was probably a fairly steady increase during most of the century, at least until football started to challenge cricket as the national game. For, at the start of the round-arm period as had been so for many years, cricket started at the end of March if Easter was early, and went on till the weather closed it down in

---

[1] Lillywhite also arrogated to himself the baseless claim that the collection was due to him and his father, than which nothing could have been more untrue on purely theoretical grounds.

October or November. The height of the season was from the end of May till early September.

There are other things which suggest a real growth in popularity: when the period began, there was no cricket annual, nor had there been for many years. Within a few years there was 'Bat's' *Manual*, which at least had seasonal averages, and this was quickly followed by Denison's *Cricketer's Companion*, itself closely followed by Fred Lillywhite's *Cricketer's Guide*, often called *Fred's Guide*. In 1864 there were actually three annuals, *Wisden* just commencing, Baily's *Cricket Annual* (very good and so far in advance of its time with its fat collection of full scores like a modern *Wisden*, that only one issue was ever made), and *Fred's Guide*, soon to cease and to be replaced by the *Green Lillywhite*. *Bell's Life* was getting fatter the whole time, and at the end of the period more frequent, as for the first time it started to encounter the competition which was to kill it. During its hey-day, it enjoyed an immense authority, and many deferred to it for knotty problems about the Laws rather than to the MCC which was carrying less and less authority[1] as the period wore on. It remains a largely unquarried source for historians of the period.

And there was one other factor – a cricket one this time – which may have helped the game on, though the evidence nowadays tends to suggest that it was the boom in the game that led to William Clarke cashing in on it with his tours all over the country, by his All England XI, formed in 1846: but this was after reporting by *Bell* had already trebled. Clarke's tours, however, and those of the United XI under Wisden and Dean, in some opposition to Clarke, must have heightened interest and probably also raised the general quality of cricket, playing fifteens, eighteens and twenty-twos all over the country.

It is a strange period of cricket, this, and it is more difficult in many ways to get the 'feel' of it than much older periods, although it is, it would seem, far better documented, and although we know much more about most of the protagonists – their cricket ability, and character too. But it is not a period *like* our own: we can see that much of the 1864–93 period, and everything since is obviously directly connected with our own time. In this round-arm period, it is difficult to see any link: it is some ninety years since elevens of the best players in England toured round the country playing eighteens and twenty-twos, and such cricket does not appeal to us as much more than a joke. Money-making maybe, and that is perhaps the only part of it which the present day can understand, with its acquaintance

[1] There were several reasons for this – the MCC made a mess of the round-arm over-arm controversy: its membership was small; it was also quite unrepresentative of the social class from which it was drawn.

89

with commercially financed teams of great players touring about the country playing minor teams on Sundays, or about the world in the winter playing not so minor teams. But there was no competitive cricket, at any rate in England: matches were hard fought anyway, and there was sufficient honour in winning without having to add to that honour two points, or whatever it is, for a win. No one could say who should have such opportunities of honour, and there was no acknowledged controlling body. Even the MCC was being challenged as the premier club by the up-and-coming Surrey Club established during this period at Kennington Oval, still in the country, as Lord's, surrounded by the ribbon development of Maida Vale and St John's Wood, was no longer. Moreover, it was F. P. Miller of the Surrey Club who provided much of the finance for *Scores & Biographies*[1] and this was something that the MCC was not even to think of doing for some fifteen years. It too lost money and only very recently did the MCC finally dispose of its stocks.

One aspect of the game in particular is strange to us now, the prevalence still of single-wicket games, between the greatest of players of the time. These were to die out before the end of the period, though they were never to vanish completely until in our own time an entirely new version of single-wicket was dreamt up. Indeed a good single-wicket game was deemed the best way to fill up time in a match which had ended early during an overseas tour, and that continued to happen into the 1880s. But previously arranged and 'great' single-wicket matches have been gone for a century now, and with only a few people alive who have ever played that game according to its proper laws, it is not possible to recapture much idea of what the public sensed and felt – save, of course, that they were watching a dour struggle between great champions.

Here is an account of one such match – the second of two that season – between Alfred Mynn and Nicholas Wanostrocht, alias Felix, for effectively the individual championship of England in 1846. It was played on September 29 and 30. Each player had two fielders only, who were there only to prevent runs. Hits could only score runs in front of the wicket, if teams were five-a-side or less: this was a one-a-side match. The account is taken from *Bell's Life*.

> The return match between N. Felix and A. Mynn Esqs for the Championship of England was played on the ground attached to the White Hart Hotel at Bromley on Tuesday and Wednesday last. Nothing could have exceeded the excellence of Mr Pawley's arrangement for the occasion. Two sides of the

---

[1] In a pique because it did not sell, he destroyed much of the stock, thereby depriving himself of profits but ensuring that those who had bought would make a handsome one. This is why the first four volumes, and especially the latter two of them are so scarce.

field were bounded by two long marquees, each extending the whole distance of its respective side. Indeed the only thing that could have made the affair a more brilliant appearance would have been that one of these monster marquees should have been entirely tenanted by the fair sex. Considering the period of the year, and the distance from the metropolis, the gathering of spectators was more numerous than we had looked for. Those who were absent sustained a loss by not seeing the admirable exhibition of batting and bowling. There was too some of the finest fielding we have for many years witnessed, by Mr Broughton, Mr Hoare and Mr Mailes. The second of these gentlemen scouted for both sides, in consequence of the absence of Mr Garland who was to have assisted Mr Mynn in that branch of the game. Every requisite preliminary having been perfected, and Mr Felix having won the toss, he went in first. The umpires were Caldecourt and Sewell. Mr Mynn soon showed that he was in good bowling, but off the fifth ball, Mr Felix obtained a run. From that period until the close of his innings, he never had a chance of adding to his score by the bat, for, although he gave a series of his best hitting, such was the beauty of the fielding that all hope of a run was abandoned almost as quickly as the ball flew from the bat.[1] At length the wicket was lowered by a cutting ripper, the score being three – one run from the bat and two for wides. Some idea may be formed of the great truth of the bowling from the fact of Mr Felix having played 42 out of 65 balls. Of this play, 24 were hits on the ground and 18 were 'no' hits.[2] Mr Mynn then took the bat but it soon became apparent, as Mr Felix was in extremely good bowling, that he had the greatest difficulty in dealing with it. He made four single runs, but in accomplishing one of them, he had nearly lost his wicket, in consequence of the brilliant fielding of Mr Mailes, who took the single stump (at the bowler's end) by a throw from a great distance. This act was loudly applauded. Mr Mynn lost his position by the thirty-first ball – a shooter. He received thirty-one balls, of which he played 28. The dinner hour had now arrived, and the bell having 'told the tale' upwards of 100 gentlemen repaired to the banquet, and abundantly refreshed themselves to their individual satisfaction. At four o'clock, the game was resumed by Mr Felix once more taking the bat, and a most brilliant display of scientific batting, bowling, and fielding was witnessed during this innings. That it was so will be readily imagined when we state that on the wicket being struck for the night, Mr Mynn had bowled 167 balls, from which Mr Felix had not been able to make any score by his admirable use of the bat. And yet many

---

[1] A reminder that he had to get 'there and back' to score.
[2] Hits behind the wicket.

of his hits were of the most powerful character. But then their effect was neutralised by the most wonderful fielding of Mr Broughton and Mr Hoare. Towards the latter part of the day, Mr Mynn had worn so deep a hole for his right foot that he was frequently thrown off his bowling balance, and thus it was that he gave the wide balls which will be found in the score. On the succeeding morning the play was resumed, and again Mr Mynn proceeded with his attacks on the wicket, and at length he succeeded in reaching it, the score remaining as on the preceding evening, namely 9 runs. Mr Mynn now went in for 9 to win or 8 to tie, and had Mr Felix bowled as well in this as in the first innings, it would have been a long time, if indeed achieved at all, ere victory would have been pronounced in Mr Mynn's favour. But the bowling was inferior, and as Mr Mynn had been practising at Mr Denison's bowling, he had become somewhat more accustomed to the slow pace, and waited to play the balls. He received 21 balls, made 20 hits, and ran off the required number in one quarter of an hour, Mr Mynn thus won the second match. The score stood thus:

		1st inns		2nd inns
N. Felix Esq.	b. Mynn	1	b. Mynn	0
	Wides	2	Wides 8, no-ball 1	9
	TOTAL	3		9

First innings: Balls 65, hits 24, no hits 18, wide balls 2, runs 1. *Second innings*: Balls 191, hits 51, no hits 48, wide and no-balls 9, runs 0.

		1st inns		2nd inns
A. Mynn Esq.	c. Felix	4	not out	9

First innings: Balls 31, hits 28, no hits 0, wide balls 0, runs 4. *Second innings*: Balls 21, hits 20, no hits 0, wide balls 0, runs 9.

Thus *Bell's Life*. There were not many people at this game, it can be inferred: there had been over 3,000 at the first game at Lord's on June 18. In that game, Mynn bowled fifteen balls before taking Felix's wicket with the sixteenth, for 0: there had been eleven hits. Felix bowled the same number of balls to Mynn catching him off the last for 5 runs. Felix had then gone in, and had received 246 balls before he was bowled off the next: he had made 175 hits, and had scored 5 runs and there had been one wide. It had been two hours before he made his first run. Other such games attracted far more spectators at various times, sometimes running well into five figures – a by no means uncommonly large crowd in those days.

Champions in those days were individuals: there is a reference early in the 1850s to a county being acknowledged champions, but the idea of a county championship was yet to be born though it came along just after the period ended. Here, however, is another distinction – the individual not the team. The Victorian idea of team spirit had not yet been born when the period began – the Victorian era was not, in many respects to begin in other than a regnal sense, for many more years, though it was well established by the end of the period.

The game at all its levels was loose-knit. It is as though one were living in an African colony in the last century, with a vague kind of Governor's Council in charge, the coastal strip to some extent administered, the hinterland a protectorate, safe enough but not neatly packaged up into modern administrative districts with the hierarchy of officials, horizontally as well as vertically organized. This is but an analogy to show that there was no organization and no administration – it was, in fact, a period of anarchy in its true sense, not of muddle and chaos, but just of nothing ordered at all. Yet evidently the need for order was felt, for after 1863 we see it all being brought about.

There is one mark of this period which is oustanding: the formation of the many great amateur wandering clubs, starting with I Zingari in 1845, and including, by 1863, Quidnuncs, Harlequins, Free Foresters, Incogniti, Butterflies, and, in Ireland, Na Shuler. Many others came later: others (for example the Band of Brothers – not originally a cricket club – formed in 1858) were concerned with cricketers from a particular county (B.B. confined itself to people of Kent), and others were simply clubs for Old Boys from particular public schools. All these clubs were, and most are, distinctly restricted in their membership, and can nowadays be assailed for their snobbish exclusiveness by those who do not concede the right of people to associate with whom they wish. In the beginning the exclusiveness was always more reasonable: competition to become members kept up a good standard of cricket, and particular school or residential qualification made recruitment easier in one sense while safeguarding against 'poaching' at the same time. If they are by now part of a bygone social scene, and even have difficulty in raising teams, nevertheless when they were founded and for many years after they provided good-class and varied opposition to public school teams and to amateur clubs all over the country: they it was whose existence made country-house cricket possible. Their rise in this period is a reflection of the increasing turnout from the public schools of young men who could play cricket well. There has always been, in cricket, a tendency to form exclusive clubs of one kind or another (as indeed in other walks of life) but these essentially 'Old Boy' clubs would not have been possible before this period for sheer paucity of candidates, and only began to become possible as the period wore on. Many other clubs were formed in later years reflecting the continued increasing turnout.

For this was when *mens sana in corpore sano* first started to grip the English mind: its full development may have been consummated in this period, if, numerically, the next was to see it finally established. Character, not learning, was the motto: an idea not held in other countries, but one which the feudal barons who finally exterminated themselves in the Wars of the Roses and under the early Tudors would have welcomed warmly as very much agreeing with their own outlook. Thus brawn and the bully-boy often superseded brain and ability in the English educational system, and held sway until our own time: an increasingly elderly generation still adheres to it.

Yet in a rigidly stratified class-ridden society, with each man in his place (or nearly: the two great Reform Bills just about straddle the period, also the Chartists), the doings of the gilded youth on the cricket field filled many columns in *Bell's Life*, and in *Scores & Biographies* too: they could play cricket well, and whoever played cricket well was looked on with a more kindly eye by the people. Baron Alderson in his famous charge to the Grand Jury of Huntingdonshire in the 1840s makes it clear how splendid it was, and how natural, that in this England, the chief lord of the county should be found playing cricket with the meanest labourer. This was true: it is even arguable that this truth, two hundred years old by then at least, had done more than anything else to make violent social revolution unlikely in England. Baron Alderson would have been the first to deplore the implications of socially restricted clubs such as I Zingari which led inevitably to the stratification of cricket socially, not only in playing ability.

It was an age which, when it began, saw a still largely rural England, and a heavily populated Ireland not yet beset by potato blight. Those who know London may find it hard to realize that when the period began, Brompton was still a separate village, with acres of market gardens spreading between it and Pimlico and other outliers of London: and Dulwich was deep in the country. Clapham Common was still enormous in extent not yet having been carved up by railways, and the famous, now destroyed Euston Arch just about to be completed.

In this rural England, each town and village had its team: some had more. Already in earlier periods, there had been some distinction in some towns between tradesmen's cricket clubs, and gentlemen's clubs. These came more to the fore. Many new clubs arose at this time: this and the next period together are when most of the modern local clubs were formed, and if many of these now pretend to a much older life, there is either no basis for it at all, or it is founded on the prior existence of a cricket ground and the knowledge that people played. But in southern England there was probably not a hamlet which had not turned out a team at some time or other, if not by the middle, then certainly by the end of the previous century: *there was no need for any club.* The need for a club arose when you wanted to organize a programme of home and away matches with other and more distant places and this did not become practicable until the railways arrived. After that it was easy to move about. It would probably be possible to plot, in many parts of the country, the date of known formations of clubs (as distinct from merely playing the game) against the arrival locally of the iron road, and to find a distinct correlation.

There was another reason for forming clubs: to enable representative teams to be chosen over wider areas. Thus it was that in this period as well as the last we continue to read of new formations of county clubs, many of which only lasted a few years: the formation was imitative and premature. The players were not yet there, nor the funds, and many of these clubs did not survive: Leicestershire, formed long before, did not last out the period: Northamptonshire with equally venerable age, did. Surrey not only lasted but grew and, as we have seen, challenged the MCC as the leading London club, for instance mounting its own Gentlemen *v.* Players match from 1857. Sussex, formed as the period started, also lasted the period out, though not without a reformation towards the end. So also did Kent, also formed early in the period, but again not without reorganizations and doubts and difficulties. There were a few clubs among the minor counties, such as Cheshire and Shropshire and Herefordshire which began in this period, and lasted well beyond it: a great similarity existed amongst these three since they were predominantly amateur and when the county clubs eventually failed, it was the amateur element which continued under the generic title of 'Gentlemen of Cheshire (or Salop, or Herefords)'.

Still there *was* an impulse towards competitive county cricket: a Maidstone newspaper had talked about a county championship in 1837 in connection with a match between Kent and Nottinghamshire, each county already having beaten Sussex, and in 1855 there was an attempt to have a knock-out competition, too early by a hundred years to succeed, and too early by eighteen actually to be launched. Surrey, Sussex, Kent and Notts played fairly regularly during the period: others were seen from time to time, as Hampshire, under a number of different disguises, whenever a club organized itself there, and that occurred a bewildering number of times in the period, or as Middlesex where every now and then some of the amateurs of the county decided there ought to be a team: or in the north, where Yorkshire and Lancashire occasionally put out a team. But it was all very haphazard.

Some of this may have been because despite the increasing interest in the game actual matches themselves were less so. Round-arm had sharply restricted

95

scoring, and scoring was only to start looking up towards the end of the period as the still illegal 'high' bowling made itself felt. The interest that the public found in the game was chiefly in the doings of the famous trio, Nicholas Wanostrocht, alias Felix, Alfred Mynn, and Fuller Pilch. All were out of the game before the period was over: all had started before the period began. Pilch was a master-player of the stature relatively of W. G. Grace, and his performances compare strictly with Grace's statistically: had he lived thirty years earlier – or later – it would have been he who would have been regarded as the great champion of the game. He stood head and shoulders above his contemporaries as a player, and it is especially noteworthy that he was throughout his career a professional, perhaps the only professional cricketer who had stamped his name on a period or on the game. (It cannot be similarly argued that, for example, Hobbs or Hammond did so.) Felix was younger and was an amateur: he was to excel Pilch as a batsman, and that was no mean feat. Felix was sometimes paid for his endeavours as other great amateurs were at that time: but he had other means, being a schoolmaster, and a by no means indifferent water-colour painter. Mynn (his name is inseparable from the famous elegy by W. J. Prowse: 'Kind and manly Alfred Mynn') was the third of the trio, something below Felix as a batsman, definitely above as a bowler; not the equal of Pilch. If we could translate it into later terms, Fry and Ranji were to Grace roughly what Mynn and Felix were to Pilch (though of course the last three were much closer in time). The single-wicket matches involving these three attracted enormous crowds: and when they were gone, there was a void for a short while. How that void was filled we can see in the next period.

The spread of the game was not confined to England: mobility made it more popular too in Scotland and in Ireland. As in the preceding period, and as in England, clubs of all descriptions were formed, including county cricket clubs and in Ireland, before the period ended John Lawrence had produced his cricket annual, modelled on *Fred's Guide* (of all the annuals which lasted any length of time in the last century, only *Wisden* owed nothing in its make-up to *Fred's Guide*: which may well be why it survived). No echo of the potato famine reaches us in news of Irish cricket in the period: there was after all no reason why this game, popular for two hundred years or more there, should not continue to be popular, for no one yet had suggested it was an English landlord's game.

Most interesting is the first international encounter, the first such tour indeed, by an English team when George Parr took his team to the United States and Canada in 1859 – a formidable undertaking in those days, and leading to cricket in a formidable environment, being played in a blizzard in New York before the

11 (*above left*).
Rev Lord Frederick Beauclerk, D.D.

12 (*above right*).
The only photograph known of a cricketer
who played at Hambledon – W. Beldham,
'Silver Billy'

13. Fuller Pilch in his retirement, with an air
about him of Abraham Lincoln and yet
also of S. F. Barnes

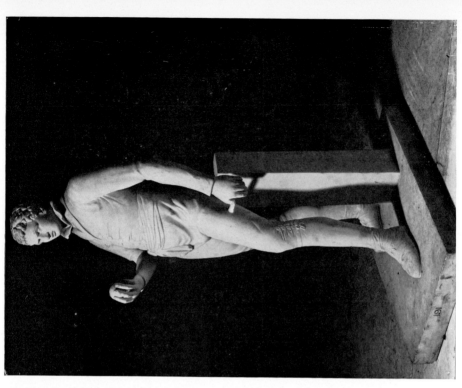

14–15. Two over life-size sculptures, by Henri Rossi, of a batsman and bowler: they show how cricket had moved yet further up the artistic scale by the first quarter of the nineteenth century, with marble sculptures thought suitable for the game: there had by then been paintings for some seventy years. The sculptures are at Woburn Abbey tour ended, with the players clad in multiple sweaters and trousers, and even gloves, John Wisden being outstanding in this respect. The game was being played in a quiet way in many towns and cities of the two countries: the great Philadelphian teams were yet to arise, though the Germantown Club had already been founded, in 1843, shortly before the first of the oldest series of international cricket matches in the world, that between Canada and the U.S.A. As we have seen Haverford College had been founded: so had the English-type schools in Upper Canada as it was then known (now Ontario). The touring team was a strong one but it found opponents certainly no worse than the average eighteen or twenty-two it would have met in England. There can be very little doubt that but for the American Civil War (which begun in 1861) there would have been another tour before nine more years passed, and if that unhappy conflict had never broken out, nor lasted as long as it did, it is difficult to see how our natural opponents at cricket would have been not Australia but the U.S.A., and, possibly Canada. One would, however, like to know just why the tour took place: not the detail of negotiations but what thought was in the minds of the English cricketers to make them accept, without query, that worthy cricket opponents existed in North America. Probably they took it for granted: the great influx of immigrants from Central and Northern Europe had hardly begun: they heard from time to time of cricket being played, there were many English immigrants from Nottingham and Sheffield who had settled in the eastern States plying their skills, and also reviving cricket in the Philadelphia area. They will all have written home: probably it *was* just taken for granted. It is we, so far removed from a cricketing North America, who do not.

The tour brought forth the first tour book, written by Fred Lillywhite who accompanied the team with his printing tent wherein he printed the latest score of each match (*were* these the first North America score-cards? It is unlikely): it is a book well worth reading for its period flavour and one wishes that the next two overseas tours by English teams, to Australia and the second to New Zealand as well, which followed in the next three or four years had been written up in similar style.

There can be no doubt about the game moving along steadily across the Atlantic: it was in this period that the first century was scored in the U.S.A., and also in the West Indies. We have little news of the game in those islands beyond the established existence of a number of clubs[1] and the certainty that there, too, inter-island rivalry was beginning to enter the heads of cricketers, for the first such matches occurred in 1865. Farther south, in the Argentine, there was little

[1] See Appendix I.

news either: the Buenos Aires Club was re-formed towards the end of the period, and there had been games in Brazil. In Central America, a well-attested cricket club had been formed in Mexico City in the 1840s: what happened to round-arm swerve, one wonders, at that altitude?

In Europe this period saw the beginnings of the game in Holland, though probably for some years there had been many quietly playing it without attracting attention before the first certain reference to it in the middle of the century. In Denmark too, the game seems to have been revived by English engineers who were building railways there.[1] In France such activity in the northern lace towns as noted in the last chapter seems to have died down, but cricket was being played by English people in Paris.

There is little news of the game in Africa: it was obviously being played in many centres: in this period here as well, the first recorded century was made, and also a game took place between 'Hottentots and Afrikaner Boers' in the Cape Province, won by the former. Is this why the Afrikaners have not till recently taken to cricket? The question is facetious because at this period Afrikaner Boers thought nothing of taking Hottentot women to themselves, whence the large South African coloured population (more of them speak Afrikaans than English) and whence also the coloured strain in almost every Boer family: such nonsense is Apartheid.

This period saw a great expansion in what was one day to be the Indian Empire: so that we find cricket being played in Kabul in Afghanistan by the troops who were soon to die almost to a man in the disastrous retreat from that town. In the lately conquered Punjab the game was being played by civilian and military teams, the record individual score in India being made and held for a time by players there. There was no large-scale participation in the game by Indian cricketers themselves, so far as is known, though the possibility exists that Bengalis were playing in Calcutta, and perhaps already Parsis in Bombay. Certainly quite early on in the period, Indian sepoys were taking part in military games: as certainly the game was being played all over India.

Farther east, cricket had already been played in Singapore as we have seen, but no later developments are known in this period, nor is it likely there can have been much on the mainland except in the other Straits Settlements. Military cricket was to be found in the newly-won colony of Hong Kong.

It is in Australia and New Zealand that great developments were taking place. In Australia the 1830s roughly coincide with the end of the first great economic

[1] Where had Hans Christian Andersen learnt the game? He certainly played it when staying with Charles Dickens at Gadshill in 1857.

boom in the Australian colonies: as a broad statement, they could have become independent at that time and been able economically henceforth to fend for themselves: they did not, and it was only later on that they even obtained responsible government: only at this time that New South Wales began to be divided up into other colonies. Yet before the 1850s ended, inter-colonial cricket had a life of some years' standing – the initial first-class matches in fact. So also had club cricket got well under way – competitive club cricket began in Victoria even before the period was out, though rather later in New South Wales. The Melbourne Club, the oldest surviving cricket club in Australia, dates from 1838: before the end three of the colonies had set up their own separate cricket associations to run the game. Seven or eight years before the period ended, the first of several commercially produced cricket annuals started up in Melbourne: yet so far no English team had appeared. It must have been Parr's tour to America which led on to a similar tour to Australia, in 1861–2: a tour of singular importance, for, in describing it, the phrase 'test match' was used for the first time, in a perfectly correct context to describe matches between the English team and each of the colonies. That we do not come across the phrase again for nearly twenty years suggests not that it was forgotten but that it was very much borne in mind and used in conversation if nowhere else. It is also of some interest that in the early 1860s a short series of matches commenced in Melbourne entitled Gentlemen *v.* Players and both the title and the idea were very much criticized as being all very well in England, but quite unsuitable in the colonies. Of course this was perfectly true: it had not yet come to mean rather than imply 'amateurs *v.* professionals', which was what was intended in Melbourne. And it was an absurd title in a land where an artisan could obtain a wage which would not be looked down upon here even now. (This is not to imply that some of the more snobbish aspects of English social life persist in strength in Australia: exclusive public schools and clubs, and a surprising number of directors of Australian companies wearing the old (Australian) school tie. Such things are far less significant in the life of the country than they still are in England.)

The two English tours (another followed two years later) showed that the Australians had good players indeed, but that they needed coaching: this was provided by William Caffyn, a well-known All England XI player,[1] staying on for many years and teaching what he could, with the effect we shall see in the next chapter.

---

[1] He had played for Sussex: was offered £400 a year and perquisites to coach in Melbourne but soon after moved to Sydney to ply his original trade of barber, though he never severed his connection with cricket.

Stephenson's team, the second of these two teams, also visited New Zealand; although cricket had been played long before this period in New Zealand, and although the country was by no means finally pacified when the period began, the game had made enormous headway in the time, and clubs were to be found in all the principal settlements: so also was first-class cricket to be seen, as many inter-provincial matches had already taken place by the time the tour began. There did not appear at that time too much difference between the standard of cricket in New Zealand from what had been found in Australia, but no English coach stayed on to lift up New Zealand cricket as had been done in Australia, and eventual progress as a result was nothing like so rapid.

In 1835 a new code of Laws had been enacted: nothing like what was to come nearly fifty years later, but still something which pulled together a great deal, and finally legalized round-arm. During most of the last years of the preceding period, round-arm had been, if not tolerated, certainly 'happening' and some discredit had been brought upon the legislators as a result.

The legislators were, of course, the members of the MCC. It is surprising to modern ideas that alterations in the Laws could be made at the annual meetings of the club *without any previous notice being given and* by a simple majority. It is not surprising that what the MCC did – or more often in this period did not – do by no means commanded the respect of the country as a whole. But then, from much earlier times, people had played the game with one or more MCC Laws modified – the length of the over being the most obvious example. This was always regarded as six-balls in country districts: it had even been used at Lord's in the previous period. There were other variations and of course the liberty given to round-arm bowling long before it was legalized, and the shilly-shallying through-out this period about the further extension to allow over-arm all helped to put the MCC into disrespect. Colonel Rait-Kerr has rightly said that the MCC's prestige was at its very lowest at this time.[1]

As he has also said, long before round-arm was legalized, over-arm was being employed when umpires allowed it. What may be doubtful is the extent to which over-arm was employed: it was probably hardly more than a slight raising of the arm above the shoulder – what in fact at first happened when over-arm was legalized. It is most unlikely that true 'high' over-arm was employed at this time, at any rate either often or significantly. But just as the gradation from under-arm to round-arm must have been quite difficult to spot in some bowlers (both were, in a true sense, though not a cricket sense, throwing) so the transition to over-arm must have been difficult to spot. What cricketers of the time ultimately regarded

[1] R. S. Rait-Kerr, *The Laws of Cricket* (Longmans, 1950), p. 37.

as crucial was whether the ball was jerked or not: with no less a man than Ranji as our mentor, if there is any real distinction between fair and unfair bowling, as the term is used in cricket, that distinction lies in the jerk. It was this which legislators of a hundred years and more ago found objectionable and it is this which is not any more in the modern Laws.

The 1835 Code introduced other changes – the follow-on became part of the Laws for the first time, though it had been practised in earlier years. Oddly enough it was another three years before the size of the ball was defined. In the mid-1840s much trouble was caused by wides, and how they should be dealt with, and after agitation the matter was satisfactorily settled by allowing runs from wides, instead of considering the ball dead and merely adding one to the score. In 1858 there was a most interesting change in the follow-on: that scoring had become much lower in this period was recognized by the follow-on limit being reduced from the 100 runs prescribed in 1835 to 60 runs in a one-day and 80 runs in a longer match. Another important change which had an immediate effect on scoring rates, was the rule permitting wickets to be swept and rolled, brought into force from about 1849.

It is worth while having a look at some of the reasons why the MCC had become a rather ineffective body in this period, and why it was all to change quite soon. By the early 1830s, the MCC did not itself command any great players: it could obtain them but it did not itself possess them, as it undoubtedly had earlier on in the century. This was one aspect of affairs. Parallel was the number of matches which the club itself played, both at home and away: in 1836 this was no more than sixteen and in 1863 it was still only sixteen, having been down into single figures, and never rising above twenty-three (in 1844: it was only twenty or over three times in the period). In the next period the figure was rapidly to double, treble, quadruple, and get well into three figures. Of course great matches continued to be played at Lord's but until the series of games between the two great touring Elevens began in 1857 (and which lasted until 1866) there was nothing really to capture the attention of the public, whatever the social attraction of some of the regular fixtures may have been.

The number of matches played by the club reflects also its small membership: there is good reason to say that it was becoming a small coterie of people, not especially representative of the aristocratic and upper class, as it had been, and was again to be, nor especially representative of cricketers either. It had an aura from the past which stood it in good stead, otherwise its situation might have become desperate. During the period the membership climbed from around 250 quite slowly to around 650: a very substantial percentage increase which, however, in no way reflected what the club should have been. It was not being well run and its members did not cope with the needful legislation properly or thoughtfully, but were the targets for outside pressure: such pressures were applied in a needed sense but surely more by good luck than anything else. Mismanagement could hardly have been better illustrated than the failure of the club to purchase its freehold, available for £7,000 in 1860: in five years time, when the full threat had been appreciated, it had to pay four times that amount to own its property. There was little chance of doing this from its own resources, let alone providing the essential accommodation that a great club needed: the pavilion was a petty affair, something that a provincial county might have had sixty or seventy years ago and far removed from the present dignified late-Victorian structure. One way to raise funds was to place a very high upper limit on total membership: the figure laid down was 5,000, and this was not achieved until around 1905. But early in the 1870s the membership had doubled, and not many years later it doubled again. This large increase in membership not only brought in funds: it also brought in members of other important cricket clubs, county and otherwise from all over the country, and removed the membership for a long time from any possible accusation of being a coterie. It meant that information passed the more readily about what was needed if there were any correction to be done: the Committee members could not sit by themselves isolated from opinion, for they encountered it wherever they went in the pavilion and in many parts of the ground itself. In short financial mismanagement led to an enormous improvement in the status of the MCC, and in its representative character, and it is strange how, in this way, so much good, for so many years, should have come out of evil. What is certain is that the club could never have fought off the building threat to its property had it remained small in numbers but would have become one of those intriguing might-have-beens of history.

There was one interesting move made by the MCC: in 1862 it attempted to lay down what county qualification should be and defined it as birth, or *bona fide* residence for two years. It was eleven more years before this was universally adopted, and the basis remained unchanged, whatever the changes in details, for many years after. This is as good an indication as any of an increased interest in county cricket.

Most of the century so far had been taken up by round-arm, or, earlier, the threat of it. One technique developed by a batsman so often leads to the bowler devising a counter to it. In the Hambledon days, Tom Sueter had been the first to leave his crease: as time went on, his habit was copied and by early in the century what was called 'forward play' had been adopted by most of the leading batsmen. It meant not merely playing forward, but going forward too. To counter this round-arm, or the 'straight-arm' bowling was devised. (It was also called, muddlingly to modern ways of thinking, 'over-hand' bowling. By this was meant that the ball was delivered from the hand with the back of the hand uppermost instead of palm up.) It was the Sussex bowlers, F. W. Lillywhite and James Broadbridge, who in due course established round-arm as the prevailing style. Both were bowlers who could bowl round-arm reasonably accurately: both were considered fast at the time: neither was as fast as Alfred Mynn, who, in some degree revolutionized bowling in his time. It has been noted that William Clarke revived under-arm successfully and it was in connection with his bowling that the comment was made that in his time no one bowled as fast as the old under-arm bowlers had: something which is very difficult to believe. Clarke was one of the leading bowlers during a good part of the round-arm period yet others were not willing to emulate him. Mynn was a man of great stature and physique, standing over six feet and weighing eighteen stone; and he was a very fast bowler indeed. It was said of him that no one had had any idea of what pace a bowler could obtain till he had seen Mynn. It is probably right psychologically to believe that all bowlers should bowl as fast as they can, just as it is also right to believe the ball should be hit as hard as one can – both beliefs being strongly held by Fijian cricketers to the present time. This belief led to many seeking to emulate Mynn who lacked his accuracy and ability, and led to what in the 1840s was called wild bowling, and the great increase in wides. Round-arm had been controllable, within reason provided not above medium pace: in the hands of a master like Mynn it was also controllable but only two or three others who approached his pace could also approach his accuracy. (It is interesting how much the same was to happen over Larwood a hundred years on: he had the accuracy to bowl what he did – others who copied him in England, and amongst West Indians, had not.) Mynn, an amateur, met his match in Felix, another amateur and in Pilch, a professional. Felix was able to master Mynn's bowling by assiduous practice against the 'catapulta' – an automatic bowling machine – which sent down the ball fast enough for Felix to learn how to play it, and so to play Mynn. Fuller Pilch, of Norfolk birth, was a tall player, like Mynn. It was said of W. G. Grace later that he was the first to combine forward play with back play, but whether or not he was the first, Pilch certainly did this. In those days it had become the custom for batsmen to be either forward or back players and they did not mix their strokes. Pilch did and he was as at home with a magnificent forward drive as with a late cut. Yet neither Pilch nor Felix had the influence on batsmen and on batting history that their own prowess seemed to demand: perhaps the low rate of scoring and uninteresting bowling had something to do with this. As over-arm started to creep in, and as it became possible to increase the rate of scoring, so the scene was set for someone with the ability to become a master. Pilch and Felix lived too early.

The effect of round-arm on scoring generally

Round-arm was not more difficult than over-arm but it was more difficult to score off because, generally speaking, direction could not be maintained consistently. Over-arm is, straight ball for straight ball, more difficult than round-arm: but if, accidentally (as in round-arm) or deliberately (in much modern over-arm) the ball is delivered off the wicket, so as to make it inadvisable, or even useless for the batsman to play the ball, then the rate of scoring, and scoring generally, must fall off. The following figures show that a 'high' was established in all but a few cases during the coming-in of round-arm in the 1825 to 1827 period – and those few cases were still after round-arm had been tried illegally. They also show that the next 'high' was established when over-arm was being increasingly widely used (though still illegal) from about 1856 onwards.

Highest individual score   – 1820: beaten 1865
Highest team total   – 1817: beaten 1859
Highest individual aggregate – 1795: beaten by 11 runs in 1834, then not till 1864
Highest seasonal average   – 1817: beaten 1871 (from 1828-58, only 9 exceeded 30)
Highest career average – established in career ending 1825, not exceeded till well after over-arm in full use
per 100 matches, 15 centuries were made in 1825, not beaten till 1859
per 100 matches, 45 fifties were made in 1828 (even then, a declining figure), not beaten till 1858
per 100 matches, 300 and over made in terms of a few every year till 1827, none till 1836, an average of one till 1856, and after that a sharp and steady rise
per 100 matches, 200 and over dropped to 13 in 1827, not exceeded till 1857 and after that a sharp and steady rise
Match aggregate record set up in 1817, of 1,047 runs: after that 800 exceeded once in 1844, then not again till 1858 after which a steady increase, the 1817 record being exceeded regularly from 1862 onwards

Over-arm did not supplant round-arm in Australia, in the best classes of cricket till after the 1873-4 tour: the very next season saw the first match aggregate of 1,000 runs achieved in Australia, and the first two team totals of over 400.

A very similar decline in scoring occurred in about 1952 in England with the increase in seam bowling, and off-the-stumps bowling, to that which followed the introduction of round-arm bowling some 130 years before.

8

THE MODERN PERIOD BEGINS:
THE AGE OF GRACE 1864-1893

(i) At Home

It has been the custom for many years to think of the modern period of cricket as starting in 1864 and it is certainly difficult to find another and more suitable date for its commencement. But it is generally wrong to divide history up into more or less independent compartments: the Victorian era did not begin in 1837, but several years later: and it can be argued either that it lasted well beyond 1901 or that the Edwardian era began in the 1890s (it certainly went on till 1914). So it is with cricket: quite a lot of things which were needed to make cricket 'modern' did not take place for a few years and in one or two cases several years – others had already happened. The period ends, however, with 1893 because what follows, the Golden Age, is a self-contained period on its own in so many different parts of the cricket world. The Age of Grace continued on well into the later period: his most astonishing feat (both in terms of its never having been done before and in terms of his age when he achieved it) was yet to come, but the bulk of his career was during this thirty-year period.

The year 1864 is usually adopted because that was when over-arm bowling was legalized: as though, there and then, the game became what we have now. Had it been like that, had there been a year when, apart from those infringing the Laws, there was no over-arm, and then the following year when it was not only over-arm, but what we imagine by over-arm, the date would be even more valid. But it was not like that: over-arm though of course legalized to the full height of the vertically raised arm was not at first used. All that happened was the arm being raised above the shoulder, and there have been bowlers to the present day who cannot have been very different in their action from the immediately post-

106

1864 style.[1] It was the Australians who brought in the over-arm which we know, when they came in 1878, and it was ten or more years before that style became prevalent. Moreover, there is in our time a tendency to sneer at round-arm, as the sort of stuff the village blacksmith bowls: there are precious few villages these days, and even fewer blacksmiths in them, but the concept is duly presented of a ball being slung with vigour and little else at the batsmen from a hand way outside the edge of the pitch. But round-arm as bowled before – and since – 1864 by top-class bowlers of the day was not of that kind: with its difficult horizontal swerve and good length, it was troublesome to batsmen of the best class. The evidence of the run-rate in the last period shows this, though it does not disclose the reason for it. Most match scores in the later years of round-arm show a very large number of wides. It can readily be guessed that many other deliveries were sent down not wide enough to be called, but in practical terms unplayable. Sometimes it was possible to score byes from these near-wide deliveries, as can also be seen from match scores throughout the round-arm period. It is none the less this kind of misconception which causes people to think of the round-arm days as close to the Flood, and so makes 1864 seem more important than it was.

It is all the same a good date: the first overseas tour to four of the countries which would be playing first-class cricket against England had taken place: in three, including also the West Indies, first-class matches had been played or were about to be played within a year or two. *Wisden* was started that year – not that it made much impact then, judging by the rarity of that issue and, apparently therefore, low sales:[2] the *Green Lillywhite* absorbed *Fred's Guide* a year or so later, and the first reckoning of county champions took place in that season. It is not likely that any of these events made the enthusiast of the time specially aware of a new period: that is something that only we can do with hindsight.

But the greatest thing of all was the rise of W. G. Grace. His first acknowledged

---

[1] See plate 26 for W. G. bowling round-arm.

[2] It is always called *Wisden*, and its formal name does not really matter. It is part of cricket's mythology because claims are made for it and beliefs held about it which differ only in degree from those which the fanatical devotees of some religions make for their own revealed books. But it has never covered all first-class cricket, it does not and has not listed (let alone without error) the births and deaths of all first-class cricketers, it does not provide a comprehensive and accurate list of records even at the first-class level, and any reasonably well-informed enthusiast could prove *Wisden* wrong. Claims for its infallibility are after all rather ridiculous for a year-book on any subject whatsoever, so that the phrase 'It's not in *Wisden*' is scarcely one to be used in praise of a remarkable feat. *Wisden* is, in fact, at its weakest in its coverage of overseas cricket but nowadays it does make an attempt at least to summarize overseas first-class matches. When all is said and done, however, *Wisden* remains the most important annual in the cricket world and it has been that for most of the past seventy or eighty years.

first-class match was in 1865 but he had made his name the previous season in making 170 and 56* in a good-class game against the Gentlemen of Sussex. The following season he was chosen, when not yet eighteen, to play for the Gentlemen of the South, the Gentlemen (v. Players) at both Lord's and the Oval, and for the Gentlemen of England. He did not do very much, his highest score being only 48. In 1866, he hit 224* for England v. Surrey, and 173* for Gentlemen of the South v. Players of the South, but only achieved 50 once in his other eleven innings. In 1867 illness and injuries kept him out of the game for most of the season, but in 1868 he made three centuries, two of them in the same match, a feat only performed twice before in all the history of cricket. He averaged 56·81. In 1869 he was sailing right away with an average of 57·39, an aggregate of 1,320 and six centuries: all quite without parallel. It was this season that made him in the eyes of all 'the most wonderful cricketer that had ever handled a bat': nor should we ever forget his bowling which was enough in itself to make his name. From then on he was reckoned 'the Champion' and it would not be at all difficult to make the entire period the story of W.G. It is enough to say that in 1875, following some stupendous seasons, it was seriously thought and put about that he was past his best, because he could only achieve 1,498 runs. So the following year he made 2,622 (his highest aggregate so far had been in 1871 when he made 2,739 runs) with a highest score of 344 and took 120 wickets. This was the way it went with Grace: hardly was the suggestion made that he was past his best or that he was retiring (quite often rumoured) than he came up with some new remarkable achievement.

Many of Grace's achievements would be rated extremely good by our standards – or rather not by our standards today which are poor, but by our knowledge of what has recently passed. By the standards of his day they were *phenomenal*: nothing like them had ever been done before, nothing like them had ever been publicized before. They were so far above the normal standards of good batsmen and good bowlers of the time when he came upon the scene as to set quite new standards, and it was *up* to his standards that cricket gradually rose during this entire period, so that by the end even some of Grace's records were being beaten or closely chased. But at the start, or in the middle of the period, there was no one who looked like doing so on the batting side: on the bowling, yes, because he made his batting his first aim. He was a very fine medium pace bowler, but something had to give if the man himself was not to. In a series of erudite and fascinating articles in *The Cricketer* in 1938 and 1939, the statistician George H. Wood (a Fellow of the Royal Statistical Society, elected as a result of a paper sent to it when he was in his middle teens) showed conclusively that W. G. Grace was far and away the finest all-rounder of English cricketers in the sixty years of cricket which was the subject of his survey. In that survey he attempted to quantify the effect of various changes in the laws, conduct and general appurtenances of the game on scoring and wicket-taking, and did so without any serious challenge: thus though his results now need to be added to, it is unlikely that any other English player has been found in the last twenty-five years, or will be found in the next thirty years, to challenge W.G.'s supremacy and it is not easy to think of any overseas player of any period who could have done so. Grace has been described as the first batsman to combine forward play with back play, but he had been preceded in this by Pilch whose example had had no permanent effect. Grace's did: no longer did batsmen confine themselves to one group of strokes, though there have always been those who have shown themselves stronger in one group, even in one stroke, than in the others. Grace made batting literally an all-round performance. Not only that: he revelled in hitting fast bowling, which is cricket as it should be played, and this was very definitely an example for others, since he showed that it could be done. He developed no one special stroke by which he became famous – he used them all, pragmatically as the occasion demanded. No one ever accused him of being a graceful bat to watch (no pun intended!) and if he had style it was that of the technician rather than of the artist. Artistry was to come later: perhaps, indeed, artistry could not come until the technical foundations had been safely laid.

This was why it is the age of Grace. But for Grace, it is unbelievable that the standards achieved by the Golden Age would have been thought of until, maybe, Bradman came along. He dominated the game, and any match in which he played: only Bradman appeared to dominate quantitatively in this way, but qualitatively, the difference was great. In fact Bradman did not do much that had not been done by one or other of his contemporaries. Grace did. Bradman had superb reflexes, but he did not possess the powerful physique that W.G. had: and with W.G. it was not just superb reflexes for he showed that what he did, anyone else could do, given application and perseverance and the massive physique to withstand punishment. But this last was not what Bradman could show. Yet . . . there had been another. Fuller Pilch had dominated the scene in his day in just such a way as Grace: statistically, the parallels between his performance and those of Grace are remarkably numerous: but Pilch does not stand out in history as does Grace because Pilch came on the scene at a period of very much lower scoring than before. He was seen in his own time as a wonderful cricketer: he never had the adulation which the populace bestowed on Grace.

Grace is important for another reason: it was not merely the first-class game which was dominated by him – he showed the way for all cricketers, and it is interesting and instructive to see how many records went by the board in minor cricket once he had shown what could be done. One question remains open: was all this because of Grace, or was it because of over-arm bowling? Or was it a little of each, over-arm being, in some respects easier to play (round-arm deliveries being so often wide of the wicket), if in others not so easy. The ball, being much straighter, had to be played, and Grace demonstrated that anyone, with talent, could play it, even if they could not achieve the summits of his own performance. It is very doubtful if any other great cricketer has ever influenced the game at all levels in the way that Grace did. It is even more doubtful if anyone ever will, or indeed if the conditions exist or can exist where anyone could: Grace's effort was a once-for-all one.

There was something else special about W.G. By the accident of his time, he became the first 'folk-hero' in modern times in England. There had been celebrated cricketers for over two hundred years from (and no doubt before) William Bedle down to Grace's own time. For the best part of a hundred and fifty years there had been great occasions when crowds of ten thousand, and later of twenty thousand and more, had gathered – formidable figures in view of the population totals and the difficulties of travel in horse-drawn days. But now, at the start of the modern era of cricket[1] there came this great man not yet heavily bearded and prefiguring Jove himself, with his fantastic performances. These performances were known throughout the country if not by the same evening then by the following morning – known to all in a far greater population (and one still increasing rapidly) than that which knew any of his predecessors. If he wished, the ordinary man could come up from almost any part of the country speedily and cheaply to see Grace play the next day. And if he could not make the journey, he might still see Grace, for Grace did not confine his cricket to London, nor to Bristol either, but toured with his team to all parts.

The late Monsignor Ronald Knox suggested in an amusingly fanciful essay that W. G. Grace and W. E. Gladstone were one and the same man: it could be argued that Grace travelled more widely and more energetically than the Grand Old Man of Liberal politics. He took his own masterful play to the people wherever they were: in first-class cricket his run total is well over 50,000 and the runs he made in minor cricket brought the known total to a few hundred short of six

---

[1] It was a modern era in so many other ways: the rise of Grace only just preceded that of Gilbert and Sullivan, yet their political and social satire is wholly comprehensible even to the young among us (though teenagers are beginning to find it difficult). Political and social satire of *two* hundred years ago was no longer comprehensible to any but the historically well-educated among Grace and his contemporaries.

figures and it is reasonably certain that, taking into account games where his score is unknown, he achieved that colossal figure, approached by no other batsman at any time. He was 'The Champion' and people thronged to see him in all his majesty of frame and cricket ability.

The dispossessed proletariat in search of an identity had found, if not an identity in W.G., a god whom they could worship. If he had not arisen at the time he did it is very doubtful if he would have caught the right moment of history: someone else, most probably in some other walk of life, might have done so. Grace did not give cricket a new lease of life – it was anything but moribund – but he gave it, and especially the first-class game, a new dimension of life. If he had arisen later, his performances would have been no less wonderful statistically but they might well not have turned him into a figure of myth and legend. Industrial England was in bad need of a hero: as Grace rose, the monarchy was withdrawing into privacy so that at the height of W.G.'s powers, there was no national figurehead. W.G. by his exploits became that figurehead and became a folk-hero, just as Pelé is in Brazilian football (in circumstances not vastly different from those of W.G., if one makes a few adjustments).

Let us then look at the scene of important cricket in the country. There had been one important development in the 1840s, about half-way through, and its effects lasted about half-way through the present period: the great touring Elevens, the All England XI of William Clarke, and the United All England XI set up in opposition. These teams, consisting of great players of the time, had toured the entire country. They were first and foremost money-making businesses, but they also spread knowledge of the game and intensified enthusiasm for it. Although these two teams effectively only lasted a few years into the period, others sprang up, the United North of England XI (with quite a short existence) and the United South of England XI, to which W.G. and others of the Grace family became attached and which late in its life confusingly changed its name to the United XI. They attracted less support and interest as the years went by, partly because of the great increase in county matches, but were finally killed because of the extensive tours undertaken by overseas teams – the first two Australian teams (excluding the Aborigines who indeed also toured widely in 1868), the first Canadians, and the two Parsi teams, all of whom followed a pattern similar to that of the great Elevens, and who must have been superficially at least, more interesting, and so far as the Australians were concerned, more attractive too.

It was this association of the Grace family with the United South of England XI which was at the bottom of the allegations that the Graces took fees for playing cricket, and it was this that led to the exclusion in due course of the youngest of them, G. F. Grace, from the Gentlemen *v.* Players match at Lord's: the MCC dictum being that a gentleman ought not to make any profit from playing cricket. This was, of course, an impeccable description of an amateur and was carefully worded so as to allow an amateur to take expenses. W.G. undoubtedly did take expenses – he openly acknowledged the fact – but what was, and is, insufficiently realized is that he had to pay for a *locum tenens* to run his practice while he was away playing cricket. What is also insufficiently realized is that he treated many poor patients entirely free: this in a period when the National Health Service was undreamt of. On the other hand, it does seem that in his earlier years, as well, probably, as with the U.S.E.E., W.G. took fees: that he asked for them is certain. This was well before he qualified as a doctor, and it was not out of line with the behaviour of other celebrated amateur cricketers before him, and for a long way back, in one form or another. Shamateurism in the game has a long history, and for a time W.G. was most probably a shamateur: no doubt there was an element of hypocrisy over all this, but W.G. was not alone in it. That it should have caused any problems in the latter 1870s, for the first time apparently, tells us no more than that this was when Victorian righteousness first interfered with cricket. It had taken a long time: it was in that same decade that bookmakers were heard for the last time at Lord's, shouting the odds. It has often been thought that the gambling aspect of the game had vanished a generation or more before, apart from whatever may have gone on between private individuals. But this is not so, and it did not vanish from the Australian scene as quickly as all that, as we shall see. Many people have been unable over the years to understand just what is supposed to be wrong about gambling: now, in a generation which sees more gambling than for many years, and in which cricket too is involved, previous attitudes must seem very strange.

But the attitude was all part of the new special aura that was springing up about cricket and cricketers, and which came to its completion well before the Golden Age was to begin: that it was somehow a rather saintly game, in which nothing mean was ever done, by players, spectators or enthusiasts, on or off the field – that cricketers were all splendid admirable fellows, and so on.[1]

[1] It is significant that the earliest known occurrence of the phrase 'it's not cricket' is in 1851 when Pycroft, referring to the dangerously fast bowling of Mr Harvey Fellows, said in his *Cricket Field*, 'Why then we will not say that anything that hardest of hitters and thorough cricketer does is not cricket, but certainly it's anything but *play*.' Before the 1860s were out the phrase was well established. It should, however, be noted that a slightly different expression had been used of the bowling of one T. Humphreys for Cowley *v.* Oxford University in 1834 when he delivered twisting underhand sneaks. These, according to Pycroft writing in 1851, had been described by the Oxonians as 'no cricket'.

Some of it is still with us: these myths take a long time to die. The very undesirable effect of this attitude was to drive anything that was supposedly contrary to the interests of the game as now envisaged, underground and out of sight.[1]

Meanwhile county cricket grew enormously in the popular imagination, helped on, of course, by the Press. By 1870 tables were being published giving the relative positions of certain counties. Recent research has shown that this kind of ranking had been going on for some time, and though the written record of it did not survive, somebody in 1887 remembered that Surrey were then champions for the first time since 1864: the playing record confirms this. Different tables appeared in different newspapers and annuals, as there were different opinions on which counties were to be included. There was no hard and fast division between what we now call first-class and second-class counties: indeed the concept of such a division had not yet dawned, and was not to do so until the 1880s. Certainly an important factor was the duration of a match but here it is difficult to understand why Derbyshire was let in, for instance, and Leicestershire excluded – except that by the end of the 1870s, when Leicestershire became prominent again after many years, the table of counties had to some extent crystallized. Yet again, Hampshire was sometimes in and sometimes out: its playing strength was poor indeed at the time, its administration often difficult to discern and both ran counter to the idea (a wrong idea!) of Hampshire as the earliest well-known cricket county. The MCC took no part in all these discussions and squabbles: as Haygarth put it, 'to MCC all counties are equal' – a preposterous idea!

So far as the counties are concerned, the period began with a large number of county cricket clubs being formed, all over the British Isles. Many of these, of course, were in counties which had had such organizations before. A number of these new formations, in and around 1864, did not last many years (Essex is such an example) and the clubs were reformed yet again later on (and sometimes more than once again: Cambridgeshire for instance). The fact remains that the actual number of such formations was unusually large: some of it was sheer fashion and even sheer snobbishness – the county in Wales, for example, which was firm that no tradesman could possibly become a member.[2] But much of it, such as the rise of Yorkshire out of the Sheffield match committee, in 1863 (it was to be reformed again some thirty years later) can only have been due to an increase in the interest taken in cricket generally. It is extremely difficult to see why this should have

[1] See page 123, for an incident concerning a member of the Grace family.
[2] Carmarthenshire.

been so at that time: if it had been the great touring Elevens which had caused this interest (and they arose out of an existing enthusiasm) then surely that interest could have been aroused many years earlier. It may have been no more – and no less – than a general public desire to see competitive cricket, to see who were champions after all. The matter was clearly of some importance for when in the early 1870s a county could pick a player who had already played for two other counties that season, the decision as to which was the champion county could have been made absurd. This led to the first generally accepted rules for the qualification of players for counties (based on the 1862 proposal), duly approved by the members of the MCC half-way through the 1873 season. Even so, the MCC was careful to see that these rules were not for a few self-chosen, or Press-chosen 'first-class' counties: they applied to all counties, and to all matches in which counties played. It would, under those rules, have been quite out of the question to play a cricketer who was still qualifying and under those rules objections were taken on numerous occasions to players appearing in matches which had no kind of competitive aspect about them, competitive, that is, from the point of view of a championship. There seems to have been some real intention at the beginning that these rules were part of the Laws, but early in the next century the rules were amended in their entirety by the Advisory County Cricket Committee, without ever being submitted to the members of the MCC. (It can therefore be argued from a legalistic point of view that the 1873 rules are still in force having been duly approved by the law-making procedure and that all subsequent purported amendments have no validity at all!)

During most of the period, from about 1870 onwards, and after the loss, apparently for ever, of Cambridgeshire as a first-class county (using the anachronistic modern term), the 'great' counties numbered nine or ten, the doubtful ones being Derbyshire (in for most of the period), Hampshire (out for most of the period) and Somerset (in for the last few years): the others were, of course, Kent, Lancashire, Middlesex, Nottinghamshire, Surrey, Sussex and Yorkshire. There arose pressure from some of the other counties for admission to the charmed circle: they already had a competition of their own, half-official (in so far as they themselves recognized it) and this pressure led to and was part of some interesting administrative developments. These were for the most part counties which would one day be accepted as first-class in the modern sense. There were very many others: every county in England and Wales has known a county cricket club, so have most of those in Ireland and Scotland, and in all the British Isles, only three counties have not played county cricket. Many of these counties were absurdly weak: early this century the MCC even, somewhat arrogantly, decided that

Scottish counties were not true counties for qualification purposes but mere clubs. That may have been true of some of them but others were true county clubs, whatever their strength. Wherever they were, these very much lesser county cricket clubs tended to play only two or three of their neighbours (this has to this day been the mark of minor county cricket) nice friendly games with a somewhat spurious air of real county cricket. They had, and many of them have, no influence on the game: they were indeed no more save in name and potential, than convivial gentlemen's sports clubs, but they all have one significance – the instinct to consider local representative cricket only in term of counties – and that goes right back to the early eighteenth century if not before.

Nor in this period were the two old Universities of great importance in the cricket field. Socially, yes: socially they were important as the Eton *v.* Harrow match was socially important, but it was only towards the end of the period that the 'Varsity sides began regularly to be good opponents for full-strength first-class teams. (But in 1878 Cambridge humbled the mighty Australians by beating them in an innings and without A. P. Lucas, probably their best bat.) They played fewer matches than they would today. It was not pressure of examination that prevented this, for few went to University then, certainly not from the cricket-playing fraternity, for scholastic reasons, but that the idea of playing cricket day in, day out was not something that appealed to the amateur mind. A professional might: if he was not playing for his county he could be playing for one of the touring Elevens, for half the period at least, and later on there was no lack of *ad hoc* matches from which he could find some reward. Some counties did not indeed run a long fixture list: their teams were largely professional. The amateur did not look on cricket in that way: all day and every day was not merely too much like hard work, it *was* hard work, and cricket was a game to be enjoyed when it was played.

More important than the Universities, whom they fed, was the rise of public school cricket. Of course there was nothing new in such cricket: what was new was the increasing number of such schools, newly founded, or newly reorganized or re-endowed, all imitations of Dr Arnold's Rugby, all preaching *mens sana in corpore sano* and all playing cricket hard. It was the vastly increased input of amateurs into the first-class game which marks this period distinctively from the last: and they came from these schools, where character was encouraged but not learning, as the schools themselves clearly stated. The cricket annuals of the period give great prominence to the doings of these schools, and that in itself reflects their importance from a cricket point of view. It stretched back even earlier in a boy's life: there was a number of what would be called preparatory schools where all or most of the masters were cricketers of some note, and where the older boys would be encouraged to play with the masters: little of this aspect of school cricket seems to have outlasted the period.

But the period saw the intensification of club cricket: all over the country there seems to have been an explosion of new clubs in the first ten or fifteen years or so of the period, some of them a reawakening, often after many years, of older clubs, some quite new as organizations. It was a time too when the older touring clubs by their existence, became an encouragement to the formation of many imitators – many were the I Zingaris that sprang up around Britain and overseas. There was no hint of organization in club cricket in this period, except in the Midlands and in the North. Competitive cricket, in the form of knock-out competitions, had arisen in the early 1880s (how was it that such cricket had occurred in this country so many years after it had first occurred in Australia?), and league cricket began in Birmingham at the end of the 1880s, and both spread rapidly during the rest of the period and into the early part of the following period till the North and much of the West Midlands – the industrialized Midlands anyway – was organized on a league cricket basis. One of the impulses towards this may well have been the element of cant that the North perhaps detected in the special aura that was being woven around cricket in the south: it may have been just such a thing, psychologically, that led to the secession of the Northern Union in Rugby football, and there has at times been an attitude towards league cricket in the south which could have led to just such a split in cricket had the whole question of professionalism not been far less important in cricket. (After all, it was only when former public schoolboys did not wish to be openly dubbed professional cricketers that any difficulty was found about two classes of cricketers, solved, if it was a solution, by abolishing any distinction among players, in competitive county cricket, though not in other classes of game.)

At this point it is worth referring to the rise of country-house cricket. There was no defined point in the history of the game when this aspect of it commenced: when a great patron in the early eighteenth century organized matches from among his own friends and tenants on his own land, was it, or was it not, country-house cricket? In one way the answer would be 'no' since such a patron was probably anxious to get together a top-rate team, whereas in country-house cricket as later understood, enjoyment was one consideration and another was the quality of those taking part, all of them friends or acquaintances of the host in one way or another. For over a hundred and fifty years there had been privately organized cricket and it was in or about the 1840s that what we would now call country-house cricket started to become noticeable. (I Zingari's cricket was almost entirely of the country-house variety for many years after its foundation and so also was that of some of the other great wandering clubs.) It lasted until the First World War, survived in an attenuated form after it and occasionally even to the present. A large number of the landed gentry and noblemen of England staged matches at their country homes, which were worthy of Haygarth's notice during the 1870s (he had paid too little attention to this earlier), and his notes on the games often indicate they were only part of a week's series. There was indeed a distinct flavour of the country-house game about the more important and first-class weeks that had been established from the time of the Canterbury week, in the round-arm period, onwards. There would be the private tents and enclosures for convivial social clubs, and for regiments as well as for principal gentlemen of the county or area: the smaller weeks graded off indefinably into country-house weeks where there was one party only, instead of many different ones. There were many county clubs which were confined to the 'gentlemen of the county': they too ran 'weeks' and their nature was very similar to the single host's week that was the true country-house game.

This kind of game is not unimportant: it was truly amateur, people who wanted to play to win regardless of other aspects, would not find themselves again invited, nor again would fine exponents but not so fine characters (and cricket has been as full of delinquents morally and socially as any other group of men). Such cricket provided an outlet for those who did not like the professional and increasingly competitive attitude in top-level cricket, and it also provided an influence on that cricket, all depending on the extent to which a county side was amateur run and led. It could have a great influence on Kent cricket, and none on Notts: much on Middlesex (who had hardly any great professional batsmen in the period, though many fine bowlers, and that was what ground bowlers were for) and later on in the period, much on Yorkshire. The game was, in a real sense, coloured by country-house cricket. Though its apogee was probably reached, in terms of sumptuousness and elegance, in the Golden Age which followed, its influence waned as first-class competitive cricket and international cricket multiplied and burgeoned: but it left its impress on the game in the present period, and that influence has lasted almost to our own time.

For the rest of the rapidly increasing population of Britain, cricket could only be had on the pitifully few days of freedom from toil that Victorian legislation had left: nor did anyone in this period think it worth while providing playing facilities, either at the board schools which were soon to be established, or otherwise.

People found a bit of ground, and played: it was easier to do then, because farming was a down-trodden industry, after the repeal of the Corn Laws, and many a farmer was glad to get a few shillings for a field which was otherwise profitless to him. As we shall see, a time was to come, and not long after the period was over, when all that changed too.

In the mid-1860s in Ireland cricket was flourishing, except in parts of Ulster where the game did not appeal to the Scottish Presbyterian temperament of the settlers there. There was we have seen, even a worthwhile cricket annual,[1] which was to last until the early 1880s. But that was when the game started dying: Parnell, a keen lover of the game itself, started his land agitation, and in some curious manner the idea got around that cricket was an alien game, a game for the English or the Anglo-Irish but not for the true Irishman. A pity indeed that it was to be nearly eighty years before Cromwell's edict of 1656 was unearthed, or the whole aspect of the game there might have been changed. It took long years to die: indeed it is not dead in and around the big cities, but as an Irish game, a game naturally played by Irishmen as a natural thing, the agitation of the 1880s killed it. None of this could have been foreseen by those who first took an Irish team on a tour overseas, in 1879, to the U.S.A. and Canada.

The involvement of the British Isles in international cricket had of course begun in the last period: it gathered pace in this. In 1868 Australian aborigines toured England: in 1878, white Australians, and thereafter every two years until 1890, and then every three: in 1880, the first team of Canadians: in 1884, the first team from Philadelphia: in 1886, the first of the Parsi teams. Going out, there had been the first tour to South Africa in 1888–9, and to India in 1889–90. The first of what came to be acknowledged as Test matches (the classification of these matches was due to an Australian enthusiast, Clarence P. Moody, writing near the end of the period) had been played against Australia in 1876–7, and the first in England in 1880. Other tours saw other representative matches against local teams. It was a great period of foundation-laying and lower-course building all ready for the finished edifice which the Golden Age brought.

There is one very important aspect of this period which marks it off from all before, and links it closely with all since – the matter of bibliography. *Wisden* for example, had begun in 1864: in 1870 it underwent its first overhaul and began to look internally very much like its subsequent issues right up to 1938: and in 1887, with the advent of members of the Pardon family to the editorship, it established a format which was to last for fifty years. The *Green Lillywhite* had started in 1865 and absorbed *Fred's Guide* the following year, to be absorbed by

[1] *John Lawrence's Handbook of Cricket in Ireland*, first issue, 1865–6, last, 1880–1.

the *Red Lillywhite* in turn in 1886: the latter had started in 1872 and was to last to the end of the century but not beyond. Thus for twenty years of the period, there were three substantial cricket annuals, and for the early part of those years, *Wisden* was *not* the most sought after. There were other and lesser annuals too. A. J. Gaston, in the first serious attempt at cricket bibliography in the 1892 *Wisden*, needed eleven pages to tell what had appeared in cricket's history till then. Neither accurate not complete, what he said is still a good guide to what was going on, and especially to the proportion of cricket books at various periods: he covers the range before 1864 in *hardly more than two pages*, much of it descriptive rather than listed material. The first known county cricket annual[1] with scores appeared in 1865: the longest lasting county cricket annual, that of Kent, began in 1877. Many others followed on. Publishers produced books of scores for various counties: publishers produced local cricket annuals: publishers gauged that there was a potential for cricket periodicals. Britain was not the first but in 1878 a monthly magazine appeared in Sheffield – the *All England Cricket and Football Journal*: it lasted a year or two, and apart from its 'real photographs' has little of interest, though its rarity (and implicitly its lack of popularity) makes it a collector's item. Another such was the *Cricket and Football Times* started as a weekly also in 1878 which lasted rather longer, until 1881, and is even scarcer – too much a kind of all sports magazine in its later development. But there *was* a demand for a cricket magazine and C. W. Alcock, the Surrey secretary and the editor of the *Red Lillywhite* (and of a football annual too: secretaries were more productive and covered a larger field in those days) founded the weekly *Cricket* in the spring of 1882. It was to last till the First World War began: undoubtedly the best general cricket magazine that has ever appeared. There was much else: instruction books and memoirs and the first of the ghosted books indeed appeared in this period. Nor was this all. For thirty years now the once immensely popular cigarette cards have not been issued (little pasteboard cards with illustrations in black and white, colour or photogravure, with advertisements, or extremely reliable texts on their backs, tucked into every packet of cigarettes, and covering an enormous range of subjects – the older generation of readers will excuse the parenthetical description). The first such dealing with cricket appeared in the late 1880s, oddly enough from an American tobacco firm and aimed at the Australian market. British firms were to follow in a few years.

All this shows clearly the hold which the game was getting on the minds of the population generally: nothing like this scale of publicity had been approached, or we may be sure even guessed at, at any previous time.

[1] Issued by Shropshire C.C.C.

(ii) Abroad

In Europe there was little to record outside Holland. The game was being played in Denmark; in 1889 ten Danish clubs formed the Dansk Boldspil Union primarily intended to look after cricket. It was played by English people all over Europe, in Russia, in Rumania, in Germany, in Austria-Hungary (probably by Viennese also for there was a Wiener Cricket und Fussball Verein in existence from 1892, which still survives as a football club, in the Prater), in Italy and Switzerland and France. In Holland it grew apace, to the extent that the need for a country-wide administrative body became apparent in 1883 when the Dutch Cricket Association was formed, the oldest of all the surviving national cricket administrative bodies in the world. And Holland was the first country outside the Empire to send its own players to tour England, and to act as host in the 1880s. In what seems a short space of time, a standard was attained up to that of good though not top-class club cricket of the time in England. And it has retained that standard.

Across the Atlantic, the game, which had something of a setback during the American Civil War, got going again with an increasing popularity: the end of the 1860s and the early 1870s saw a number of American-produced cricket books, instructional and factual, and not confined only to the Philadelphia area. It was still possible for a New York newspaper to talk about cricket as being the national game of the country though if it ever had been, since colonial days, much evidence to that effect must have been lost (however, as late as 1915 American newspapers outside Philadelphia still boasted 'cricket editors'). The war between the States, which had affected the revival or growth, of modern cricket, had provided opportunities for the growth of baseball as a game demanding less in time and space: baseball came generally to be called by that name early in the 1830s, following the publication in 1834 of rules referring to it by that name, those rules being otherwise identical with an earlier edition in 1829 in which the game had been called rounders, which, of course, it basically still is. Baseball rapidly became extremely commercialized, and this commercialization assisted its popularity, but at the same time encouraged many Americans, in an age when it was still possible to move relatively slowly, to adhere to or take up the essentially amateur game of cricket.

The idea of cricket being essentially amateur was a notion basically as wrong as the much earlier American concept of the English constitution, and it was much more of an American idea, in revulsion from baseball, than an English one.

It may, in the long run, have been responsible for the virtual death of the game there, anyway as a first-class game. One of the great exponents of the idea was the Merion Cricket Club which was founded in 1865 and eventually of the same status as the older Germantown Cricket Club, both of which still survive under those names, and with their lovely grounds and once excellent pitches, given over to lawn tennis. Three years after Merion was formed, E. Willsher took a team to North America, and in 1872 this was followed by a team led by R. A. Fitzgerald, the then secretary of the MCC. The team (plate 17) consisted entirely of members of the MCC so it could be argued that this was the first overseas tour of the MCC, if, however, unofficial. Both tours aroused great interest, and helped on the game enormously: in 1874, there occurred a tournament at Halifax, Nova Scotia, which was won by Philadelphia and led to competitive cricket in Philadelphia striving for the possession of the trophy won at Halifax. Then in 1877, the *American Cricketer* was founded, weekly till the end of the century, monthly until its demise (though very irregular towards the end) in 1929, and thus the longest lasting of any cricket magazine. In 1878, the Cricketers' Association of the United States was formed, as the governing body of cricket, adopting the MCC Laws except as modified locally. The same year saw the first Australian team to England visit Philadelphia and have the worse of the draw in an eleven-a-side game. The Australians had complained about umpiring in England during their tour, alleging that all the umpires were professional cricketers, and in the pockets of the amateurs: now they did the same in Philadelphia, and tried to abandon the game: they were persuaded not to do so only by very severe threats from the American Committee, but too much time was lost for the game to be finished. An angry mob jeered at the Australians as they left the ground.

After this, tours flowed regularly to America from England and Ireland, nine visits in all in the period, and two more by Australians (in the second of which they were first beaten by the Philadelphians by an innings: it was to happen again) as well as the first overseas tour by a West Indian team in 1886. In the other direction, the U.S.A. visited the West Indies in 1887–8, playing what was the first international match involving a representative West Indian team (which lost by 9 wickets), and the Philadelphians twice visited the British Isles.

The great clubs of Philadelphia grew fat on the proceeds of the many representative matches played against these visiting sides, and built their palatial pavilions as a result (plates 33 and 34). The game was played in schools, and Haverford, though now the only one, was not by any means alone in this period, when there was a regular inter-schools competition. Nor could the game be kept out of the Universities, and several were known to run their own teams. Nor again, was the game confined to Philadelphia though it was always best there: New York came next perhaps, and Baltimore, Boston, Chicago and Pittsburgh were all cities which competed in the U.S.C.A's inter-city trophy competition.

The game throve, and if all could see the flowering of it in Philadelphia that was to come in the Golden Age, none could see, or be justified in seeing, its decline and demise not long after the Golden Age was over. Philadelphian cricket was not all amateur: there were many English professionals who were employed as coaches, and there was a regular Gentlemen v. Players game in Philadelphia, not always won by the amateurs, which is enough to indicate the quality of the professionals. One of these, A. M. Wood, who had played in England as an amateur, settled down there as a professional but later turned amateur again and was one of the few exceptions to the unspoken rule that Philadelphian teams only included native-born Americans (another being J. A. Lester after this period).

In Canada, the prospect seemed every bit as bright: the game was, anyway, being more widely played than in the United States, it was well established in schools in Ontario; there was a large number of clubs playing, the game spread into the prairies as the population did too. The international match with the U.S.A. was revived in 1865, and then for some reason lapsed again until 1879 after which it was played pretty regularly until 1912. All but three of the touring teams who visited the U.S.A. also played in Canada, the first All Canadian team to play an English team doing so in 1868 (twenty-two against eleven, and the XXII could only make 28 against the XI's 310–9). Yet somehow Canada did not attain the same standard of cricket: was it too diffuse? Was the American centralization on Philadelphia its playing strength, if its weakness in other ways (which would explain why combined U.S.A. could sometimes lose to Canada, even if only thrice in this period)? There was enthusiasm for the game, though: a Canadian cricket annual which had appeared once in 1858, revived for two issues in 1876 and 1877: and a Canadian cricket magazine appeared in 1882, but lasted no more than the year. What did not assist Canadian cricket at all was the attempted tour of England in 1880. This tour, designed to emulate the Australians but with a side so much weaker as to make the idea laughable, was captained by a man who turned out to be one Trooper Dale, a deserter from the Royal Horse Guards, who was eventually arrested on the field of play and hauled off to court-martial: there, having been sentenced to thirty-five days (a mild sentence no doubt in recognition of his cricket and marital abilities for, after he had fled to Canada, he had married twice and fathered six children): he then broken loose and jumped into the street outside, where he was caught by a passer-by, re-arrested, and given another 300 days. The team had already been no attraction, though, and the arrival of the Rev. T. D. Phillips (whose active career spanned over sixty years – he was a very redoubtable Canadian player) in June, did nothing to save the tour. Seven years later a properly organized Canadian team made a very different impression indeed. When we refer to Canadian cricket in this period, we should also recall a once-famous English cricketer, W. R. Gilbert. Gilbert was a first cousin of W. G. Grace's, and had taken part with W.G. as a member of the U.S.E.E. This team ceased to exist after 1882, and, no doubt finding living difficult as an amateur (and giving indirectly a further indication of the fees that the Graces must have obtained from their matches for the U.S.E.E.), he became a professional at the start of the 1886 cricket season. He played in one or two matches, was featured in a special article in *Cricket* and then no more is heard. He had been found in the act of stealing in the dressing-room from his fellow players: the scandal was hushed up by the Grace family, and he emigrated to Canada, where he died in 1924, having, however, taken up the game in his new country and made many fine scores.[1]

The first country-wide governing body in Canada was formed in 1892: thus both Canada and the U.S.A. very easily preceded other first-class cricket countries in forming their own national administrative organizations.

The first tours to and from the West Indies took place in the last ten years of the period. Inter-colonial cricket had started in 1865 in a match between Barbados and what was till lately British Guiana: four years later British Guiana played Trinidad, and in 1891 the first inter-colonial tournament between those three territories took place. Jamaica is not seen, except as furnishing players for the tour to North America, in this period. There is little known about the game apart from the facts that club cricket was widespread and schools cricket too: not of a good quality, on the whole, probably through lack of fashionable regiments in the garrisons as much as anything else. But things were astir, and in the next chapter on the Golden Age, we can appreciate the better how much must have been slowly preparing during this period for the days when the West Indies would enter the international fray.

In South America, the same kind of slow half-unconscious preparations must have been going ahead, particularly in the Argentine with its ever-increasing English population, building and running railways and trading generally. It was in or shortly before the period that the leading clubs in Buenos Aires, and also in Brazil, were founded, and shortly after the beginning of it, the Argentine first

[1] Another indication of the recurring instinct for suppression was a suggestion to me that if this story had not appeared in print before (it has not) it should not now!

sent a team to play Uruguay. And, in 1881, an instructional book in Spanish (*La Tranca* by J. W. Williams) was produced in Buenos Aires, with such delightful terms as '*batador*' for batsman (naturally) and (less expectedly) '*boleador*' for bowler. Books of this kind do not appear unless there is a need for them: this is a clear indication that the Spanish-speaking population was becoming interested in the game, an interest it does not appear to have maintained despite the often lengthy reports of matches that have appeared in Spanish in Buenos Aires newspapers.

There was of course a great deal of cricket played by visiting ships of the Navy against local expatriate communities of businessmen, and of course not only in South America, but around the world generally.

The Navy has been responsible as much as, if not more than, anyone else for propagating the game among the Pacific Islands, and it was in this period that cricket in Fiji, and Samoa and Tonga, and in other islands first began to come to notice. Even before the cession of the Fiji islands to Britain, a club had been formed in Levuka, and within a few years Fijians themselves were playing the game. It made great progress towards the end of the period, largely owing to the enthusiasm of J. S. Udal, a colonial judge and a well-known cricketer in England before his appointment, and it was just after the period ended that Fiji went on its first overseas tour, to New Zealand. P. A. Snow has written a fascinating account[1] of the game in those islands, and for any lover of the game, or the Pacific, his details are extremely rewarding.

Not so far away as distances are measured in the Pacific, there lie the Samoan Islands, at this time and almost to the end of the period, another independent kingdom: here too the game caught on amongst the native inhabitants, and became a fever, of such danger to the country's economy that it had to be prohibited by law: this prohibition has been reimposed at later times in the history of the islands, when economic circumstances, or the results of a hurricane have compelled it. The reason is simple: the Samoan version of cricket provided for an entire village playing another village, all of them fielding. Batsmen queued up to go in, the head of the queue a pace or two from the batsman still in, waiting to rush to the wicket when he should be out – for, if he did not get there in time, he might be bowled by the opposing bowler before he had time to take his stance! An entirely delightful version of the game, and an excellent substitute for war!

New Zealand must be considered both as part of the Pacific, and as part of the Australasian continent, in cricket terms: an outlyer, with contacts in the islands,

[1] *Cricket in the Fiji Islands* (New Zealand, Whitcombe & Tombs Ltd, 1949).

but heavily influenced by Australian cricket. 1864 saw the visit by George Parr's team, coming over from its Australian trip, and which established the first cricket contacts between England and New Zealand. 1894, the year in which the next period, the Golden Age, began, saw the establishment of the New Zealand Cricket Council. And the opening year of this period saw also the first century made in New Zealand too. First-class cricket had already begun before the previous period ended: where else has first-class cricket commenced without a century having been made in any class of cricket? Inter-provincial cricket increased greatly during the entire period but it was well after it that the Plunket Shield was established, so that all games were on a friendly basis. It was a period that saw much coming and going between New Zealand and Australia and it is noteworthy that the first Australians, on their preliminary tour of the colonies before visiting England lost by 6 wickets to a Canterbury XV: Canterbury had wanted to play on level terms but the Australians had scorned this! It was in this period too that Maoris are known to have taken part in the game, as they still do, but never with the enthusiasm they lend to Rugby football. And just before the end of the period the first of three issues of a New Zealand cricket annual appeared: publicity being welcomed by the game's enthusiasts here as everywhere else at that time, and indeed in one sense more than elsewhere; for in 1879 a small historical pamphlet had been issued, of great rarity nowadays which seems likely to have been the first publication outside the British Isles on the historical aspect of the game locally.

In Australia, the period saw the game being brought on to a higher level than ever before – indeed the highest level, with the playing of the first Test match ever in 1876–7. This was after a time of building, covering a state when the Australian cricket was weak, so weak that even its strongest combinations, and never even eleven-a-side, were no more a match for an English team than the twenty-twos such a team would have encountered in English provincial towns, to a time when it was able to beat an English team even-handed: and all that inside fifteen years. And if the representative character of that English team be doubted, another five years saw a truly representative English team beaten at the Oval and thus giving rise to the legend of the Ashes. This legend arose through the printing of a mock memorial notice in remembrance of English cricket, in a sporting newspaper, with the intimation that the Ashes would be cremated and taken to Australia. Not long after, Ivo Bligh, at a dinner in London, said it would be the aim of his team to try and recover 'those Ashes', and they did so. But much of the detail of the story is not generally known, least of all that there was never any intention that the Ashes should become a kind of spiritual trophy to be contested for (though never actually moving from their glass case in the Imperial War Memorial Gallery at Lord's).

In that same speech, Bligh said his team would play three games against W. L. Murdoch's 1882 Australians (the Third Australians) and one or two matches against Combined Australia – a combination which would evidently be stronger than Murdoch's team since then, as now, it was the general rule that countries are stronger at home, for obvious reasons of availability. It has sometimes been supposed and very often stated that the one match which was eventually played against Combined Australia was an afterthought, but this is not so. For not only did Bligh refer to it several months before it was played, but a fixture list, which was published in Australia just after the first of the three games against Murdoch's team, clearly showed it already as a fixture. That it eventually began one day later need be no surprise to us now who are familiar with venues and dates of Test matches being switched for non-cricket reasons at very short notice indeed.

Bligh, as we know, had the best of the three games against Murdoch's team and accordingly some ladies of Melbourne burnt the bails used in the third of these matches and put the Ashes in the small urn which is now so familiar.

More than ten years later, an Australian, Clarence P. Moody (who first set out the accepted list of Test matches) referred to contests between English and Australian teams as being for 'the Ashes' but there is no evidence that the term was in colloquial use and it has not been possible to find any other references to the term in the intervening period (though this does not imply the certainty that it was not used). Indeed the term should not have been used in the sense Moody now gave it, *since the relevance of 'the Ashes' was solely to matches by English teams against Murdoch's 1882 Australians.* If this had not been so, if all matches between English and Australian teams were taken into account, the Melbourne ladies would surely not have prepared 'the Ashes' after the third match but would have awaited the fourth match (known for several weeks as a fixture and not hastily arranged after the third – it is from this wrong supposition that so much of the muddle arises), if not indeed the more recently arranged fifth Test at Melbourne which was, however, cancelled very late in the day. Moody was wrong, then, and he seems to have been very much a lone voice in talking about 'the Ashes' until P. F. Warner announced in 1903 that it was his aim to 'recover the Ashes'. His appears to have been the first English reference in print to the term in twenty years: but he was well-read in cricket history (unlike so many Test cricketers) and he was not averse to dramatizing his own part in the making of it. He can be excused for this to some extent for he had a desperately hostile Press when he was appointed the England captain in 1903, and the Press too had some reason for this, since, as it pointed out, he had never played in a Test match (the few matches in which he had played against South African teams were not then regarded as Test matches nor for a few years to come). It is then partly Warner's historical sense, visualizing himself as St Ivo, and the very title of the book he wrote recounting his success – *How we recovered the Ashes* – which has led to the erroneous habit of thought which treats of all Anglo-Australian matches as for a trophy, and which arose from that time. It is the fashion now to deplore the habit of thought, and it is no contradiction of the modern tendency to play for trophies that this fashion exists: it is one thing to have a trophy for one match, and quite another to allot it notionally for a series in which the only result may be in the first game and the remainder stalemated as draws. It may be easier to abandon this habit of thought now, once it is realized that it arose in error, prolonging into perpetuity one of those heavy-handed Victorian jokes which was itself spun out over some six months.

What was responsible for the vast change in Australia? Two things, or rather two people: one of them William Caffyn, who had stayed in Australia after the 1863–4 tour and undertaken very much coaching, coaching which had its effect on willing learners, and the other the man who came to be known as the Demon bowler, F. R. Spofforth, who is generally credited with introducing true over-arm bowling to England: that is with the arm raised as high as possible. To those two cannot be added the influence which W.G. ought to have had when he visited Australia in 1873–4, because in twenty-three innings he could only hit one century and his average in the better-class matches was under 34.0. Even so, he and his younger brother G.F. (who hit two centuries) did twice as well as anyone else in their side. If it did nothing else it led to the spread of first-class cricket outside Victoria and New South Wales, when a Victorian team met South Australia in 1874–5, and when, shortly after, the South Australian Cricket Association was formed: the fourth of the colonial, or as we should now say, State cricket associations to be created, and to be followed by Queensland and Western Australia shortly before the end of the period. (Queensland was met by New South Wales for the first time in 1863–4, and Western Australia met Victoria thirty years later, thus completing interchanges between a colony and at least one other.) And just before the very end of the period, after Lord Sheffield's tour, which brought W.G. a second time to Australia, Lord Sheffield presented the Shield which is named after him and which was competed for in 1892–3, for the first time. It was not the first inter-colonial trophy: there had been an earlier one in 1880, which had been won outright by Victoria, in competition, however, only with New South Wales.

The period seems to divide itself into two, if we study not only inter-colonial and international cricket at around 1880, so far as Australia is concerned: a division which can also be vaguely discerned in English cricket too. Before it, scoring was on a relatively low level: after it, it was not only every bit as massive as in England, but came very often to exceed it. Six hundred and more became a relatively common score in Australian club cricket: eight hundred was exceeded in Australia in first-class cricket in 1886–7, and the way was opened for the first total to exceed 1,000[1] (some thirty years later, twice more exceeded in Australia, but nowhere else even now). It is understandable that Australian bowling should have enabled Australia to beat England: how was there, after that bowling had established its pre-eminence, any possibility for such extensive batting feats to be achieved? Wickets were, of course better in Australia than in England, but this must have helped English batsmen in Australia also, as indeed it did in several instances. I am inclined to think that the new rate of scoring reflected, just as it did in England, the straightness of over-arm bowling and the necessity for playing every ball – and so of often scoring: it took time for the new style to be mastered, for its tricks and deceits to be discovered, but once learnt, the batsman became freer to make runs than ever before since round-arm came in. And Australian over-arm bowling was over-arm bowling taken to its ultimate, or nearly so (i.e. excluding what is called throwing).

It was not only in first-class cricket that high scoring was achieved: the King's School, Parramatta, was one of the first teams in Australia to make 500, in 1877–8, so schoolboys were in it too. School cricket all through this period was of considerable importance in Australian cricket life and Clem Hill signalized his own greatness by making the then Australian record score of 360* for his school in December 1893. University cricket too came on the Australian scene with the first match between Melbourne and Sydney Universities in 1870 – the first of a long, but in its earlier years, a rather irregular series of matches.

Club cricket had been competitve in the principal cities from an early period, in 1860–1, as for example in Victoria: this too had its direct effect in raising the level of the game generally, though towards the end of the period the predominance of some leading clubs which succeeded in attracting a majority of the better players, tended to make matches one-sided and to detract from enjoyment. This aspect will be referred to in the next chapter since it was then that the cure largely took place.

The long series of tours from Australia in the period (eight of them) introduced many fine cricketers to the English public, and also made a great amount of

[1] 1,094 by Melbourne University against Essendon on the University ground.

16. The old Albert ground in Sydney: one of the few photographs of a big single-wicket match in progress: 12 of New South Wales *v.* 7 of England on 27 January, 1874. W.G. was the only one to bat on the English side, knocking off all the runs that were needed. The English side is in the field

17. W.G. in his early twenties, the centre of a group of R. A. Fitzgerald's team of MCC members which toured Canada and the U.S.A., 1872. The ground is at Montreal and Mount Royal can just be seen in the background. The Hon. G. Harris, later Lord Harris, is fourth from left

18. Not Eton *v.* Harrow some years ago, but the coach enclosure on the Merion ground, U.S.A., in 1897

19. The celebrated Rood en Wit club of Haarlem in 1883 in a costume which would not have been unusual in England at that time, though not necessarily for cricket

money too for those who took part in the tours, often limited to no more than twelve men who played every day of the week right through a four-and-a-half-month season: they were men in those days, even if they did make a handsome profit out of it. Amongst these great players must be mentioned in particular the two bowlers, C. T. B. Turner and J. J. Ferris. Turner actually succeeded in taking 283 wickets in first-class matches in the English 1888 season, by any standards a remarkable performance and rendered more so when his average of 11·68 is considered. Turner is the only bowler to have taken 100 wickets in an Australian first-class season. Ferris's performance (199 wickets) is second only to Turner's on that tour; but for Turner's presence, he might well not have done so well, as he used to pitch in Turner's footprints!

There was also the man sometimes known as 'the Australian W.G.' – George Giffen. He never quite showed his full batting form in England, so he has left less of an impact here, but he is still well-remembered in Australia. He was entitled to the description of himself not as a batsman but rather as an all-rounder: he was the first Australian to achieve career figures of 10,000 runs and 1,000 wickets, and only four others have since achieved them, all players whose career was largely in England (F. A. Tarrant, who also played in India, A. E. Trott, G. E. Tribe, and S. M. J. Woods). Moreover, in terms of his career batting and bowling averages, only five players have exceeded both Giffen's (W. G. Grace of course, way out ahead, G. H. Hirst, W. Rhodes, F. E. Woolley and, again, F. A. Tarrant). Giffen was born in 1859, played his last match in 1903 and died in 1927: his life-span corresponds with W.G.'s, but his playing career was much shorter. A number of Giffen's feats are noted in the Appendix on Australia: here it is enough to say that he made 100 runs in an innings, and took 10 wickets in a match six times in first-class cricket, including on one occasion 271 and 16 for 166: and he made 100 runs in the match and took over 10 wickets on three other occasions, including on one occasion 20 and 82, and 17 for 201. He is a member of the small company of cricketers (mostly in minor cricket, as in Giffen's case) who have made a century in an innings, and taken 10 wickets in an innings in the same match: Giffen's feat though in minor cricket in formalistic terms was in first grade Adelaide cricket, no mean standard. He was the first Australian tourist to do the 'double' in first-class cricket in this country, a feat he performed three times in all: four others have since done the 'double' as tourists (it is a sobering thought that no Australian tourist has done the 'double' since 1921, and only one tourist since 1928). As a bowler, he bowled slow medium, and he also had a slow ball, sent down very high which seemed to be coming well up to the batsman but which pitched short and gave Giffen many wickets caught

E

and bowled. Giffen was, by the way, not a good captain and tended to keep himself on too long, a fault to which almost every Australian captain who has also been a bowler seems to have been prone.

English teams to Australia also made money: they did not go there purely for the pleasure of cricket, and W.G. had in fact demanded and received what was correctly described as the monstrous sum of £1,500 to go on the tour of 1873-4, as his personal fee, expenses being in addition. W.G. was at that time no more than a medical student, hardly even that indeed, and the sum he obtained would be the equivalent of about £10,000 now. From Parr's team in 1863-4 to the end of the period, there were in all eleven English teams, the last nine playing first-class matches. Not all of them made money: the two teams who toured simultaneously in 1887-8, did not, and on one or two other occasions deplorable dissensions amongst Australian cricketers (usually those who had just been on an English tour, be it noted, and could afford to dictate terms) caused a lack of interest in particular matches.

But all this might never have come about. There had been trouble, of quite a serious nature, with the Australian team in Philadelphia: more especially with its captain, D. W. Gregory, who certainly made no move to restrain his team but rather led it into inopportune protest. This trouble had followed a tour in which there were several incidents in which the Australians complained about umpiring in England, all of which had been very much magnified in the Australian Press. There had been one other incident, that involving W. E. Midwinter.[1] He was born in Gloucestershire and he had played for Gloucestershire in 1877. Long before the tour began, Australian newspapers had pointed openly to the probable trouble that would be caused if he were a member of the team. They were right: there came a point in the tour when W.G. descended upon Midwinter when the Australians were preparing to play at Lord's, and removed him to the match Gloucestershire were playing at the Oval. W.G. used some robust language at which the Australians took offence for which W.G. subsequently apologized – but that was the only thing he needed to apologize for, as the Australians were clearly in the wrong, and if, as some of the Australian Press asserted before the tour, Midwinter had a contractual obligation to Gloucestershire, his selection for the tour was a first-class blunder. Thus, the first Australians did not make themselves loved, and when they returned to Australia there came a final incident at the Association ground in Sydney in the match between New South Wales and Lord Harris's XI. Again Dave Gregory – on his home ground now – complained about

[1] He was, incidentally, the first batsman known to have scored a double century in Australia, in 1869-70 at Bendigo.

the English side's umpire, and refused to play. To some extent incitement by bookmakers in the pavilion had something to do with what then occurred, for an angry mob of members as well as other spectators invaded the pitch, and threatened the players. In the presence of the Governor of New South Wales, mounted police had to be used to restore order, and there was no more play that day. Profuse apologies were tendered by the civil and cricket authorities, and the game was resumed the next day: something of the value of the apologies was lost when it became known in Australia that Lord Harris had written a complete and, so far as one can judge, an eminently fair account of what happened and sent it to the English Press.

The result of all this was that when the 1880 Australians came to this country, they found it extremely difficult to get any fixtures at all against reputable teams, and though the ice did start to melt some time before the tour was over, the fact remained that most of the first half of the tour was taken up playing minor matches against eighteens and twenty-twos. But their captain, W. L. Murdoch, was a different kind of man from Gregory – indeed he came to be much respected in English cricket and eventually settled in England to play for Sussex – and in due course he was able to prevail upon Lord Harris too to resume friendly relations. Had it not been for that reconciliatory attitude by Lord Harris, the tour would have been a certain flop, and the first Test in England would never have taken place when it did (and it came late enough in the season, in September) and arguably might never have occurred. For there might not have been another tour to this country from Australia for many years, and if the second Australian tour had ended in financial and social disaster, there would have been sufficient ill-feeling engendered to inhibit the frequent English tours to Australia that were to occur in the near future. It is, in short, by no means fanciful to suppose that Test cricket as we know it would have developed along quite different lines, and very much later – and might even never have developed at all.

The organization of Australian cricket was anomalous. As each colony became strong in cricket, each had formed its own Association. In New South Wales, it had even been intended that the Association should own its own ground and indeed the present Sydney Cricket Ground was intended to be the Association ground and was for very many years so called. But for legal reasons it had been vested in Trustees, and these Trustees adopted an independent existence, sometimes in opposition to the best interests of cricket: it needed a High Court action to settle it, but the N.S.W.C.A. still does not own its own ground. Nor does the Victoria Cricket Association. Unlike the older colony, Victoria had during the last half-century and for some years to come in the next only a weak governing body: power and prestige, as well as the cricket ground, was owned by the Melbourne Cricket Club, which organized some of the tours out of Australia, and invited many of the teams in (in conjunction with the S.C.G. Trustees). It led the way in local organization too, and there was a time when it came perilously near occupying a similar position if not in Australian, then at least Victorian cricket, as does the Marylebone Cricket Club in England. Happily this did not occur. In South Australia the Association owns, or is at least the direct tenant, of its ground and was so from its inception. It was thus, as a body, more powerful than either of the other two. General dissatisfaction with the running of Australian cricket as a whole, however, led to the formation of the Australasian Cricket Council (though New Zealand never took any part in it) in 1891–2, but 'player-rule' was not diminished, and this 'player-rule' being considered a bad thing, the Council was, early in the next period, dissolved.

North from Australia the first of a long series of matches between Hong Kong and Shanghai took place in 1866, when Hong Kong made the high score for those days of 430, and almost at the end of the period, we find Hong Kong meeting, and shortly afterwards, visiting Singapore to play the Straits Settlements. Cricket was played by the English community in Tokyo and Yokohama very shortly after the period began, and there was a long story of 'inter-port' rivalry from Japan down to Malaya and Java which has lasted in a diminished form into our own time. Though the Malays have never exhibited much enthusiasm for the game, they are known to have been playing it in the 1880s, and of course there are records of the descendants of the Dutch settlers also taking part. But most of Malaya only fell into British hands in the latter half of the period. In Singapore the game had been played much earlier.

About the beginning of the modern period of cricket, there was the commencement of the modern period in Thailand (then known as Siam). There was a general up-dating of the country's economy comparable with but less intense than what went on in Japan about the same time. Some of the political pressure for this was British and arose from the British-Indian take-over of Burma: it led to a fair number of Thai children from the Thai upper class receiving an education at school and University in England. Some of them not only learnt cricket, but liked it too and, five years after the first known cricket club (the Bangkok City Cricket Club) was formed in 1890, a letter appeared in the *Bangkok Times* from 'a Siamese' appealing to other Thais interested in cricket to join him in forming a cricket club or, alternatively to join the existing Bangkok City Club. There is nothing to show that such a Thai cricket club was ever formed, but Thais had been playing in Bangkok as early as 1890. Thai cricket has, however, remained very largely expatriate, including Pakistanis, Indians, and Australians as well as British, but there are still Thais who play the game and some of them are equal to the best in the country from the expatriate community. Thai cricket might have achieved a boost in the 1890s had the Singapore Cricket Club not turned down an invitation to visit Bangkok for fear of cholera. This fear evidently lingered on long after its justification had vanished, for until the middle of the twentieth century, Thailand saw little of cricketers from elsewhere apart from those on visiting warships. Now that teams from other countries touring the Far East find a visit to Bangkok enjoyable, and with Thais still attending schools and Universities in Britain, there is some possibility that the game may flourish a little more.

In India, not yet an Empire, the game was flourishing: widely played wherever there was a cantonment of British troops, and played also by the commercial community in the big cities, this was the period when a serious interest in the game started to be taken by Indians themselves, with the establishment of clubs by Parsis, by Hindus, and by Muslims in Bombay, and elsewhere of clubs which had no community restriction, as in Madras and Calcutta. In the United Provinces, instructional books appeared in Urdu and Hindi: probably elsewhere and in other languages judging by the success of the game in the Bombay area. In the 1870s, there had been talk of a Parsi tour to England, and indeed also to Australia but neither came off, though later in the 1880s two tours to England by the Parsis were undertaken. In 1890 Lord Harris became Governor of Bombay and within a few years the Parsis were strong enough to take on the Europeans of the Bombay Presidency and so began just before the end of the period, the first of a long series of Presidency matches in Bombay, in 1892–3. Already there had been an English tour to India, led by G. F. Vernon against whose team the Parsis had shown their strength, and in 1892–3, Lord Hawke's team played All India. There was so much good-class cricket in India in the period that the future looked much brighter than it turned out to be. A case can even be made for India's first first-class match having been played at the very start of the period when Calcutta met Madras in 1863–4 for the first time. Certainly during this period, the game spread into Indian schools, as well as schools for Europeans, in India: before it, there had undoubtedly been Indians playing but, as we have seen, not so as to constitute any organized endeavour. A vast country, and an enormous population made it difficult to control or even chart what was going on, and it was only in large centres of both population and education that some organization was able to emerge: it was many years before even a Province could have its own administration, let alone All India. India, after Egypt, had always taken the cream of the Army and overseas civil servants so there was much European talent available to demonstrate and encourage the game, and especially in these optimistic years in the middle of which the Empire was proclaimed.

Ceylon came to notice at this time as teams to and from Australia, starting with Ivo Bligh's which recovered 'the Ashes' in 1882-3 called in *en route* to play a one-day match. This long series of matches did much to raise the standard of cricket in Ceylon.

Southern Africa was not, at the start of this period, anything like the homogeneous white-ruled block that it appears to be now: the Zulu wars were still to occur, the Prince Imperial still to die, Rhodes still to be thought of, diamonds at Kimberley still to be discovered – or gold on the Rand: the Boer republics were still young with Pretoria still to be founded. There was nothing approaching first-class cricket when the period began: when it ended the South African Cricket Association (an all-white body) had been formed, in 1890, and the Currie Cup had been initiated in 1889-90,[1] and a team was being considered for the first South African tour to England to return the tours undertaken by Major Warton's team in 1888-9 (captain, C. Aubrey Smith, the famous actor of later years whose manner of bowling earned him the nickname of 'Round the Corner') and W. W. Read two years later (the last being the only occasion on which an English team has played a non-white team in South Africa: illustrating a colour prejudice too often found later on, the English amateurs refused to take part. Non-white cricket had been played for many years before, of course). The first South African Cricket Annual, a pretty small local affair confined, despite its pretentious title, to Cape Town, had appeared in the 1870s: another, much better, was to appear a decade later in Natal. And in 1884-5 there occurred the third of the Champion Bat Tournaments, the first having been in 1875-6, but the first which could seriously be considered first-class. The tours by Warton's and Read's teams saw the first matches played by English teams against combined South African elevens, but no one then thought of calling them Test, nor did the first historian of South African cricket, Luckin, do so in 1914: indeed, it is difficult to sustain any argument that these matches should have been first-class, quite apart from the fact that the South African tour to England in 1894 was not.

It was a period when school cricket in South Africa began, when non-white cricket started to flourish on a scale comparable with Indian cricket in India – but when few if any Afrikaners were found playing the game. Yet it was President Kruger who first sanctioned a grant of land in the nascent Johannesburg for the Wanderers Cricket Club, at the end of this period.

[1] In the second Currie Cup Tournament, the only match played lasted seven days, the first first-class match in the world to last so long.

134

There were now national organizations in Canada, the U.S.A., Australia (though it was to fail and be succeeded later by a much more powerful body), South Africa, New Zealand, Holland and Denmark: yet so far nothing in England, for the Cricket Council there established had come to an untimely and indeed unnecessary end.

(iii) Conduct of the game and administration

The legalizing of over-arm in 1864 did not eliminate the many grounds for complaint, if it did indeed quieten them. Edgar Willsher of Kent had defied the then law in about 1857, but his bowling had not been unfair[1], it had been said, whereas that of others was. Wherein lay the difference? Objective consideration suggests that the only difference there can have been must have been between over-arm 'bowling' and over-arm 'throwing'. Jackson of Nottinghamshire and Tarrant of Cambridgeshire were categorized as dangerous bowlers at the end of the 1860s: why? Presumably because they bowled bumpers, but was it only that? Round-arm bowling was usually round-arm throwing – it is very difficult to separate the two: but when the arm was raised higher the difference between 'bowling' and 'throwing' must have become clear to onlookers and to batsmen, though not immediately, nor to all. Hence it is likely that immediately after 1864, 'anything went' and hence the dangerous bowlers who, most probably, threw, and were in that case the first 'throwers' under the amended Law. People had not become accustomed to discerning that there could be a difference in over-arm which hardly existed in round-arm, nor to realizing that legalizing over-arm did not mean automatically legalizing all 'unfair' bowling.

For a time all is quiet, then the Australians arrive with their new 'high' delivery, and within a few years this style has been imitated widely: and within those few years there began to arise a new school of over-arm 'throwers'. J. Crossland and G. Nash (both of Lancashire) were the two most prominent of such bowlers: subterfuges were used to call them out of cricket, for either no one could define properly what was involved, or no one wanted to if the affair could be swept under the carpet, as it were. It was not: it festered on well into the Golden Age, and only then was the 'illegal' action finally condemned and stopped: it was to remain so for almost fifty years, until weaker and less able men were at the helm.

Over-arm wrought a revolution in the game, and it affected scoring generally.

[1] *Scores & Biographies*, IV, 377.

There was no other innovation which had, or could have such a drastic effect in the actual conduct of the game.

Yet this piece of legislation was passed at a period when the prestige of the MCC as a law-making body was at its lowest. Proposals for a more democratic cricket parliament were widely circulated and supported not only in the north, but from county sources in the south too: yet they fell to the ground, and it was many years before anything else arose. Meanwhile, in 1883, the MCC decided to recodify the Laws in full and after wide circulation in draft form overseas they were adopted in 1884. It has only rarely been observed that these Laws had one fundamental change, because that change did not apply to two- and three-day cricket, i.e. not to first-class cricket. First-class cricket was always in a minority: for the overwhelming majority the MCC now bowed to almost universal custom and sanctioned six-ball overs in all one-day games, at the captains' option. In 1889 by one of these strange and meaningless compromises so often found in the running of cricket, five-ball overs were introduced into English first-class cricket. This too was the year when declarations were first permitted (though, long years before, something like what we would call declarations seem to have occurred). It was also the year when an immemorial custom came to an end, that of a bowler being allowed to bowl two overs in succession when he changed ends. Strange that it should have lasted so long: strange also, from another way of looking at it, that it should have been abolished.

In the wider administrative sphere, the MCC had had no say, apart from the question of county qualification. Interest in and concern with the conduct of county cricket generally having greatly increased, a County Cricket Council was set up in 1887, taking over part of the agenda which the meeting of county secretaries, from 1882 onwards, had dealt with. It did a lot of good work, and proposed a good and workable plan to classify the counties, but came to an abrupt end in 1890 as a result of a motion to suspend the meeting of the Council *sine die*. There was a tied vote, and the chairman improperly cast his vote in favour of the motion and the Council never met again. There are two points to note: first of all, the chairman should have cast his vote against the motion since the motion precluded further discussion, and a casting vote should always allow discussion to continue in such cases, the *status quo* being maintained: the second is that the motion did not necessarily mean the end of the Council. It was always open to the officials of the Council to reconvene it, but their legal training was such that they never did: what happened to its funds is not known. Not for the first time, nor the last, have those in charge of cricket administration shown themselves ill-informed and incompetent. Thus, in the gaping void left, it fell

20. Style in cricket – Hon. F. S. Jackson epitomizing the 'Golden Age'

21. The well-known photograph of Victor Trumper which perfectly sums up the man and his approach to cricket

22. A (postcard) team photograph of the South of England v. Australians at Hastings in 1902, showing many who made the Golden Age famous

SOUTH OF ENGLAND XI V THE AUSTRALIAN

ITCHMARSH   BROCKWELL   TOWNSEND   G. JESSOP   MASON   BOARD   ABEL   WEST
(UMPIRE)   C. B. FRY   LOCKWOOD   GRACE   RANJI   HAYWARD

to the MCC to take a hand in county classification for 1894, and willy-nilly, into everything else, as time went on. It has always been a pity that the reform movement of 1863 and thereabouts (there had been earlier ones too) did not come to anything.

By the end of the period, a warning light was already being shone for cricket: more people were watching football on each of several grounds on Saturday afternoons than watched a day's play in a Test match. Many drew attention to this at the time, pointing out the contrast with cricket: but cricket was about to enter its Golden Age and no one was willing to heed the warning when everything seemed so glorious.

E*

9

THE GOLDEN AGE OF CRICKET
1894-1914

(i) At Home

Some have argued capably that this period from 1894 to 1914 was not in fact *the* Golden Age of cricket: that it can rather be found between the two World Wars. Such things are a matter of opinion, but there is one major argument in favour of so considering the twenty years before the First World War: that it was, or seemed then, or sometimes seems now, to have been a 'Golden Age' in so very many other things. We are still very much captives of that period generally and still liable to look at it romantically: maybe in fifty years' time, there will come others who will persuade themselves and others that it was a period of black iniquity disguised from the general view by highly painted and gilded lath and plaster work. There are, however, some good cricket reasons why it should be regarded not as *a* Golden Age of cricket but as *the* Golden Age of cricket.

In this country, it was the period when a Board of Control was set up: when Test-match selection became a central responsibility: when overseas tour selection became, in a slightly different form, also a central responsibility; when the control of county cricket was also centralized; and when minor county cricket was first organized. It was a period which spanned the first South African tour to this country and the Triangular Tournament of 1912: at the beginning it almost took in the start of the Currie Cup in South Africa, and even more closely almost took in the start of the Sheffield Shield in Australia, while the start of the Plunket Shield in New Zealand came later on in the period. The New Zealand Cricket Council was established in 1894: the South African Cricket Association a shade earlier: the Australasian Cricket Council just before, but ended not long after the start and was replaced after a few years by the Australian Board of Control. Its commencement very nearly saw the start of the Bombay Tournament in India: shortly after that it only just failed to see the first All-India tour to England but did succeed in seeing it just before its close, while almost throughout it saw that great Imperial symbol, Ranji. Its start just missed the rise of international touring in South America, and almost completely took in the rise of West Indian cricket. It saw the greatest age of Philadelphian cricket. And at home, it saw the formation of the Scottish Cricket Union, the formation of county competitions in Scotland and in North Wales, and the very early beginnings of what was to become the Club Cricket Conference. The serious development of League Cricket came about during the period and the start had preceded it by only a few years. In legislation, the last modernizing changes in the Laws took place: the six-ball over, the optional follow-on, the raising of the limit of the follow-on, the first new ball rule, and the steady extension of the period within which one could declare (not finally consummated till after the Second World War), and facts were faced, however unpalatable, in recognizing that drawn matches were inevitable when points were awarded for a first innings lead towards the end of the period. Some attempt also was made to make the first-class game more popular by tentative experiments with a Saturday start. (Great matches had generally started on Mondays and Thursdays for very many years.) To mention but one statistical point, no other period comparable in length has seen so many individual scores of 300 or over made, in *all* classes of cricket: at least 78, the majority being in England and Australia. Both between the wars, and since, the figure has not reached sixty. Finally, Yorkshire, to its praise, in this period became the first county to ensure all the year round payment for its players as well as to establish a provident fund for them when retired: a very significant social change, and not hitherto attempted or even thought of by any other county and by no means fully emulated by all counties up to the present time. It is difficult to think of any other period of the game's history when so many important things happened. But its importance is itself an indication of its hue: it was the magisterial structure which was being erected everywhere for the game: ever since, we have been living in an increasingly old-fashioned house, more and more ill-adapted to modern needs, but then up-to-date and shining. There is no other period with such a structure, and if some think that the years between the wars saw the Golden Age, let them consider whether it was not because of the mellowness of the background to it, all built well before.

Of course much of what emerged in the Golden Age was a result of previous growth: but it was the emergence of the flower which makes it Golden, not a previous period when the seed was sown. In my view it was not only the Golden

Age, it was the greatest age of cricket: it was the age when cricket could *seem* to have reached a degree of perfection, the age from which everything has fallen away since, just as it has politically and socially (or at least from the standpoint of a great many people: and if there are many others who disagree and who would have hated to have lived in that period, many of them, in turn, would have much rather played *and* watched cricket then than now).

Why 1894? Conveniently, because that is when the MCC, plunging at last into the maelstrom of county cricket squabbles, from which it had always held most carefully aloof (treating all counties as equal as Arthur Haygarth recorded faithfully; his own last volume – the fourteenth – appeared in 1895), decided to classify Derbyshire, Essex, Leicestershire and Warwickshire as first-class, and at the end of the season Hampshire too. This led to an enormous increase in first-class cricket and led in turn to the establishment of new cricket records many of which survive to our own time, or almost so: in other words it seemed to make cricket then continuous and comparable with cricket now, in a way which is not felt with earlier periods. So, the following year saw the Minor Counties form their own Association and competition, three years later the Board of Control for Test matches was established, and six years later, the Advisory County Cricket Committee to the MCC: the administrative set-up for major cricket in England remained thus and unchanged until 1969. 1899 saw five Tests played for the first time. 1905 saw provision made for the last Test in England to be played to a finish in certain circumstances (this proviso lasted till just after the Second World War). And marl was first used on wickets on a considerable scale around 1895: for some the most important development of all as it ensured good lasting wickets.

But dates of events like this do not amount to a survey of any kind: the dates are set out in full in the appendices, and they reinforce what has already been said about events in this period: they tumble over one another.

A year after the period started, W.G. made his thousand runs in May, an astonishing performance for a man of forty-seven: he also made his hundredth century: a year after the period ended, W.G. died: in some sense he epitomized the life of the game, although the game has gone lingering on, as he himself did not once he had played his very last match in the year the war began. But the aura of W.G. overhung the period at the start, and was never quite absent from it at the end. For, during that period, the standard of the first-class game had generally risen to his own high standard, and without his own example it is questionable if it ever would have risen so high. Within a few months of the period starting, some of his own long-established records were broken, and most notably by K. S. Ranjitsinhji, whose first game in first-class cricket was in 1893, and whose first regular season was in 1895. But in 1896 he made 2,780 runs and beat a record that W.G. had set up in 1871: in 1899 Ranji made 3,159 runs, the first batsman to pass 3,000 runs in a first-class season, and in 1900 he made 3,065 averaging 87·57 and beating Arthur Shrewsbury's record average of 1887 (also beaten more decisively by R. M. Poore with 91·23 in 1899). The 'silken-shirted Hindu' remained in the country for most of the period, though he had to give more and more of his time to managing his own State's affairs in India. To the English public, he typified the broadmindedness of Empire, as it was supposed, and he gave them a different mode of playing too. In Sussex, the county of his choice, he found another great player, C. B. Fry, who had likewise first played in 1892, and then regularly from 1894: arguably one of the greatest, after W.G., of all English cricketers, and certainly the most knowledgeable and literate of all: rivalled, perhaps, in knowledge much later on by Bradman.

C. B. Fry scored 3,000 runs in 1901, thus emulating Ranji from whom he learnt much also. Yet both were dropped from Test teams the following year, and this, more than anything else, shows the great strength of English cricket at that time. If, however, one man is needed to epitomize the period, it is F. S. Jackson, later Sir Stanley Jackson. The photograph of him (plate 20) shows more than any amount of words what was meant by style in cricket at that period: the photograph itself comes from one of the most fascinating books on the game ever issued – two volumes with text by Fry and carefully taken photographs by G. W. Beldam, of Middlesex, on *Great Batsmen* and *Great Bowlers and Fielders*. Jackson first played for Yorkshire in 1890: it was he who three years later gave Ranji his 'Blue' at Cambridge – and he a few years later who established a feat not equalled before or since: he scored three centuries in three successive first-class matches spread over four seasons. There, surely, is an example of what 'class' means when applied to a batsman. (Many 'Golden Age' cricketers are illustrated in plate 22.)

One thing becomes clear, and it is that these, and some other, cricketers who started to make their name just before the period began and who by no means all played throughout it, put their stamp upon it. It would not have been the 'Golden Age' without such players as Ranji, Fry, Jackson, MacLaren, Mason, and others. Yet by the end of the period, all of them were either out of the game or playing only intermittently: their place was only partly taken by such renowned cricketers as J. B. Hobbs, F. E. Woolley, and others. Hobbs, it is fascinating to know, was described by P. F. Warner, when he first saw him, as a young professional who played just like an amateur. This was true and it was always the mark of Hobbs's batting: strictly professional in its application and near-perfection, it was strictly amateur of the best sort in its style and approach, attacking and chivalrous, and in this it differed from that of virtually all other professionals since his time. In Hobbs's time the great amateur batsmen set the example: Hobbs was not the only professional to follow it, but the one who most successfully professionalized it! Indeed, since Hobbs's time, it may be said that only D. C. S. Compton, amongst professional cricketers, showed the true amateur spirit in his attitude to the game.

Hobbs was a very great batsman and also one of the finest cover-points ever known: he was also a fair bowler, and opened the bowling for England in more than one Test. Yet he was never an all-rounder in the usual sense of the word and did not aspire to be. Above all he was an astonishingly great partner as an opening bat: perhaps the most successful opening bat who has ever lived, he was so successful because he had an instinctive understanding of his partner, whether it was his first, Tom Hayward, or Andy Sandham, or Wilfred Rhodes or Herbert Sutcliffe. His partnerships with Sutcliffe were more successful than those of any other opening pair of batsmen in the world, more successful by far. Yet it is arguable that he was not the greatest batsman: in his determination to amass runs, he did not approach Bradman who had weaknesses which Hobbs never showed, and though his first-class figures well exceeded W.G. he was W.G.'s 'follower' – W.G. had pointed the way, and had W.G. been able to start his career when Hobbs did, and play for the next thirty years or so, there can be little doubt that his record would have been far more wonderful than Hobbs's – and W.G. *was* an all-rounder. Hobbs, too, never made a thousand runs in May.

Cricket expanded, first-class cricket, and arguably all cricket in England, in this period, or from shortly before it: as to first-class cricket this expansion was beyond question the reason for the establishment of so many new records in batting, bowling and fielding during its first few years. The calibre of the cricket can be judged by the great number of those records which still stand, or which have only been beaten in quite recent years, or which, though beaten, have only been beaten once. When these statistics are massed together they tell a story which cannot be ignored: if one cites only one group of them – the records for wicket partnerships in England by English players – for seven of them, what is now the second-best was made between 1890 and 1900. Cricket was borne up on to a plateau in this period, and we are now far below it.

The amount of first-class cricket was more than doubled in the period: after the admission of Derbyshire, Essex, Leicestershire, and Warwickshire for the 1894 season, came Hampshire at the end of it, Worcestershire in 1899, and Northamptonshire in 1905. It was not merely the almost doubling of the number of such counties, it was the increase in programmes apart from that. The two Universities played more matches each than they had before. From 1902, there were few seasons without a first-class touring team, sometimes two. There were many other matches which made the programme interesting and full: no doubt this number was much exceeded between the wars, and again after the Second World War, but the general quality was different since the proportion of competitive county matches rose to such a great extent. Just below the first-class county level was that of the Minor Counties, as they are now called, but as they were often called at the time, the Second-Class Counties: what is not now generally realized is that many of these counties were exceptionally strong in talent. Both Worcestershire and Northamptonshire showed this by their own promotion, while there were others who lacked the finance or the desire to be first-class but who would always have provided a match for many of their supposed betters: invidious perhaps to mention any, but Norfolk was one such, and Norfolk was also one that did not wish to be first-class and did think that much of the joy had gone out of minor county cricket when it became competitive. They expressed the amateur attitude, that cricket was a game to be played and enjoyed and if possible in pleasant surroundings.

This was the hey-day of country-house cricket too, where the class of play could very well be right up to first-class standard – or no more than pure holiday fun. Country-house cricket of the old type is dead now[1] – few private individuals can afford to maintain a cricket ground and find the labour to do so, and it was already dying between the wars as death duties took their toll of estates. But in this period, the apotheosis of the wealthy upper-middle-class as well as the last fling of the country gentry, as such, before years later they resurrected themselves as hard-working farm managers, cricket grounds were a status symbol: and even more status attached to the ability to attract great cricketers to play. (Yet one who took part in such cricket – H. D. G. Leveson-Gower – expressed his opinion in 1903 that the great days of country-house cricket were over, gone with the enlargement of the county championship.) 'Weeks' were held up and down the country, from the north of Scotland, even down far into Cornwall, and across the Irish Sea at (to name no other) Bray. Three games would be played, and the

[1] Here and there a ground is maintained for a one-day game but there is not much putting up of players at the house. An example is Hovingham Hall the home of the present Duchess of Kent before her marriage, and others include Arundel, Everdon, Marchwiel Ascott, Hoveton and Highclere.

great touring clubs such as I Zingari, Free Foresters, Incogniti, as well as well-found service teams, would be the guests: an amateur cricketer of merit could spend a happy August staying in one great house after another, playing good class cricket all the time, and well housed, fed and wined – paying no more than his travelling expenses and suitable tips to the staff. Nor were only amateur cricketers involved: professionals without a fixture at the time would often be invited to play, and in September when county cricket had ended, many more would be attracted to these friendly games. There was thus an interchange of play between the great, the near-great and the not-so-great which is wholly absent nowadays, and which had not existed to such an extent since the final passing of the great All England Elevens and their progeny, in the early 1880s. First-class cricket was interwoven with minor county and club cricketers in this way, and it went further: for the better clubs, touring or otherwise, invariably had some two-day fixtures in their programmes such as few are able to boast nowadays: inevitably a two-day game provided cricket of a better class.

Social changes were to drive country-house cricket almost out of existence in the ensuing seventy years, but the interchange of play between first-class and club cricketers diminished largely because of the great increase in county championship cricket brought about as a result of the promotions at the beginning of the Golden Age. They made it much more difficult for amateurs, other than 'Varsity students and those in the teaching profession, to play any first-class cricket: they certainly diminished the possibilities of both amateur and professional playing in cricket at lower levels. Yet such matches at lower levels had been part and parcel of the whole ambiance of cricket at this time when the great could play, and still get some relaxation, and the less great could have the chance of learning from example – and the local onlooker might see some well-known cricketers whom he could never have seen otherwise. These possibilities continued to exist in all overseas countries, and continue to exist to this time except in Australia (yet even in Australia there is still a marginally greater possibility of playing against the great in a minor match than in England). It is, after all, not by watching potential talent playing that its ability can be judged so much as by playing against it: such opportunities hardly exist now, and though in England club cricketers often encounter first-class and Test players, in almost all cases they have to be described as 'former first-class' and 'former Test players': not at all the same thing. Nor is it the same thing that there is keen competitive cricket at lower levels such as in the leagues.

In 1888 league cricket had commenced in the Birmingham area and within a few years leagues had become the normal way to play club cricket in much of the

Midlands and all the North of England and later spread into Scotland and Wales. This led to cricket being played 'harder': it was not in accordance with southern taste nor was it to be for nearly three generations, and those who played in country-house cricket adopted a hostile attitude towards the league game. The argument – a fair one – was that highly competitive cricket is not, basically, cricket as it should be played: the unfair argument also used was to involve cricket as the 'sacred game', the home of a special sporting spirit and so on. Cricket is surely a game to be enjoyed and if it is not possible to play it other than in a highly competitive way, it must become the plaything eventually of external business interests. The northern leagues have not, but their example has pointed the way for the intrusion of such interests elsewhere: the engagement of overseas players, and indeed of great players of our own, on a highly paid basis was not the best way in which to enjoy cricket, and the long-term effect has certainly been to lessen playing interest in the game in Lancashire, if nowhere else. But in this period league cricket played as great a part in the popularization of the game and in raising the otherwise low standard of local cricket in the north as, in a quite different way, did country-house cricket in the south.

School cricket in this period meant public school cricket: this was a period when a young man would stay on until he was nineteen or even twenty, in order to play for his team, and if he could establish a reputation thereby, obtain a place to University despite a poor scholastic record. It had a following amongst the public too, and was able to command commercially worthwhile sales for a cricket annual[1] largely devoted to the doings of public schools. It was all part of the business of preparing the young men of England for the 'great game' which, it was felt, would be upon them before many years were passed, and which, from about the early 1900s came to be actively wanted by a small but not uninfluential section of the upper– and upper-middle classes. For, looking back on it all now, there can be no doubt that however much Britain may have desired peace, a large element in Britain, or at least England, really did wish to go to war with Germany: it was from this element that the young men came in their thousands to lay down their lives in the First World War, and it was this element which thereby committed social suicide as, four hundred years before, had the Barons. It was this element which thought of war as a game of a special kind: of such a kind indeed that all other games were to be suppressed when it began – not indeed Association Football, but certainly cricket which was 'their' game, which enshrined the Arnoldian and bourgeois virtues of Victorian England. It was this element which could produce an Archie MacLaren with his abusive and offensive

[1] *Ayres Cricket Companion*, first issued, 1902; last, 1932.

comments[1] in the *World of Cricket* after the First World War began, and who proposed to stop publication of the magazine, notwithstanding subscriptions paid, who could attack one who questioned his attitude in opprobrious language; for there were many *then* who did not regard Germany as an enemy, nor a *casus belli* established. Of these, time has shown the former view to be wrong: but the latter almost certainly right.

Beyond school cricket, there was club cricket of the more local variety. All over England this was established and thriving: it was an age of under-employment, and there was plenty of labour to keep the grounds and pitches in order, plenty to run the secretarial side of things too. It was only in and around the great cities, and especially London, that trouble was being experienced: it was nothing new, the demand of the builder for land, and the desire of the landowner to get what he could for his money. Nearly a hundred years earlier the Portman family had uprooted Thomas Lord: now other families were to uproot other clubs, as London started spreading out, as the electric railways themselves spread out to bring more and wider areas into close touch with the centre. Playing fields which had known no machinery more sinister than a mower and seen no smoke other than from a farm labourer's cottage, were now to be inundated with bricks and mortar. All this started as the period started slipping towards war, in its last seven or eight years: it already aroused dismay but no one envisaged what would happen when the war was over. Yet already the seeds were sown of the organization which under a different name, the Club Cricket Conference, would combat it and other problems.

But there was one large mass of people for whom no effort was made at all: the majority of the school population of the country, who had to content themselves with play in asphalted yards with scores of other children running around, or with street lamp-posts as wickets down some cul-de-sac, or on one of London's remaining commons, if the pitch had not been pre-empted by some local club with alleged prescriptive rights. It is something of a mystery how a boy from that background ever could discover his talent, and it is perhaps relevant to the growth of the northern leagues that there were, by and large, more good professionals forthcoming from the north than from the south, then, and indeed since: for, in the highly organized northern leagues, there were chances for the youngster to show some talent, to be given a trial, to be given encouragement. He

---

[1] 'That crowned madman, William of Hohenzollern, has committed the greatest crime against civilization of which any ruler has been guilty since the days of Napoleon. Through his restless ambition and insane lust for dominion, the whole continent is likely to be shortly in the throes of a desperate struggle.' (*World of Cricket*, 15 August 1914, p. 426). In the next issue he called the Kaiser 'the hog in armour'!

could find it too in the country in the south: but not in the great cities, and not in London. One of the earliest provincial towns to take to cricket was, we have seen, Leicester: it was Leicester who, in 1893, became the first to organize local school cricket properly, but it was years before the example was followed elsewhere. (It had been Leicestershire who had been the first county to agree a match with the 1878 Australians.)

Before we leave English cricket, let us turn from that humble sphere about which few knew and even fewer cared, and read a description of the setting of a country-house cricket match: it is fiction, written many years ago by a retired Civil Servant, who was something of a *littérateur* and had translated one of the sagas: that it is fiction does it no harm, for it tells us what such cricket was like – or perhaps what it was thought to be like, and that is more important if we are to understand why the age has been called the Golden Age.

'Time, you know, is a curious business,' said Lord Anmering, tilting his head forward a little to let the brim of his panama hat shade his eyes; for it was tea-time, and the afternoon sun, from behind the cricket field below, blazed out of cloudless blue full in their faces. 'By Jove, that's the style!' The ball, from a magnificent forward drive sailed clean over the far fence, amid shouts of applause for six. 'If you let your boy go and smash my melon-houses, knocking the bowling about like that, I'll tell you, I'll have no more to do with him,' he said.

They looked back for a minute to the great west front of Anmering Blunds, where it ranged beyond green lawns and flower-beds and trim deep-hued hedges of clipped box and barberry and yew: long rows of mullioned windows taking the sun, whose beams seem to have fired the very substance of the ancient brickwork to some cool-burning airy essence of gold. Lady Southmere waiting on the silence a minute, might hear as undertones to the voices of the cricket field (of players and lookers-on, click of wood against leather as the batsman played) the faint far-off rumour of tide-washed shingle, and from trees, the woodpecker's rustic, slumbrous, suddenly started and suddenly checked discourse. From golden rose to larkspur a swallowtail butterfly fluttered in the heat. 'Just too perfect for words,' she said, turning at last.

Fifty or sixty people, maybe, watched the game from the western side where the tents were, and garden chairs and benches, all in a cool shade of beech and chestnut and lime and sycamore that began to throw shadows far out upon the cricket field: a pleasant summer scene as any could wish, of mingled silence and sound, stir and repose, white hats and white flannels and coloured caps and blazers contrasting here and there with more formal or darker clothes: a gaiety of muslin frocks, coloured silks, gauzes and ribbons, silken parasols and picture hats: the young, the old, the middle-aged: girls, boys, men, women: some being of the house-party, some the belongings of the eleven that had driven over with Colonel Playter from Hyrnbastwick: some neighbours and acquaintances from the countryside: wives and friends, parents, sisters, cousins, aunts. Among these their host with Lady Southmere, now threaded his way, having for each as he passed, the just greeting, were it word, smile, formal salutation or private joke. 'Sorry uncle,' said Jim Scarnside, as their paths met, he on his way to the pavilion, 'ingloriously out for three. Just as that chap Howard was walking back the way he does to get properly wound up for one of those charging-buffalo runs that terrify the life out of a poor little batsman like me, I remembered, Lady Southmere, didn't Mary make me promise that you should have the first brew of strawberries and cream, because they're so much the best and isn't it long past tea-time, and now they'll all be gone? So there, and Nigel Howard sends down this beastly yorker. Is it fair? Really Uncle Robert, you ought not to allow ladies to look on at serious cricket like ours. All very well at Lord's and places like that; but here its too much of a distraction.'[1]

(ii) Abroad

Cricket in Holland was yet young as the Golden Age began: the two divisions in which eight or ten clubs played competitively had begun in 1891, and it took the entire period to double the number – a period in fact of very slow but steady growth, and more in the quality of the cricket played than in any large increase in numbers. The ground was being laid for the great expansion which took place during and after the First War. It was in this period that Holland first played at Lord's, and that the MCC first sent a team to tour in Holland, in 1902: the first overseas tour by the MCC in modern times, not forgetting that a generation earlier they had paid a visit to Paris. In 1910, at the Brussels Exhibition there was a four-team tourney involving Holland, the MCC, Belgium and France (both the latter largely British residents). An outstanding Dutch player of the time was C. J. Posthuma who still has some fame in this country as W. G. Grace brought him over to play for his London County team – Posthuma was well up to English first-class standard.

In Denmark there was little development: the game was, as in Holland,

---

[1] From E. R. Eddison, *A Fish Dinner in Memison* (New York, E. P. Dutton & Co., 1941), quoted by permission of Mrs J. G. R. Latham and the publishers.

making slow progress, but Denmark, too, got involved in International cricket at this time, her first visitors, somewhat surprisingly, being the Royal High School from Edinburgh.

Elsewhere in Europe the game was the prerogative of British expatriates, and tours to Portugal or to Spain had something of a country-house quality about them, and did not involve the natives of the countries.

In Turkey, on the Bosphorus, at Smyrna, and in one or two other ports where British influence was strong, there was a certain amount of expatriate cricket – again not involving the inhabitants of the country. The same too was true of Egypt where both merchants, civilians in Government service and the British forces there were able to entertain visiting teams, once again including the MCC, and provide good opposition.

In Africa itself, it was a period when, in both east and west cricket first started being taken seriously: and also, in the west, there already it was being pursued and overtaken by soccer. But it was in this period that the first matches took place between the Gold Coast (now Ghana) and Nigeria, and matches by Africans themselves. In East Africa, the game was overwhelmingly a settlers game. In southern Africa, development was both fast and large: the Currie Cup had already been established, the first two English tours had occurred – and cricket had moved, with the invaders of Rhodes's chartered company, into what is now Rhodesia. In 1894 came the first tour by a South African team to this country: none of the matches was reckoned first-class, and when one studies the playing record and the teams to which it was opposed,[1] one can have no surprise. It was the first occasion on which the South African colour bar was brought forcibly to the attention of the cricketing public in this country for an outstanding coloured player, T. Hendricks, had not been chosen for the tour, and the reason was colour and nothing else. The captain, H. H. Castens, of English origin, did not pretend to defend the decision, unlike the attitude taken up by so many since. After the return of the team there was a proposal to choose Hendricks for the traditional Cape Colony match, Colonial Born v. Mother Country – obviously Hendricks was qualified for the first-named – but the proposal was ignored. A few years later, during the South African war, many British officers and men noticed the strange attitude by the South African whites to the very idea of coloured players, and commented on it in letters home. There can be little doubt that, had the Boer War been conducted by other than a Tory government (which

---

[1] Many of them were not even in name first-class and the actual composition of those that were was well below first-class strength for the most part. Of the ten matches against nominally first-class teams they lost four and drew four.

had earlier sanctioned a colour-bar bill in Natal, disallowed by the previous Liberal government), coloured combatant troops from other parts of the Empire, including, in particular, India, would have been used, and that the Boers would not have been able to enforce in their peace treaty, which otherwise surrendered everything, one stipulation: that there should be no coloured voters in the former republics. This is where the evil began.

Yet it was this country which, remaking itself after its war, was able to claim Test status in its tour here in 1907, having earlier played what must be considered its first true Tests during the first MCC tour there in 1905–6. It was this country which, through the person of Abe Bailey, set on foot a proposal for a Triangular Test tournament, which duly took place in 1912: but not until the proposal had led to serious trouble[1] between England and Australia, her oldest Test opponents. Trouble indeed which was very quickly put right as administrators recovered their sense of proportion, but it was an early illustration of the power of South African gold in influencing policies in Britain. The negotiations which led to the Triangular Tournament involved a South African visit to Australia, which was not successful from a cricket point of view, nor indeed a financial one: but a member of the South African team was the only man who has been openly avowed as a coloured man (there have been plenty who have not) – C. B. Llewellyn, the Natal-born professional who played under qualification for Hampshire. He was tormented by his white fellow tourists to such an extent that for peace and quiet in the hotels where the team stayed, he had to take refuge in the W.Cs and lock himself in. His chief tormentor was J. H. Sinclair, the leading Transvaal batsman. This kind of thing should never be forgotten when South African cricket is referred to.

In India, where the Bombay tournament had been firmly established, Lord Harris was Governor of the Bombay Presidency from 1890 to 1893. His love of cricket, and his own indulgence in it as governor helped its popularity enormously. He adopted on the cricket field the attitude that all cricketers are equal, regardless of colour, and this attitude became widely known and made him a much respected governor at a time when governors were thought of as necessarily aloof from the general Indian populace. Bombay was always rather a special case in India, of course, because of its cosmopolitanism, and much of that cosmopolitanism was due to the presence of the large Parsi community whose team was now fully equal to the best that the Europeans in India could field. It

---

[1] The counties refused, in the summer of 1908, to accept the Australians on their own in 1909. They were brought to their senses rapidly by a masterly letter by the Hon. F. S. Jackson to *The Times* of July 9 1908.

was not many years before the Hindus achieved the same eminence, nor many more before the Muslims emulated them, so that the Bombay tournament became first triangular and then quadrangular. There was other cricket in India: Ranji was to be found playing for the old Maharajah of Patiala's team (father of the captain of the first All-India side to tour this country in 1911), as well as many other fine cricketers. There was a project which was almost consummated for an Indian tour in England in 1904: had it occurred, the Indian team would have been at a strength greater than any which have since made the trip. Ranji was not indeed the only Indian playing in first-class cricket: a name now little remembered was the Afridi Pathan, Ahsan-ul-Haq who played for Middlesex. But a list of great Indian cricketers would be a long one. The game had been slow in achieving its then quality and strength: now it seemed to leap ahead as cups were donated for school competitions and as teams of fair quality sprang up all over the country: as teams from universities toured far afield; as clubs visited overseas countries such as Ceylon, and Burma (technically part of India of course). In 1911, the first All-India tour took place: it was not a playing success but it could have been if the young Maharajah of Patiala had not been ill and if he had released his secretary, Colonel K. M. Mistri, to play for the team when he was away from it. All the same, the public was given some idea of what India might one day do: much of what they then attempted had been the result of assiduous coaching by leading English professionals,[1] and others were to continue to play a part later on. It was in this period that cricket literature from India began to multiply: the fact is enough to indicate the popularity of the game because such books did not on the whole, appeal to the English public, yet they were directed to the English-speaking Indian population.

Ceylon has always been a rather special cricket case. Its position on the sea route to Australia enabled it to see many of the great teams from England or Australia passing through: perhaps Ceylon has seen more great cricketing visitors than any other country in the world, and seen them playing, and all this has had an enormous effect on the quality of the game. Many have sneered at the one-day cricket played in Colombo by teams passing through only later to realize that all the time lessons were being learnt so that when three-day matches came to be played, Ceylon was found to be no pushover. It was in this period that the first of many Ceylon cricket annuals appeared: and also that the first extended tour by a team from Australia took place, just before the war began.

[1] W. Brockwell (Surrey) and J. T. Hearne (Middlesex) were brought out by the old Maharajah of Patiala in 1898 (Brockwell had come the year before) and were probably the first. In 1898 Ranji, too, played for Patiala, reasons of state keeping him away from what was to become his own principality.

Farther east, cricket in Malaya continued to be the preserve of settlers and planters, and other expatriates. It was played in a few schools, it is true, but the important matches were when teams came down from Hong Kong to play Singapore. Hong Kong itself could produce a powerful team, though it had already lost one complete team in a marine disaster. Shanghai could match Hong Kong, and was also able to feature a Parsi Cricket Club, perhaps the earliest Indian club outside India proper. There was a lot of other cricket played in the Chinese Treaty ports, as well as in Yokohama and Tokyo in Japan. There is little record of any being played by the natives of the two countries, though there was certainly a Chinese team, made up largely from ground staff, which played occasionally in Shanghai.

In Australia where the Sheffield Shield had just been commenced, cricket in Melbourne and Sydney in the 1890s was in a dull condition. It was rather the opposite of the present situation in Australia: then the trouble was that a small handful of clubs in the principal cities monopolized the best players, and this was depressing for others. Competitive cricket had been in existence for years but it was ceasing to be competitive with only a few very strong teams and many more not up to their standard. The answer was 'district' cricket, where clubs could only draw from players in their territories, with special provision being made for University players. This meant, inevitably a spread of players around nearly all the clubs, which made for competition, attracted crowds and revivified the game. It did not happen all at once: Sydney first, Melbourne some years later, but with an earlier reorganization of cricket there which went some way to repopularizing the game. Adelaide and Brisbane followed four years after Sydney, and Tasmania later still, but Tasmania has never quite been able to decide whether district cricket is a good thing, and the different scale of area and population perhaps makes it a matter not of great importance. (Perth did not go over to district cricket till after the Second World War.) It was not only the re-arranging of competitive cricket that enlivened Australian cricket at this time: it was the rise of two of Australia's very greatest cricketers about whose relative merits there can still be argument (though in my view none!) – Victor Trumper and Clem Hill. Clem Hill had been a schoolboy prodigy making the then record Australian score of 360* in December 1893. His first-class playing career very nearly coincides with the Golden Age for he played his first game in 1892–3, and his last in 1924–5, but he had effectively gone out of the game by 1914. Once again for a short while, he held an Australian record (for first-class cricket only) when he made 365* in 1900–1. He was a very fine batsman but opinions have differed whether he was a good Australian captain: one selector told him towards

23–24. Cricket in London, 1900 – (*a*) on Parliament Hill, (*b*) in the street

25. Mitcham Green at the turn of the century: cricket has been played on this ground for very nearly three centuries and it is probably the oldest cricket ground with continuous use in the country. Note the period costumes in the foreground

26. One of G. W. Beldam's photographs of
W. G. Grace, showing him bowling in his
usual style – an undoubted round-arm by
modern standards

27. A fine action photograph of the American
fast bowler John Barton King, certainly one
of the six leading bowlers in the world of
all time, and arguably the best. He was also
a fine batsman

28. An unusual view of Lord's which could only have been seen for a few years in the 1890s: it
was taken from the old Stand 'A' (where the Warner Stand now is). On the other side can be seen
the Mound, which gave its name to the Mound Stand that replaced the old Tennis Court which
can also be seen, and extended over the Mound itself. The Mound was made of soil excavated
from the foundations for the then new Pavilion

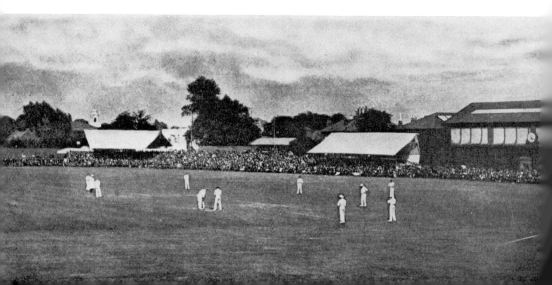

the end of his career that he was 'lousy' and was hit on the jaw for his trouble. Clem Hill was a record-breaker more of the Bradman type though he never came near Bradman's mechanical perfection – people did not try to in those days because there was still an attitude, even amongst top-ranking Australian batsmen, that cricket was a game. Victor Trumper – both his names conjure up a special aura – was not of that type: he made runs, and could have made far more, but was not interested in record-breaking as such. What impressed people was his style, his ability on no matter what kind of wicket and his own exceptional kindliness of character which endeared him to small boys, older boys, new opposing bowlers in much fear of what he might do to them, and a host of others. His schoolboy career was something to talk about though details of it are now, unhappily, lost, and his first-class career also approximates to the Golden Age for he first played in 1894–5, and last in 1913–14. It is Trumper whom Australians of an older generation (and the more earnest students of a younger one) set up as *the* great Australian cricketer as opposed to Bradman. To some extent this is nostalgia – the past was ever better (though in the case of cricket an extraordinarily good case can be made out to support such a thesis), but it is the 1902 season which seems to decide the matter. Bradman never played through a wet English season, but as is fairly natural, his play on wet wickets was not up to his hard-wicket form, even if it was still well ahead of any others. But Trumper batted through that wet season as though the wickets were as good as his usual hard Australian ones: he made 2,570 runs (the top aggregate) and averaged 48·49, yet his highest score was only 128, showing well how often he made runs. This was beyond question a wonderful performance: his average was beaten by only one batsman, who played far fewer innings.

The Australasian Cricket Council had been established to control the game in 1891 but it did not get full support, especially from the New South Wales authority, and it was dissolved in 1900. It can be said with hindsight that the reason for its weakness was its refusal, as a body, to exclude active cricketers from consultation in running the game. It was succeeded in 1905 by the present Australian Board of Control for Cricket. This body, or a section of it made up of the powerful New South Wales Cricket Association (never afraid to discipline its players however famous) and the weak Victorian Cricket Association (who wished it could get control of *its* players!) decided that players should have no say in the running of cricket or in the choosing of teams to go on overseas tours nor have any access to the often substantial profits from such tours. This was the basis for the eventual blow-up in the season of 1911–12 when half a dozen leading Australian players, including Hill and Trumper, found themselves in opposition to the Board and were not selected for the Triangular Tournament tour. It is also true that the way in which the Board was set up was open to serious legal questioning: but the ultimate point at issue was whether or not cricketers were to have control, to any degree, of what went on. Ever since the decision went against such control it has been a matter for consideration whether Australian cricket has been better off as a result – or better off than English. Is a virtually self-appointed council or committee, some of whom have played first-class cricket, the right body: or is a much smaller group of men, often prominent businessmen, appointed from each constituent organization, each such organization itself being on an appointed basis from its constituent clubs, and very few of whom have ever played first-class cricket, the better answer? In terms of actual organization and efficiency, the Australian model would seem correct, but if so it must be remembered that it only came about as a result of ruthlessness and a considerable element of dishonesty. Thus although, from a playing point of view, cricket in Australia at this time very much partook of the Golden Age, the administrative squabbles tarnished the gilt.

Early in the period occurred the first of, so far, five attempts to float an Australian cricket magazine, and the last two attempts, to float an Australian cricket annual (other than sponsored by one of the State organizations). Something in the Australian cricket atmosphere has not seemed to encourage writing about the game outside newspapers.

New Zealand saw rather different developments. The first year of the period, 1894, saw the establishment of the New Zealand Cricket Council, the governing body of New Zealand cricket to this day, and possibly the only cricket governing body – at least of a Test-match country – never to have inspired violent criticism or controversy. (One qualification – the selectors are always fair game, but they need not be identified with governing bodies!) In the same year, the last of the provincial cricket associations was formed, making ten in all. New Zealand cricket has been represented to a predominant extent by four of these provinces, Auckland, Wellington, Canterbury and Otago, known as major associations, and for many years the only competitors for the Plunket Shield (established 1906–7): two others once were eligible to compete for it, Hawkes Bay and Southland, and were therefore first-class also, and much earlier Nelson and Taranaki had been reckoned first-class.

New Zealand cricket has been quite highly organized from that time onwards: towards the end of the period the Hawke Cup was instituted for competition amongst what are known as minor associations, which include the non-first-class provinces and many subdivisions of provinces. If major associations can be considered on a par with first-class counties in England, then the minor associations correspond to the minor counties with the difference that nowadays they are probably stronger than our minor counties although sixty or seventy years ago the reverse was true. Nearly every city or large town has its own local competition: district cricket was imported into New Zealand from Australia in 1903–4 (Auckland followed by Christchurch 1905–6, and Wellington 1909–10) but it has never found favour and it is not to be found anywhere now. Conditions were not similar: a mistake that many New Zealanders make when they seek to take over an apparently good Australian idea. Two years after the Plunket Shield competition was organized, the Heathcote Williams Shield was presented for competition amongst all New Zealand secondary schools: the idea was good and the competition lasted for some years but two schools tended to make a monopoly of it, and so it has become dormant. In 1906–7 the first inter-college match took place (both colleges are now Universities). There were many interchanges of tours between Australia and New Zealand, more than in any period since, and New Zealand saw all the leading Australian players of the time. The Marylebone Cricket Club sent its first team to New Zealand in 1906–7: it has to be spelt out in full since the other (one of the many!) MCC, from Melbourne, undertook two tours in this period also. There was never any question of New Zealand's cricket authorities emulating rugger, and sending a cricket team to England then however: but attempts were made to get the South Africans to extend their Australian visit to New Zealand in 1910–11. The lack of success of Australian cricket annuals has been mentioned – it was the same in New Zealand till after the Second World War, but the first few years of this period did see four issues of an annual, the second attempt since Brittain's at the end of the previous period.

Fiji first came to prominence in the cricket world at this time. The earlier developments of the game there have already been touched on: in 1894–5 Fiji felt strong enough to tour New Zealand, playing eight games of which four were won and only two (against Auckland and Canterbury) were lost. Seven of the team were British expatriates, the other six Fijian chiefs. The game was by this time exceedingly popular in the islands and played at every reasonable opportunity: the extent of its popularity and the quality of its cricketers may much better be judged by what happened a few years later in 1907–8 when a team from one island alone, Bau (not very much larger in extent than the whole area occupied by the MCC in St John's Wood, judging from a low altitude photograph in Snow's book[1]) toured Australia playing State teams six times (two of them lost)

[1] P. A. Snow, *Cricket in the Fiji Islands.* See plate 31.

and many country teams and others. It is doubtful if such a small area has ever before or since provided a team which could take on other teams of near-first-class status (they were not the full State teams), and the tour was a remarkable performance. The main characteristic of Fijian cricket then, and since, has been a desire on the part of the batsman to hit the ball as hard as possible and as far as possible: and on the bowler's part to bowl as fast as possible. Slow bowling is looked down upon – and also found difficult to play for lack of adequate practice against it.

Elsewhere too in the Pacific the game progressed but in one area it regressed; for the Sandwich Islands, or Hawaii, became a territory of the United States and were flooded with American settlers.

It was during the Golden Age too that the standard of cricket in South America was first brought to the notice of the cricketing public elsewhere.

The first interchanges of teams in South America had taken place at the end of the previous period. Though there were three more tours between Brazil and the Argentine in the Golden Age what was of real importance was the establishment of competitive cricket in Buenos Aires in 1897–8: a second division followed in 1903–4, and a Saturday competition the next season. In 1899 what eventually became, in 1913, the Argentine Cricket Association was formed, to have control of all cricket in the country. The standard of play was perceptibly improving and the game was firmly established being played in the English schools as well as in the English sporting clubs and by English businesses and industries in the Argentine. Towards the end of the period came the first tour from England, a MCC team led by Lord Hawke: not really a strong team, though it included A. C. MacLaren and E. R. Wilson, and only just capable of being thought of as first-class, it lost one match to Argentine, and won the other two, one of them by only two wickets. But the First World War happened soon after or much more might have been heard of cricket there.

In Brazil, the old Rio Cricket Club had been reformed in 1898 and there was a considerable amount of cricket played by the large expatriate community though it never dug itself in deeply as it has in the Argentine. An inter-State competition was begun in 1908, for a trophy presented by the then Portuguese Ambassador to Brazil, and it is played for to the present day. Apart from the three exchanges with the Argentine, Brazil saw no international cricket in the period.

Cricket in Chile was always of much smaller note than in the Argentine, and there is nothing special in this period. But the existence of cricket in South America, with the game being played in the North American winter, offered opportunities to the English professionals employed in the United States of lucrative and enjoyable off-season duties. One of these was Bob Brooking, a brother of a once well-known cricket writer in this country, G. A. Brooking, whose name will often be found in old issues of *The Cricketer*, and later one of the founders of the Brazil Cricket Association.

In the West Indies the game was coming right out of its local shell. The first team from England toured in the first winter of the Golden Age, led by R. Slade Lucas, and two years later two English teams came out, one led by Lord Hawke and the other by Arthur Priestley.[1] Priestley's team played the first match by an English team against a representative West Indian eleven, and lost by 3 wickets. In 1900 the West Indies sent a team to England – it was captained by P. F. Warner's elder brother R. S. Aucher Warner, and it included Learie Constantine's father: it was not reckoned first-class but the second team in 1906 was. Lord Brackley took a team out in 1904–5 (following R. A. Bennet's) and during it occurred some disagreeable behaviour by some of the amateurs with the team: a forerunner of shemozzles of various kinds that have come to be associated with the visits of English teams to these islands. Shortly before the First World War began, the MCC sent two teams to the West Indies, both led by A. W. F. Somerset, in 1910–11 and 1912–13; in all six 'tests' were played and the MCC won all but one which they lost by an innings. So the West Indies were already showing how, on their day, they could be formidable.

Inter-colonial competitive cricket had started just before the period began, but it remained confined to matches between Trinidad, Barbados and British Guiana, Jamaica being too far away to be able to take part as steamer communications went via Panama! The smaller islands were not reckoned to be equal competitors, though if grouped together they might well have been. Inter-colonial cricket was strictly amateur, so was competitive club cricket in both Trinidad and Barbados at that time: this had the effect of keeping out of important cricket many coloured cricketers who were professionals: there was a kind of rather ineffective colour bar, symptoms of which linger on in the islands to this day, but not enforceable in populations of such very mixed origins as those are, and something that vanished after the First World War in cricket – except

---

[1] In passing it must be remarked that both tours took place through the stubborn and ill-mannered mulishness amounting almost to insufferable arrogance on the part of Lord Hawke: he was to behave in a similar way later, in England, when he demanded that a professional cricketer throw up a contracted engagement in order to play in a match with which he was concerned. This was A. E. Relf contracted to play at the Hastings Festival whom Hawke seized for the Rest *v.* the Champion County (see *Cricket* (1909), p. 411): it is worth mentioning to explain why there were two tours simultaneously, and also to illustrate how the running of cricket at that time could be arbitrary in the extreme.

for naming West Indian captains. Cricket was played at the top level on turf, except in Trinidad where matting was used from the turn of the century: perhaps the relative strength of Barbadian first-class cricket has its origins in that change by Trinidad.

The period saw a Jamaican cricket annual produced – one issue only – and a long run of a Barbadian cricket annual which ended only with the outbreak of war: from it a clear idea of the strength and keenness of West Indian cricket can be gathered, and it is noteworthy that the first elevens of leading schools were deemed strong enough to compete with the men's clubs – two of them possibly the strongest clubs in the world at that time in playing ability – Wanderers and Pickwick.

There seems little doubt that but for the First World War, Test cricket on an official basis would have been played by the West Indies much earlier than it eventually came about, in 1928, and there are some ready to argue that the most powerful West Indian team of all time could be found from pre-1914 players.

Cricket in Bermuda came very much to the fore during the Golden Age: records of the game there go back to the early part of the nineteenth century but there had been little sign of any good standard being achieved. The visit of the Philadelphia Zingari in 1891 may have stimulated interest in the game: fourteen years later the Hamilton Club visited Philadelphia and that was the first of many visits by Bermudan teams to North America. The Philadelphians went to Bermuda again in 1907 and then four more times before the First World War, with other visits after: and teams from New York and Canada also have paid short visits. There were fourteen matches in all played between All Bermuda and All Philadelphia and Bermuda won five of these, losing only four. Bermuda was obviously up to first-class cricket with such a record as that, and it is indeed arguable that some of these matches should be treated as first-class. Bermuda has also had contacts with the West Indies, but for cricket purposes has not yet been considered as part of West Indian cricket: yet the strength of the island is not what it once was, and though she can produce fine players, they can have no great future if Bermuda continues on her own. Bermuda entertained Australian teams just before the First World War and did not do badly, and on a number of occasions from the time of the visit by Sir Julien Cahn's team in 1933 has entertained English teams: in 1969 a representative Bermuda team made a tour to Denmark and Holland – an enterprising innovation.

In the United States, this was the hey-day of cricket in and around Phila-delphia – cricket which sustained the game in Boston and Baltimore, in New

York and even in an almost typically English country-house form in Virginia. Cricket in America is so much regarded now as a joke or a curiosity that it is difficult to realize that it was in this period that the prospect of Philadelphia actually playing Test matches one day was not to be laughed at. Let us just consider a few of the events of the Golden Age of cricket as they affected Philadelphia: for four years around the turn of the century, there were two competing monthly cricket magazines in that *city* – two! Few countries are able to support one nowadays. One of them – the old *American Cricketer* revamped itself at the turn of the century to become one of the best *productions* that has been seen amongst cricket magazines at any time. There was an annual which ran right on until the First World War began, sponsored for the latter half of its life by Spaldings, much as Wisden's firm sponsored one in this country, and replete with detailed statistics (F. Fitzmaurice Kelly, its editor in its latter days was second only to F. S. Ashley-Cooper in his time as a cricket statistician and historian). So much for the literature, which was no new feature of the game in Philadelphia. Look at the tours: from 1896 to 1914 Haverford College undertook five tours to England to play other schools, and clubs. It was many years before any English school toured abroad. The Gentlemen of Philadelphia came here three times, and each time their record was good and some of the play remarkable. Three of the constituent clubs each made tours here to play clubs and county teams and Service teams. There were six trips to Bermuda and to Jamaica. Twelve teams from these islands made tours to North America and chiefly to Philadelphia, and these included Kent, the first county to tour abroad, the MCC, and many of the leading players of the time, Ranji among them. It was an extremely pleasant ending to a cricket season to cross the Atlantic in early or mid-September and play on till October in the marvellous surroundings to be found there. There were three Australian tours, official in 1896 (when again they managed to lose to Philadelphia in one of their matches by an innings) and 1912, and unofficial, but hardly less powerful in 1913. And Philadelphia was never found to be playing above its class.

The leading clubs in Philadelphia were found in this period mostly rebuilding, either after a fire, or for expansion, and provided amongst the world's best settings to play and to watch the game: crowds of twenty thousand could be found on occasion watching an international match. Domestically, cricket was highly organized with any number of different leagues and cup competitions. Domestically too, it was progressive, experiments being made with eight-ball and ten-ball overs whilst English first-class cricket was still dallying with five-ball overs. Indeed eight-ball and ten-ball overs were adopted officially for certain competitions though the general opinion was that ten-ball overs were too long. Although it cannot be proved it seems likely that the Philadelphian eight-ball overs must have made their impress on the Australian cricketers who visited the city.

Philadelphia had one very great player, of world class – John Barton King: a fast bowler who maintained his speed for twenty years, and had perfected a controlled swerve which he used but rarely and then with deadly effect. He headed the English bowling averages in 1908[1] with a figure not to be achieved or beaten for another fifty years, and never since approached by a touring bowler. (He was not the captain in 1908 as is sometimes stated.) He was also a fine batsman and set up the North American record. He was not a wealthy man, as so many of the Philadelphian cricketers were, and was subsidised discreetly by them. The Americans eschewed professionals: how they swallowed King is something to wonder at! American cricketers regarded professionalism as the potential ruin of cricket, as it had been, in their view, of baseball, leading inevitably to arrant commercialism, and warnings were uttered occasionally about England's professionalism. Only in our own time, half a century after, can we see the bitter truth of those warnings, as commercialism seizes and manipulates cricket to advertise itself.

Why did all this wonderful scene collapse? Partly because it was amateur and depended on the leisured and wealthy amateur for its existence and after the Wall Street crash years later there were few enough of these: partly because the magnificent cricket clubs turned themselves into all-sport country clubs, and a time came when a majority of members were found to prefer the shorter and quicker game of lawn tennis: partly because there was very little real junior cricket, without which the senior game could hardly thrive naturally: partly because the great Philadelphian Eleven of the 1890s was, with only a few changes, still playing twenty years later, not so much because no one else had come along as that the team was all-powerful in itself. There were one or two who saw the portents, but they did not speak up enough nor were their somewhat muted voices heard by others. One thing is certain – that the entire hey-day of Philadelphian cricket fits into the span provided by the Golden Age.

Nowhere else in the United States was cricket so popular, nowhere else was it

---

[1] 1894 T. Richardson (Surrey), 196 wickets, average 10·33
   1908 J. B. King, 87 wickets, average 11·01
   1958 H. L. Jackson (Derbyshire), 143 wickets, average 10·99
King does not appear in the record books as the line is, for some reason, drawn at 100 wickets, but you would have to find someone who took less than 40 wickets to beat King's figures in that sixty-four year period!

29. The attacking style in cricket demonstrated by
J. H. Sinclair, the South African batsman, still used
thirty years later in club matches by another South
African, Herbie Taylor (see pages 169–70)

30. C. B. Llewellyn – the coloured
South African bowler

31. Bau Island from the air: from this one small island in the Fijis went a team to Australia in
1907–8 strong enough to hold its own against Australian State teams

32. Country House cricket, believed to be photographed at Crabbet Park, Sussex

33 (*right*). The Merion Cricket Club's ground at Haverford, U.S.A., in the 1890s during a big international match, showing the imposing pavilion and stand alongside

played to such an extent by native-born Americans (this was one of the great boasts of the Philadelphians): that it was far more widespread than now is true, with inter-State and inter-city matches and many interesting tours not confined to the eastern half of the country. But rarely was it outside Philadelphia a truly American phenomenon. On *that*, all we need say is that it was in this period not long after the turn of the century that the last matches of 'wicket', that ancient game brought over by the early colonists, were played: that version is now dead.

Cricket in Canada profited by the 'fall-out' from English tours to Philadelphia, and from tours by clubs from that city; and the standard was sustained to a considerable extent by the need, or the desire, to match what Philadelphia or its clubs could do. Canadian cricket never quite matched up to the Philadelphian standards, despite the fact that in this period, Canada won five of the sixteen finished matches in the International series *v.* U.S.A. Not that the game was not widespread: it was played and well-organized in British Columbia: it was played in the Prairie Provinces, where an inter-provincial tournament was organized: it was played in the leading English-type public schools in south-western Ontario: it was played at universities. There ought to have been a good substratum for the game to grow: at this distance in time, all we can say is that it was enough to ensure that the game continued at that standard fifty and more years later, no more than that. It is perhaps relevant that in all this period, only one Canadian team came to England, from the Canadian Zingari club, in striking contrast to the doings of the Philadelphians. Yet the period also saw, at the start, a detailed history of the game in Canada covering the previous sixty years, and towards the end, a second attempt at a Canadian cricket magazine: if the public was not adequate, it was at least thought to be. Some explanation of the contrast in the way the game has gone in the two countries may lie in the greater readiness of the English expatriate to 'Canadianize' himself than to 'Americanize' himself, with as complements, a greater unwillingness of the Canadian to anglicize himself than of a certain type of American from the Eastern States and with a private-school-cum-Yale-and-Harvard background.

There is one part of North America to be referred to for the first, and for the last time: Newfoundland. For it was in the last few years of the period that the game finally died out (sporadic attempts to revive it in the 1920s got nowhere): it seems to have been fairly popular into, and past, the 1890s (there had even been an annual issued in 1897) and then fell away rapidly. Economic reasons may have played their part, climatic ones no doubt also. The game must have been hard to establish, and it is unlikely it will ever get a footing again in what was once our oldest colony and is now Canada's newest province.

(iii) Conduct of the game and administration

There were some important changes in the Laws during the Golden Age, changes which finally made the game very little different from what it is now so far as first-class cricket is concerned: lesser cricket is much less affected by such changes – new ball regulations, follow-on, and such-like play little part in one-day matches and none in afternoon cricket.

The limit for a follow-on had remained at 80 runs even in a three-day match for forty-four years during which time the game had been transformed. The persistence with this low limit was, it was believed, what was wrong with the follow-on law – not the fact that it was compulsory. It is perfectly true, of course, that by raising the limit, you eliminate most of the cases where compulsion is unjust but you do not eliminate them all, and it took two major incidents (of bowlers bowling wide so that their opponents could not follow-on) to raise the limit first of all, in 1894, and then six years later to abolish the compulsion. The first raising of the limit was, itself, only to 120 runs, and evidently not enough: in 1900 it was raised to 150 and there it has stayed ever since although 200 runs are now sanctioned for a match of longer than three days duration. Australia, however, did not follow this legislation, establishing it as 200 runs in 1896–7 and compulsory until 1907–8. In this Australia was behaving in accordance with what the first-class game required: declarations for instance, did not take place in Australian competitive cricket until that ceased to be timeless in 1927–8, and there was strong objection when Warner declared in a match in 1903–4. The period within which a declaration could not take place in English cricket was fiddled about with during the first decade of the century and continued to be until years later, after the Second World War, one could declare at any time – the obvious and sensible answer. As so often it took cricket's legislators a long time to arrive at it.

The trouble that had arisen in the 1870s and 1880s over throwing had not disappeared, merely died down, and around the turn of the century, it livened up again until it was very decisively dealt with by the English captains naming the supposedly guilty bowlers. The action was disavowed but it had had its effect. Towards the end of the trouble, the Laws were changed to make it clear that either umpire could call no-ball if not satisfied with the fairness of the delivery. There was rather more support given to the umpires at this period than in the previous one, or than there was to be sixty years later – for it took nearly all that time for the trouble to arise and become serious again.

162

In 1900 the over was increased for all other than one-day matches to six balls: this brought the small minority of two-day and three-day cricket in England into line with all other cricket in England, and also in line with much first-class cricket abroad. It is extremely difficult to understand why it had taken the English authorities so long to make universal what was anyway almost universal, six-ball overs having been used in country cricket – which meant most of it – very early on; and even, as we have seen, at Lord's in the Eton v. Harrow match of 1827.

In 1907, largely in order to clear up misunderstandings about when a new ball could be taken – the shorter life of balls in days not long before had meant more than one being used in an innings – it was decided to allow a new ball after 200 runs (the MCC had proposed 150 runs, which nearly agrees with the modern run equivalent of overs after which it is allowed, but this was turned down). The aim was not to provide swerve bowlers with a new ball solely to regularize an existing custom. It had, as we shall see, a most evil effect and the effect has been heightened by allowing the new ball after so many overs instead of after so many runs: if the ball comes into use when so many runs have been made, the game does keep moving, but if after so many overs, the fielding side can and do just play possum with negative bowling till the new ball is due. Once again, an obvious situation but not yet seen by the legislators.

Two attempts to change the Laws failed – one was to widen the stumps by an inch and that of course did eventually happen some thirty years later, but was not necessary at the time of its proposal (or, in my view, later): there was some horror at the high scoring that was seen at the turn of the century, and there was a desire to limit it, as, for some reason, there always is when high scoring comes along in first-class cricket.

The other was a more important proposal to change the l.b.w. Law virtually to make any obstruction by the batsman sufficient to give him out. It was defeated and it may well be thought it was a very great pity that it was: the tale is told how Ranji once came in deploring that there was a ball mark on one of his pads. Pads were never intended to protect a batsman's wicket, only his legs, and the old children's law of 'hit the leg three times and it's out' has a great validity.

These were the only changes in the Laws at this time but they were far from being the only changes in administration, for this was the period in which the MCC took over control of much of English cricket at the top level. The MCC had never wished to be involved in anything else but declaring what the Laws were, and as we have seen and will continue to see, these were by no means always observed either locally in England or overseas: that they were the accepted standard is one thing but they were no more than that and if special conditions prevailed locally, then the Marylebone Laws were ignored.

The MCC came into the administrative picture *faute de mieux* soon after the Cricket Council had gone out of existence. Something had to be done: it was ridiculous, for example, that just because Somerset could arrange fixtures against the other first-class counties, she necessarily became first-class, so the first step was taken by the MCC in 1894, of approving which were and which were not first-class. It is interesting that those new names on the first list (Derbyshire, Essex, Leicestershire, Warwickshire) were all counties which had customarily played three-day matches against the accepted first-class counties: the newspaper classification did by now ignore what cricketers themselves *felt*, and the promotion of Hampshire echoed this feeling. (There can be less satisfaction with the later promotions of Worcestershire and Northamptonshire, the result more of skilful lobbying than any feeling generally that they merited it.) This was not all. Faced with this problem of controlling county cricket, the MCC set up an Advisory County Cricket Committee in 1904, and this lasted until 1969 when it was merged in a new structure. In 1898 a Board of Control for Test matches at home had been established: something long overdue since, till then, teams for Tests had been chosen by the ground authorities – the MCC had failed to choose Ranji in 1896 though he was chosen elsewhere, and on this form, ought to have been chosen at Lord's too. It was the first but no means the last occasion on which the MCC showed insensitivity over matters of colour: thirty-three years later they were to omit Ranji's nephew, Duleepsinhji, under South African pressure. Of course a Board had to be established before the 1899 season when there were to be five Tests for the first time at home: a fantastic situation would have arisen had five different bodies picked their own people. The curious thing was that the Board was *only* for home Tests. The idea that there should be control of overseas tours had not occurred to anyone: it did after the 1901–2 tour by Archie MacLaren to Australia when either he refused to pick Yorkshire players, or Yorkshire refused to allow him to choose their players (it is not clear to this day which it was) and as a result had a much weakened team. This led directly to the MCC taking a hand in 1903–4, and from that time on the overwhelming majority of teams and certainly all Test playing touring teams from this country sailed under MCC auspices. It has not on the whole been a satisfactory business though: the selection of teams has often run counter to general opinion, and even to what the English selectors have wanted, the MCC adding in their own selectors who often overruled the remainder. The financing has not been satisfactory either – secretaries being provided for managers, but sometimes no scorer, and any eventual share-out to counties being until 1969 a matter of grace on the part of the MCC. But it lasted over sixty years before a more satisfactory solution was reached, even if it is not yet all it should be.

With MCC control established in one form or another, the then more important cricketing countries all had their central authorities and it is not surprising that in 1907 a movement should have originated to create a kind of world authority. Only it was not a world authority – it was to be an Imperial Cricket Conference, and thus excluded Philadelphia, arguably more powerful at the time than the surprising proponents of the idea, South Africa. The Conference was, however, established in 1909 and has continued ever since, to become International after over half a century had passed. Its origins clearly introduced politics into cricket, and that introduction came from South Africa!

As to the actual conduct of the game in this period, perhaps the most notable from our point of view so many years later (though not noticed at the time) was the evident freeing of the game from the set fielding positions which had for so long been laid down in instructional books and in cricket annuals ('for a slow left-arm bowler', 'for a medium-pace bowler round-the-wicket' – two of the sillier examples!). Such diagrams continued to appear, but they were now guides, and they often showed some exercise of intelligence: this too was now being exercised by captains who now were setting fields in accordance with what a bowler needed. It went beyond that: the more famous bowlers of the period, such as S. F. Barnes (arguably the best bowler ever produced in this or any other country) would set their own fields, sometimes operating through the captain – and sometimes not. Bowling had not yet become fossilized into the pattern set up after the First World War, when, under the influence of the example set by the famous Australian pair, J. M. Gregory and E. A. McDonald, every first-class and many another team seemed to open with two fast bowlers, one at each end – no thought of variety as had hitherto been the case (and as must surely be correct?) and the further pattern that started to be set up between the wars of new-ballitis – 'must have a new ball, *must* have swerve bowlers'.

But at the time, what must have struck people most was the introduction of googly bowling. It was B. J. T. Bosanquet, of Middlesex, who made this famous on the first MCC tour to Australia in 1903–4, and the ball used often to be termed a 'bosie' (or 'bosey') after him, and still is in Australia. In England it has always been more usual to call it a googly. It is quite uncertain who first bowled this ball, or where: something like it seems to have been known in the early 1890s: and the word 'googly' seems to have existed in Australia several years before to describe a similar kind of delivery: whatever the truth may be, it was Bosanquet who both perfected it and made it famous. The idea was taken up by several South African bowlers who together formed a powerful attack against the MCC batting in 1905–6, but who were less successful with it when they came to this country in 1907: and after that it has become a free-for-all with many bowling it who had insufficient control over action or length. However, all the way down since then, there have been bowlers who could perfect this type of concealed delivery – for that is all it is, bowling one thing when you seem to be bowling another – and such bowlers have always reaped their reward. The reward is due to them because it comes only with very hard and assiduous practice.

The top-class players, however, soon became so expert at dealing with the googly that by the time of the Second World War it was not, in itself, reckoned a great wicket taker: A. P. Freeman, for example, in his great days (some of them very great: the only bowler to take over 300 wickets in an English first-class season – unkind critics said it was because he was Kent's only bowler!) used it very rarely except against left-handers. The great players of it got out to the pitch (or even, like Duleep[1] and the older Nawab of Pataudi[2] volleyed it) and what they couldn't reach that way was short enough to be comfortably watched off the wicket. In either case it did not matter which way the ball was breaking. The good county batsmen found most googlies easy to 'read', far easier than the top-spinner. And some quite humble performers coped successfully by playing everything on or outside the off-stump as a googly: if it was they middled it, if it was the leg-break, it went away harmlessly!

[1] Duleep was K. S. Duleepsinhji – Ranji's nephew, or rather one of many of them – who was a wonderful and graceful batsman, with every stroke but with one which will ever live in the memories of those who saw it – his late cut. He contracted tuberculosis and from 1932 was out of the game for ever. Had he remained fit, it might be he whom we would rate as the greatest batsman of the period, not Bradman.

Duleep has to be mentioned for another reason: on page 149, the incursion of South African racial attitudes into cricket was noticed. These attitudes recurred over Duleep: chosen for the first Test against the South Africans in 1929, the tourists objected, and he did not appear in the remaining four games. He never toured South Africa – but those were the days when it was not necessary to send the best team to that country. In later years when serving as Indian High Commissioner in Australia, he stated that he had agreed to stand down, not wanting to cause trouble: he was always a gentle creature, not like his uncle, who was ever ready to stand on his rights and his dignity (and would never have been the Jam Saheb if he had not) and who was furious over the whole affair. But then Ranji remembered what is nowadays forgotten: the MCC *had not chosen him* when he was at the height of his powers in 1896, to play against Australia. The MCC was properly snubbed by Lancashire and Surrey who saw to it that Ranji played at Old Trafford and the Oval.

[2] The older Nawab, father of the present Indian Test captain, had not the grace though much of the brilliance of Duleep, and was a fine aggressive batsman.

In referring to the new regulations, mention has been made of its effect on swerve bowling. It had been developed in this country by George Hirst, the Yorkshire all-rounder (assessed by a very fine statistician – George H. Wood – as second only to W.G. as an all-rounder in the whole period from the late 1870s to the outbreak of the Second World War) the only man ever to make 2,000 runs and take 200 wickets in the same English first-class season, in 1906. It had been separately developed by J. B. King in America. Probably Hirst's example had the greater influence but King's can hardly be negligible, and many others followed. That led (via the new ball fetish – so unforeseen are these decisions) to the 'two-eyed' stance and short back-lift and to the dreary seam-bowling we see so much of today.

One other relatively minor matter was regularized in the period – the question of how many runs were scored if a ball was hit over the boundary line, rope or fence. It had been the custom only to allow a six (or, in Australia, a five with the batsmen having to change ends) if the ball was hit right out of the ground itself, and four runs otherwise: now it became necessary only to hit out of the playing area. It must always have been arguable on some grounds (and probably Lord's was one of them with a carriage road running right round the ground, so that it was possible to run some hits out as the ball disappeared into the throng) whether the ball was 'out of the ground' or 'out of the field of play'. Precision and definition about these big hits meant that in future batsmen would score more for the same strokes than they had in the past: when W.G. began playing, all runs had to be run out – when he ended, one could very well score a century without moving from the crease. (One of W.G.'s critics said 'Pilch played cricket, W.G. plays boundary'.) There can be no doubt that the gradual 'solidification' of boundaries was a large contributory cause of the higher scoring which came to stay from the beginning of the Golden Age until the early 1950s: it may also be responsible for the decreasing physical fitness of the cricketers of modern times. Boundaries do not, or more correctly, did not originally exist for any cricket purpose at all but purely as a means of more efficient crowd control. As the extract from Nyren shows,[1] crowds used to part to allow ball and fielder through.

The great characteristic of the Golden Age was style. The Age of Grace had been to a great extent a matter of perfecting technique, learning how to use every stroke and not just a few: in a word, application. All these matters are, of course, generalizations, but the Golden Age is not famous for technique – that is taken

[1] See above, page 62.

for granted and if from time to time some players were faulted it was not because their technique was wrong, but because it was ugly, or lacked style. G. L. Jessop, the great hitter of the period, and perhaps the greatest of all time, was known as the 'croucher' because of his stance at the wicket: it was a crouch too, bent quite a lot, and from it he would leap forward and smite the ball all over the ground. He was no unscientific village-cricket slogger: he was a skilled batsman and certainly one to be considered for an England team of all time. But he was not typical of the period: nor, if it comes to that, was Ranji. Ranji was a marvellously fluent stroke player, doing everything just that much better than his contemporaries because he had an amazing eye and wonderfully quick reactions – he would late-cut the ball when the wicket-keeper thought it was safely past the wicket. Style may first have been seen with L. C. H. Palairet, of Somerset, who was often spoken of by those who saw him as the most graceful player they had ever watched: but there were others who showed style, Archie MacLaren, C. B. Fry, Jackson (already mentioned), R. H. Spooner, and of course Victor Trumper. A most typically stylish stroke was the off-drive with a full back-lift and a full follow-through: stylish play was generally thought to exclude leg-side play whereas the off-drive was thought to be the most beautiful stroke of all. Yet Ranji immortalized one leg-side stroke – the leg glide, a kind of forward stroke played across the flight of the ball, with the face of the bat turned towards square leg, and the ball deflected so that the bat may be said to have slid across the ball. Only one with perfect timing could have played such a stroke, needing a crooked bat and across the flight of the ball. In Ranji's hands this must have been a beautiful stroke to watch. Returning to the drive, however, there is little difference in the beauty of the straight drive, lofted safely over the bowler's head, from that of the off-drive, and both have been seen from Peter May and Ted Dexter in recent years, Dexter being an especially fine exponent of the drive. Style was the product of exquisite timing combined with the proper use of power: it made strokes seem effortless, and even if effort was to some extent visible as the batsman moved out to the ball, any thought of it was forgotten in the effect of the stroke itself.

Style was a product of amateur cricket at the top level, and that was in turn a product of careful coaching at the great public schools: the coach was often nominally a professional cricketer – until the 1890s frequently one who was still active in county cricket in the smaller county programme of those days but more realistically there were one or more great amateur players on the staff of the public schools, and their influence, by example and exhortation, was probably far greater than that of the 'pro'. R. A. H. Mitchell, at Eton, was one of these

34. Manheim, Philadelphia, 1903. A Halifax Cup match, with the Germantown side in the field

35–44. The attacking style in cricket demonstrated by J. B. Hobbs
who, as 'Plum' Warner once said, 'batted just like an amateur'. Here
he is seen playing the high drive to the off

coaches, and one of the most famous. There have been many others down the years. Scholastically, some of them may not have been up to much but their cricket ability and their ability to instruct at the game was high, and that, after all, was what they were there for in those days. But it took time for the utilitarian and the pragmatic to be clothed in splendour, so it was long after coaching had seriously started in the public schools that its results began to show in beauty. Palairet, of course, and others with style, were playing long before the Golden Age began: yet the great flowering of amateur stylists took place in that age. It all had a marked influence on the professionals most, but by no means all, of whom to some extent modelled themselves on the amateurs: although some, in the northern counties, remained content to make runs without bothering too much how they made them.

Many readers will know of photographs showing batsmen of the Golden Age, and indeed earlier, standing to receive the ball with their bats held high. W. G. Grace was certainly one player who did it (he was not the first), Lord Harris was another, and the most familiar photograph of it is no doubt that of A. C. MacLaren. This was no pose: it was how the great batsman of the period received the ball and C. B. Fry, according to Donald Knight, was the greatest and most powerful exponent of this fashion. Fry would start the back-lift before the ball ever left the bowler's hand, before the bowler had reached the crease even, and so had completed the downward stroke and was in a position to meet the ball with all his force when it reached him: he would, as did others like him, do this to fast bowlers as well as slow. Knight confesses that this ability was beyond him (and he was a fine batsman in his own right). It is a way of playing that is never seen now, certainly not in first-class cricket in this country, yet it is, of course, entirely logical: instead of letting the ball hit a motionless bat, or one to which no back-lift worth the description is given at all the method enables the batsman to deal with the ball with great power. It is an aggressive method of batting, and it is one which needs a good eye, good judgement and good timing – none of them impossible to acquire or use. It went right out of the game many years ago: probably Fry and MacLaren were the last, or almost the last, players of any note to use it.

Yet it lingered on as the following tale will tell: during the late 1930s the Hon. Charles Lyttelton (now Lord Cobham) was out in South Africa for his health, and played a few club games. In one of them R. J. Crisp, the South African bowler then playing for Worcestershire, was bowling and Lyttelton was at mid-off. An elderly grey-haired man came in, and proceeded to punch the ball hard to the boundary, off the back foot, with Lyttelton having no chance at all of

F*

stopping it. Mystified as to who it was and puzzled how it was done, he asked Crisp who the player was and was told it was Herbie Taylor, who must then have been close on fifty – he had first appeared for South Africa in 1912 and initially played first-class cricket in 1909–10. So Lyttelton asked him how he did it and Taylor replied, 'I have my bat up at the start and bring it down to meet the ball – I don't just start raising it when the bowler delivers the ball like the modern custom' – and Lyttelton wished he had played the ball that way all his life. Perhaps his few fine innings many years later when Governor-General of New Zealand may have shown that he put Taylor's words to good use. (Could it be that they will be read by some modern batsman who will profit by them and give back to the game some of its lost attraction?) Taylor by the way was coached at his school in Natal (Michaelhouse) by George Cox, sr. of Sussex – one year Fry's junior, so the line of transmission seems obvious.

Such was the amateur approach to the game: it remained in English first-class cricket till after the Second World War; and what makes the passing of the true amateur player lamentable is that there is no aesthetic influence left in the game. But even before the amateur had largely departed from the game, the negative and defensive attitude derived from modern coaching theories had already started to diminish the attractiveness of their batting. No amateur of the Golden Age could have written 'when I play a defensive stroke, nothing else is present in my mind but the absolute necessity for safeguarding my wicket'. With that, the openly expressed belief of a modern English captain, no wonder the modern game is dreary. And just as the influence of fine style spread downwards, so has the negative influence: it is found now in quite low grades of cricket and no wonder young men do not enjoy playing any more.

10

THE FIRST WORLD WAR

In a curiously subconscious way, those who lived before and took part in the First World War seem to have been aware that great, indeed enormous changes would result from that war, in all sorts of ways which they could hardly guess. Indeed, the full working out of these changes would not come until the Second World War, partly because the awareness had been subconscious rather than overt. This is, of course, why it is that those who came to mature thought after the last war are unable to grasp what the general social set-up was before it, whereas those who came to mature thought after the First World War can very well understand the pre-1914 period. Both, to the present generation, are now history: but to the generation of thirty or forty years ago, not even the first seemed to be history. Yet there seems to have been this subconscious awareness of something enormous happening. It can be seen in the way that cricket came to a halt in August 1914 for all but a very few games – not only county cricket but club cricket too. It can be seen in the way that young, and not so young men went cheerfully, even joyfully to their fate. It can be seen, in its darker side, in the utterly fantastic war hysteria which gripped responsible citizens. There was a real break in the continuity of many things, as there was not during the Second World War: but, of course, there was constant change and adaptation going on socially in the Second World War, of a type of which there was no hint at all in the first, and often very rapid.

There was no serious cricket, not even cricket of a good standard, over most of England from 1915 to 1918. True, some southern professionals went to northern leagues and established there some wonderful performances: those of Jack Hobbs in the Bradford League are worth mentioning, so are those of S. F. Barnes. But this was Saturday afternoon cricket, an organized recreation for factory workers in heavy industry: it did not occur in the south, nor – the south not then being industrialized – was there need for it. Appeals for volunteers creamed off the cricketing talent: creamed it off as soon as they left their schools, and in those days, it must be remembered, few State supported schools ran cricket teams, so 'schools' means public schools and grammar schools of the older type. A boy at about fifteen or sixteen became increasingly aware that his next move after he had reached his sixth form was not to University but to the trenches: hence, indeed, compulsory training in the O.T.C., which spared him doing duty as a private soldier. There was nothing like the Second World War system whereby very few indeed obtained direct commissions: all had to go through the ranks and be recommended – and some were not, nor were all their successors afterwards: one who was to become an England captain was evidently judged not to be of officer material when he went before his selection board. There was indeed club cricket in the south but it had to struggle hard to keep going: hence the formation of what was to be the Club Cricket Conference, which had its origins in charitable assistance before the First War.

School cricket was played: the MCC scraped together players from amongst their older or less fit members to provide some opposition, but that was all. In 1918, as the summer drew on, and victory started to seem a possibility, a few one-day matches of better status were played, but nothing like the 1945 series of Victory Tests was arranged. There was no inter-county cricket: there was exceedingly little two-day cricket even. Yet travel was far easier during the First World War than it was ever during the Second. Cricket was, for the first time in its history, seen, reluctantly, and unavowedly, to be one of those childish things which men put behind them. It is true that from about 1917 there seemed less 'disgrace' about playing cricket, partly no doubt because there had been no let up in football but also perhaps coinciding with, and because of the introduction of conscription.

It was worse in South Africa: there was no first-class cricket from after the MCC tour of 1913–14 until the A.I.F. team visited the country in 1919–20: no Currie Cup tournament from 1912–13 until 1920–1. South Africa had her own serious internal problems: the attempted Boer revolt, supported from German South-west Africa; the necessity for clearing up that colony, and after that of going on to German East Africa, later Tanganyika, now Tanzania, to help the British in their not by any means successful war against the celebrated German general, von Lettow-Vorbeck, who conducted a remarkable 'bush' campaign until, indeed, after the armistice in Europe. South Africa was very much involved, and did not play serious cricket, nor did the leagues on the Rand continue during the war or elsewhere.

In Australia, the 1914–15 Sheffield Shield, and all district cricket by contrast, continued as though there were no war: even the 1914–15 tour to South Africa was not cancelled until quite late in the day, and then from the South African end. But after that one season, Australia took life as seriously as England, and no more organized cricket was played until 1918–19, when a fairly full programme of inter-State fixtures took place, as well as a revival of matches between district clubs. New Zealand, in further contrast, saw only two seasons without first-class cricket, 1915–16 and 1916–17: and the Plunket Shield was only omitted in those two seasons and in 1917–18. Competitive cricket at district level continued in many centres.

In India, where the war had little effect on the people as a whole, there continued to be much good cricket, and a number of English professionals found wartime jobs there as coaches, so that better-class cricket was sometimes seen than previously, as was to happen again during the Second World War.

In Canada, cricket continued much as usual, and throve in British Columbia: but the level was not high, nor ever had been, compared with what went on south of the border. There cricket continued just as though nothing whatsoever were happening. Indeed nothing was happening: the U.S.A. were neutral until 1917, and even their entrance into the war did not affect the game largely – it did little more than introduce American cricketers to England where they played amongst others in matches between hospital teams, many of which came from the Philadelphia area. All the various competitions went on in Philadelphia (except only in 1918), and the great clubs continued to furnish strong, but ageing teams: it was not that the young were not coming on but rather that they were not quite good enough. There were even a couple of minor international tours by a club from Bermuda. Farther south again, in the West Indies, good club cricket continued, as well, of course, as school cricket, but there was no attempt at first-class cricket.

Generally in the world, there was much unorganized cricket in the forces, but it never attained the level to be seen during the Second World War in England, or in Egypt, or in India. The game was put behind: but not quite always. There is the well-known account of how the newspaper placards announced in 1915 'Death of a great Cricketer': it was Victor Trumper. That same year saw the passing of W.G.: Trumper was undoubtedly premature in his death, he was 37, and W.G. not an old man at sixty-seven by our present standards, but the heavy physique he carried no doubt had worn him out over the years.

Yet during these years, there was one new development: the eight-ball over. It had first been tried in a local Sydney competition in 1909, and was generally adopted for local cricket there in 1915–16: it spread to other States, and became law for Australia from 1918–19. It spread too to New Zealand and was generally but not universally adopted in the same season (after that New Zealand had periods when she used the eight-ball over, and then reverted to six balls, and then back again to eight balls). South Africa, under the Australian example was certainly playing eight balls in competitions on the Rand not long after the First World War, though she did not formally adopt it till many years later.

Many strange proposals were put forward in the autumn and winter following the First World War and one was later to be adopted: much later, after the Second World War. It was from F. S. Jackson, of all people, and it was that boundaries should be shorter. The idea was hotly attacked, and cogently, by the editor of *Wisden* in his 'Notes' in the 1919 issue pointing out that it would lead to high scoring (oddly enough it did not), that it would kill slow bowling (and that has certainly been true) and that they would practically destroy fine outfielding as the ball would reach the boundary too quickly for the ordinary mortal to reach it (again proved true). It is strange that he did not realize it would also have a deadening effect on the game, for with boundaries scored more easily, it is easy to knock up a relatively high total with relatively little action. It is a simple argument: four runs an over sounds a lot (and should indeed mean nearly 500 runs in a day) but if it is by way of one boundary an over it can be very dull: but if it were by way of four singles, two two's, or even a four all run, there is action and excitement and a crowd tingles.

11

BETWEEN THE WARS

(i) At Home

The First World War ended in time for Australia to organize non-competitive inter-State games, and for New Zealand to organize the Plunket Shield (then still on a challenge basis). The rush to play cricket again exhibited well the yearning to get back to 'normal'. Yet for some extraordinary reason, 'normalcy' in England meant, in first-class cricket, at least, something quite abnormal – two-day inter-county cricket playing very long hours. It is difficult to find out just what were the overwhelming arguments in favour of this experiment: those against it triumphed in the end and are public knowledge but there must have been some good reasons in favour of it. At least so one would suppose, but it is possible the whole thing was one more of those strange compromises: some counties thinking they could not sustain a full 1914–type programme, and others quite sure they could, and someone having the 'bright' idea that if they played two-day games all would be well, and all would be happy. At any rate the majority in favour of it before 1919 was as heavy as that against it after the season was over. The experiment failed, and everyone was happy when matches reverted to three days in 1920. But that the experiment failed was due more to its circumstances than anything else. The hours were no doubt long, and made to seem longer in the then chaotic conditions of rail travel, with as many as three matches a week, going overnight between venues twice, and with only Sunday for a rest. There was nothing inherently wrong with two-day matches of long hours: that is what all minor county and most good class club cricket was when it was not just Saturday afternoon cricket, and there has never been any problem about getting results.[1]

[1] To paraphrase C. Northcote Parkinson, 'cricket expands to fill whatever time is allotted to it'.

There was all the same this intense desire to get back to normal, and cricket was resurrected as it had been in 1914. Only two men who had played for England v. Australia were killed – Colin Blythe and K. L. Hutchings – but they had finished with Test cricket, so, superficially, cricket in England had suffered little. But there were substantial losses amongst those who had already done enough to show they were likely to be candidates for an England place: Booth, Jeeves, Alec Johnston, Jaques, Jennings, G. B. Davies, Chester (through losing his right hand), let alone others such as John Howell, A. D. Denton, G. W. E. Whitehead who had not done anything of note in first-class cricket but were known to be good. Of course some would never have fulfilled their promise: but others would have. And there was a serious effect on players who were about to enter the first-class game in 1914 and lost four years before they could consolidate their game: it must have been a terrible handicap to such as Herbert Sutcliffe and others like him.

That first season was very much 1914 again. The clubs, too, got back on their feet – or tried to. So did social life generally – or tried to. That was the hall-mark of the inter-war period: the attempt to behave as in pre-war days, and that necessitated first and foremost a stable currency, not the inflation that had affected prices so much in 1919 and 1921. The stabilizing of the currency meant deflation, and a stagnant economy, and unemployment of proportions never experienced in England and hardly ever over long periods in any other country before. It was, however, the background to cricket in England in all those years: it explained why amateur cricket was often so good, why the standard of professionals attained so high a level, why so many played to ages far beyond those now encountered amongst paid players. Country-house cricket continued but *not* as before the war: different hosts, different and fewer grounds, but no less sumptuous than before 1914: labour was, after a brief period, cheap and plentiful, and for those with money, life was easy, if no longer quite as easy as before 1914. Club cricket experienced some vicissitudes: during much of the period, and especially the first half of it, there were endless threats to grounds by speculative builders, and speculative landlords too, and many grounds were lost, and with them the clubs which had played there. But as London doubled in extent, fresh clubs were organized farther out, and the balance was just about maintained. Quite early in the period, Sunday cricket started to be played and there was lots of it by 1926: but there was some intolerance of it in some quarters, of a nature hardly to be imagined now when every kind of competitive cricket, including Test matches, is played on Sundays. This led to some clubs disguising their teams under other names, while others shut their eyes to what was going on. It

is interesting that Denis Compton first came to notice as a youthful and fantastically successful member of one of these 'semi-clandestine' Sunday teams. Apart
from the Butterflies, the great wandering clubs held aloof from Sunday cricket
till after the Second World War.

There was no real lack of money in the game: pay was good, relatively to other
trades (three times the annual wage of an unskilled labourer, from the best
counties) for the professional, there was no thought of television except at the
end, as a rich man's toy, no motocracy, nothing to compete with the game as a
summer attraction. Even unemployment helped to increase the crowds: you
could get a seat in the sun for a shilling a day, you could find your beer and
sandwiches at something less than the over-priced products now to be found in
most big grounds, or you could bring your own – and if you went to Lord's you
could, after 1925, even find free covered seats. It is too often forgotten that many
of the big pre-1939 crowds were from the unemployed: some of them hopeless
for work and regular attenders at the only thing which gave them joy. Their
shillings (half price after tea) helped to swell the counties' revenues and there
was little need to appeal for members: indeed members had to overcome several
hurdles before they could get in. Of course there were always some weaker
counties in the Midlands or in the south which could never attract crowds,
either because the crowds were not there, or because of their own play, and who
continued to run into trouble: more than one county was within measurable distance of being wound-up between the wars, and more than one depended just a
little too much on wealthy patrons to become properly independent. There is no
doubt that up to half a dozen counties should have been got rid of at that time,
to the greater eventual good of cricket in this country – but the rural population
of England was still large even if unemployed or underemployed, and rural
gentry were still numerous, not having taken in the full implications of the pre-
war land taxation: and rural pride preserved these teams so that they are all still
with us, and now hardly a one with more than two or three cricketers born
within their borders. But it could only have been done by some of the stronger
counties saying they were no longer going to offer fixtures to those tottering on
the brink of bankruptcy.

More and more first-class matches were played as the years went by, eventually
achieving a seasonal total well beyond anything the majority of pre-1914 players
would have thought reasonable. This can be readily shown. Though one unfortunate individual played seventy-five innings in 1895 (the record) that was
the first time sixty innings in a season was attained, and it was attained by from
one to four batsmen in a season from then until 1913 except in 1897–9, and 1908.

But in 1961 no fewer than thirty-five batsmen had sixty innings or more. And that total is only one less than all the batsmen who had *forty* innings in 1903. Before the First World War, to have *sixty* innings was a penalty paid by a few players at the top, and you would not fill two cricket teams with those who had *fifty* innings until 1923. And then the figure really starts rising. In that same 1961 that saw thirty-five players with sixty innings or more, fifty-seven others had fifty to fifty-nine innings. Nor does this take any account of the many Sunday matches played till 1968 for someone's benefit, and now for the Sunday league: no wonder players have been getting stale. It is no longer cricket: it is slave-driving, and there is no wonder that players do not enjoy it any more. It is important to realize what the effect of this really was on the first-class cricketer. For the vast majority, it meant playing first-class cricket, some of it Test or representative cricket, on every day from the beginning of May to the end of August and for some time beyond. It is something a few top-class players can do, and have always been able to do, though they have always needed to recuperate (some of the pre-1914 Australian teams went through a season with only one or two reserve players) and before the last war they were generally able to do so during the winter – because, generally, there was not an overseas tour every winter as there is now and, more important, only the tour to Australia demanded the very best: tours to the other countries consisted of teams never better than an England 'A' Eleven and sometimes not better than an England Second Eleven. Before 1914 – well before – the top-class player had also played every day of the season: but he had *not* played in first-class matches, or anything like first-class matches, every day. He had interspersed his county games against local fifteens, or eighteens or twenty-twos: or he had played for some wealthy patron in what were essentially holiday games where he could try himself out and if he had recently been making mistakes, seek to cure them. By the end of the 1930s there was no such opportunity for any player, top-class or otherwise. Top-class players suffered: mediocre players very much more, and the occasional sparkle they had shown tended to become a very small spark indeed. It was at this time that the seeds were sown of the modern boring game: it was at this time that swerve bowling commenced to take up so much of the day's play, though its proportion seems, in retrospect, small compared with what is now to be seen. And all this was in the name of finance!

It was argued by some counties, that since they had to pay players for a full season, then they might as well employ them for a full season: and since, on the whole, each additional match tended to show a profit, even if small, over its expenses, each additional match helped the county's balance. These were the days of the unpaid secretary in many counties still, and of county committees consisting predominantly of country gentlemen and landlords: if the former were much better in their approach to the game than the modern paid secretary, the committees tended to look upon the professional cricketers as their own labourers, as though on their own estates – sometimes benevolent (for the most part benevolent) but sometimes with a degree of inhumanity that is unbelievable nowadays (the Sussex treatment of the celebrated Maurice Tate is an infamous example of this – sacked in the last month of the season without prior warning) but whether good or bad, it was the master–servant relationship, and it was only mitigated by a strong captain. Since the captain was still an amateur of more or less the same origins as the committee, there was only some mitigation when the situation was not made worse by the very background of the captain. On the whole a private soldier could claim to better treatment as a human being in a good regiment than the average professional cricketer: but the latter was not subject to blind discipline, and was well paid, so he stuck it, and even encouraged others to go into the game.

Two of the really great players arose between the wars – W. R. Hammond, one of England's greatest batsmen and a fine all-rounder and second only to Bradman. There also arose one of the finest bowlers ever seen, Harold Larwood, whose speed and accuracy were later on at the bottom of the body-line controversy in 1932–3.

The ordinary clubs had been losing cricket grounds before the First World War and continued to do so after it. During the First World War there had arisen what is now known as the Club Cricket Conference: it was to be the first alliance of non-competitive clubs in the country, and it achieved great strength and influence. On one matter it showed itself to be quite remarkably reactionary: very early on in its career it had set its face, and by a unanimity of votes from its members, against competitive cricket, and it persisted in that attitude right down almost until our own time. It thus made club cricket in London and the south-east essentially the same as it had been ever since the modern period of cricket began and it did more than anything else to perpetuate the myth about cricket and its character-building qualities. To this extent it has been damaging the game: in other respects the Club Cricket Conference did nothing but good, helping clubs to retain threatened grounds, and fostering the movement to enable playing-fields to be acquired by local authorities, something now taken for granted but unheard of till the early 1920s (local authority cricket and other games had been played in park land or on common land, there being no question of the actual acquisition of ground). And in that period began the first stirrings of a social conscience amongst cricketers, when movements arose (one, like other similarly charitable movements, taking its name from Oxford) to provide the opportunity for the boy from the working-class family, from poor environments generally, to play cricket elsewhere than in a cul-de-sac or in a tiny school yard. From this was to emerge after the Second World War the Lilleshall coaching scheme: an admirable idea for that time of twenty years before, but no longer wanted when it did begin, and disastrous in its restrictive effect on boys' methods.

Cricket at the public schools tended to become more of a dogma than ever (though not so much amongst the boys): yet it was in that same period that a loosening of the dogma began to be felt, as first one school, and then another, allowed boys to play lawn tennis, and it was a sign of the times that at one famous school, a housemaster who had been an England opening bat, one day found his house could not field a cricket team in the school competition, largely because of the prowess of its rowing members (two of whom were to find themselves a little later as the presidents respectively of the O.U.B.C. and of the C.U.B.C.).

Between the wars the political and social process of female emancipation was brought many steps nearer completion. Begun before 1914 by the Suffragettes, given an enormous impetus during the First World War by the large number of women workers in factories, offices and shops (before then there were few women assistants in big departmental stores, and no women assistants in business premises), the first big step was taken when women over thirty were 'trusted' with the vote in the 1918 election. In time for the 1929 election, Stanley Baldwin gave the younger women what was derisively called 'the Flapper vote', thus providing the United Kingdom with universal adult suffrage for the first time. The process, if we are to believe our contemporary politicians, is to be consummated by all women being paid on the same terms as men by 1975. Feminism, as it was called, was still rampant in the 1920s and it was as part of this movement that the Women's Cricket Association was formed in 1926. There is no such thing as women's cricket as a separate object of study in cricket history: it is part of our social history.

There is no period when we can be certain that the allegedly weaker sex has not played the game, in child or adult form: it has done so naturally in country districts when the game was far less sophisticated – it has done so to furnish semi-bawdy amusement in and before the Age of Rakes. It has done so in its own right without publicity for nearly a hundred years now, but it was only between the two world wars that it felt any need for an organization. Legendary tales exist that Lambert had a wife or a sister who accidentally originated round-arm: a more frequent but less plausible tale is that it was one of John Willes's relations.

They make a good yarn, the woman bowling with her arm right out to avoid her skirt, but there is no reason to think this is how round-arm began: indeed round-arm had been tried in Hambledon days. Then, late in the last century, women experimented with a dark blue ball, and found it unsatisfactory. There is no special impact that has been made by women on the game, and the two incidents mentioned are slight enough. The game's popularity among women is declining now much faster even than among men: it has always been exceedingly difficult for women to keep it up once married, and those who have done so have been exceptions in many ways. Already, the English magazine *Women's Cricket* has been unable to survive, and although there is more international women's cricket than ever before, with some prospect of the West Indies being involved soon too, the long-term outlook for such cricket is poor. It is an interesting specu-lation what might happen if sexually un-segregated cricket were ever to be introduced at a serious level.

Details are given in the Appendices of the many international tours conducted by women's cricket teams and the remarkable thing is that international cricket occupies a vastly more important position in the women's game than it does in the men's. There are around one hundred women's cricket clubs in England and it has been guessed that there are some fifty thousand men's cricket clubs: there are about fifty schools where girls play cricket, but there are ten thousand in-volved in the English Schools' Cricket Association, which comprises boys' schools only. Thus English women Test cricketers are about one per cent of those women currently playing. Bearing in mind the near-impossibility of an accurate computation of male cricketers, at any one time, current Test cricketers cannot be more than one per one hundred thousand. The women's cricket effort is a highly devoted one, but essentially that of a small minority, almost indeed negli-gible but for one thing: they play cricket to enjoy it, the only good reason for playing.

In the middle 1920s the name of a sports journalist came to notice in the north of England, and later to the world. He wrote under the name of 'Cricketer' in the *Manchester Guardian*, and when he published his first collection of essays, he revealed his name as Neville Cardus (he had been known in his youth as 'our Fred' but Fred Cardus might not have been a name which would have rung down the years!) He wrote not merely very fine prose – he wrote what was rightly judged to be literature of a high order – and he was certainly the first sporting journalist to do so, and arguably only the second (E. V. Lucas being the other) to write literature on the game since Charles Cowden Clarke became Nyren's 'ghost'. He has been prolific – over the years perhaps a little too prolific – but much of what he has written will last and will recur in anthologies or will be purchased in years to come and lovingly re-read. He may, however, have done the game some harm: he inspired imitators amongst his fellow-journalists and with few exceptions, whose names will come readily to mind, they have not come up to his own best standards, and then not consistently (but then he has not been consistent either) – he has also inspired other genuine writers who have loved the game to write about it also in a literary way, amongst whom it would be right to single out Alan Ross since the Second World War. However, the effect of so many would-be Carduses is to reinforce the approach to the game as a ritual which it very definitely is not. That approach was no new one when Cardus first saw a game of cricket but his writing may well have helped to perpetuate that attitude long after it was, socially speaking, out of date. He also made the game seem something of an art: caring, it seemed, little about what happened but much about how it happened, the style in which it happened. This was all right when those playing were unconscious of the 'art' aspect of the game but it is doubtful if it has been a good thing for that aspect to have been publicized and emphasized. It may not have done too much harm to top-class cricketers, who probably never read him and his imitators anyway, but it may have done harm further down, and it may have created a kind of revulsion amongst the 'plain men' who do not want to read of an innings by Woolley as though it were a Beethoven symphony but as a part of a cricket match. His influence has been great and will remain, for good and ill, and but for the example he gave and the opportunity he thereby created, it is doubtful whether any of our better cricket writers who are now well-known would have been heard of.

(ii) Abroad

No real attempt was made to maintain contact with Philadelphian cricket after the First World War: the Incogniti sent a team in 1920 (having been refused entry by the State Department in 1919), and a team called the Philadelphian Pilgrims came over in 1921. The name was a mistake:[1] it came from the club of Philadelphian internationals, and had no other significance, but it suggested a pious visit of nostalgia, and it was treated as a holiday trip, and was so called in *Wisden*. It was not the intention at all. It is just possible that had that visit been followed up the next year by a county team, or a strong MCC team, the great Philadelphian Clubs would not have started demoting cricket in favour of lawn

---

[1] Quite recently it was most improperly adopted by a collection of minor cricketers from that area who had no connection with their fore-runners.

tennis from 1922 onwards: just possible that the game could have been kept alive at a high standard, just possible that it would have survived the Wall Street crash – well, it did that anyway, for the game was an unconscionable time dying. Haverford, the first school team of all to tour abroad, sent its last team here in 1925: though there were visits to and from Bermuda, by the time Sir Julien Cahn took his team to America in 1933, cricket in Philadelphia had so far deteriorated for that city to be no longer worth visiting. In 1929 the last issues had appeared of the *American Cricketer*, the first ever of the many cricket magazines.

In Canada the situation was rather different: there were several serious efforts at keeping the game going, and maintaining it at a high standard, two or three important tours to this country, two or three in return, with colts or schoolboys' teams also being involved. There was even a really first-rate magazine started in Montreal in 1933, but it did not even have a handful of issues. Cricket had never been qualitatively so strong in Canada as in and around Philadelphia, but it did not lose such quality as it had, and it may not have lost in quantity during the period. Provincial matches continued to be played in the west, and Ontario continued to play Quebec, and so long as there was anyone to play, and any cricket worth playing in the U.S.A., teams would wander south as well. Canada too started entertaining Bermuda. Canada could still hope, as the Second World War began, to see a better cricket future: only a born optimist could hope for that in America.

Yet, it was those two countries that saw Bradman in 1932: Bradman, who was never seen in New Zealand or in South Africa, or in the West Indies, took part, with several other leading Australian players, in a long and exhaustive tour of both countries led by Arthur Mailey: and it was Bradman who established the Canadian individual record. It was the last tour in North America by an Australian side which could have been ranked first-class if it had played any matches against first-class opposition: as it was, it scythed down such opposition as it encountered, losing, inevitably, the odd game in such a long tour. It could well have been this long and tiring tour which to some extent exhausted Bradman when it came to the famous 1932–3 tour of Australia by Jardine's men.

As one country loses prestige, so others gained it. The counterpoise here was the West Indies. Just before the First World War the West Indies had shown what they could do at home to a not quite good enough MCC team – to two such teams indeed: and then came the 1923 tour, made famous by the Scarborough match in which a virtual England side was set 28 to win, and lost 6 wickets in doing so, and should have lost another (when the rest might well have gone too) to the bowling of G. John and G. Francis. This led on to the MCC tour of

1925–6 to the West Indies, and to the granting of Test match status to the West Indies in 1928, when the tourists did not come quite up to expectation.

Nevertheless, this was when the West Indies established their international reputation. The 1929–30 MCC tour did nothing to detract from it, for if E. Hendren could have a fantastically successful batting tour, and if England could pile up the total of 849 in the fourth and last Test, the West Indies could reply, thanks to George Headley, in such style as to suggest that they might have won had time permitted. George Headley was often known as the 'black Bradman': he was a much more interesting player to watch than Bradman, and of course – and therefore – more fallible, but he made some wonderful scores. The following season, the West Indies in their first Test tour to Australia (in many respects something of a disaster from a playing point of view) nevertheless managed to win one of the five Tests played, and won it on merit. Cricket had long been the national game of the West Indies and the West Indian Cricket Board of Control was the first 'national and all West Indian' representative body in any walk of life: the game was then (and still is) haphazardly organized, but it was played in quantity in almost every island then under British rule (excluding always the Bahamas where the game exists but never seems to have caught on), as well as in British Guiana (though not in British Honduras). Those who nowadays visit the West Indian territories come back amazed at the game's popularity: they would have been more amazed, perhaps between the wars when the game was very much more popular in Jamaica (and even in the other territories) than it is now. But they would also have found that there was still very much of a 'white-ocracy' in the running of cricket, even if the black professional was at last recognized for his worth as a cricketer. On the other hand they would have found a flourishing annual on all sports in Trinidad, which appeared in most years between the wars, and which gave much space to cricket.

South American cricket was relatively much stronger between the wars than it had ever been before, or has been since. Three tours, one by the MCC, were rated first-class, and a combined South American team came here in 1932 and played a short programme of first-class matches. There was a larger, and probably a more leisured, British colony in Brazil and Chile in those days, and the expropriation of British-owned property in the Argentine was not even written on the walls in those days; the three countries played each other at a first-class level, and the domestic competitions in all the Argentine were of a good standard. At one time the possibility seemed to exist that we would one day see Test matches against South America, but that possibility faded after the last war. The cricket played between the wars was up to the best amateur club cricket in England: and

45–52. Some frames from a 'thumb-flicker' demonstrating Bradman pulling the ball to leg, one of his favourite strokes, of which he was a master

54. W. R. Hammond's leg glance, the stroke made famous years before by Ranji

53. Don Bradman's parents at their country home: the character of the cricketer can be well seen in his parents

that meant a high standard, fed the whole time by the English schools and clubs out there.

In the Pacific, there is little to be gleaned of cricket in the islands: the Fijian spurt before the First World War seemed to have petered out, and such cricket as was played was either at a club cricket level, or of the local variety. But in New Zealand the matter was different: if Arthur Sims's Australians had mopped up New Zealand in the last season before the First World War, displaying to them Victor Trumper in so doing, his tour had been a powerful influence on the game. After the First World War there was at first a lot of touring between Australia and New Zealand – two Australian teams in 1920-1 and 1927-8 (the last of any kind from Australia till after the Second World War), a New South Wales team, a Victorian team, and a strong Melbourne C.C. team. There had also been MacLaren's MCC team of 1922-3. It is likely that when the first New Zealand team to visit England came in 1927, it came two or three years later than the peak of New Zealand cricket of that time: granted no Tests, it played extraordinarily well, and played bright cricket into the bargain, contrasting with the rather dour cricket against Australia the summer before. This led to a series of Tests in New Zealand in 1929-30, and the first series in England in 1931. It led also to the 'poaching' by English counties of a number of leading New Zealand cricketers such as R. C. Blunt, C. C. Dacre, W. E. Merritt (all world-class players), who were a great loss to the game out there. Domestically, there had been little change in New Zealand cricket from before the First World War. The eight-ball over had been generally adopted (and then abandoned, and then re-adopted once more)[1] just after the war: district cricket, found unsuccessful, was for the most part abandoned, though it lingered on in one or two centres.

The Plunket Shield became competitive instead of on a challenge basis (though the Hawke Cup remained on the challenge basis to which it had reverted just before the war) and was, to start with, on a play-to-a-finish basis, though it came on to a three-day basis later on. The national competition among New Zealand schools continued but much later on it fell into abeyance since only one school seemed able to win! There was a first-class history of the game produced, in two volumes. There was obviously a great deal of interest in the game, but there was not so much money available for it: the 1927 tour resulted in a substantial loss, to its backers (it was financed by an *ad hoc* limited company – an interesting development that might have been tried elsewhere, and might indeed still be tried elsewhere: one way of circumventing restrictions on money transfers, for example).

[1] They kept it till after the Second World War, then dropped it, and in 1968 adopted it again.

It is, however, in Australia that we find the most significant events, and the most significant personality, in cricket between the wars, possibly in cricket since the First World War generally. He is, of course, Sir Donald Bradman.

Australia would have been powerful in 1912 but for the 'great Australian row' of that year: a reunited Australia, and an Australia reinforced by new discoveries from the Australian Imperial Forces teams which toured England in 1919, became as powerful again in 1920–1, against a badly chosen and moderately led MCC team. It murdered our Test teams in 1921, chosen with even more apparent lack of consecutive thought than usual (doubtless the selectors were handicapped badly by the illness of J. B. Hobbs). In Australia, the Sheffield Shield was still a competition between three States, each match of unlimited duration, and since of unlimited duration, played on wickets to last: and since wickets to last, therefore batsmen's paradises.

Here is an example of what happened on one such paradise, although the game was over inside four days. It is quoted not because it is the world record score without any qualification but because of the manner in which it was made. The season of 1926–7 was the first season in which Queensland took part in the Sheffield Shield: and, for that same reason, was the last in which matches were played to a finish. The idea exists – has a firm and even ineradicable grip, one might say, on the modern mind – that all such matches were dreary and lengthy. The truth is the opposite: the notional time allotted to a 'play-to-a-finish' match was four days and the modern mind would be astonished if it were to tabulate these matches and find how many were finished in that time, and even in three days. Not many went beyond four days, and comparatively few into six. Beyond six was very much the exception even in Test matches. Victoria *v.* New South Wales at Christmas 1926 followed the normal pattern. The teams taking part were about at their full strength at that time: New South Wales lacked Macartney, ill, then at the end of his career anyway, and H. C. Steele who had been showing good form as a bat. Macartney was, of course, an all-rounder, and therefore a more than useful bowler: otherwise New South Wales had its full bowling strength of that season. Victoria might have been slightly below her full batting strength, without K. Rigg for instance, who was admittedly to show his skill as a batsman in years to come.

On Christmas Eve, on a perfect pitch, New South Wales toiled to 221, Victoria using six bowlers and took all day to do it. On Boxing Day, Victoria made 573 for 1 wicket (that of Woodfull out for 133 with the total at 375 made in four hours. *Made in four hours.*) And when Woodfull had gone, Hendry joined Ponsford and together they added another 198 unbroken in just under a hundred minutes. It is nowadays taken more or less for granted that some Australian bats-man or other will make a double-century in an Australian season: indeed that someone will make two, or even more: but until Ponsford attained 200 on that day, no one had ever before made two double-centuries in an Australian season. The actual play that Boxing Day lasted five hours twenty-two minutes: in his 334 Ponsford hit 36 fours – it is very difficult indeed to hit a six on the Melbourne ground – and Woodfull and Hendry hit another 12. In other words, over 360 runs were run out (and probably quite a number of unnecessary runs were made before the ball reached the boundary): this was no game of 'boundary', but a game of fast-scoring cricket, and made in half an hour less that the usual period of play found in this country. New South Wales made what turned out to be a disastrous mistake in that Woodfull should have been easily run out when he was 10! Next day a big crowd turned up to watch Ponsford beat Clem Hill's record of 365 in the Sheffield Shield: that feat was to be achieved by him the following season when he became the only batsman in any class of cricket to make over 400 twice in his career, but he fell some runs short on this occasion. The crowd saw something else instead. Ponsford was out with the total at 594 and his score 352. Hendry followed 20 runs later having just completed his century. Ryder had come in on Ponsford's dismissal, and was now joined by Love, who made 6 out of 17 before being stumped by Ratcliffe off Mailey, and Love was followed by King who suffered the same fate when he had made 7 out of 26 more. Those figures tell a tale also: for Ryder was hitting. Ryder's was a sensational innings – a far greater one than Ponsford's. Ponsford had been in almost six hours for his runs: Ryder hit 295 in 245 minutes, and he managed to score six sixes, and thirty-three fours. Ryder used the now old-fashioned long-handled grip. Again New South Wales had bad luck: Ratcliffe who had helped Mailey to 2 wickets in the 600s (he had caught Woodfull to give Mailey his first wicket) saw the ball pop out of his gloves when Ryder was yards down the pitch, deceived by Mailey's flight, when Ryder had scored 135, and the total was not yet 800. With Hartkopf who made 61, and then Liddicut who made 36, and finally Ellis, Ryder took the score past the thousand, and eventually to 1,043 before he was out. He had taken 115 minutes to make his first hundred, but only thirty-two more minutes to reach another 50 and his score of just under 300 was made in just over four hours. All this is supposedly dreary play-to-a-finish cricket. The departure of Ryder was not the end of the innings: that went on until the total was 1,107, made in ten hours thirty-three minutes, the fastest sustained scoring by one team over two days that the game has ever seen (much higher aggregates have been obtained in two-day matches by both teams in minor cricket, of course, but this is the best by one team). Nothing like it had been seen before, and nothing like it has been seen since. Reports of the game praised the keenness of the New South Wales fielders: 'even after the 1,000 had been signalled the fieldsmen were running in to meet the ball, racing round the fence with the same dash and keenness as during the first hour of the innings'. Mailey had the appalling analysis of 4 for 362, and had many droll comments to make about his experience, one of which was that 'it was a pity Ellis got run out at 1,107 as he was just striking a length'. New South Wales used eight bowlers: perhaps a little surprising by English standards but illustrating the Australian habit of playing the game hard and not using forlorn hopes. And the next day, their batsmen failed again, and they were all out for 230. The next time the two sides met, just a month later in Sydney New South Wales had Macartney (who took 5 for 24 in the match). Victoria were all out for 35, and the match was over in three days. It was not the only Sheffield Shield match finished in three days that season. Cricket was enjoyable in those days.

One important point should be noted about this world record: it was not made by a strong team against a weak team as have so many high scores. In terms of the match, it was the batsmen who let New South Wales down, not the bowlers.

Australia produced, of world wonders, first of all W. H. Ponsford and then D. G. Bradman. Bradman arose at the right moment, when an ageing Australian team was doing badly against a far from youthful, if youthfully led, team headed by A. P. F. Chapman in 1928–9. By the time he came here in 1930, he was already a legend. The legend was thought to be no more than that when England won the first Test: and again, when she batted on till near lunch on the second day of the second Test, many thinking that her overnight score was enough. So it might have been in a three-day Test, but this was four days: so it might have been had there been no Bradman. It was then that the quite infallible, utterly boring,[1] cricket machine was exhibited in all its inexhaustible power. Fascinating to watch the inevitable runs: but boring, because after a bit, it was obvious that they were inevitable.[2] This *was* Bradman, until 1932–3, and skipping that, until his illness after the 1934 tour here. There has never been a batsman like him, and it is to be profoundly hoped there never will be another such batsman, for per-

[1] But a marvel of interest by comparison with some of those who pass for Test batsmen now-adays.
[2] But he was hardly ever defensive: never a safety-first attitude from him. He was aggressive almost from the start of his innings. On one occasion he was not: George Geary bowled two or three maidens, but when the Don got down to his end he remarked, 'Well George, that was a nice little rest: I'd better be getting on now' – and proceeded to murder him!

fection is dangerous in any walk of life, and most of all in what is supposed to be a game to enjoy. When you get perfection set against you, you either give up, or seek means, of no matter what kind, to overthrow it. Some gave up: Australian cricketers did, on the whole, and certainly his own team-mates tended to (Australia had a marvellous Test record during Bradman's career: but study the results of the Tests if Bradman failed to make a century, when playing, in one or other innings, hardly anyone else took his place): others sought means of no matter what kind. Whether the 1932–3 leg-theory was justifiably called 'body line' is a moot point: in my view it was not since it was remarkably accurate as bowling (bowling *at* the wicket *not* the batsman, that is – statistics support this view): but it was undoubtedly hostile and intimidating, and Bradman was intimidated. Some, however, at the time argued that Larwood took his wickets with his straight balls having first 'softened up the batsman': it was not even a unanimous Australian view. Bradman was not the only Australian batsman to think that cricket of that type was hardly worth playing: but he did not get out of the game as one or two others did. On the other hand he did not face the bowling confidently; as a few others such as McCabe and Fingleton and Bill Brown at least appeared to do. After it was all over, he was still a marvellous runmaker, but the infallibility had gone, and he became to the ordinary watcher a far more interesting batsman. His career lasted for two or three years after the Second World War, reluctantly on his part, it is known: yet almost to the end he was an enormous success and pathos was felt by all who saw and read of it that his last innings at the Oval in his last Test should have been what it was. But his career figures remain staggering and unequalled over such a period – even if for much shorter periods, the activities of other batsmen can be made to compare with him. In one way, this manner of run-getting, he appears supreme, but few competent judges allow him to be equal to Victor Trumper, many would place Hobbs above him, and none would remove W.G. from the topmost pedestal of all. Which all goes to say that one must not judge a cricketer on his figures alone.

Bradman was a shy man: he hated the adulation that his fame brought him, and it led him to great unhappiness, with his family having to go on holiday without him for fear of the crowds. Nor could he 'unwind' in an important match in the evening, and envied those many others who could. He by no means stayed as long as he might have done when batting, and would get out deliberately when he thought enough runs had been made for his side (he ran out of partners when he made his own record of 452* an innings which, it has been computed, might well have gone to well over 600 had he not). And when he did this

189

he would ask the wicket-keeper[1] who was the most deserving fielder – or bowler, and manœuvre accordingly. He was and is a great student of the game and of its history – one of the few really great players who has been, and he is thus admirable as a cricket administrator nowadays on the Australian Board of control. But he never forgets his body-line experience and he let England have a taste of intimidatory bowling after the war – not of course bodyline or anything like it. It was not the best way to encourage good cricket relations between the two countries. He is also stubborn; he would not accept that there was much more than prejudice involved in the great outcry over Australian 'chuckers' in 1958–9 and it took all Harry Altham's powers of friendly persuasion to make him agree even to look at some films: once he had seen them, he was a total convert, and to him more than anyone else in the world, do we owe the stamping out of throwing in Australia in our own time. He was one of the few really great cricketers the game has seen.

The Australian scene generally had already become highly organized domestically before the First World War: that organization was but reinforced during the early 1920s, and the administration of the game hardly differs now from what it was forty years ago, or even more. Closely-knit leagues in each city playing 'district' or 'electorate' cricket (everywhere save in Perth; that came after the last war); competitions for schools, some of which played in the lower division of the competitive leagues (they are hardly ever called leagues in Australia, and the term is only used as 'shorthand'); many other competitions for clubs less interested in sheer point-gathering but more in a happy game. The Sheffield Shield was enlarged by the admission of Queensland in 1926–7, and this meant the cessation of play-to-a-finish matches the following season in that competition, and Western Australia started playing the eastern States in earnest. There was much talk of a second division to the Sheffield Shield with Western Australia and Tasmania in that division playing the second elevens of the other States. It used to be argued that those matches could not then be first-class: but recently in South Africa both Transvaal and Natal field second elevens in the Currie Cup without question as to their status. There also arose an Australian cricket magazine, consciously cashing in on the Bradman legend, which lasted some four years, the longest any Australian cricket magazine has lasted. Yet towards the end of the period, and partly as a revulsion from bodyline, partly as a result of Australian lawn tennis prowess, interest in the game seems to have dwindled: it was perhaps good for Australian cricket that the war provided a break.

[1] From one of whom this story (and this view of Bradman) comes – but it is also told, and may well be equally true, of Trumper.

To the north, in Malaya, cricket reached a relatively high standard during this period, the peak being reached with the defeat of a strong Australian team at Kuala Lumpur by All Malaya in 1927. All the same it is arguable what the status of Malayan cricket was: it was no better than that of Hong Kong, or of Shanghai, where, in those days, the game was played predominantly by expatriate officials and business men or planters and traders. There is a general difficulty over status at this period; any one of the more powerful English clubs accustomed to playing two-day matches, and with teams composed of serving officers, former Blues or schoolmasters on holiday, was probably strong enough (save, perhaps, in bowling) to meet and beat a county. They never had such encounters, so there is no line that can be drawn: but these overseas teams in Malaya and Hong Kong and Shanghai – and in parts of India – were of that very type. The game was played by Indians, by some Chinese too, in Malaya: it was played by both in Hong Kong, and to a much lesser extent by both in Shanghai: but it was in this period for all intents and purposes a European game still.

Across the sea westwards, cricket was flourishing at all levels in Ceylon, as it had for so very many years and where, despite a discouraging amount of rainfall, it still does. The first MCC tour in Ceylon, as distinct from a visit, took place in conjunction with the first MCC tour to India under Arthur Gilligan in 1926–7. It was the first serious participation of Ceylon in international cricket, leading to the All Ceylon tour to India in 1932. Ceylon is one of the few places where inter-school cricket still arouses, and has aroused for very many years, the same enthusiasm as it once did in this country.

Three countries were admitted to the Imperial Cricket Conference in 1926 and soon after granted Test match status – New Zealand and the West Indies were two; the third was India. Cricket there had been gradually growing in strength: growing as more and more Indians took part in the game, as more and more benefited from the patronage of Indian princes. It had not ceased during the First World War, and it continued after. It had been played for very many years at leading schools in India, whether for Europeans, Anglo-Indians or Indians: it had also been played at some of the Universities. In this period, the Punjab University played each year against very strong teams of players and later on other Universities started taking part in competitive cricket against each other in the Rohinton Baria tournament founded in 1935. Competitive first-class cricket did not exist on a nation-wide basis until the latter part of the period, when the Ranji Trophy was founded in 1934–5 for competition between the various Indian provinces (as they then were) and the semi-independent Indian Princely States. There was the Bombay Tournament, on a quadrangular basis, and due to become a Pentangular in 1937. This attracted the best players from all over India: there was the Lahore tournament but it was only played in occasional years and its players were of a similar status. There was the Sind Tournament whose standard was a little below the level of those other two tournaments. There was a tournament for the Viceroy's Cup in New Delhi, but it did not attract first-class teams. There was the Moin-ud-Dowlah Gold Cup tournament in Hyderabad (Deccan) which did, but it became an occasional affair, and lapsed into insignificance at the end of the period only to be revived twenty-five years later as a first-class competition. Finally there was the Madras Presidency match between local Europeans and Indians, and there were occasional similar matches in Calcutta at the New Year.

All this provided rather incoherent first-class cricket, and gave no opportunity, or insufficient opportunity, for cricketers of the top class to meet each other, nor any opportunity for the development of powerful provincial teams. The general incoherence of that state of Indian cricket can well be seen from the muddle over what was, and what was not considered to be first-class during the first MCC tour of India in 1926–7. The institution of the Ranji Trophy, on a knock-out basis in the first instance, and admitting only obviously strong teams (a policy since departed from to the general detriment of Indian cricket) in 1934–5 led to a change , and enabled the Indian Board of Control to come to grips with *Indian* cricket – to deal with it separately from cricket played by the British who could never, it seemed, be qualified to represent All-India. However, the selection of teams to tour England, in 1932 and 1936, was unfortunate, each being captained by Princes (the Maharajah of Porbandar and the Maharajkumar of Vizianagram) none too well known for their cricket abilities: there was little unity among the team members, and one from the 1936 tour had to be sent home early. The matter was the subject of an inquiry by a High Court Judge, but it was never properly resolved, and it was generally felt at the time by Indians, and since by most other critics, that the cricketer involved had been hardly done by. The basic trouble was the attempt at perpetuating into Indian cricket control the military-cum-feudal regime which had to all intents and purposes governed India since the Mutiny: a Prince as captain who could hardly play cricket (a very amiable man and highly knowledgeable about the game though he was), and a manager who was an officer of the Indian Army. Not a happy combination nor one likely to run a cricket team happily: and they did not. These two tours to England and the two MCC tours to India, led by Gilligan and in 1933–4 by Jardine, together with an unofficial Australian tour organized by the Maharajah of Patiala (the same who had captained the first All-India

55. The scoreboard as the players came off the field on 28 December, 1926, at a few minutes before six o'clock, Victoria having just completed the world record score in any class of cricket: the details are shown in full. Though such boards have been in use in Australia for at least seventy years, and are to be found in New Zealand and the West Indies, there is only one such in England, at Trent Bridge

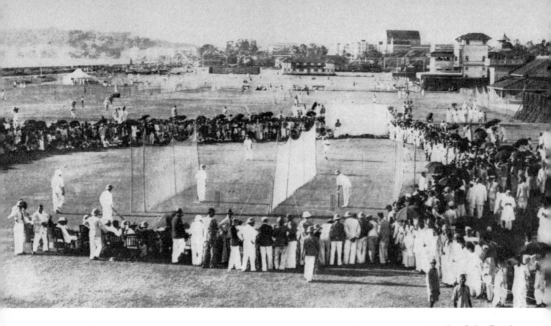

56. The Australian touring team of 1935–6 in the nets on the extensive grounds of the Parsi Gymkhana in Bombay. The Parsi Gymkhana was the first of the leading Indian cricket organizations in Bombay and though the Parsis spearheaded the path to first-class cricket by Indians, they were almost certainly not the first Indian community to play cricket

57. The Hague Cricket Club's youth team in 1944 – the date is important, because after five years of Occupation the Dutch could still dress their boys up in whites for cricket

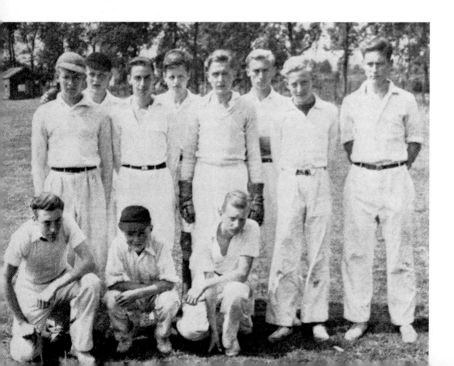

tour to England in 1911) and another led by Lord Tennyson, made up India's international cricket up to 1939 – never forgetting the constant flow of teams to and from Ceylon. It is false however in the case of Indian cricket to make 1939 any kind of a dividing line, just as indeed it was to make one of 1914. The game went on in the same way the whole time: the best dividing point for Indian cricket would obviously be 1947 when it became split between two countries. Burma during most of this period was part of the Indian Empire, and such cricket as there was there was mostly expatriate or Indian. Burmese have indeed played cricket, especially at schools, but it has never taken root there as it did throughout most of India.

The period saw the rise and fall of three distinct Indian cricket magazines, of which the last failed only owing to the war and was, as a production, one of the most distinguished to have been produced anywhere: it saw also an output of a large number of cricket annuals and other books on the game all of which pointed to its increasing popularity. The Indian Cricket Board of Control was formed as the governing body of the game in 1927, and shortly after many of the present-day provincial organizations were formed, thus providing an administrative sub-structure for the Ranji Trophy competition when it followed in 1934. Somewhat as a would-be rival to the Indian Board, there was also founded the Cricket Club of India, originally in New Delhi but it moved soon after it was formed to Bombay where it built a sumptuous cricket stadium, pavilion and club house. It was the intention to make it a kind of 'MCC' of India, and its membership list was star-studded with Princes and with leading British officials, and Indian businessmen. It aimed far higher than it could achieve, for it possessed no apparent ability to discern the future. But it has given Bombay a marvellous cricket ground, and that should be enough for it to earn some gratitude.

There was of course a great deal of impressive cricket played by British civilians and military during the period – members of the Free Foresters in India could certainly field a first-class team, and often did: there was much that was reminiscent of the more expansive Edwardian era still to be found in playing cricket in India between the wars. And the widespread provision of good cricket grounds for the benefit of British troops in India helped, of course, the development of the game amongst the Indian population.

In Africa, between the wars, there was much cricket of a good quality played by the British forces in Egypt, at Alexandria and at Cairo: hardly surprising in view of the presence of battalions of the Brigade of Guards the whole time. They attracted a number of tours from this country, notably led by H. M. Martineau (one of whose teams was the first ever cricket team to travel by air), but they in no way involved Egyptians in the play. Cricket in Egypt was thus expatriate as it positively was not in India.

Farther south, the colonization of East Africa from this country was in its early stages during this period: cricket in all three territories was played, but mainly on an 'Officials *v.* Settlers' basis, and inter-territorial cricket did not arise. But the great influx of Indians to fill the lower levels of government service and on the railways provided a basis for a considerable expansion in the game which duly came about after the Second World War. On the other side of the continent, cricket was now less popular, having given way to football: but games between Nigeria and the Gold Coast continued on a regular basis, always involving African cricketers, so that it is true to say that Africans took part in international cricket earlier in West Africa than in East Africa. There might well have been an English tour to West Africa, led by Sir Julien Cahn, had not insuperable accommodation difficulties arisen, just before the Second World War began, so that it was another thirty years before a team from England was seen on the west coast, and then in one-day games only.

Much farther south, it was at the beginning of this period that Rhodesia was divided into two distinct colonies, North and South, but until the dissolution of the Central African Federation in the early 1960s, Rhodesia at cricket comprised the whole area. Rhodesia had taken part in the Currie Cup quite early on but then lapsed and did not take part again until many more years had passed: economically it did not sustain a large enough population to make any cricket impact of importance until after the second war.

In South Africa, cricket underwent a slow and steady development, all the while along separate racial lines – not merely whites alone, but Africans, Cape Coloured, Malays, and Indians all separate, with their own separate organizations: if anyone doubts the Nationalist government's perpetual references to 'our traditional customs' he has but to look at the organization of cricket in this period, for it was only after the Second World War that the non-white cricketers all came together. But it was a South African Indian team that made the first 'non-white' tour out of South Africa to visit Mohun Bagan, the well-known football and cricket club in Calcutta, in 1922.

As to white cricket, the Currie Cup was revived after the war, and played whenever there was no touring team in South Africa, and on one or two other occasions when there was a desire to have trial matches rather than the rather unbalanced inter-provincial matches, in which one or two provinces were paramount, and one or two others always bottom. At first, as before the First World War, the Currie Cup was often played in one centre, in a massive succession of matches on a few grounds, sometimes one match being finished the same day as another began on the same ground (easy enough on matting wickets): later it came to be played on a visiting basis like similar competitions elsewhere. The older system meant less time given up by cricketers – the more usual one allows more people to watch. Although on the Rand sumptuous living had not become a fixed and certain matter – and did not really do so until after the gold price changes in the 1930s, cricket in South Africa was then, as it still is, an amateur game in the real sense of the word. But during most of the period between the wars, playing opportunity was insufficient, and was on matting wickets: turf wickets became general only just before the Second War. This all helped to keep South African cricket rather below a standard it could have attained otherwise. South African cricket generally proved attractive to onlookers in England, but did not gain so much attention during its sole tour to Australia in 1931–2 and of course Bradman never visited South Africa.

Club cricket was strong, and well organized into competitions on the Rand, where eight-ball overs were used quite early on in the period (though not generally adopted till 1938): cricket was also much encouraged in the English-type public schools, but it was not to be found in the Afrikaner schools, which, because cricket was an English game, preferred to go in for athletics – and rugger; though how they could argue that rugger was not English is difficult to understand. (The Scots however do, saying it comes from the Borders.)

And in all this period, there was no official contact between white cricketers and the others, nor any arrangements made for touring teams to play non-white teams.

Back to Europe. Cricket in Malta and Gibraltar, and in Portugal and Spain was all expatriate: so were the few matches played in European Turkey during the Allied occupation after the first war. There was much cricket played in the (first) BAOR – and the old pre-war German clubs in Berlin got going again, eventually to send a team to tour this country in 1930. But cricket has never had any real hold in Germany. In Holland it was different. The game was already well organized, and widely played, and it continued to grow in popularity, if confined largely to the west of Holland – where pro-English sentiment was chiefly found: in the east of Holland during most of the period the sentiment was pro-German. In 1931 their weekly magazine *Cricket* was founded, which continues to this day, and in 1935 came the first visit by an overseas touring team, South Africa. The game continued to look well, even if only played, or largely played, by adults in their own clubs. Very much the same thing happened in Denmark: the game continued to grow, under the administration of the Danish Ball Games Union –

only after the Second World War did a proper cricket administration get formed: and in 1930, the Danes founded a cricket magazine (called *Kricket* – but later *Cricket*), which, like the Dutch, also continues – and like the Dutch was also published during the German occupation. The game was played at a reasonable club cricket standard, but not much outside Copenhagen, and North Jutland where the game was much encouraged by Baron Rosencrantz of Skanderborg Castle (the only 'patron' of cricket known of in Europe who followed the style of such patrons in this country). It grew slowly, and grew steadily: but it did not show the popularity it has had at all comparable periods in Holland.

(iii) Conduct of the game and administration

Cricket broadly echoed social history during the period between the wars, certainly in Great Britain, and to a considerable extent overseas. This was natural: socially, most countries tried to restore the *status quo ante bellum,* sometimes dealing with abuses sometimes not: it was a period of resistance to change, as apparently threatened from Russia, and this desire to resist change reinforced the desire to get back to things as they had been.

There is thus very little to record in the running of the game during this long period. The Imperial Cricket Conference enlarged itself informally in 1926 to include three further countries: quite how this was done has never been made clear especially since there was no governing body at all for cricket in India, or the West Indies, yet the status of their delegates was unquestioned. That Conference did nothing else of note, except to discuss then and eventually approve four-day Tests in England, though the feeling amongst some observers was that it would have been better to change to five.

Legislation in the period was small beer indeed, or so it would seem at first sight, though the change to the l.b.w. Law had a long-term deleterious effect.

One that did not was made in 1927 when it was discovered that cricket balls had, apparently, for years been made smaller than they should have been, so it was decided to legalize the smaller ball and to recognize the *de facto* situation.

A change which might have had a more serious effect was the optional enlargement of the wicket in 1931, by an extra inch of height and, if enlarged, by an extra inch of width. The aim behind this was to return to the bowler some advantage that had, it was thought, been lost as a result of the much improved and more durable pitches by now being provided everywhere, in England as well as in Australia. There was a great horror of the increase in drawn matches in the county championships: a horror not apparently echoed by the cricket-watching public which wanted nothing better than to see batsmen make high scores, and since a first innings decision meant points to both sides, it was something to go for. Certainly the second innings in such cases might become redundant, but there were far fewer spectators on such a day, and in any case the rate of run-making was high – much higher than now – so that there was usually some interest on the third day. Captains had not yet learnt to destroy the meaning of the game by a so-called declaration, often contrived between them, in the second innings. They did however start contriving phoney declarations in the first innings, in rain-affected county championship matches, but the habit was severely censured by the MCC, and there were not very many instances in all: it is interesting how times have changed and that the MCC now shows no signs at all of condemning the post-war phoney declarations. These are, after all, much worse than those between the wars since they render nonsensical all the play, during the greater part of two days, that had gone before, whereas the declarations between the wars provided a much greater time in which to conclude a rain-affected match. They were praiseworthy rather than culpable.

In 1938, following permanent adoption or experiments elsewhere, it was decided to try out the eight-ball over in this country in club cricket first and in 1939 in first-class cricket: it remained in force until 1945, and there is no evidence that it was unsuccessful or disliked, but it was not persevered with after the war.

But the most important change was that in the l.b.w. Law. This Law merits a little retrospective history. Basically, it is a Law intended to deal with a specific form of obstruction: obstruction of itself was not illegal in the seventeenth century and was not made wholly illegal until 1787. In 1774 however, leg-before-wicket had been made illegal: it was probably understood to be so in many forms of cricket by that time – what is said on page 44 about the custom in 'wicket' is relevant, as is the survival of that custom in children's games generally. The first Law put the striker out if he put 'his leg before the wicket with a *design* to stop the ball': in other words the umpire had to judge intention, an always irksome and sometimes impossible task. Fourteen years later there appeared for the first time a reference to the ball having to pitch 'in a straight line to the wicket' – or between wicket and wicket as it is now worded. There seems to be no real reason for this restriction – except only as a means of relieving the umpires who no longer had to judge intention, and would otherwise have had an enormous number of possible cases to adjudicate, and it is unlikely that such a rather convoluted thought was in the minds of the then legislators. Why then did that clause come in? It is taken for granted now, though there is no reason why it should be: and perhaps the explanation of its origin may help to clear the minds of modern legislators. At the time this clause was introduced, the visiting side had the choice of where they pitched the wicket (though it had to be within thirty yards of a point chosen by the home team).[1] This obtained from 1774 to about 1811: before 1774, the side which won the toss chose the pitch. This presents an enormous advantage to bowlers, who could pitch the wicket on a suitable slope, and thus be able to bring the ball in far more sharply than any flat wicket would have done. From 1811 the pitch was to be selected by umpires, at first, and until 1823, within thirty yards of an agreed point, later anywhere (and in Law, they had this power right up to the 1947 Code when, for administrative reasons, it was taken from them. (Other examples of administrative convenience affecting the conduct of the game will be noted later on.) But no one thought to remove the now redundant clause in the 'l.b.w.' Law: in a way of course it was not entirely redundant since some grounds were heavily sloping anyway, and, among first-class grounds, Lord's slopes to this day. The fact remains that as the century wore on, grounds got flatter, slopes got less, and the need for this clause vanished. First introduced to meet a very specific possible abuse, it has remained when it has no further justification but clouds all attempts to improve the Law. In 1863, the Law would have been amended to something quite clear and reasonable, by making it again, in effect, a purely obstruction Law, but sufficient notice had not been given to the change, so the resolution in this sense was out of order. It would have removed the clause about pitching between wicket and wicket, but would also have put the striker out even if the ball had not been going to hit his wicket. It is surprising that no attempt was ever made to change the Law again in that sense. In 1888 the Cricket Council recommended a change in the Law to the MCC Committee who turned it down without stating its reason: but the amended Law was adopted in the United States, and remained the Law there until 1896 – the adoption there was in what the Americans felt to be the moral certainty that the amendment would be adopted eventually by the MCC. The amended Law removed the clause about where the ball pitched, but provided that the striker, when stopping the ball with his person, should be between wicket and wicket, and that the ball would but for his inter-position have hit the wicket. (Incidentally the same meeting of the United States Cricket Association adopted the six-ball over as 'practically all the matches in the USA had used six-ball overs for a long time past': and also made a new follow-on Law providing for a compulsory follow-up if one side scored 40% less than the other.) In 1901 things at last came to a head, and the 1888 proposal was put and carried at a

---

[1] Incidentally, would it not be rather splendid if that old Law were reintroduced for Test matches?!

special meeting of the MCC, but not by the requisite two-thirds majority: it fell short of that by some thirty-nine votes in a meeting of some 447 members. Eventually, in 1937, after two years' experiment, the present Law was introduced which puts the striker out if the ball pitches outside the line of the off-stump (as well as between wicket and wicket). It was a compromise: it has remained now for over thirty years. There is much talk of change at present, and many different suggestions but it is safe to say that all are wrong which do not set out to simplify the Law: and that any which set out to make it even more complicated are even more wrong.[1]

Body-line, or leg theory as it is better to call it, has already been referred to but the MCC also, in due course, called it direct attack. During the 1932–3 tour of Australia, the Australian Board of Control framed a local regulation designed to make body-line impossible. The regulation was not adopted by the MCC in its original wording, but in due course the MCC made its own regulation prohibiting 'the persistent and systematic bowling of fast short-pitched balls at the batsman standing clear of his wicket'. After the 1934 season, when such methods of bowling recurred (having been non-existent in 1933), the MCC took assurances from all the counties to stop it. It did then cease, but many will wonder whether they have not seen something very similar to it (like the definition of direct attack, that is) far too often since the last war.

One reflection that has to be made upon changes in the Laws in this period – and since, as well as to some extent before this period – is that far too many of them were designed to meet trouble which had occurred in first-class cricket: they did not have regard to the vast mass of cricket generally, where such troubles virtually never arose. For that reason, the vast mass of cricketers did not protest at such changes since they were not affected directly; but the principle of universally applicable changes in the Laws to meet a special situation occurring in one restricted class of cricket seems to be a bad one. It has become worse since the Second World War, for whereas before changes in Laws had to be sanctioned by two-thirds of the members of the MCC at a special general meeting (which meant very few changes indeed) nowadays they are effected by the MCC Committee through changes in, or additional 'notes' to the Laws, the pretence being that 'notes' to the Laws are not Laws. Other more substantial changes are put into force, although actually changes in the Laws themselves, on the grounds that they are temporary. *Il n'y a rien qui dure que la provisoire*, and there can be little doubt that the chief mentor of the MCC between the wars, Lord Harris,

---

[1] My comment stands in view of the 1970 experimental change which reverts to the 1935 law but re-introduces the 200-year-old matter of 'intention'.

would have disapproved strongly of present-day procedures: not that they did not occur in his time but they only occurred rarely and in exceptional circumstances, instead of every year in a number of different instances and as a habit.

There is a further reflection that can be made about cricket's importance in a much wider sphere. The West Indian Cricket Board of Control was established in 1927 – one of the first, if not the first all-West-Indian authorities to be established in the West Indies. It foreshadowed eventual political unity, as it had done elsewhere, but in the case of the West Indies that unity did not come until the 1950s. This was much too late, as events turned out and the Federation did not last. But the concept of West Indian unity continues to exist: West Indians think of themselves as West Indians, and they only think of themselves as Jamaicans, or Antiguans, as Australians may think of themselves as Victorians or Tasmanians, or as we may think of ourselves as Yorkshiremen or men of Kent. Professional historians who fix their gaze too much on political events fail as a result to detect happenings vital to their field which occur, for instance, in the world of sport. One hears such comments as that Australian unity was not 'realized' until Gallipoli. But of course it was: it was realized when Australia beat England in the first Test ever, just short of a quarter of a century before the Commonwealth came into existence. Australians were very clear about their basic 'nationality' over half a life-time before Gallipoli and while it is certainly not true to say that international cricket was the cause of that unity, there can be not the slightest doubt that it strengthened the feeling of unity immeasurably. Exactly the same can be said about the white population of South Africa – the national cricket governing body was in existence some twenty years before Union came, the first official Tests were played three years before that event, the first unofficial ones five years before, and for another fifteen or so years earlier more or less representative unofficial South African sides had played English and Australian teams, and toured. Everyone is aware of the economic reasons, and the purported political reasons, for the uniting of the Australian, and of the South African colonies but an historian who ignores these important sporting events does so at the peril of being unaware of the sociological groundswell which made the economically desirable unity, politically possible. It may well be that the future in the West Indies is a Caribbean unity not confined to the former British islands but it will be the sense of common interest that those islands have, not just because they were once British, but because they played cricket, and other games, together, that will help to strengthen that much larger unity.

58. Denis Compton, showing his famous 'sweep'

59. After their tour to New Zealand, in 1948, the Fijian team played a match against the rest on their return to Suva: here they are going on to the field in their traditional dress and in their usual single file

60. Indian boys playing in a Calcutta street in 1969. Compare plate 24b

61. A recent photograph of cricket being played on the Maidan in Calcutta on a relatively quiet day: on a really busy day it would not be possible to distinguish individual games. The area shown is barely a tenth of the total available

12

THE SECOND WORLD WAR

Quite unlike the First World War, the Second tended to encourage cricket rather than the reverse. There were many different reasons for this.

In Holland and Denmark cricket is, or is usually thought to be, a peculiarly English game, and playing cricket under the German occupation was an extremely good way of showing defiance to the Germans. The game went on in Holland, after a brief hiatus at the start of the 1940 season, right the way through, organized on a fully competitive basis, and with the official Dutch cricket magazine continuing throughout: until liberation in 1945. Then competitive cricket was abandoned, and hundreds of matches were played instead against the many British units who had helped to free the country. As for the magazine, that had had to change its name from *Cricket* at the behest of the Germans in 1943, but when the Dutch Cricket Association pointed out that they used it for their 'Official Communications', they were allowed to bring it forth instead under that title: its contents needless to say hardly varied. An interesting tale is also told of how the game was enabled to continue after the German occupation: maintaining bats, or even making some kind of bat, was not difficult, but balls were quite a different problem: what did they do? The answer was that two wise men toured the entire country buying up hockey balls, and then painted them red. The magazine almost ground to a halt at the time of the Liberation, since paper, in satisfactory supply until then, became almost non-existent. Damage was done to very few grounds and for the most part consisted of embedding large stakes to prevent gliders from landing: as the wickets were matting anyway, no lasting damage was caused. And since not only men's cricket had been kept going, but boys' also[1], the game came through the war well.

[1] Plate 57 shows the Hague Cricket Club youth team in 1944.

In Denmark conditions were very similar with the small difference that since the country's internal administration was left more or less intact, there was no trouble over the Danish magazine: and it, and the Dutch magazine, both now called *Cricket*, are the second and third oldest such periodicals in the world.

The very widespread dispersion of British forces, on a scale never before known in history, helped the game also, wherever they went (even if with no lasting effect), and also helped it to retain its popularity with them, helped them in fact to visualize themselves as the peace-loving civilians that, at heart, they remained. Canada is an example of cricket being played on a scale, if not, maybe, of a quality, not before encountered, and many places in the United States which had never heard of the game found it being played: some fillip was given to its members in Philadelphia too.

The West Indies knew no break to their cricket: the Inter-colonial Tournament was interrupted, never to be resumed, but first-class matches of a high order and often with wonderful feats of record-breaking, took place throughout the war, and of course club and school cricket never ceased. In South Africa and Rhodesia, though first-class competitive cricket came to an end during the war, the presence of RAF trainees helped to make up for the absence of many famous South African cricketers in the East African and Middle Eastern Theatres of the war.

The Middle East, indeed, saw the largest concentration of British personnel by far, outside the United Kingdom, until 1944, and they were by no means all British: besides South Africans, there were Australians, New Zealanders, Indians (though no well-known cricketer among them) and many others. The leading cricketers somehow managed to gravitate to Cairo and were to be seen almost any Sunday in the summer playing at the Gezira Club in one-day matches of virtually Test match standard in terms of those taking part: and the troops in their thousands watched, around the tree-lined turf-covered ground.

Beyond, in India neither divided nor even at that time expecting such a fate, cricket never ceased at any level: the Ranji Trophy went on without interruption, so even did local international tours with Ceylon (where conditions were very similar). The entry of the Japanese into the war, and into the Indian Ocean caused some interruption locally (the word is comparative for, in a country the size of India, locally would involve millions rather than thousands): and later with the build-up of British, Indian and allied forces for the South-East Asia campaigns, there came many famous cricketers from England, too, the most notable being Denis Compton: he and others were able to entertain thousands, British troops and Indian public, at Bombay and elsewhere. Farther south, in Malaya, the Japanese interrupted cricket, but it revived as soon as their occupation was over, just as it did in Hong Kong, and just as it did for a brief moment before flickering out, probably forever, in Shanghai.

Cricket in Australia and New Zealand went on much as it had in the first war, competitive first-class cricket being played in both countries in 1939–40; after that Australia had one season more of first-class matches, until 1945–6, though New Zealand was able to play some major matches each season. Australian troops were committed not only to the Middle East and Malaya but also very much to New Guinea and the north of their own country: there was much dislocation of all grades of club cricket, and nothing like that situation had been encountered in the first war. New Zealand's troops, when not in the Middle East, were largely concentrated at home or in island dependencies, and there was much opportunity for good class Forces' cricket, as there was in the United Kingdom.

The start of the Second World War had been slow: there was much talk of business as usual, there was little attempt at vast recruiting drives, for the automatic machinery of conscription took men in as fast as the Forces and their equipment could absorb them: thus when the appalling events of the early summer of 1940 hit Britain, they hit a country still by no means mobilized for war. That summer was a curious mixture of very very hard work indeed by a great many people, no relaxation of watchfulness or combativeness by a great many more, business as usual, which meant club cricket as usual at least, for part of the summer, and the desperate need for some kind of recreation later on. Though 1940 was not typical: the remaining seasons were. It was out of the question to keep the increasingly well-armed Fortress Britain from recreation, and a wise Prime Minister made it clear that the country as a whole could not do without it, whether in uniform or out, as all were doing their bit towards the country's safety. One or two powerful scratch elevens were formed (the British Empire XI was the most notable, with some continuity of organization and existence), various of the overseas forces produced their own teams too, and several of the counties played county matches, for the most part one-day games; a few of these games were of as high a standard as any pre-war first-class matches. Club cricket[1] continued on much the same basis: not only did it provide local recreation but it coped with evacuees who needed a game, with isolated Forces' units and individuals, furnished grounds on which the game could be played by others

---

[1] Most of the great wandering clubs closed down and the few that did not only played a few matches. But these wandering clubs are no more representative of club cricket as a whole than are first-class counties.

than themselves (tragic that for reasons, it seems, of inverted snobbery, one or two well-known old club grounds such as that of the Gentlemen of Cheshire were commandeered for war purposes, and never thereafter saw turf again), and provided opponents for major Forces' units in the vicinity. The famous slogan 'Is your journey really necessary?' made tours out of the question, and cricket was more restricted geographically than it had been since the start of the railway age, for there was no petrol available for cricket teams either. The year 1944 saw the departure of so many men on the great adventure in North-western Europe; 1945 saw many of them back playing in the first first-class games for six years and attracting enormous crowds to the very attractive cricket that was being played.

It was an interesting period, and it was then that the first attempts at central cricket organization in this country were made: they did not last long, because no one seized the obvious opportunity. They arose in this way: sports goods, like almost everything else, were rationed; priorities, as between one club and another, one school and another, had to be determined: the authority recognized by the government officially to deal with all this in each county was the county cricket club. From that much good might have come in the immediate post-war years but people were far too keen to get rid of any kind of rationing to be remotely aware of the possibilities offered for the fundamental creation of a national cricket administration.

But out of all these war years, the game emerged apparently even stronger than before, and certainly this appearance was seen in all the old cricketing countries.

13

THE POST-WAR YEARS

(i) At Home

The immediate post-war years, and a few after that period too, constituted a period of delusion, in which the game's apparent popularity blinded far too many people to the signs of the social change which has so greatly affected the game at all levels in Britain. For the first few years, there were the late afternoons and evenings of the young pre-war players whom everyone wanted to see in their prime or something near it. That was one reason for the crowds: another was the reaction from being in uniform and absent for long periods abroad (Eric Linklater had a tale which exactly captured this spirit, when two young soldiers reach the Elysian Fields, and find a village green, and a cricket match in progress) – to sit in the sun and watch placidly the 'run-stealers flickering to and fro' was pleasure enough. A third reason was that it was almost the only pleasure available: it was the early 1950s before petrol rationing was abolished, and from that moment to this you can draw a straight line graph for county and other clubs correlating the decline in attendances directly with the rise in motor-car registrations. A fourth reason was that television was by no means in every household; it had been in few enough before the war, and it was a long time before TV aerials became the accepted cityscape, so that one could not sit at home if the weather was none too promising, one had to go out and chance it.

There were other factors which would militate against cricket: the once famous Beveridge plan, accepted by all parties, aimed to reduce unemployment permanently to a level somewhat above what it was in late 1968, and such a reduction from the horrors of inter-war unemployment was regarded as marvellous. But the creation and subsequent maintenance of full employment was bound to lead to a cheapening in the purchasing power of money: it had already fallen a lot since 1939, and was to decline very much further indeed as the years went by and as an inflationary, but productive, economy seemed to replace a stable, but stagnant, one. The greater spread of much better education, and especially of higher education would inevitably cramp the style of the young man who only went to Oxbridge to get his 'Blue'.

At first, the post-war years seemed like a bonanza to county treasurers and secretaries: there was no shortage of members and potential members, and it seemed quite unnecessary to raise subscriptions when there was enough money coming in from the increased membership to meet all expenses. And it did not seem terribly important to raise wages for professionals, not at first, or at any rate not by the amount that the declining purchasing power of money should have dictated. There was no repetition of the treatment given to the Kent professionals in 1920 when they had been asked what the then grossly inflated cost of living made their required annual wage bill, and on their submissions as to the amount, the club negotiated. Nor was there, of course, any sudden inflation such as took place after the First World War and soon subsided: the inflation was insidious and gradual and its effects were simply not appreciated by the relatively uninstructed and unsophisticated men who administer cricket at the top levels. Consider the wage bill of the Yorkshire Club which has for most of the last eighty years been well in advance of all other county cricket clubs in the way it has treated its professionals: it has trebled since 1955, yet the full membership fee merely moved from two guineas in 1946 to three guineas in 1958 and only in 1969 to four guineas. The Yorkshire Club is of course an exception in very many respects, not least in the amount of support which it has in the county: but there can be no doubt that little attempt at all has been made to find the revenue it needs from its members by frequent and timely increases in membership rates.

The effect of not increasing membership rates, and not therefore increasing revenue except by obtaining new members, has been to preclude county clubs from finding the finance needed to pay the players properly. Football can think in terms of a few thousand pounds a year *per player*: cricket can only think in such terms *per team*.

It is an axiom of commerce or of anything else involving money that what is wanted has to be paid for and the cricketers whom the public saw in the immediate post-war years were almost all gone by the middle 1950s. They had been well paid by the standards of the date when they first came into cricket, three times the annual wages of an unskilled labourer, against a background of unemployed never less than one and a half million. And that money excluded what they could get from Tests, tours, advertising and so on: they were relatively well paid in a world where jobs were not easy to get. They were not replaced. Those who came of age since the last war have only known full employment: and that has not only meant that a cricket talent is not a way to get a living when no other exists, but that wages fully comparable with cricketers' could be obtained in other work and games, and as time went on not merely comparable pay but very much better. It needs some intelligence to play cricket well: it needs also quick reflexes which can also find adequate reward in many other types of employment. No one of intelligence, nor even anyone possessed merely of quick reflexes will go into cricket as a career if he can get better pay elsewhere: this lesson has still not been learnt by cricket administrators. The inevitable result was mediocre recruits to the game. It has affected also the intake from the class of society which produced the amateur of bygone days: institutions of higher learning are no longer interested in the merely brawny or athletic young man – they will only take a man who will get a good degree, and nowadays getting a good degree precludes playing much first-class cricket. In order to get a good degree, the candidate for university has to have done well at school: this means good 'A' levels, and they in turn can and often do preclude days of cricket at school. And because school work precludes serious cricket, other games and sports less demanding of a boy's time have gained some popularity. Even when they have not, the boy, when grown, will hardly play much cricket however keen: he is likely to get married at an early age, well before twenty-five, often well before twenty-one, and he will have little or no time for cricket. This applies not only of course to the social class which produced the amateur, but to all elements of society: other demands, the car, the motor-cycle, the wife, the family have all led to a vastly diminished active participation in the game,[1] and nearly twenty-five years after the last war, it was possible to see commons and parks where once a great number of cricket matches were being played, sometimes even in *mid-week*, now totally deserted at *weekends*. Well-known touring clubs have found increasing trouble in getting up teams: local clubs have encountered in south-eastern England an influx of London 'commuters' who do not (whether they will or not) mix with the local cricketers, and thus further diminish interest: clubs in the northern league areas of England have lost support because of the hopelessness of playing against teams with an outstanding international professional in the opponents' sides. All over the country, in almost all grades of cricket,

[1] Football, especially, and lawn tennis as well as other games and interests, such as athletics, have encroached into the summer season or competed with cricket for attention in that season. Some of this competition is of long standing; some much more recent. And some of these sporting events show their own declining interest, though not at the same rate as cricket's.

matches are now played before a mere handful of spectators, sometimes even none at all. Forces' cricket had become a farce within ten years of the end of the war, as the five-day week led to a virtually complete efflux each weekend from units: and the effect of the five-day week has been quite the same in other walks of life: it was one thing to go and play on a Saturday afternoon when you worked all the week including Saturday morning and would have the Sunday at home anyway, but now the car can whisk you (both) away on the Friday evening.

On top of all these unforeseen consequences of the social revolution in England since the war are others created by cricket itself, or, rather by its administrators. Years after it had been needed, a central coaching establishment was set up to provide basic coaching for 'boys who would otherwise never see a cricket bat': an anachronism, but made much worse by the dreadful uniformity of it all, the dreary emphasis on defence rather than on attack, and by a kind of 'trade union' having grown up which tends to deny a coaching job to a cricketer, however talented, unless he has obtained a coaching certificate from this establishment.

The result has been a kind of cricket which is predominantly defensive, both batting and, more to the point, bowling: it is not pleasant to watch, and it is not pleasant to play and the more adventuresome type of young man who would, in former days have enjoyed a year or so in county cricket before settling down into a job will not now touch the game even at club level and would, he knows only too well, not enjoy that type of game, entirely lacking the patience or the will to let bad balls entirely alone over after over.[1] It is extremely questionable whether in England first-class cricket is 'better' than other cricket: it is certain that it is nothing like so good to watch, but it is also putting people off even attempting the more enjoyable type of game. And that game, too, is losing some of its joy as defence more and more predominates.

Nor has the game been helped since the last war by the almost religious aura still attached to it as a result of the Victorian attitude towards it which amounts to near sanctity at Lord's: it has become – except among the northern leagues – too much identified with an outmoded social division in the country, with a now powerless but still moneyed class which does not reflect the general outlook of the country in its perpetual half-strangled appeals for 'proper behaviour' and 'good form', and the rest of it. It does cricket no good to be identified with that outlook: nor is it fair that the game should have been, but it has no chance of losing this identification so long as the higher administration of the game remains in the hands of people heavily imbued with that background and those ideas.

---

[1] In 1968 two leading English Test batsmen, in together, received eleven full pitches in three overs and scored off one!

208

At various points in the course of this history the point has been made that it is not reasonable to expect all cricket everywhere to be played under precisely the same rules and regulations, not to mention Laws. It can be argued that in most other games this is possible, that, for instance if you play for Pevensey Bay Extra XV at rugger, you play under exactly the same rules as if you play for England against the All Blacks. But there is an essential difference between cricket and rugger and indeed most other games. The actual playing period is always the same in rugger (always excluding the exotic end-of-season seven-a-side game) no matter what the class of the game, within a few minutes: and the same is true for many other games. Even where there is no fixed period, as with golf, or lawn tennis, either the goal remains the same (as in golf) or the number of 'combats' is reduced (as when saying the best of three sets instead of the best of five in lawn tennis): but the actual playing conditions remain the same.

It is not so with cricket: originally a game where matches had to be played out, i.e. to a finish, it has become over the years a game where a finite period is allotted, and that period differs according to the type, or class, of match. An ordinary, comparatively low level friendly club game is got through in an afternoon (even though it is rarely taken into the second innings these days), and there is every variation up to the six-day Test. Obviously in such conditions those Laws which are directly related to the duration of the game need modification for various differing classes of cricket: hence the differing amounts needed before a follow-on can be imposed – four in all.

However, there is, or should be a world of difference between the fundamental Laws of the game, which should be unvarying at least within any given country, and what are not properly Laws at all, but are playing conditions and which should depend on the class of game. Consider three different propositions: the length of the over is the first. There never was agreement on this: only since 1900 has the length been uniform within the U.K. even (apart from the years when the eight-ball over was tried out) and different countries have had different approaches to the problem. It ought in theory to be possible to reach agreement on this as it ought to be regarded as a fundamental Law of the game. Next, consider the follow-on already referred to. In this case the amount required to enforce the follow-on should be regarded as a playing condition, and taken right out of the Laws proper (so by analogy, should the *detail* of new-ball legislation) which should merely state that the follow-on exists in certain circumstances and may be enforced by the team having the lead, leaving the amount to be defined according to the special requirement of the class of cricket involved. The third matter is the actual result of the game: there ought to be no possible scope for difference in this, yet (writing in 1969) Nottinghamshire engaged in three matches within five years in which the scores at the close were level but where, in each case, the opponents lost fewer wickets than Nottinghamshire. Before the 1947 Laws, each match would have been regarded as a tie.[1] But now, as two of these matches were played under no Laws of cricket at all, but special competitive regulations, the results for Nottinghamshire were a defeat, a draw and a victory! This was absurd: and what was wrong was that any competition regulation could *alter* a fundamental Law of cricket. The 1947 Code had said that such a result should be a draw: then it should have been a draw in each case.

There has been far too much tampering with fundamental Laws. The great Lancashire and England fast bowler Brian Statham said in his autobiography that he was not sorry to be getting out of the game before the 1969 season began as he would have had to play under five different sets of rules, and it is possible to think of five more in which he could have been involved without difficulty. Two of these sets of rules are for commercially-sponsored activities in which the basic principles of the game are openly flouted for the sole purpose of obtaining a result – a so-called result one is bound to call it in some cases – in a period which is obviously not sufficient for a result except by means of artificial contrivances. In the 1930s the MCC condemned such contrivances: now it gives them its blessing and it does so whilst pretending that it is in the best interests of the game that a wholly artificial element is brought into a small number of matches in an attempt to save from bankruptcy sixteen often ill-run and unrepresentative clubs. But it is not in the interests of the game at all that there should be so many different kinds of regulations.

It is a curious reflection that the worst regulation of those affecting Test and first-class cricket is the one concerning the tea interval. It only became formalized in this century, tea being taken on to the ground (as cold drinks are now on hot days) and consumed then and there: but now the whole affair has been surrounded by so much verbiage that it is doubtful if there is one person alive who can accurately state the full purport of the tea interval regulations. Cricket was not meant to be as complicated as this, least of all in matters which have nothing to do with the game but are purely administrative.

Yet, for all its diminishing appeal in England as a game to play or watch, cricket still manages to retain a surprising amount of interest: television has

---

[1] It is difficult to understand why, after so many years, any change was thought necessary unless for one reason only: to make the adjudication of points in competitions easier, where such competitions allowed points to be earned for a first innings lead. If that was the motive for the change, then the matter should have been dealt with by a playing regulation for the competition concerned, as had been satisfactorily done in the past.

helped this as much as it has deprived the game of crowds of spectators. It is difficult to tell what sort of an interest this really is: whether for example it is on its way to becoming something like the Derby which almost everyone is interested in even if only a fraction of the population is otherwise interested in racing. Is this indoor, somewhat bookish, interest anything which can really keep the game going? Only the next generation can answer this, but as it has been known, in its first-class dress, as a 'Varsity or public school sport, as a popular recreation, and as a spectator sport', it is either dead or dying: and all that would seem to remain of a future for it is as a minority sport, such as, for example, table tennis.

(ii) Abroad

In some ways, but only in some, the history of the game since the last war abroad has paralleled English cricket: the most important being the necessity for imitating the negative defensive cricket which has been the product of an underpaid overworked unenthusiastic group of cricketers of mediocre ability for most of the past twenty years in England. And this was true long before seven-days-a-week cricket began. In other and important respects, there has not been a parallel, because the social circumstances have been different, and in one or two cases radically different.

The fact that Germany was defeated, the fact that cricket is an English game (or is thought to be), the fact that the troops liberating both Holland and Denmark were British has all contrived to make the game there far more popular than it was. In both countries, right up to the time of the rise of Hitler (and even after in respect of a very small minority) there had been large sections of the community who admired Germany and German culture. It was often said that Dutchmen aspired to the ways and clothes of either a German junker, or of an English country gentleman: the war removed one choice entirely, and cricket has benefited accordingly: lately for the first time, there has been some possibility of the game being played in Dutch and Danish schools, on which a useful comment is to note the assiduity with which cricketers in both countries have always brought on their young, knowing that if the young idea can be captured, the game is safe. The game is, of course, as it almost always has been, a one-day affair, with only occasional representative cricket going into two days: but the standard is far from low, and it is a matter of history that Holland was able to beat the 1964 Australians, both sides playing true cricket, attacking and not attempting to put up the shutters. What Holland has once done, Denmark could well do, because there is little difference in the standards at representative level in the two countries. The game thrives and is well supported in Holland by – to the ordinary English mind – a surprisingly large output, and of good quality, of cricket literature, both in permanent form and periodical; in Denmark only the periodical is to be found.

Elsewhere in Europe the game does not really exist except amongst English expatriates, and in the British possession of Gibraltar, and Corfu. As we have seen, the game was implanted there during the British occupation of the Ionian Isles, and is still played locally, having had something of a boost in recent years from clever publicity. But it is not important from any but the curio point of view.

There was a time when in Egypt there seemed a chance that some of the inhabitants of that country would start playing the game in earnest: there was even a tour to England by Egyptian cricketers, but as they came from a pre-dominantly upper-class and pro-English environment, they were sadly hit by the social and political changes in that country. Elsewhere in what as a result of the last war is so often wrongly called the Middle East, the game was played only by British forces or civilian expatriates, and died when the one was removed or the other dwindled in numbers. Yet, in one small area, Kuwait, it was possible recently for an Australian club team to find the score of the match kept in Arabic.

In Africa generally, the development of the game was partly hindered by the departure of the British, and partly encouraged by the presence of native players and administrators anxious to show their own merit. Only later did other political events make things more difficult. In West Africa the game took several strides forward in the Gambia, in Sierra Leone, in Ghana and in Nigeria. Inter-colonial matches now became international ones: but these ceased as politics took too much out of the spirit of three of these four countries: what the future can hold can only be guessed at, but as there had hardly been the slightest sign of encouragement from Britain, as no other cricketing country of stature ever offered to tour West Africa and show, if not the flag, the bat, enthusiasm is too narrowly spread, and the outlook is not good.

In East Africa there had been a great spurt forward after, and possibly as a result of, the war. Matches were played between all three territories, and during the period there has been a number of international tours, from England, from Pakistan and from India (not to mention a coloured South African tour in which Basil d'Oliveira first showed his mettle to the outside world), and the standard exhibited was high. The game was played in many schools, and it was not only those of European and Asian origin or descent who played but Africans too.

212

Despite that, it did the game no good when very large numbers of Kenya Asians chose to leave for England or India and Pakistan, as they had formed the solid backbone of the game, just as they had of commerce and much else in Kenya. Political strife in Uganda did not help, nor the quarrel between Britain and Tanzania over the Rhodesian question. Again the outlook does not seem set fair, but there are all the same far more people devoted to the game in East Africa than on the other side of the continent, and, if the game is to die out, it may well take a long time doing so. It may even get support from a surprising quarter: in the late 1960s the former Australian wicket-keeper of between the wars, Bert Oldfield, took a team of Australian schoolboys to play in East Africa and in Ethiopia. The game was watched with favour by the Emperor, and it was later learned that an Imperial instruction had gone out laying down that cricket was to be played in future at all Ethiopian secondary schools. It will be ten or fifteen years before any outside effects will be felt from this decision, always allowing that it is being fully implemented.

Cricket was played by the settler and mining populations of Northern Rhodesia, now Zambia, and in Nyasaland, now Malawi: Zambia is a multi-racial state, and sent a multi-racial team of schoolboys to play cricket in England, but how long cricket will still be played in the schools of the country, or anywhere else, is difficult to forecast. The so-called European population will obviously go on dwindling, and so long as there is a white racialist regime in Southern Rhodesia, let alone in South Africa, it cannot seem in any way an attractive and splendid thing for Africans to play a game in which some of the nearest white men they know are unwilling to let them take part; as for example happens in South Africa, and as has begun to happen in Southern Rhodesia where school games between pupils of different racial origins are no longer encouraged. On the other hand, since many Africans play in South Africa, there may be some eventual counter-weight to attract their northern neighbours. The political troubles in Southern Rhodesia have of course been tragic from a cricket point of view: once a country had gone into rebellion, there could be no question of making a case for treating cricketers differently, even if it did mean that one of the most brilliant fielders the game had seen, Colin Bland, could no longer appear abroad, but he was, after all, a supporter of rebellion from the outset.

The future of the game in Southern Rhodesia can go one of three ways: it will either come more and more closely to resemble the situation in South Africa, if the solution to the political question favours the minority settler population, a large part of whom are, it should be noted, of Afrikaner origin. It can become confined to a dwindling settler population if the solution is along the lines favouring African government: or, if there is a genuine multi-racial development politically, then we may well see the game embracing all sections of the population there. The likelihood is of course the first.

Inter-racial cricket in South Africa has been very scarce indeed, and multi-racial, in the sense of including in one team players of no matter what origin, non-existent. But there have been contacts: even under the Nationalist Government, there have been inter-racial matches, and, despicably though South African 'white' cricketers have sometimes behaved in the past towards others not of their alleged legal hue, it seems very reasonable to suppose that Basil d'Oliveira would, had he been ten, or twenty years older, have played for South Africa.

The arrival of the Nationalist party in power was bound to occur sooner or later, for purely demographic reasons. So long as constituencies were delimited so as to give the weightage in favour of the rural districts, instead of putting the towns on an even basis, there is bound to be excess support to the Nationalist vote. It came sooner, and there are plausible grounds for believing that the arrogant manner in which the Smuts Government displaced the Wanderers Club from their long established ground – from that concession granted by President Kruger – in what had become the centre of Johannesburg, lost that government a great many votes by way of both abstentions and of a positive swing. If so, it is interesting that one of the world's political tragedies should have developed when it did because of the inept way in which a cricket ground was appropriated.

The structure of cricket organization in South Africa facilitated the carrying-out of Nationalist policy: there had been organizations for each different race, for the 'whites', for the Bantu, for the Asians, for the Coloured, for the Malays. Apartheid, as understood strictly, was intended to segregate all these different races: there was no special theory behind that desire, it was a smoke screen to cover the separation of 'white' from 'non-white' and it looked better if it purported to be a thorough-going separation. Cricket has organized itself along those lines: true, the 'governing body' – *as recognized by other countries* – did not specifically purport to be 'white' but it had no affiliations from non-white, and none of its constituent unions admitted any one or any club other than 'white': it was thus, however it attempted to muddy the issue in external discussions, a racialist and segregationalist organization, and as we have also seen, had been from the outset. The non-white organizations made haste to unite and now constitute the South African Cricket Board of Control, a non-racial (as distinct from multi-racial) body, and it represents by far the largest number of cricketers in South Africa who play in miserable and even pitiful, conditions.

214

Yet such is their fervour that more than one of these down-trodden cricketers could have represented the country as a whole and a team drawn from them would in most years since the last war have been a match for the weaker counties at least. The only time such a team has ever played outside South Africa was when one toured East Africa and played against properly mixed teams there. Cricket thrives amongst the 'non-white' population in spite of every discouragement: it is almost impossible to imagine what its progress would be if 'non-white' cricket were properly integrated and fostered – except that a majority of a representative South African team might well, in ten or fifteen years, be 'non-white'. Other cricketing countries have done little or nothing to assist these 'non-white' players: they have never been invited to England, and attempts to get teams of 'coloured' origin to visit and to play them have all failed except a tour by Kenya Asians several years ago. It is understandable that leading West Indian and other Test players should be discouraged from visiting South Africa by reason of the appalling personal indignities to which they would be subjected: it is all the same a pity that they have not, for their presence, playing top-class cricket, might have made a breach in the wall.

But for the 'whites' the picture is entirely different. The greatest possible facilities are available – all those facilities that can be commanded by an economically well-endowed class of people, able to command an abundance of cheap labour. The cricketer from boyhood up plays on a fine ground, on a turf wicket, with good coaching: he has, when he gets old enough to represent his Province, enough leisure to do so for a few years at least, or enough resources, which amounts to the same thing. It is an ideal kind of pre-1914 amateur cricket that is to be found in 'white' South Africa, and it produces a remarkable number of fine cricketers, few of whom however play in the top class for more than a few years. They know they have to earn a living and in this respect they do not resemble the pre-1914 amateur English players, so many of whom did not need to earn a serious penny all their lives. The effect of this is not only to make opportunities available the whole time to the up-and-coming young players: it ensures that the top-class players do not suffer from the boredom of continually playing modern Test matches. Indeed, this 'boredom' is much less for the 'white' South African since he will never encounter the West Indies, Pakistan or India, but even with these omissions reducing opportunities, the turnover of top-class South African cricketers has always been large and remains so, and is likely to continue so.

However, within the last fifteen to twenty years, a remarkable change has come over 'white' South African cricket: the Afrikaner who hitherto was notable on the cricket field by his almost entire absence, has begun to take part, and to do so in a very big way. The game is no longer an English, and therefore an alien institution: it is a South African game, and now that the political connection with England has been severed, the Afrikaner can play cricket with a quiet conscience. He can do more: he can read about it, to the tune of several pages in each issue of his daily paper, when a Test match is on, a coverage equalled perhaps nowhere in the world nowadays. He has even started acquiring books on the game and aspects of the game in his own language. South African politics require that so much is withheld from the daily press of what is really going on in the outside world, or even in the country itself (much of the best information on what has been described as a 'vile society' can only be derived from outside its borders) and the result is newspapers filled with sport to a remarkable degree.

All this has certainly given cricket an enormous boost in South Africa, and with the more than doubling of the 'white' population playing cricket there could well be a very considerable rise in the standard of the top level, if it has not already taken place.

Many South Africans, disturbed at the prospects of political isolation, are using every endeavour to keep the country's name prominently before the eyes of those abroad who, they think, will support their cause. The result has been a flood, compared with what happens in respect of every other country, of club teams and schoolboy teams visiting England, and in turn being invited to visit South Africa. It has all helped the expensive propaganda campaign of the South African government, but it has missed the essential point which is that the people whom they thus think to influence are themselves without effective influence in England, and in so far as they represent a racialist outlook in England, represent only a small part of the population. They are, unhappily, far too representative of cricket players and administrators. However, apart from the obvious political implications of all these tours, there can again be little doubt that they have helped to boost the standard of South African cricket, at all levels.

It is as impossible to foresee the future of South African cricket, 'white' or 'non-white' as it is to foresee the political future of the country, but there seems some possibility that the present and recent cricket 'boom' amongst 'whites' might collapse if the cricketers themselves get frustrated at their inability to play enough top-class cricket, i.e. Test matches. Such a collapse would, of course, do little more than to set the popularity of the game back to what it was some twenty years ago, when it was far from small. On the other hand, the financing of first-class cricket may become much more difficult if profits from Test tours are no longer available, and that in turn may have an adverse effect on the game

62. Children playing cricket in the West Indies in rough conditions

63. An international match at Hjørring in Denmark – note the Dannebrog flying proudly over the pavilion

64. A riot scene in the West Indies during a Test match against England. The first notable riot associated with cricket was in 1787 at Hinckley as a result of a match between Coventry and Leicester, although there was one less well authenticated eleven years earlier at Tilbury (and, if true, the most serious as it involved fatalities). Australia, U.S.A., India, Pakistan, and East Africa have all seen major disturbances at important matches during the last ninety-two years, as well as the West Indies, and in all cases in matches involving touring teams

65. Kensington Oval, Bridgetown, Barbados

at lower levels: but there is plenty of money in the country, until gold becomes effectively demonetized in the world outside: and when that happens the future may well become suddenly very gloomy for the country and its cricket.

There is however one influence capable of doing harm to the game which is lacking in South Africa, though it is uncertain if it will remain lacking, and that is television, of whose effects in other ways the Nationalist government is very afraid. Broadcasting, of which there is plenty, does the game no harm at all, rather the reverse: television keeps people away wherever it has spread.

Australia is indeed a good example of this, yet the effect has been nothing like so drastic as in England. Oddly enough, there is something of a habit of watching a game on TV on one of the weekend days, and watching the match itself (or another if there is one locally) on the other: the weather is of course not as in England, and it is unlikely that bad weather prospects combined with TV would ever keep people away because the weather is rarely doubtful in Australia: it is plain certain, one way or the other, or tends to be. But the usual other out-door influences have also been at hand, notably the motor-car, which has made it easier to get away to some rural or seaside or mountainous spot than in England.

In some respects, Australian cricket resembles South African 'white' cricket. It has a firm basis in excellent facilities at the schools, and it follows this up by highly organized competitive cricket in each city. There is one gap – a failure, reported by good schoolboy players, to catch the boy as he leaves school and take him into one of the lower grade district teams, which leads to the loss of many boys who might have gone on to play eventually for their State. Apart from that, however, the organization is excellent, or so it would at first sight seem: it is a game open to everyone, which is how a country with one-fifth of the U.K.'s population can play cricket on level terms.

There are however flaws in the Australian cricket scene. One of them is that, with the exception of Tasmania, which has not yet been admitted to the Sheffield Shield, each State team represents its capital city and nowhere else in the State. The country boy may well be in the team as a player from a district club, not as a player from, for example, Bowral. It does not seem necessary for a State team to be confined so rigidly to the capital, and one would have envisaged good players from Newcastle being able to play in their own right. This is where equality of opportunity does break down a little, because that equality is only for the city-dweller, though to be sure the city-dwellers of Australia represent an enormously high proportion of the population as a whole. There is a second, the tendency for hero-worship to pull enthusiasts – Australia wins the Davis Cup, so many flock to lawn tennis – when she stops doing so, the flow will be another way. It has always been like this in Australia, and to a certain extent cricket has learnt to live with it.

A third flaw is the altogether depressing effect that playing cricket has in vast untenanted stadiums built for the crowds expected at another kind of game, and is especially so in Melbourne, Adelaide and Perth, with Melbourne by far the worst of them. The Melbourne Cricket Ground can seat 120,000 people at an Australian Rules Football Final: it can have a quite respectable cricket crowd of ten thousand and appear empty. This does not only apply to the Melbourne Cricket Ground, it applies to several other grounds in Melbourne which have increased stand capacity for the football crowds. It applies to a lesser extent in Sydney with Rugby Football, because the Sydney Cricket Ground has not yet been turned into such a stadium. It does not help the cricketers to know that the TV cameras are bringing their doings to a crowd the size of a football crowd and indeed much larger: they are no longer people enjoying a game, they are public performers, and they need an audience, and they are getting it proportionately less in Australia even than in England. There is a fourth flaw and that is the somewhat cramping effects of District cricket, as have recently been evidenced. The original idea of District cricket was a good one, but the rather rigid boundaries combined with the expansion of the population out into suburbs beyond the effective reach of many existing District clubs does not assist the encouragement of the game. There may well be a case for abandoning District cricket now, and for allowing clubs to recruit as best they can: it would be better by far for there to be six to eight first grade clubs but all full of very keen cricketers who are even ready to travel a bit to play for them, than for twice that number of District clubs with rigid and exclusive boundaries. In Sydney there have been good attempts to redraw the boundaries, but the system is at fault, and it is that that needs revision or abandonment.

There is a fifth flaw which also arises out of District cricket. When District cricket was first thought of, there were very few Inter-colonial (as they then were) matches in a season: six between the major and Sheffield Shield States, sometimes a couple more between New South Wales and Queensland which by no means always involved the full N.S.W. strength, sometimes a couple more between Victoria and Tasmania which again by no means always involved the full Victorian strength, and an occasional game played by or in Western Australia. Only every four or five years when there was a team from England did the programme fill up. In these circumstances, the absences of top players from District cricket were few indeed, and sometimes no District cricket was played at all during such a match in a particular city. But over the years the picture has changed: first Queensland was admitted to the Shield, and some twenty years later, Western Australia at first on a part-programme basis, later as a full member. First-class matches in the non-legal sense have more than trebled, from six to twenty, and there is rarely a season when there is not an International tour taking place. Circumstances have entirely changed but the social background has not: the top class Australian cricketer is still an amateur and few derive any other pecuniary benefit from their playing, and it is now many years, nearer half a century, since a professional cricketer was to be found in Australian cricket (if we except imports from overseas, such as Lock and Milburn and Sobers now sanctioned on a regular basis). Thus so far from the top-class Australian player taking part in almost every round of District cricket, a situation has been reached where the demands of Test matches keep him away even from his State team on many occasions, and he has little time available, in terms of the actual programme, to take part in Saturday cricket: many find that even when the programme permits, they have enough of their own work to catch up with, and some are to be found only at the very start of the season, in early October, and then not again until the very end, for the final rounds.

Thus, the ordinary club cricketer, at District first grade level (numbering well over six hundred players) is deprived of a regular opportunity of encountering the Test, or even the State stars, and often of any opportunity at all: and so is the spectator. This has undoubtedly affected gates in District cricket, and perhaps at first-class matches too: sixty years ago, a cricket enthusiast could reckon to spend almost half the Saturdays of the *year* watching Victor Trumper for little more than his tram fare to whichever ground he was playing on, whereas now he would not be certain of seeing him anything like so often if he were rich enough to pay the air fare to Perth.

The outlook for Australian cricket then is likely to be a slow and almost imperceptible decline, continuing what has been going on for the last twenty years, but at such a rate as always to put its popularity and standards well above those in England. How the gloomy forecast for English cricket, though, may rebound on Australian cricket is another imponderable. Meanwhile for many years, generations ahead, there will continue to be a fresh output of intelligent and able cricketers, much along the South African lines, rather less amateur in their approach, and staying rather longer in the game.

This slightly less amateur approach can be particularly seen in the post-war pioneering of extensive tours from Australia to Britain, and eventually round the world, of teams of cricket players. Never before the South Australian club cricketers in 1955, organized by one such cricketer C. A. Skitch, who died tragically just as a second tour was about to begin, had there been tours by other than first-class cricketers on such a scale or for such a distance, and his pioneering effort led the way to other Australian teams doing the same thing, until the idea that a major tour could only be carried out by a team of first-class players (an idea that perhaps arose during the inter-war depression, when the substantial tours by teams from North American clubs and schools ceased) has been finally exploded. It was Australia more than any other country which made it plain to a cricketer that, if he could pay his way, he could go on a cricket tour anywhere, provided only that he had some ability.

The outward face of New Zealand cricket is so similar to that of Australia, the reality so different. Cricket, of course, has never been a national game in New Zealand, merely a rather grudged summer game, an interlude in playing and preparing for rugger. Unlike most other countries where it is played, Rugby League in New Zealand is not purely a professional game, but it is severely secondary to Rugby Union in popularity, a game which is by definition amateur but taken so seriously in New Zealand as to have some of the aspects of a wholly professional game. There has never been, as a result, money sufficient to put cricket on to the same level as it is or has been in other countries, and there is probably relatively less now. New Zealand cricket teams, of Test status and lower, right down to *ad hoc* club teams, and including of course both local and representative school teams, have more than taken their part in international cricket, but with diminishing success as one goes higher in the scale. Money is the problem: much more than in the far richer Australian and South African social spheres, New Zealand cricketers cannot stay long in the game at the top level, that is to say the international level, but they do stay rather longer at the Plunket Shield level, where the majority of matches are completed during the Christmas and January holiday period: and this may have the slight effect of preventing up-and-coming young cricketers. At all events, New Zealand does not produce any more the bright young stars who still come forth elsewhere in the Southern hemisphere – good young players, yes, but not stars. Money is the problem in a more important sense, for it is a country where labour is in short supply, a country more urbanized probably than Australia but with its urban population far less concentrated, and yet dependent to a dangerous extent on one type of export for its economy, dairy farming for the U.K. market. The labour shortage is evidently the reason why there have for years been complaints by visiting cricketers about the nature of the wickets in New Zealand, not merely the match wickets (that there should be complaints about *them* is quite bad enough) but about practice wickets too. It is as though the idea has grown that any bit of turf will do for a man to practice his strokes or his bowling: an absurd idea, and it would be better for matting-covered concrete wickets to be laid down notwithstanding the difference in the way they play from turf. Bad wickets provide no encouragement to the learner, nor any kind of assistance either, and the trouble goes deep.

It is not the only thing which is wrong with the set-up of New Zealand cricket. There is probably too great a diffuseness as a result of too many teams existing that are not strong: if there are only six first-class teams in Australia, it is difficult to see how as many can be justified in a country whose population is less than an Australian State, and whose entire social arrangements reflect an Australian attitude, but at a lower standard of living, and where cricket is not the idol which it has certainly been in Australia on many occasions in the past.

It has been argued well, by those who were in favour of increasing the number of first-class teams from four to six[1] that only thus would the opportunity be created for players away from the four largest cities to play first-class cricket. Before the enlargement of the Plunket Shield, in theory each of the four major associations drew from each of four areas of New Zealand, Otago having the smallest to draw on: in actual fact they rarely did so, sometimes a player from a smaller town would up sticks and move, more usually he would stay, for the prospects were never good except for a quite outstanding performer. Now he no longer has to do so, except in the very large area still available to Canterbury to draw on, and possibly in Southland and outlying parts of Otago. But the counter-argument can be put forward that it was the method of selection that was wrong, not the number of teams, and in a small country such as New Zealand, with all the increased mobility that the motor-car confers as its only benefit, it ought now to be possible to ensure proper selection as well as opportunity for playing without the player having to move his abode (after all a county captain in England not long ago lived two counties away from the side he headed). In that case, four first-class teams should more than suffice, and would almost certainly raise the standard of the game, just as in England, or in India, a reduction in the number of teams would have the same effect on first-class cricket.

Cricket in New Zealand is not a plant that can be taken for granted, and it needs encouragement of a sort it rarely gets: there have for instance been only four country-wide first-class tours since the last war, and one of those was from Fiji: the others were from the West Indies, MCC and Pakistan. This is not

---

[1] The 'major' associations of Auckland, Wellington, Canterbury and Otago were now joined by Central Districts which included all but one of the minor associations in the Wellington major association area as well as Nelson and Marlborough, and Northern Districts which included all the minor associations in the Auckland major association area.

enough to sustain spectator interest, nor to provide adequate top level match practice. The habit of adding four to six matches in New Zealand at the tail end of the season to extensive tours by teams in Australia has also done little good – and has taken much money out of the country (New Zealand has an adverse balance of payments in terms of cricket expenditure, since she not only has had to pay for tours abroad, which have brought too small a profit but also has had to furnish large, some would consider exorbitant, guarantees to teams from abroad). The weather has often been adverse, and players have had little recent first-class match practice by the time these major tourists arrive: on top of all that, it has not been unusual, especially in the case of the MCC teams though rarely with others, for 'star' players to be allowed to return home and not go on to New Zealand. A lackadaisical approach has often been equally obvious on the part of these tourists.

Australia carries a big responsibility for her attitude to New Zealand first-class cricket: the nearest cricketing country to New Zealand, she has yet allowed precisely one official Test match against New Zealand since New Zealand obtained Test status forty years ago: many Australian teams have toured New Zealand, it is true, more than is often realized, but there has been no top-class Australian side in New Zealand for over forty years, and Bradman was never seen there though he had been seen in Canada which did not play first-class cricket! There has been no kind of excuse for the Australian attitude (coincidence of seasons is obviously no reason at all, or there would never have been Australian tours to South Africa), which has shown much more than signs of pure arrogance: one example of this is the number of Australian writers and statisticians who will not accept any matches in New Zealand as first-class except those played by New Zealand representative teams. (Yet Canterbury recently beat the Australians.) At a lower level, there is a fine interchange of teams – schools, colts, and so on, in which the Emus from the country districts of New South Wales have played a big part. If New Zealand had as big a share of international cricket, played at the right time of the season, as even South Africa has (limited though hers is by politics) let alone as other countries have, there might be some chance for New Zealand cricket to look up: young men would be encouraged, older players would be, and above all spectators. One has only to look at the vast difference in touring by rugger teams, no matter which code, to realize how hardly done by cricket is, and how much better done by it could be.

Oddly enough there is no lack of sponsorship for cricket in New Zealand: but in the last resort a game needs only one sponsor – top-class international players, whether guests or locally produced. There have been only seven New

Zealand cricketers, excluding always Grimmett, who have been in that top class, since the first war: C. S. Dempster, C. C. Dacre, R. C. Blunt, W. E. Merritt, M. P. Donnelly, J. R. Reid, and B. Sutcliffe (K. C. James, a very fine wicket-keeper, might make an eighth). Only Pakistan can show fewer, but over a much shorter period.

There is a lot of cricket played elsewhere in the Pacific: local varieties such as that played in New Caledonia, or that played more widely in Samoa and other islands, as well as the accepted version. Samoan cricket can still take up the time and manpower of whole villages, and can still, as over seventy years ago, require the authorities to ban it to get any work done. The normal version is played there too, and is of a reasonable standard in terms of club cricket. But the cricketing power in the Pacific is Fiji, which has sent several teams on tour to New Zealand since the last war, resuming a pre-1914 precedent, and which have attained a high standard, and not only that, an approach to the game which in itself was always enough to draw expectant, and duly satisfied crowds. One team has been to Australia since before the first war, and beat a strong New South Wales team in a one-day match. No representative teams have toured Fiji in this period, though the opportunity to do so has been available to more than one. There is a strange kind of selfishness which seems to have hold of cricket administrations, world-wide nowadays, and it cannot be due to financial fears except if their financial ability is small, and they fail to appreciate implications. You cannot operate on a basis of all take and no give: if you only take golden eggs from a goose, and feed her not, the eggs will certainly stop coming. Elsewhere in the Pacific, there have been attempts to revive the game in Hawaii, but this belongs more properly to American cricket now than to Pacific cricket.

Turning west once more, cricket in China is dead, but not in Hong Kong, and the island colony has attracted international teams in fair number since the last war. The game there is played by all sections of the community, but the majority of players of any standard are European, Eurasian or of European education and culture. The top standard reached is good, and might, with a good representative team, equate to that of a weaker first-class county. All the same it is difficult to foresee any satisfactory future there for the game especially since the Leased Territories, very much more than half the total area of the colony, must revert to China in 1999. It is not that many years away: and other political events in Asia may alter things drastically before then.

In the Malayan peninsula the game thrives, and once again with all sections of the community taking part, but, once again, with those of a European background of education or culture and the better educated Indians predominating.

There is much competitive inter-state cricket: Singapore – an Independent State now – has its own strong team too but still no stronger than one of the better-equipped Malay States. Cricket is played in the schools, and it is popular amongst almost all the non-indigenous and Chinese population. Whether it will ever 'take' with the Malays or the Chinese generally is an open question: that the Chinese are interested is obvious to anyone who has seen the Chinese crowds around a match there. Though a question would arise in the onlooker's mind: just what were they doing, because most of them seemed to have their backs to the game? The answer is that the Chinese in those parts are quite inveterate gamblers, and have found cricket an unsurpassed medium for betting: whether a named batsman would score any runs off the fourth ball of the over, and if so how many – and so on. Just as in England football pools have perpetuated an interest in soccer which might well otherwise have dwindled, it could be that in Malaysia and Singapore, gambling will eventually cause the Chinese to take part more actively in the game.

Cricket used to be played by both Dutch and British expatriates in various centres in what is now Indonesia: with few of either left now, and with no indication at any time that the Indonesian himself was interested in the game, it must be regarded as just one more of those areas where expatriates play but no others.

The game is dead in Burma: the departure of almost all British expatriates and commercial firms, and of – the process is still continuing – Indian expatriates too combined with the lack of interest shown by Burmese in the game, all this coming on top of the havoc caused by the last war has served to kill the game for as far ahead as one can see.

It is not at all so in India, nor in the other succession State of the Indian Empire, Pakistan. The game has had a long history in India, and it continued to thrive right through the last war: nothing, not even Partition, has stopped it doing so. On any holiday, and on many other days, you can see that vast open area of Calcutta known as the *maidan* covered with hundreds of games going on simultaneously, with fielders occupying most dangerous positions having regard to the game going on behind. You can travel round in villages remote from any big town in the south of India and see little children, half naked in the heat, playing on a dusty bit of ground a game which, to your delighted astonishment, you suddenly realize is cricket, just as, *mutatis mutandis*, it might be played on a waste lot of ground in a slum area of England. It is played in many, though not all, of the many hundreds of secondary schools: there are a few towns without some kind of a cricket club, and the game is properly organized from the grass-roots up, with well-managed competitions on an All-India basis for school, as

224

66. An example of mixed cricket: South African non-whites of various origins with an East African team of various origins, including European, in Kenya in 1958. Basil d'Oliveira is third from the left, front row

67. Basil d'Oliveira

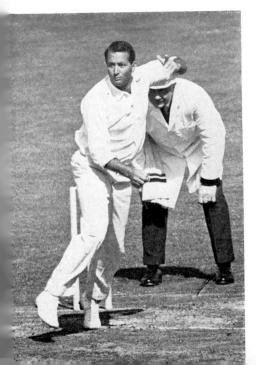

68–69. The New Wanderers ground at Kent Park in Johannesburg from the air: *below*, the demolition of the Old Wanderers ground in the middle of the city

well as university cricket. And then above that there is the Ranji Trophy played for on an Inter-State basis but with certain other teams of equivalent playing strength (Services, for example) taking part: and above that again, the Duleep Trophy in which the State teams are grouped into zones. These zonal teams are, nowadays, usually the non-Test match opposition that a touring team encounters.

Indian cricket is rich, as it always has been, in good batsmen, who learn their trade on hard unyielding wickets, but poor in bowlers of great merit, unless spinners. Yet her batting strength is not what it was when Merchant, Hazare, Modi and Umrigar were piling up quantities of runs and establishing new world records. There are reasons for this: there are few if any professional cricketers in India, other than those who were once supported by Indian princes, and can be no longer. A man has to earn his living in a country which is essentially poor, and with a quite appalling balance of payments problem. He can no more stay long in the game than his counterpart amongst amateurs elsewhere: true, a few have indulgent business firms as employers, but they do not affect the general argument. There is plenty of money in India for cricket to be derived from the very large crowds who attend matches, not always Test matches either: more still could be obtained for the capacity of big grounds is nothing like enough for those who wish to watch a Test match, yet capital funds to undertake the necessary works are lacking. It is a vicious circle.

Against that, there is far too much cricket so-called first-class in India: too many teams in the Ranji Trophy for instance who would stand no chance at all against any English county or New Zealand Plunket Shield team. The zonal teams do something to remedy this situation but there is not enough zonal cricket, and far too much Ranji Trophy cricket. The standard of cricket at the top is slipping rather than improving. What is needed is some way out of the vicious circle of accommodation: if that could be provided, starting for example with the unfinished stands at Eden Gardens, Calcutta, and continuing at other grounds which are insufficient still, then so much more money could be raised that, if properly directed, it would be possible to employ a number of Indian cricketers professionally. They in turn would provide the nucleus of more frequent zonal matches, and so the standard would start rising again. But it is difficult to see where the money is going to come from. People in India only watch international games now. It is not possible in the circumstances of India's existing adverse balance of payments for money to be made available for transfer abroad by visiting teams to India: it is even difficult to get finance to cover the cost of Indian teams going abroad, and when they do, their profits are not great, for Indian teams in recent years have not been popular visitors because, again, their standard is no longer sufficiently high. Once more a vicious circle: there is of course one solution to this, as has been said before: if host pays all and takes all, no trouble over international exchanges of currency arises nor of dwindling gate receipts owing to increased membership, and only when the other cricketing countries see the obvious merits of this proposition will there be much chance for India to build up reserves in her cricket organizations.

India has indeed done her fair share of international touring and of acting as host, even to sending first-class teams to East Africa (only Pakistan and England have done so otherwise), and she deserves some more understanding treatment by other countries. But even with that, will there ever be a truly fast Indian bowler? This seems doubtful: the climate militates against such a possibility, and the only part of undivided India where a fast bowler might have arisen is now in Pakistan, or disputed Kashmir. This is part of the damage which Partition did to India, for it created two below-average Test countries where, before, had existed one with hopes and reasonable chances of showing herself equal to older countries.

At first when Partition took place it was supposed that it need not affect cricket, and indeed the tour to Australia in 1947–8 was that of a team as though from undivided India. But the massacres of populations, the vituperations of politicians on both sides, the evil actions of more than one British expatriate official, all combined to divide up cricket as the country and people had been divided too. Cricket would have been in a bad way in Pakistan had not the first Governor-General, the Qaid-i-Azam, Mohammed Ali Jinnah, a Muslim from the old United Provinces of India, been himself a cricket enthusiast. The old quadrangular tournament in Karachi was revived for a space, an inter-provincial competition along the lines of the Ranji Trophy was organized, bearing his name, and the game received very much encouragement, at all levels, from schools upwards. What seemed like a disaster turned into a near-miracle of success so far as cricket was concerned. Jinnah's successors as Governor-General, and later Presidents, were keen cricket enthusiasts, and President Ayub Khan supported the establishment of a zonal tournament similar to the Duleep Trophy in India, for a trophy bearing his name: the Pakistan Board of Control is fairly identified with the government, in a way not found in any other country. Tours abroad have been many and often successful, and Pakistan's record in international cricket is far better than India's. Yet when she plays India, neither side dares lose, and there has been a long series of very tedious draws between the two countries. There have been many fine players from Pakistan since Partition, with Hanif Mohammed, the holder of the record individual first-class score, the best known, and several other younger players showing an approach to the game which can only be described as unusually gallant – such as in that wonderful innings by Asif Iqbal in the final Test at the Oval in 1967, and it was not his only fine innings.[1] (He has not done so well since entering English county cricket.) The outlook is not however clear: to the extent to which cricket was supported by and identified with President Ayub's regime in Pakistan, it may now suffer.

Turning from politics directly, but perhaps remaining with them indirectly, there is the abandonment of cricket by the Pakistan services: not a helpful nor a good sign. Like India there has been a proliferation of teams which do not justify the title of first-class and the Ayub tournament, designed in some measure to correct this, has itself admitted weaker teams than seems reasonable or prudent. There is the failure of certain sections of the population to play the game at all, or in substantial numbers anyway, such as the Pathans, and to a certain extent, the Bengali Muslims. There has been far too much petty quarrelling between organizations leading to some childishly absurd situations: in fact, things have occurred at quite high levels in Pakistani cricket which are unheard of in any other country and ought never to have occurred in Pakistan. It is a personal opinion only, but it does seem to the writer from what he knows of both countries and peoples that the outlook for the game is far more promising long-term in India than in Pakistan: though he hopes that his forecast will be proved wrong.

Ceylon has gone from strength to strength since the last war although she has not yet achieved her desire of Test status: and not yet achieved her wish to send a team on tour to this country. She has acted as host in the period to 'Commonwealth' teams, to MCC teams, to teams from the West Indies, Australia, Pakistan and India: she has toured both the last two countries, and at a lower level than first-class she has sent a touring team to Malaysia and her schoolboys to Australia. There is much emphasis on schools cricket in Ceylon, both at the 'public schools' and what are called the 'national' schools where the game is as much fostered as at the former. Being a small island, it is difficult to arrange an extended tour by an overseas side, such as would give opportunity to many players other than those of the top standard, and she suffers as a result. But an all-Ceylon team with all those playing instead of some being unavailable (as has happened with some of their leading players employed in England), could be a certain test for even a strong visitor, and this has been demonstrated against the West Indies, where Ceylon could force a draw, and Pakistan, whom Ceylon could beat. It is most unfortunate that the 1968 tour to England was called off, but no one could

[1] He had learnt his cricket in India where he had played in first-class matches.

have expected the selectors to be so venial as to choose themselves for the tour, although that may not have been the only, but rather the ultimate factor in the cancellation of the tour.

Having completed a tour of the Old World, we must have a look at the New. In the Caribbean lie the islands and mainland territories which have produced some of the greatest players of modern time: George Headley and Learie Constantine before the last war have already been mentioned but since then have come so many more: the three 'Ws' – Worrell, Walcott and Weekes, the spin bowlers Ramadhin, Valentine and Gibbs, the all-rounder Sobers, the always lamented 'Collie' Smith, the fast bowlers Hall, Griffith, King and even the ill-famed Gilchrist – a good fast bowler whatever else is said about him – and many others. These players, members of teams which have toured every other Test match country than South Africa, and acted as hosts to most in turn and more than once, come from a quite chaotically organized cricket community. But for the fever which lives in every West Indian, and makes cricket far more the national game in many of the islands than it has ever been anywhere else, it is not possible that West Indian teams should have done so well. There are plenty of well-organized leagues for school and club cricket in Guyana, Trinidad, Barbados and Jamaica, and much other cricket played in smaller islands: but there is no regular competition between territories, despite sponsorship by Shell. The chief grounds, as in India, are quite unable to hold the crowds that would attend a Test, and indeed often other matches, and as in India, again, there are no funds available to build more stands, but, unlike India, great profits accrue when West Indian teams go abroad. (Though what reaches West Indian hands is of the order of one-third of the large takings at Tests when they visited England, and often less: the reason is that crowds are restricted by all seats being numbered and reserved, so that the outer gate, which is all that tourists get a share of in England, was lower than it would otherwise have been while the extra profit went to the home country. That system would be admirable on a host takes all and pays all basis: but, as I said, an unusual selfishness has crept into cricket administration in recent years. Tourists get no share of the TV fees either.)

So far as the game itself is concerned it is so popular in most territories that its long-term future might seem to be assured. It has never been so popular in Jamaica and now partly because of a poor and large working population living alongside the jet set in the extravagant tourist resorts, it is much less popular than it used to be. Unfortunately, except in Barbados there have been distinct signs of a loss of popularity of the game elsewhere in the West Indies. People do not watch first-class matches – they throng to Tests – but they are also becoming less interested in playing at lower levels. It is, though, a part of the world where little boys play almost before they can walk and speak and in many places it is the only possible game: for many years to come, whatever falling off there may be, there should be more than enough players to keep club and school cricket going. Yet twenty years ago few would have forecast the almost total collapse of interest in first-class cricket in England and an enormous loss of interest in the game at other levels: it may be rash, then, to make any forecast for the West Indies. It is certainly at the higher levels that one starts worrying: there seem no adequate reasons, not even the absence of the Test players on tour for several months a year elsewhere, why there should not be inter-island games each year, no adequate reason why funds should not be built up to improve spectator facilities at the important grounds – none is adequate by the standards of any other Test country – no adequate reason why just receipts should not be obtained from overseas tours, and profits accumulated for building. None of these things is done. At the root of it all is perhaps local jealousy which made the West Indian Federation unworkable, and which demands that each territory has its proper share of representation in Test and touring teams (how 'proper' is to be interpreted must be asked from those who demand it). All this would probably preclude expenditure on one ground and not on others, and would probably not even permit agreement on a priority scheme to allow all, in due course, to be improved. Something might be done if there were an international agreement about the proper treatment of Test and tour profits, and which would necessitate local pooling in place of the present tendency to scramble nationally, and then locally, for the biggest share possible.

Control of cricket at the top level is inadequate too. It ought not to be possible for nepotism to be alleged in the selection of teams, yet it has not only been widely alleged, in the present as well as in the past that this has occurred, there is reason to suppose that it actually happens. It ought not to be possible for a player of European extraction to be earmarked years ahead for future West Indian captaincy to the exclusion of better players of African origin: nor, equally, should it be possible for the converse to be true. Top level control is still to far too great an extent kept in the hands of a small and limited circle, not by any means necessarily white, but often markedly lighter in colour: rather than abdicate their own power, they abdicate instead decision and responsibility – they do not assert but rather deny authority.

It is all bound up with Caribbean politics: there are in power in each territory governments which are, to an enormous extent, the old colonial authority in a local guise and not truly popular governments. So long as these relatively anachronistic governments exist, so long will control of cricket remain in the hands of non-representative people, however hard-working and devoted, and indeed able, they may be. As the C.I.A. is often supposed to be behind some of these governments, they may last a long time – or may explode. Cricket has already exploded in riot in all three territories where some progress has been made – it cannot be called much more than that – to *true* independence: but it has not yet exploded in Barbados where the political regime is more backward and cricket much more popular ('Fine game, teaches discipline,' one can hear someone muttering). Cricket is identified as a part of European culture and that culture brought by the English. Now that culture is being questioned, riots take place at Tests against England but not against other countries, not against Australia. Riots are not anti-white – they are, in a deep sense, anti-English. Cricket was the only way the master race could be beaten; it still is, and if that race is not beaten, there can be riots – and there can also be a loss of interest in cricket as people ask themselves just why they bother about this English game anyway.

Part of the answer is that, till now, sociologists would be hard pressed to classify West Indians as anything else but coloured Englishmen: that is a situation which may be changing more rapidly than is generally realized. Still, if that is what West Indians are, they probably share the characteristic said to be typically English of muddling through: muddling through is how West Indian cricket is run, and it may well be that the future of cricket there is all right, if it can be held together – if, for there has already been talk of Jamaica seeking independent cricket status, and eventual Test status. Others might follow, and if cricket fragmentation were to follow political fragmentation, just as cricket unity preceded political unity, it could well happen that cricket in the West Indies, except as a pastime, will dwindle right away.

Far away in the Atlantic is Bermuda: another jet-set paradise, but with a keenness and ability at cricket amongst the population rivalling the true West Indies. Cricket there has been referred to earlier: it continues to thrive, upset admittedly by local squabbles. But that Bermuda can produce a strong team is not in doubt though she would find some difficulty in beating an island side from the West Indies. She is still a venue for teams touring from the U.S.A. and Canada, and still sends teams there as also occasionally to England. She has produced one quite outstanding player, Alma Hunt, who has been well-known in this country, when he played as a professional for Aberdeenshire.

Canada and the U.S.A. must be considered separately: their history has been separate politically, as has their cricket experience. In Canada, there have been most strenuous efforts to publicize and popularize the game since the last war: Colts' teams have toured this country at regular intervals, and Canada has been the host to many other touring teams from across the world – Pakistan, Australia, New Zealand. The game is played in a scattering of schools, chiefly the equivalent of English public schools, in Ontario and British Columbia: it is played by a considerable number of clubs, again chiefly in Ontario and British Columbia, but with a certain amount going on round Montreal and in the Prairies. But it is only in Ontario and British Columbia that those taking part would be a majority of Canadians, as distinct from ageing British exiles. There is cricket of the latter sort going on all over Canada, except in Newfoundland where the game is now dead but it does not help the game there for British expatriates to strike specifically British attitudes to the game which tend to rouse hostility in North America. There have been vast and manful efforts on behalf of cricket in Canada, but they result in little: the standard has not improved since the war, but has actually gone down in the last ten years or so, and members of Colts' teams are conspicuous by their almost total absence from representative Canadian sides. The whole social climate is against the game, as well as the meteorological one. Canadians see little point in hanging round a town at a summer weekend: they are out to the shack in the woods or by the lakes: cricket is thought, wrongly, to be a British game and this no longer helps in a country which is more (unconsciously rather than consciously, though the latter too sometimes) anti-British than any of the 'old Commonwealth' countries. The game will no doubt always be played in Canada, but the long-term and perhaps the short-term future must mean at a far lower level of intention. Canada will never in our time play a Test match, and she is not a match for a strong county, maybe not for a weak one either: T. S. Eliot said that life was a matter of making the best of second-best, and Canada should face the facts and do this: perhaps her governing body is doing just that.

As we have seen, the past in the U.S.A. was at a vastly higher level of endeavour and performance than in Canada, yet now and for so many years, it is vastly lower. There are very few native-born Americans who play and most of those who do are of West Indian origin: there are a great number of Americans of recent Commonwealth origin who play but they are expatriates in spirit whatever the colour of their passports. The game is still played at Haverford, and there are still some long-established clubs who play, right across the continent: and more recently a United States Cricket Association has been revived after very many years. Everything in the social, but not the physical climate is against cricket in the U.S.A. nowadays, yet there is some chance that it will get stronger rather than weaker in the long run. In a population of two hundred million there

231

is room for a wide variety of individuals, just as there are possibilities for viable support for specialist magazines not remotely possible in smaller countries. There is also the periodical reaction by Americans from the more nauseating aspects of the 'American way of life' which can make some turn to cricket, as from time to time they have turned to it in the past. Cricket could, in short, become a kind of esoteric cult: much of its background is ideally adapted to such a purpose in that country. But if it does not become that, then it has no other future than that of a minority sport played by expatriates.

In Brazil, Chile and the Argentine the game continues to flourish, and the three countries have played matches amongst themselves almost every year since the last war, and have been at home to minor representative and club teams from England, and from Australia. The quality of the game differs in each country: in both Brazil and Chile it is essentially an expatriate game played by the British community in the big cities. In the Argentine there is a large settled British community however and the game there takes on much more the aspect it would have had years ago in Australia, or in any other 'white' colony. It is played in English-speaking schools, there are several strong clubs, there are some beautiful cricket grounds, there is an English-language daily newspaper to chronicle matches in the Buenos Aires League and other more important games. There is also a millionaire to support the game – Harry Martin of Biro pens. The standard of cricket has declined a great deal since before the last war, and can no longer be reckoned first-class – nor could even a combined South American team be so reckoned nowadays. But it is up to a good club cricket standard, and more to the point, the game is enjoyed. Its future there seems as secure as that of the British colony: in the other two countries it is more likely to dwindle. Cricket is also still played in Peru, and the Lima club sent a team down to the Argentine recently, but it is strictly an expatriate sport there. But in the Argentine you will find cricket reported in Spanish, for many of the British colony can no longer speak English.

(iii) A Note on the Wicket

It is in the period since the Second World War that turf wickets have come to be used exclusively for Test matches, and in all but one country exclusively for first-class matches also, and some attention to the history of the wicket itself is therefore appropriate. From the beginning, it has been assumed that cricket originated on turf of some sort: it is an entirely reasonable assumption whether it originated in these islands or in Europe, as there is little open space which is not,

70. The Adcock Playing Fields, Port Elizabeth. On this, and other grounds such as this, the South African non-whites are forced to play even their top-level inter-provincial matches. What is involved is not apartheid but out-and-out cultural repression

71. The crowd at National Stadium, Karachi, to watch the MCC Under-25 team play Pakistan in 1967

72. A private cricket ground, laid out for Mr Harry Martin on his estate, Martindale, near Buenos Aires

73. Pukekura Park, New Plymouth, during the unofficial New Zealand v. Australia Test match in February 1967 (the first time New Zealand beat Australia). Most of the trees are pohotukawa, the New Zealand 'Christmas tree', and a few tree ferns are visible. The pavilion is tucked away in the trees (*middle right*); the Press is housed at the top of the middle distant terrace. 8,000 people are easily accommodated on the wide grassed terraces

or perhaps more correctly, was not turfed. Even if the game may very early on have been adopted into back-yards or side-streets hardly alters the conception of it as, properly speaking, a turf game. In this form it was almost certainly developed in England, and in this form it was most probably first exported to America (though the game 'wicket' was often found as a street game later on). So far as North America is concerned, it is only since the First World War that games of any standing at all have come to be played on matting wickets: in the great days of Philadelphian cricket all games were on turf and no one expected anything else. In the West Indies, Trinidad was the only territory which used matting for first-class matches and then only for a period of some fifty years: otherwise almost all organized cricket is played on turf. This too is the case in South America.

South Africa is the only major cricket country which used matting wickets for all grades of cricket till comparatively recently. Presumably turf wickets of some kind must have been used early in the last century but found unsuitable owing to the climate and the soil, and for good-class club cricket of the time, matting wickets are known to have been in use by the early 1880s. The change over to turf for first-class matches only began in the later 1920s, but it was completed for all first-class matches including Test matches by the end of the 1930s. Much other cricket and all non-white cricket is still played on matting. In East Africa both matting and turf are used depending more on location than the status of the cricket played.

In India and Pakistan there are centres, such as Lahore, Delhi, Bombay, Calcutta, Madras and quite a number of others where turf wickets have 'always' been used. Prestige on the one hand, and access to water (irrigation or rain) have been the governing factors. But though in both countries a number of grounds used for first-class cricket have been converted to turf in the last twenty years or so, matting wickets far outnumber turf in India for first-class cricket, though now against the competition rules in Pakistan (the Qaid-i-Azam competition introduced turf wickets compulsorily in 1959–60, and the Ayub competition followed six years later). But in other grades of cricket, the nature of the surface depends on finance and climate. Three different kinds of surface are to be found: turf, which is probably the cheapest of all in a well-watered area, matting, which tends to be expensive as a strip will do well if it lasts out a season, and hard sun-baked mud which will often be found for the outfield anyway. This last surface is a wonderful one to play on: very fast, and dangerous against a fast bowler who can do anything, but the batsman finds his compensation in the speed with which the ball reaches the boundary. It is this speed of the ball on the surface, by the way, which has led to the development of a distinctively different technique by Indian and Pakistani hockey players. It is, again, that speedy surface which has been responsible for some of the remarkable scores in quite minor cricket, as well as in top-class cricket, in the Indian sub-continent. But in a town like Calcutta turf wickets are no problem: that vast expanse called the *maidan* has only turf wickets: such a plethora of turf wickets would be out of the question in a similar area in Delhi, though, again, not in Dehra Dun in the foothills. And although Lahore may be more generously endowed with turf wickets than most towns in Pakistan, it is doubtful if it could sustain such a number as Calcutta. In India there is no limitation of Test or first-class matches to turf though only two grounds with matting wickets have been used for Tests (Kanpur and Lucknow) and the first of these is now turf.

Ceylon has turf wickets: so has Malaysia, and so has Hong Kong. In Australia cricket of any distinction in the leading towns and cities has always been played on turf but in country districts matting is more frequent, laid over a concrete or composition surface: once again, there is a problem of climate. In New Zealand there is no such problem and wickets are turf.

In the two cricketing countries of Europe – Holland and Denmark – matting wickets are generally used and though long ago turf wickets were occasionally used, the fact that most cricket grounds are used for two-thirds of the year for football means that turf wickets are precluded nowadays.

There is however probably no country in the world where *all* cricket is played on turf or matting. At lower levels there is not the money to pay a groundsman nor buy the matting. And at higher levels, maintaining turf wickets has become something of a problem. They need a great deal of care by men who are not only devoted to their task (they are liable to be called out of their beds at night as the ordinary gardener is not) but who are born with 'green fingers'. Such men are getting older, and are retiring younger: and generally speaking in the more developed countries the pay is nothing like good enough to attract suitable entrants into a highly skilled and specialized task.

At the same time there has been an increasing tendency to cover the wicket, not just the two ends, nor only when play has finally ceased. The tendency is, indeed, towards a more or less standardized product the world over: it is far from being achieved yet, and it is most improbable that it will be so long as turf wickets continue. It seems a logical step to turn away from turf wickets in future. It has been possible for some years to construct artificial wickets of materials which will reproduce many desired characteristics: not all of them of course, as the 'mix' has to be varied to achieve any difference. Rather than make a match depend on the accidentally acquired ability to play in unusual conditions (such as heavy rain on an otherwise perfect surface causing those 'glue-pot' conditions that used to be known at Sydney and Melbourne many years ago) it may well be far better to lay down on each major ground a number of artificial strips, two of each different characteristic (to allow for repairs) and let the toss decide which of these different strips is to be used. This would be going back to an older Code of Laws and would retain the useful element of luck. These strips would need a certain amount of rolling and repairing and even slight remaking (like repatching a road surface) but both the task and the responsibility of the groundsman would be very much lightened indeed. For the outfield needs a different kind of care which can, nowadays, be applied more or less easily by mechanical means. It would hardly be necessary to cover such strips against rain and, indeed, as a broad statement, play would only stop when rain was actually falling, and would in most cases be resumed within minutes of the rain ceasing – tropical thunderstorms always excepted. Nor is there any question of such artificial surfaces being favourable only to the batsman: they can be made favourable to almost any kind of bowler, slow, fast, spin, seam. The batsman would be favoured in one important sense: he would no longer be faced with one of those ambiguous wickets which, without favouring the bowler, cramps the batsman, and keeps him from scoring and makes for a dull game. No bowler would worry about that kind of favour to batsmen.

Early in 1970, news came of an intention to play Test matches in England that year on artificial wickets in certain circumstances. There can thus be little doubt that it is already sufficiently recognized that these wickets are likely to be the wickets of the future.

14

CHANGES IN THE GAME
SINCE 1939

There have been very few changes in the conduct of the game in the last thirty years, but what few there have been have had an often far-reaching and also unforeseen effect, and these effects can be seen at all levels at which the game is played. The first is a working-out of the full effect of the change in the 'l.b.w.' Law which took place, of course, in 1937 after an experimental period. It was designed to curtail the apparent mastery which the bat had achieved over the ball during the 1930s but in a different period, with a different outlook, and on wickets by no means prepared as paradises for batsmen (or anyone else if it comes to that), it has come to have what most observers feel to be an evil effect on the first-class game, and also on its imitators at lower levels down even to school cricket. This, of course, is excessive pad-play to the ball on the off, a purely defensive form of play, and without any merit to it at all. It has also led to the really dreaded double-shuffle-cum-forward-defensive pad. There can be little doubt that the Law would be changed if there were any sign of general agreement what the change should be, but of that there is little at the time of writing. (See, however, the footnote on page 199.)

The English experiment with the eight-ball over, following on the more general adoption of an over of this length in the cricketing world generally, was abandoned after the war: there seems to have been a fairly general agreement that there was nothing objectionable about it, and the only solid reason for its abandonment seems to have been a desire to return to 'normal' after the war, and 'normal' meant, to most people in England a six-ball over. It did not take long for New Zealand and the West Indies to follow suit (though New Zealand has since gone back to eight balls) but it was several more years however before South Africa abandoned eight-ball overs: Australia clings tenaciously to it, and

236

is unlikely to change. Eight balls are still used in some parts of the Pacific, and also in parts of the United States where the longer over was first tried out and adopted.

One of the worst things about modern cricket, in its upper levels, is the ubiquity of seam bowlers, depending on the new ball for their effect.[1] The original new ball legislation was intended to clear up what had become an obscure matter: at what point in an innings did a ball become sufficiently worn to justify replacement? That was all there was to it. However, during the second war, shortage of materials led to rationing of cricket balls, and instead of the statutory 200 runs, which was well-known so that nobody thought too much about it, replacement was determined by so many overs, fifty-five in the first instance. These overs were signalled specially from the scoreboard: the result was to draw attention to the approach of the new ball in a way that had never been done before. Indeed, the scoreboard told the fielding side when 200 runs were scored: now instead it was counting up the overs, and the result, the direct result, was that when only a few overs remained to be taken before a new ball was due, entirely negative bowling was adopted, designed to get through the overs without giving away any runs. Despite no fewer than seven changes in England in twenty years on when the new ball should be taken, this habit has grown stronger. The period before a new ball can be taken is now eighty-five overs in England, and the extension of the period has only tended to extend also the dreary period of negative bowling to suppress runs: as this is followed by the equally dreary seam bowler doing what he can with the swerve while the ball is still fresh, the overall result has been to reduce the possibility for interesting cricket to about half a day per full day's cricket. There seems to be no cure for the fetish for the seam bowler, but if the period for a new ball were measured by runs, there would be little or no negative bowling at the end of each period. Better wickets might help to reduce the awful seam bowling, so might a change

---

[1] One unresolved question in connection with seam bowling concerns the ball itself. Swerve is generated by the boundary layer of air surrounding the ball coming apart from the ball owing to the roughness of the seam – the matter is a complicated one and requires several pages of physics to explain the effect. Before the last war, the seam of the ball was much smaller than it is now: the stitching used was what is called five-cord stitching but it is now eight-cord stitching, almost twice as large. The result is that the seam itself is very much bigger, and so the ability of the seam to cause the boundary layer to separate from the ball lasts much longer than it did before the last war: in turn the ability of the seam bowler to achieve his skills persists longer in terms of each ball than it used to. And so, in turn, the seam bowler is much more used than he ever used to be. The change in the seam occurred somewhere at the end of the 1940s or very early 1950s. Thus it may not be anything more than a change in implement that has caused such a disastrous change to the game itself: and if so, the remedy is clear. (This information comes from T. E. Bailey on the BBC during the third Test against New Zealand at the Oval in August 1969.)

in the 'l.b.w.' Law: but a different attitude of mind is really needed, such as getting rid of notions (held by an England captain) that spin bowling is unduly expensive.

Towards the end of the post-war period, there had grown up a habit of 'dragging': at its worst quantitatively in Australia, but with its worst practitioners in England, it had become a serious menace. Bowlers (fast bowlers at that, because obviously there was no problem with slow bowlers, or with very few, and not much of one with medium-pace bowlers) were effectively reducing the length of the wicket to eighteen or nineteen yards. It is uncertain when the habit began, and it may even have begun well before the last war. When however effective measures were taken to terminate 'drag', the result was remarkable. The first full season where drag was limited in Australia resulted in run-scoring right back to the level of the 1930s, though wickets were no longer the batsman's paradises they had been then. It was clear that the insidious shortening of the length of the wicket forced on cricket by 'draggers' had made the reaction time for too many batsmen too short for dealing effectively with the fast bowler, and that the imposition of restrictions on drag restored the reaction time to what it had been. The longer term effects of this restriction have yet to be seen, but since the tendency everywhere seems to be to invent new and more wonderful ways of playing negative cricket, we may see fewer genuinely fast bowlers, and more 'seamers' of medium pace, especially with first-class cricket seven days a week.

Allied with drag, in many people's minds, has been the question of 'throwing': very evident when a man 'threw' from eighteen yards. Much ink has been spilt on the question and no honest attempt has been made to deal with the problem, nor will it be so long as it is thought that special protection must be given to a man earning his living from cricket or to an overseas tourist in England (no such protection is given to English tourists abroad). The post-war resurrection of the problem, dormant save for a few very isolated instances since the turn of the century, arose quite simply because the celebrated umpire Frank Chester was told by no less a pillar of the cricket establishment than Sir Pelham Warner that he would get no support if he no-balled C. N. McCarthy, the South African fast bowler, during the first day of the first Test on the 1951 South African tour. Although Chester did not reveal in his book that it was Warner, it was common knowledge to cricketers of the time and Chester himself did not disguise it. It was completely typical of Warner, whose behaviour at the time of the 1932–3 tour in Australia had been equivocal to put it mildly. From that point, the trouble got worse and worse, and there can be very little doubt that one of the worst offenders was an English bowler.[1] The whole affair came to a head when as many as four leading Australian bowlers were found, or believed to be, throwers in the 1958–9 season. In the end the Australian Board of Control took very strong action indeed, and the matter has been cleared up in that country, but not elsewhere. Throwers are alleged in New Zealand, the West Indies, and, still, in England. Photographic evidence is cited in support of these allegations: no camera has yet been used for such photography with the technical characteristics which would enable anyone to justify or refute such an allegation. But the quarrels, often journalistically inspired, have led to bad blood between more than one pair of countries: any resolution of the problem has not been helped by a competent authority *encouraging* an umpire not to 'call' a visiting bowler, as has happened on at least one notorious occasion in England long after the Chester incident in 1951.

The Law is quite specific on the matter: it is also simply not enforced, nor outside Australia are umpires adequately supported who do enforce it, and there is clear evidence of this. Some of the present difficulty arises out of a desire to define throwing: to define the illegal act, rather than to penalize anything which seems other than legal (an indefinite thing and bound to lead, as it has, to differing interpretations). Readers will recall how 'bowling' was abandoned some two hundred years ago, in favour of the pitched under-arm ball and that all under-arm actions, other than strict bowling, as well as all other forms of delivery are throws. Hence the difficulty about defining the throw. Ranji many years ago said it was the jerk that gave it away: but the jerk is no longer illegal, and hence even more difficulties. The problem is made much more difficult of solution because of the more or less modern habit of bowling a number of 'bumpers' at the batsman in each over: it is far more intimidatory bowling, if it can be called bowling in any sense at all, than was the 1932–3 leg theory. Yet much less is done about it: no doubt umpires warn bowlers, no doubt bowlers desist, but the practice continues: and it should not. Administrators are fearful of legalizing 'throwing' for fear that it would lead to the 'thrown bumper' but it would be possible both to legalize 'throwing' and to prevent 'bumpers' no matter how delivered, by laying down the 'length' shorter than which the ball must not be pitched. In due course, no doubt something like that will be done. Some fear that legalized 'throwing' would lead to an even more monotonous type of bowling than seam bowling: it would be worth experimenting to see.

---

[1] It was not, incidentally, strong action by umpires that had kept throwing out of the game till then – it was prompt and early action by county committees in eliminating suspect bowlers early in their careers.

Apart from these matters, any changes in the Laws have been minor: the new 1947 definition[1] of a tie – quite the contrary of what had been accepted for many years before as one: another has been the attempt to define a catch on the boundary. The position just now is in an illogical state: a fielder may not go over a boundary *line* having made his catch, but he may lean against, and indeed over, a boundary *fence* to make his catch. But these and other minor matters hardly affect the conduct of the game. Yet many people are full of complaint year after year about continual changes in the game: these changes for the most part affect either notes to the Laws, and are of no significant character, or the scoring of points in competitions, and other legislation for competitions, such as the abolition of the follow-on one season in the county championship. They are irksome and they do attract much publicity: but they do not affect the overwhelming number of games played in a season. Matters that do are attempts to limit polishing the ball: this was a good example of how something that may be good for one level of cricket (and even that is arguable) is positively harmful at another level. It is rather extraordinary the way a desire is found in some quarters for all legislation to operate at all levels of cricket: it is not possible to enforce it, and we have already seen that the majority of matches played in any season are not played strictly under the Laws, modified or not officially, but under a local league variation or even simple understanding between captains (as for example the failure to insist on a second innings when there is plenty of time). The nature of cricket at different levels is far too diverse for it to be feasible or desirable to insist on complete uniformity of observance, in every detail.

This attempted uniformity is something that has come out of recent lengthy negotiations to form a national cricket authority in England. It is the intention that every club in the country shall belong, numbering at a conservative estimate some fifty thousand, affiliated through local and county organizations to a national body: that this in turn shall join with representation of other interests in cricket, school, county, and so on, to form a Cricket Council in whose hands will lie, it is intended, the control of the game in all its aspects in England. It is too early to discuss something which has only recently been finalized, in any intelligent terms, but the structure does not suggest anything markedly democratic about it, with far too much influence left in the hands of the MCC nominees and representatives. That influence may diminish once the new organization has been in existence for a little time. It will not, however, have any regard

---

[1] Formerly if runs were equal irrespective of the number of wickets down, the match was a tie: now it only became a tie if the team batting last had lost all its wickets.

to the Laws of the game which, illogically, will remain in the control of full members of the MCC. It seems oppressive either that these members shall be asked to 'rubber stamp' decisions made by other bodies or that they shall be in a position to frustrate such decisions, and it would seem that the law-making power should pass from it to the International Cricket Conference, which should in turn delegate local legislation to the constituent countries.

The International Cricket Conference is the lineal successor of the Imperial Cricket Conference, originally contrived by Sir Abe Bailey before the First War. It now embraces as full members all Test match countries save South Africa, and as non-voting, but as events are showing by no means powerless members, nearly every other country in the world where there is a national cricket organization. With the accession of Canada in 1968, few important cricket countries (save of course South Africa) remain outside, and there are the makings of a true Cricket Parliament. This however, will not develop so long as the affairs of the Conference are operated on an unpaid part-time basis from a back room at Lord's, with one meeting a year for one day at which the majority of decisions have to be referred back to the member countries if they have any real importance. It is arguable whether Lord's or indeed London at all should be the centre for the I.C.C.: it is geographically not the most convenient centre, and less mileage would have to be flown by delegates if meetings were held in Australia or indeed one or two other countries. Yet the I.C.C. already has one law-making power: it determines in general terms what a first-class match is, though it leaves the detailed application of this to the several countries. It is not a negligible body already: and despite the desire of at least one major cricketing country to limit the authority of the I.C.C., it is likely to grow in strength and authority in the long run.

The international cricket scene since the last war has displayed a variety of experience such as would have astonished pre-war enthusiasts: seven Test match countries, each playing Tests home and away against all others, with two main exceptions: the notorious one of South Africa, who will only play three other countries, and what ought to be as notorious, Australia who will not entertain New Zealand to Tests (though New Zealand visits and has entertained all other countries for Tests), and has only once, right after the war, played a Test against New Zealand in New Zealand. Just as there is something very badly wrong with South Africa's attitude generally, there is something equally, if differently, badly wrong with Australia's attitude to New Zealand.

In addition to all these Test tours, there has been a great number of other tours mostly of minor nature, but involving other than Test match countries.

That South America and North America should receive touring teams of first-class and even of club strength from not only England but other countries is but in line with an old tradition: that Fiji should send (but not yet receive) first-class teams will be of no surprise to the student of the game, but of great interest to many others (what a pity that in the glorious summer of 1959 a Fiji team was after all unable to tour England): that Ceylon should entertain teams who are visiting the sub-continent is again of no surprise. But it is a different matter when Hong Kong and Singapore see first-class teams, and they have not by any manner of means been the only ones to see touring teams from afar.

All the same, though in prospect all these tours have been exciting, the actuality has been less so. Test matches in particular have proved dull affairs except a few years ago when West Indian cricket seemed on top of the world, and many remarkable finishes took place, including the famous and only tied Test, at Brisbane in 1960–1.

Part of the reason for this has been the abolition of play-to-a-finish Tests,[1] which has meant far too many Tests, and indeed whole Test series, given up to playing for draws so as not to lose the rubber: an impossibility when one Test in each rubber must be finished (and itself an incentive to finish others). Defensive cricket at its very worst has far too often been seen in what ought to be cricket at its very best: but it is no new thing for Test matches to seem dreary to onlookers. There were those who thought so in the 1890s when they only had to see three days' worth (in this country: and at that time only three such matches).

Familiarity breeds contempt: apart from war years, it is now forty-five years since there was an English season without a first-class touring team, and forty-three since there was one without a Test. There is the same clogging up in Australia, and, though there are anyway far fewer first-class matches in New Zealand, that country is becoming almost as frequent a host as Australia: and thirty years ago who would have dreamt that there might be two teams of first-class character, if not status (India and Fiji), in New Zealand at the same time?

The contempt may derive from the lack of really outstanding cricketers since the Second World War. The first few years saw the last of Don Bradman, still

---

[1] The abolition of play-to-a-finish Tests was also the abolition of the old idea in cricket that all matches shall be played out. It had dwindled as the nineteenth century drew on in England: it dwindled in both Australia and New Zealand as competitive first-class matches ceased to be timeless in the 1920s. Once again non-cricket reasons of administration have had their effect on play. It is a common misconception that the essence of games is that they are to be completed in a definite time. Golf and the large number of games played with racquets know no such limitation.

outstanding, but not quite so much in command as he had been before the war (yet he was not old by English cricket standards) and there has been no one, there could hardly have been anyone, of his stature or ability. There have been attractive enough Australian batsmen (Neil Harvey, Norman O'Neill) and efficient enough Australian batsmen – Bobby Simpson, Bill Lawry: but they have not matched the giants of pre-war days. There have been fine Australian bowlers, on the whole probably better than those since the earlier 1920s, to name only Keith Miller, Ray Lindwall, Richie Benaud, Alan Davidson, Graham Mckenzie: how they compared with Gregory and McDonald, Grimmett and Mailey, or O'Reilly, of between the wars is a matter of opinion. Few enthusiasts however go to watch bowlers: perhaps there would be a greater following for the game if they could understand bowling better, as a spectacle.

In the period, New Zealand produced two cricketers of world class, Bert Sutcliffe and John Reid: and many others of good county standard, but hardly any better. We have already seen that the famous Indian names arose during the last war, though the great Pakistani names inevitably arose after (few with great names came into Pakistani cricket from undivided India). South Africa has produced a great number of flourishing young, and not-so-young cricketers, always with one or two in each team of world class, and at the present time with rather more of above average first-class standard than usual, so that it can well be argued that South Africa has the best playing team in the world. With the Pollock brothers, and Barlow, as a nucleus, with Trevor Goddard as an all-rounder still available, it is a powerful claim, and could only be challenged by a match against a West Indian side which is now on the downgrade. Of the great post-war players, only Sobers remains, and there can be two opinions about his greatness: that he is a remarkable and versatile cricketer is certain, but whether he is really a contender for a hypothetical world team of all time is quite another matter. Far too often he does not succeed in Test matches: far too often when he does succeed, it is against a less powerful country, or in a match whose ultimate result is of no importance. The same can be said of so many post-war English cricketers. The period saw the last half of the sadly interrupted careers of Len Hutton, Denis Compton and Bill Edrich: no one has replaced them, and the old amateur cricketers who would once have done so, do not, or will not, stay the pace; an example of this is Peter May.

Denis Compton needs a word to himself. Compton was something of a genius – as notable a judge as Lord Cobham has said he was certainly the best batsman England had produced in the last thirty years and supported his judgement by saying that a batsman's real merit lies in his attitude and that Hammond and

243

Compton were all aggression and could not be contained even by the best bowling. This is perfectly true, and it is why it cannot be said that there has been anyone since Hammond who could be counted as the greatest cricketer in England for the simple reason that Compton, genius that he was, had flaws so that he could not stay on the peak he once reached: indeed, he probably did not want to, and could not have done had he wanted to owing to serious and recurring knee trouble which eventually put him out of the game, a few years prematurely by pre-1939 standards, but already a veteran by modern ones. Compton was all aggression, and he had some perfectly extraordinary strokes which are not capable of description for they were no real strokes at all: he would advance down the wicket as if to drive, find that the ball coming to him simply was not of that sort at all, try to glance it to leg, and finish up almost spread-eagled on the ground having finally achieved a kind of hook: and from that position he would attempt an impossible run, to his partner's dismay. But he had all the usual strokes – it was just that any innings of his would be likely to contain, depending on its length, several of these entirely invented shots which no one else in his time in the world would even have attempted. But Compton had also one other stroke which must be mentioned: the sweep. The sweep (not as has been described at times, a leg pull) was invented by George Parr and it used to be called 'the George Parr sweep'. Parr made great use of it – he must have had a wonderful eye, and wonderful reflexes. And then it more or less went right out of use, except by uninstructed tail-enders in first-class cricket: for it was and is a dangerous stroke, using a cross bat swept round horizontally in a plane intersecting the trajectory of the ball at ninety degrees, intended to take the ball right out of the ground on the leg side fairly square on. It is obvious that the slightest error in timing, if the ball is straight will mean the loss of one's wicket, and if it is not, a great probability of putting up a catch off the bat's edge. It is an ugly stroke, yet it is also a glorious one because it is so dangerous and all concerned know it to be: so that when it comes off, as in the hands of a master it so often does, one can only applaud. Compton must have had as good an eye and as perfect reflexes as Parr: he played the sweep often and effectively and to the delight of all who saw him, and to the bewilderment of many a bowler who could not really accept that the stroke was feasible. And in this Compton's example has had a very bad effect: nowadays, you will find all sorts of batsmen, in reputable batting positions, attempting the sweep off good balls early in their innings, yet with no evidence at all of the ability to judge the stroke that Compton showed so obviously. And of course, they either get out quickly, or allow themselves to be scared at their narrow escape and go into a defensive hutch. It is a stroke only for geniuses: not for the mediocre (though it is always allowable to an uninstructed tail-ender). See plate 58.

Compton was not by any means only a batsman, he was a fine fielder, and he was a very much underestimated left-arm bowler who could produce the 'Chinaman' (which is the left-hander's googly. This ball, by the way, was not named after the West Indian Chinese bowler, E. Achong, who used it; the term arose much more crudely in the more arrogant days of the past when it was the custom to make snide remarks about foreigners and Asiatics and orientals. 'Chinamen' as they were called, were thought to be 'wrong 'uns' and this delivery is the left-hander's 'wrong 'un' in cricket parlance, and hence the term.) Compton nearly did the double one season, and was always a useful county bowler: he was rarely used in Tests when he might often have broken a prolific partnership in the period before an interval – at some expense no doubt, but better than no wicket at all. But Compton's Test bowling came at the beginning of the play-safe attitude which does not believe in buying wickets, and even thinks spin bowling expensive, so he was under-used. He occasionally captained teams (his county, and England, as vice-captain on tours) but his attitude was too unorthodox for success: yet many of his ideas were sound – why not, after all, open an innings with one fast bowler, and one slow? But no one else in his time seemed to think it worth trying. English cricket has been much poorer since Compton went out of the game. Yet he was not great in the sense that Hammond was, though he could have been.

Tom Graveney in the evening of his career has shown what graceful cricket and reliable cricket can be: omitted from Test teams for much of his earlier career, because of the belief that he lacked temperament, now towards the end of it, he has shown that he no longer lacks it. The belief had some justification: in his earlier years he did not stick his head down and keep it there, he got out far too often off stupid strokes when he should have been well set, and this indicated a lack of concentration at least which suggested an inadequate temperament. Of bowlers, there have been two great ones, and two or maybe three nearly great: among the first are Lock and Laker, despite Lock's suspect action which in much of his career must have earned him many wickets, and the other three are Statham, Trueman and Bedser. Perhaps one of these five would make a post-1919 England team. For the rest there have been as many dreary hacks amongst batsmen as amongst bowlers, and it is amongst wicket-keepers that we see some sparkle in the period. Godfrey Evans led the field (though competent judges put him well behind Ames) and was far ahead of the next two, Roy Swetman and John Murray; Alan Knott is a young player who fits well into an old Kentish tradition of fine 'keepers. It will be recalled that we had a similar number of fine wicket-keepers between the wars. But maybe things are somewhat easier nowadays: he seldom stands up to the bowling, as his predecessors between the wars did to some extent, so he misses the chances of stumping: but he takes the catches which should have gone to first, or even second slip, to make his bag much greater than those before him could have attempted. Seam bowling moreover encourages the snick to the 'keeper: so does the batting! Evans took a far greater proportion of wickets which fell than Ames, in Tests: yet Ames is reported to have missed only four chances (was it?) in his entire Test career. Standing back does not however help the bowler psychologically, as standing up does. Bedser was a far better bowler to the England wicket-keeper Evans standing up than to his county 'keeper McIntyre, standing back.

Thus one can see most of the reasons why this plethora of international cricket has not been the great crowd gatherer that it would certainly have been had the cricketers of between the wars been taking part. It could be that we are in an 'in-between' state: my own view is that the game is on the decline, and especially in this country. What we do in England has an enormous influence on what others do: can the still almost youthful enthusiasm for the game at so many levels in the rest of the world survive the increasingly moribund state in which it finds itself in England? Can it, more to the point, revive it in England?

It may do, but it will not come about by means of the too ready hiring of international cricketers from elsewhere even if Australia now copies us: such hiring can only make less money available for the home players, discourage them in the first place, and render the international stars stale. And even if such a revival does come about it will be in the long run of a temporary nature only, for a more profound and subtle reason. (See statistics at page 250.)

For rather more than the last hundred years, the upper-class element (in educational terms) in England has been brought up so as to retain an essential childishness all its life, and in complete contrast to what is to be found in any non-British territory (except the U.S.A. where it is also to be found for other reasons in a rather worse state). Everywhere else, when a man grows up, he puts behind him childish things: but in the British, or more specifically the English and English-influenced areas of the world, he joins Old Boy clubs, he retains strong links with his school even when he does not join a club, he wears an old school tie, and goes out of his way to favour those with a similar background: he may join later on a more adult kind of organization but any onlooker is inclined to regard these more adult organizations as no more than a further projection of childlike desire and longing. This childishness leads him to cling to taking part in and watching sport in a way foreign to most other countries. This is not to say that other countries do not watch sport in their millions: of course they do, but the manner of a football crowd is not the manner of a largely upper-class crowd watching cricket. It is the manner essentially of the populace provided with bread and circuses as by the Roman Emperors of old, or of the soma-drugged masses in *Brave New World*. The football crowd anywhere in the world is a different kind of crowd from that which watches other sport. In English-influenced countries, those crowds are clinging tenaciously to their childhood: the childlike attitudes in this respect of nearly everyone in the Army is noteworthy compared with the far more technological attitude of the Air Force and the Navy, for the Army is too often even now but school writ large, with NCOs and officers but prefects and masters with more power: the Air Force and Navy have been for many years technical factories, where grown men work.

One of the most significant changes in the status of cricket in recent years has been the collapse of the Eton *v.* Harrow fixture at Lord's as a social event. It was, till not long ago, one of the Events of the Season, by which is meant the social season. It is no more. It had been such an event for very many years, well beyond living memory, back almost till its first occurrence at Lord's. It was one of a number of events in the social calendar which included Garden Parties at Buckingham Palace, Royal Ascot (but not Ascot Heath), Goodwood (to a slightly lesser extent), Henley, and to some extent Wimbledon if confined rather to the feminine sex. It can be seen that there is no common factor to these occasions: they were not, and are not, all sporting events. But all except the Garden Parties are. And though people go to Ascot and Goodwood and Henley and Wimbledon for the social occasions that they are, very many also go because they are great sporting events. Henley, it is true, has diminished as a social event in recent years, but it has not collapsed and it may even have a relatively larger number of rowing enthusiasts present than in former years as it has taken on more and more the aspect of a top level international regatta: thus the decline in one aspect of it has been to some extent offset by its more fundamental aspect. Wimbledon was never quite on the same level as the others, but it has hardly receded from that level, and its importance as a lawn tennis event is even greater now than in recent years since the coming of open championships. Royalty attends Ascot, and is to be seen at Goodwood: Goodwood has its own charms in other ways, and both are top level racing events. But Eton *v.* Harrow was never a top-class cricket event: it was never more than a school cricket match, a match admittedly between schools who by their numbers, by the age of their teams, by the quality of their coaching, would generally have the edge on other school teams: generally but not always. Eton *v.* Harrow was a great social occasion: just possibly the biggest social occasion in the country at which Royalty was not formally present. Crowds have exceeded twenty thousand on each day in the past: five figures were common a hundred years ago and until not so many years ago. Between the wars it was virtually not possible to find a place to watch from if one arrived late: tents and marquees would be pitched in the Nursery Ground at Lord's. There once used to be attractive wooden 'bowers' which would be gaily decorated with flowers and bunting – replaced not long before the last war with the concrete arcading under which cars are now parked but which were intended to fulfil the same function as the 'bowers' and the tents as temporary homes for social clubs and 'old boy' institutions where those watching (watching?) the match could get high quality summer food and drink in picnic, but appropriately sumptuous surroundings. Moreover, many of those attending were people who had never been to either school, nor had any children there, and in no small number of cases had no relatives there either – and were not at all interested in cricket. For it is generally true to say that few indeed went to watch the cricket. Some of the cricket was good – some of it poor: like schools cricket anywhere at any time. The quality has not varied over the years in this game, except in so far as the quality has varied in the game at any *instructed* level in this country. People went to the game because it was one of the most important social occasions: because there they were pretty sure they would meet everyone, and anyone, of importance in the entire English 'establishment'. (And that very definitely included archbishops and bishops of the English established Church too: it was not unusual to hear one such dignitary greeted by a silk-hatted friend with, 'Didn't know you liked cricket, Ambrose,' and the greeting answered with, 'I don't, but I always come to this match.')

It was, in short, a gathering of English 'top people'. It has so far ceased to be that no tents are now pitched, few people turn up, the President of the MCC (usually having been at one of the schools) can appeal for a greater attendance in future: well he may since all he sees is a tiny scatter in the vast emptiness of Lord's, about as many as used to watch London Clergy *v.* Southwark Clergy.

All this has happened inside ten or a dozen years. And it has not happened to the social participants at any of the other social sporting events: that is, gone from vast crowds to nothing at all – to the point when *prudent* managers of Lord's cricket ground would not stage the game any more as wasteful in resources.

Part of the reason of course is that the public schools have ceased to occupy

74. Young cricketers practising in a derelict sixteenth-century Portuguese cathedral at Bassein Fort, near Bombay

76 (*overleaf*). The Artillery Ground in Finsbury, London – far removed from its rural eighteenth-century surroundings

75. Is this the future of cricket? An indoor game which originated amongst the Danish minority in South Slesvig and is played amongst schools in Denmark in the winter, in pleasant conditions when ice freezes the rivers and the sea and makes land travel difficult. The boy batting is himself a German (of the Danish minority) – the others are Danish boys

the position they once held as the preserves from which the governors of the country, lay and religious, civil and military, should come: being no longer these preserves, it is no longer appropriate to flaunt, or to celebrate their status as once they or their alumni did. For this game was the archetype of public school cricket matches in that sense: it epitomized and exaggerated all that the ordinary man felt about such establishments – a large gathering of the obviously well-to-do, *and* the only such school sporting fixture to have attained that particular kind of social status. In other words, Eton *v*. Harrow is no longer felt by English 'top people' to be an appropriate focus for a gathering.

The collapse of this fixture as a social event can therefore to a great extent be explained on non-cricket grounds, just as its popularity as a social event had little to do with cricket either – those vast lawns at Lord's were for ladies' pretty heels, not for a cricket ball and spiked boots. All the same, cricket comes into it: for the collapse of Eton *v*. Harrow as a social event reflects also a half-instinctive appreciation that cricket is no longer important. Its mystical aura no longer exists, its special kind of ethic; its special appeal to 'top people' as in some way reflecting 'proper' values – all this has gone. Above all, though self-appointed members of the 'establishment' still try to run the game as their own preserve, condescendingly and grudgingly admitting those from other parts of society, the game itself is no longer conducted by such people. Professionals captain counties, captain England, sit on county committees, sit on selection committees, chair selection committees: the sphere of the amateur (*sc* 'gentleman') has not merely been invaded, it has been occupied: and so cricket has far less of an attraction to the 'establishment' as a whole. Secluded, once, in their schools, in their universities, in special changing rooms in cricket pavilions, they now retain that seclusion only in their schools, and not all that much either: the rest has gone. No special place gives them a special authority: they are forced to be equal – more to the point, they are forced to grow up.

But England has as a whole, started to grow up in the last ten years or so: students, faced with life as it is, and what have half-facetiously been called 'child marriages', are no longer concerned with pretending still to be at school – they want to live and to earn a living. Keenness on sport, on games, is part of childhood: so it ceases. This attitude will spread over the years and generations to other English-influenced countries, and this is why there is no real future for highly organized cricket at Test match or first-class level, nor, in the long run, for cricket annuals, periodicals, or literature generally. It is notoriously difficult to write credible cricket fiction, partly because what happens in real-life cricket can be in itself beyond credibility had it not actually happened. No one can really accept that the hero will win the vital game, or that the villain will success-fully foil him: in any case it is all trivial compared with life itself. Thus just as there is very little credible cricket fiction, so as cricket falls away as a serious interest for grown men, it is hardly likely that its literature will any longer survive, except as folklore: rather indeed as Charles Cowden Clarke's *Nyren* has survived as folklore till now.

Statistics on the Decline of English First-Class Cricket

Just as the figures of the round-arm period illustrated the effect of that period on scoring, so do figures over the last seventy years or so illustrate the decline of English first-class cricket since the last war and in particular since about the years from 1952–5. The following is a selection from very many which all underline the point.

Since 1949, no batsman has made 3,000 runs in a season except in 1959 and 1961: yet it was made sixteen times between the wars.

2,000 runs in a season was made in twelve seasons between the wars, by at least nine batsmen in each of those seasons: since 1953 only four seasons have seen nine batsmen doing so. 1963–8 saw an average of only three batsmen doing so, the lowest for any six-year period since 1900. In 1967 the highest individual aggregate was only 2,089 runs, the lowest since 1898.

At least one batsman made 300 runs or more in all but nine seasons from 1914 to 1950: since then only four seasons have seen such innings.

The average number of innings of 200 or over in 1963–8 was four, the lowest for any six-year period since 1897.

Only 149 centuries were scored in 1965, three more than in 1958, and both the lowest since 1910: the average number from 1956–68 was some sixty per season lower than from 1919–35.

For the first time since 1891, a total of 500 was not achieved in 1968 nor in 1969 and the 1969 total was the lowest since 1878. The average number of times 400 was exceeded per season from 1953–69 was some fifty lower than from 1946 to 1952, or from 1919 to 1939. Only three seasons saw 600 exceeded since 1951 but from 1895 to 1951 only eight seasons failed to see such a score. No bowler has taken 200 wickets in a season since 1957, and only four have done so since the last war. From 1922 to 1939 only two seasons were without at least one such taker.

Only five bowlers took 100 wickets or more in 1969, the lowest since 1889, and 1969 saw the lowest aggregate of wickets (109) by the leading wicket-taker in a full season in the last hundred years.

From 1895 to 1939 the average number of cricketers doing the double per season was about five or six, the lowest being one in 1895: from 1946 to 1969 the average has been under three with four seasons with no one doing it and six with only one.

Though run-rates are not known for seasons, they have been established for Tests and there has been a steady decline world-wide in the rate of scoring since about 1950, from a fairly high level from about the mid-1890s, with only a slow decline since the peak was reached just before the First World War until the big slump about 1950. A slight tendency to rise in recent years does not even restore the level to pre-1950. It should be pointed out in this connection that, in terms of a 120-over playing period, a difference in a run-rate per over from 2·4 to 2·7 makes the difference between below and above 300 runs in the day, a difference of considerable psychological importance to onlookers and more distant enthusiasts. Such a difference is highly significant.

Similar figures can be produced for other countries which tend to show the same general falling-off in batting and bowling ability. The term ability is used: some may say that what is in question is a defensive attitude, but this, surely, is ability, or its lack.

Afterword

The theme of this book is of rise, life and decline. It is my view that by the end of this century cricket will still be found, fairly world-wide, but played as a game for pleasure (even at the club cricket level) as all games and sports should be played or indulged in. Its rise was an accident of geography and social history, and, maybe, of one or two other local factors: its esteem during the best part of its healthy life was something quite definitely accidental as it became a kind of hand-maiden of the British Empire: and its decline was as inevitable as was the decline of that Empire.

A little parallel is worth drawing here. There was a book known as 'Cole's Imperial Military Geography',[1] at one time obligatory for candidates for the Staff College. One of the book's important theses was that the non-self governing part of the British Empire was a British-Indian Empire. Of course there were some areas where the statement did not apply but from Durban to, in those days, Shanghai, Indian police or troops, Indian civil servants, Indian traders – one of these groups at least – were involved as well as their British counterparts. Even outside that wide arc round the Indian Ocean and beyond, you can find Indians in Fiji, Trinidad, Guyana, the West Coast of Africa and even in the so-British Gibraltar. Thus the moment the decision was taken to relinquish any hold on India, the whole basis for the British Empire, its *raison d'être* and its manpower, disappeared. No politician in Britain showed any signs of realizing this: no leading military man showed such signs either though the thesis must have been well-known to them. I had preached this to my friends from 1947 on: one takes no credit for seeing the obvious, least of all when it has been revealed by others.

This is what has been happening in the world of cricket. Those that run it

[1] Major D. H. Cole, *The Imperial Military Geography* (8th edition, 1935).

have been burying their heads in the sand and have refused either to see what is happening to the game or the altering social circumstances in which it has been played, and they have refused to study any remedy. The decline has been much worse in some countries than others: because of this, those in control in this country have pointed to where there has been very little or no decline as though this made up for what has been happening under their own noses. They have for the most part been men of little intelligence and little status: it is only necessary to compare the composition of such a body as the Committee of the MCC now with that of thirty years ago to realize what a change there has been. It is not now a body which commands much respect, and one of the reasons is that too much is said on its behalf which is at best only partly true, or, often, misleading: too much is done for reasons lacking proper validity: too much takes place which smacks of veniality, of self-interest, and of straightforward vanity. It is doubtful if any other controlling body in sport in this country commands so little respect from the very type of person who, in another age, would have been automatically expected to respect it. The decline of cricket in this country started in the early 1950s: just when the prestige of the MCC started to decline, and it may well be no coincidence that it was about that time that the MCC decided it ought to treat the Press more kindly. It can see where that has led it.

For the best part of twenty years nothing has been done to stop the decline: new rules, new laws, new competitions, new regulations have flowed out from St John's Wood but the basic trouble, which may be summed up in one word as over-professionalism, has never been touched. It never could have been touched by people who think of the initials 'MCC' as a kind of talisman to be attached to everything, of cricket as almost a holy game, and of Lord's as a kind of mediaeval cathedral. If they had not been so conscious of their own importance, if they could have seen that Lord's is just another ground[1] like Kennington Oval, or the Basin Reserve in Wellington (what a name for a cricket ground!), that cricket is just a game and not an ethic, then something might have been done.

I personally think the game will last but, as a result of mis-government, not even on a minor key, but as something rough and ready, something for which there will be no money, something where the present-day implements (already terribly expensive) will be replaced by much cheaper ones (metal bats are not

---

[1] There is for instance nothing more natural than to take one's tie off on a hot day when watching cricket, but members, and not only of the MCC, are still told at Lord's that they may only do this on the top of the pavilion.

against the Laws) and longer-lasting even semi-permanent, wickets, and so located as not to interfere with the summer game of football. It will become a boy's game again, for an occasional afternoon, or sometimes the evening: a grown man may feel the urge from time to time to smite the ball or to bring off some stupendous running catch, and some of them may occasionally get a game up playing in their ordinary dress as was the case at the highest level little more than a hundred years ago. *Wisden* will long since have ceased publication, but old copies will be much sought after by real statisticians for the fascinating distributional problems it provides. Cricket literature will be regarded as a wondrous thing, and cricket libraries as valueless and odd aberrations, though some of the books they contain may be found to have a rarity value, and others may be of great interest to sociologists and psychiatrists of the next century. For if the first-class game declines, the club game will go too: and as the first-class game has declined it is only too easy to see also the decline there has actually been in the club game in both quantity and quality. All of this might have been avoided.

Twenty years ago, I wrote a detailed memorandum which pointed out, with the knowledge of those days but without the hindsight of these, that factors such as full employment and the taxation of the well-to-do would make the continuation of the first-class game impossible along the then lines: the lines it still follows. I suggested a two-divisional county championship, both divisions first-class with promotion and relegation: I suggested two-day cricket of long hours at weekends, on public holidays, and in mid-week in August: I pointed out that the number of days needed for a county to complete a programme was well within the weekends, public holidays and during the individuals' own annual holiday. I showed that the true amateur, who has hardly ever played in first-class cricket in England (though he has overwhelmingly done so overseas), would be able now to play: that the waste of money on ill-paid mediocre professionals could be concentrated into retaining two or three outstanding players per county, any of whom would be unlucky not to be chosen for England, instead of in the state then, and far more so now, lucky to find themselves even on a short list. There were a few murmurings about this scheme: but nothing was ever done, and when I elaborated some parts of it in 1963 in *Cricket Quarterly* I knew already that it was too late; for in the meantime there had been vast social changes in England.

These are still continuing. Twenty years ago it was still possible to consider counties credible as a part of England's structure. Now they are no longer credible, and county cricket teams are not viable. In each of the four countries of the United Kingdom, responsible government commissions have recommended the replacement of counties by other authorities. So far as cricket administration is concerned, the majority of first-class, of minor, of Welsh, and of Scottish cricketing counties will cease to be identifiable (as, for instance, Middlesex has already ceased to be identifiable) with their successor authorities and those that can be will have greatly altered boundaries. Indeed so far as playing cricket is concerned, first-class teams can no longer be found from counties: county clubs – which C. B. Fry showed over sixty years ago in his own magazine are mere bodies of season ticket holders, and not representative in any way nor, for the most part, were real cricket clubs either (even fewer are such clubs now) – are no longer able to find teams which can even claim to be first-class without hiring overseas professionals, or rejects from the one or two strong counties which remain. It is plain then, that any scheme based on counties is by now a non-starter: what is needed is a grouping of counties to provide, from the limits of the new grouping, teams strong enough to play first-class cricket: teams somewhat comparable with Australian State teams, playing four-day cricket in mid-week or, in some weeks, at weekends. Such teams would, no doubt, be professional rather than amateur: but they would be viable. There is no sign of any present interest in such grouped teams: the talk is of four-day mid-week county cricket, and there is no prospect of that kind of competition doing any good at all.

Yet it may be in the end all for the good: it is good that nations grow up. It is good that they cease from childish things, and it may well be that, without in the least realizing it, the MCC has done the English and some other nations much benefit. There is one thing they may ponder: in 1969 half a million people, young people, assembled in a public park to hear a pop group. The most sedate crowd at cricket could have taught them nothing about decent behaviour. These young people do not need, nor do they want, cricket.

Or is this all wrong? Is first-class cricket just in a trough? It has been in troughs before. Its precursor was in a trough in the mid-eighteenth century. It was in a terrible trough in America after the Revolution but arose stronger than ever before, though it is all gone now. It was in a sad trough in Australia in the 1890s, first-class and lower, but rapidly climbed out of that with intelligent changes in organization. It was in a trough here in the Napoleonic wars, in the early years of round-arm, in the early years of the Age of Grace. But if it is in a trough now it has been settling deeper into it every year for twenty years, as long as ever it has been in a trough in this country before. What is undeniable and notwithstanding local keenness, is an overall decline in interest in the game at

255

school and club levels, which outweighs the local maintenance of enthusiasm. How can the game possibly emerge from this?

One thing seems certain: the minutely detailed organization which has now 'assumed charge' of cricket in England (in the words of the MCC official announcement in 1968), at a cost of many thousands of pounds a year[1] is not likely to be the source from which the resurrection of the game may come. It was thrown together in the fashion which Professor C. Northcote Parkinson has made familiar, and it should be remembered that Parkinson considers that comprehensive organizations only come into existence when the need for them has ceased.

Even as this book was being prepared for the printers, the MCC furnished yet another example of the apparent inability of cricket's administrators to look forward. It is the stated policy of the government of this country that all measurements shall be in metric terms by 1975: proper metrication does not, however, simply mean just putting imperial measurements into metric equivalents – it involves using measurements which would be natural in metric terms. Yet the MCC announces that there will be no changes in cricket's measurements, thus condemning the youth of the future to play on pitches, and to measure out pitches, measuring 20·12 metres. Cricket's administrators are not prepared to sacrifice the odd three inches to get a nice round figure in metric terms, a change as small as four parts in one thousand. It is noteworthy that in athletics no one is proposing to run 201·2 metres as the equivalent of 220 yards: the figure is being rounded to 200 metres, and the fact that 200 metres has long been used in competitions in countries which use the metric system is relevant only to the extent that we are now moving on to the metric system and must use normal metric measurements.

This is no trough into which the game has fallen: it is a decline into the grave. Does it matter? To those who have enjoyed playing, watching, reading, talking, writing cricket all their lives, of course it does. But in not so many years we will all be dead. Americans have largely forgotten their own great cricket past, of barely sixty years ago, and even those in England who should know about it, have forgotten that past too. So it will be here, as the decline grows apace. Many can remember when many thousands, even twenty thousand people would watch Eton v. Harrow, and now it is barely possible to count as many score. It has vanished within a few years as though it had never been. I mention it to show how sudden and complete has been the decline in one small aspect of the game. It will

---

[1] Try as one will, it is very difficult to understand how such sums can be spent on the central administration of cricket.

continue, and in less than a hundred years, those who have enjoyed cricket will probably be a handful of dodderers; an episode in the social history of England, and to some extent of the world, will have closed. Part of the purpose of this book is to provide for those who live a hundred years hence some reasoned account of how and why it all happened, and what its effect was.

I

Chronological Appendices

with decorations by Bernard Hollowood

Notes on the Appendices

The Appendices which follow are intended to provide the dates for all the more important administrative, touring and record-breaking events, in no matter what class of cricket, which have occurred. With one or two exceptions the births and deaths of cricketers are not shown. Nor is any attempt made to show all the very many tours which have taken place: even before the 1950s when they were relatively infrequent. Nor, again, is any attempt made to show something about every country where cricket has been played. It must have been played in every country in the world at some time or other but, for the most part, by British expatriates, civilian or military. But, with few exceptions, and those not intentional, something has been entered about every country where cricket is played to any substantial extent by the local inhabitants.

Appendix I shows cricket in one table, up to 1850, world-wide. From then on is covered by Appendix II, split into different headings: England, Australia, Southern Africa, West Indies, New Zealand, India, Canada and the U.S.A. to 1946, Pakistan, and 'Other countries' (including Canada and the U.S.A. from 1947). A number of references to the minor countries appear not only under 'Other Countries' but also under the main countries if tours to or from the main countries by the minor countries have occurred. Competition results, where worth showing, are complete to the end of the 1970 season.

No one would pretend that a collection of dates, facts and figures such as this is entirely without error or completely comprehensive within its own terms of reference. I am indebted to David Gallagher for assistance in removing errors and if any remain he is not to be blamed.

On the other hand, a number of differences will be found between what is stated here and what will be found in some other sources. In almost every case, the reason is that the latter have not been soundly based. Though important in themselves, they are but details in a work of this scope and it has rarely been thought worth while – let alone practicable in terms of space – justifying different statements made in what follows.

I should however welcome corrigenda and addenda for future editions.

Appendix I

DATES IN CRICKET HISTORY
WORLD-WIDE TO 1850

13th century	'*Crosser*', French verb meaning to play '*crosse*'. This was a catch-all term covering any game played with a clubbed staff and a ball and included golf, hockey and cricket
1300	First probable reference to cricket ('Creag') in England, in the Wardrobe Accounts of Edward I, the locality being Newenden in Kent
Early 14th century	Depiction of game resembling cricket in illustrated MSS in the British Museum (Royal MS. 10E. iv, f. 94 b)
1478	'*Criquet*' referred to in north-eastern France, in what was then Flanders, in the vicinity of St Omer where, in 1593, the Jesuit school which became Stonyhurst was founded. (See plate 1.)
Early 16th century	Depiction of game resembling cricket in Flemish Book of Months in the British Museum (Add, MS. 24098, f. 21 b)
1523	'Stoball' or stool-ball first referred to, another catch-all term including rounders and cricket
c. 1550	Cricket played at the 'Free School' at Guildford (mentioned in a court case of 1597. The date was set down as 'the Monday after the feast of St Hilary in the 40th year of the reign of Elizabeth', i.e. 17 January 1597 Old Style which is 1598 New Style). (See plate 2.)
1598	G. Florio's Italian-English dictionary mentions cricket. (It has not been possible to confirm a report that it was published three years earlier in Italy, despite extensive searches)
c. 1610	'Cricketing' between Weald and Upland against Chalkhill near Chevening Kent
1611	Cricket mentioned in Randle Cotgrave's French-English dictionary
1621	Stool-ball played on Thanksgiving Day in Massachusetts
1622	Six parishioners prosecuted for playing cricket in the churchyard on Sunday at Boxgrove, Sussex
1624	Jasper Vinall killed accidentally at Horsted Keynes, Sussex, through batsman attempting to hit the ball twice to avoid being caught

1629	Cricket being played at Ruckinge, Kent, by 'persons of repute and fashion'
c. 1635	Cricket often played on Sundays at Maidstone before this date, but by then suppressed (see 1640)
c. 1636	Cricket at East Horsley, Surrey. (A supposition that a cricket ground was made here about this time is based on a misreading of a late seventeenth-century document)
1640	Cricketers found guilty of playing cricket on Sunday, in a court case at Maidstone
1646	First recorded cricket match at Coxheath, Kent. All those taking part were of some social standing. The match also involved the first record of betting on cricket
1647	Probable reference to cricket being played by Winchester scholars on St Catherine's Hill, in a Latin poem by Robert Matthew
1652	Unsuccessful attempts to prosecute several inhabitants of Cranbrook, Kent, for playing 'the unlawful game called cricket'. (N.B. – there is no evidence that it actually was unlawful, except on Sunday)
1654	Seven parishioners of Eltham fined for playing cricket on the Lord's Day
1656	'Krickett' proscribed by Cromwell's Commissioners throughout Ireland; all 'sticks' and balls to be burnt by the common hangman. A possible, but unprovable reference to cricket in New Amsterdam, later New York
1658	Cricket balls as such first mentioned
c. 1665	John Churchill, later first Duke of Marlborough, played cricket at old St Paul's School
1668	Decision by J.P.s at Maidstone concerning sale of beer at a 'kriceting' indicating that cricket was already a spectator sport on an appreciable scale. Mine host of the Ram Inn at Smithfield rated for a cricket field thus indicating that cricket was already a business
1676	First certain reference to Englishmen playing cricket abroad, when on holiday at Aleppo
1677	The Earl of Sussex, son-in-law of Charles II, present at cricket on Dicker Common near Chiddingly, Sussex
1679	Birth of William Bedle, accounted when he died in 1768 as 'formerly the most expert cricket player in England' – the first of a long line
1685	Cricket known to have been played on Mitcham Green
1693	Spectators at a cricket match in Sussex fined for 'riot and battery'
1694	2s 6d paid for a 'Wagger' [sic] about the cricket match at 'Lewis' [sic]
1697	A 'great' cricket match played somewhere in Sussex, and reported in a London paper
1700	Cricket being played on Clapham Common
1705	Match between West Kent and Chatham at Malling
1706	First full description of a cricket match, in a Latin poem, In certamen pilae, written by William Goldwin of Eton and King's, Cambridge
1707	Mitcham challenged London and London played Croydon on Lamb's Conduit Fields

1709	First county match, Kent *v.* Surrey at Dartford. William Byrd III of Westover, playing cricket with his friends on estates along the James River, Virginia
1710	First mention of cricket at Cambridge University
1719	Kent beat London in White Conduit Fields, Islington
1721	Mariners of the East India Company played cricket at Cambay, India
1725	Cricket being played at Boston in New England
	First recorded match on the Artillery ground, Finsbury. This ground has continued in being ever since, belonging to the H.A.C.
1727	'Articles of Agreement' governing the conduct of matches between the teams of the second Duke of Richmond, and Mr Broderick of Peperharrow, clearly supplementary to a code of Laws which has not survived. G. B. Buckley was certain that earlier articles must have existed and had reason (which he did not give) to believe that they had been used in 1722. First mention of cricket at Oxford University. Twelve men over seventy (three over eighty) celebrated Restoration Day by playing cricket. Horace Walpole said cricket was then common at Eton
1728	César de Saussure, a Swiss traveller, records the great popularity of county cricket at that time
1729	Date of earliest surviving bat: inscribed 'J. C. 1729' (J. C. was John Chitty), it is to be seen in the Oval Pavilion. First reference to cricket at Gloucester – a very early reference for that part of England
1731	First reference to cricket in Essex
1736	Crews of H.M. ships at Lisbon playing cricket there. First recorded tie: London 4 and 19 *v.* Richmond, Fulham and Barnes 18 and 5, on Lamb's Conduit Fields
1737	Mention of cricket in Georgia, N. America. First reference to cricket in Hertfordshire
1739	Earliest known depiction of cricket, under the name 'The game of cricket' by French artist Gravelot: twenty years later he published the same illustration in France under the name '*le jeu de la crosse*'. (See p. 36.)
1741	Cricket played on Christmas Day at Savannah, Georgia (Savannah had been founded only eight years earlier). First references to cricket in Bedfordshire and Northamptonshire. First recorded two-day *fixture* – Hill *v.* Dale at Maidstone, August 21 and 22
1742	Highland Scots celebrated St Andrew's Day in Savannah by playing cricket
1743	Picture of a match by Francis Hayman, now at Lord's. First recorded match lasting two days, between London and Sevenoaks, August 23 and 24, on the Vine. London won by 6 runs. First reference to cricket in Suffolk
1744	June 18: the first great match of which the full score has been preserved, Kent *v.* All England on the Artillery ground (a less important match was played a few days earlier, whose score also survives). The match, won by

1744	Kent, was described in full by James Dance, alias Love, in his 'Cricket: a Heroic Poem' published the same year. The first known issue of the Laws of Cricket, undoubtedly a recension of an earlier code, and drawn up by the London Club whose President was Frederick Louis, Prince of Wales, father of George III, who died as a result of a blow from a cricket ball in 1751. First recorded charge for admission: 2d to the Artillery ground (raised to 6d for the match following, Kent *v.* All England, evoking much protest). At this time the toss conferred choice of pitch and innings
1745	First reference to cricket in Norfolk
1747	Cricket being played in New York
1749	First reference to *a* cricket *match* in Hampshire (at Portsmouth)
c. 1750	Cricket being played by the military at Perth in Scotland
1750	In the match between Dartford and Addington, five of the Dartford men in their second innings were dismissed with consecutive balls, the first recorded instance of even as many as three such dismissals
1751	Old Etonians play the Gentlemen of England. Cricket mentioned as far north as Yorkshire and Durham, and as far west as Somerset. First reference to cricket in Berkshire. First recording of the fall of each wicket. Match in New York between New York and a London XI 'played according to the London method'. Presumably this will have been in accordance with the 1744 Code which by now differed sharply from the much older version of the game still being widely played in North America
1752	First reference to a Marylebone club, playing against an XI of London on August 31. This had no connection with the 1787 club, but in each case the expression used signified no more than a group of people in a particular locale playing cricket. In the case of the later club it became formalized and so a permanent name, even when it moved to another locale in 1811, in St John's Wood. (The recently defunct Borough of St Marylebone which also included St John's Wood only came into existence in 1888.)
1754	Cricket being played in Maryland. First known match by Cambridge University, against Eton, who won
c 1754–61	At about this time, the Duke of Dorset, then at Westminster, playing for the Town Boys against King's Scholars, 'had an innings that might have lasted till the time Bacelli (his mistress) ran him out had not the other side given up the game'. This could have been the earliest century scored. The match, then described as the 'great annual match' (thus indicating it had been played for several years) was at the time of its lapse during the last war the oldest annual cricket match in the world
1755	First reference to cricket in Buckinghamshire. Laws revised by 'Star and Garter' Club from which sprang the cricketers who played on White Conduit Fields and eventually the Marylebone Cricket Club
1757	First reference to cricket in Derbyshire

1759	The great Dartford XI twice beat the Rest of England
1760	'Winchester beat Eton' in Port Meadow, Oxford
1761	First match eleven *v.* twenty-two: Dartford *v.* twenty-two of Essex at Woodford
1763	First mention of cricket in Wales (Pembroke). First reference to an Inn with a name certainly connected with cricket: 'at the Sign of the Cricketers' at Rainham in Kent (there are earlier possible references which are, however, more likely to be concerned with the insect)
1766	Horace Walpole watched cricket at Neuilly-sur-Seine, near Paris. William Pett of Sevenoaks sold eleven bats at 2s 6d and two balls at 3s 6d to the Duke of Dorset. First reference to cricket in Northumberland
c. 1767	Formation of the Hambledon Club: matches were played first on Broadhalfpenny and later on Windmill Down, and All England was often defeated. The great days lasted until the early 1790s, though the club survived as an ordinary village cricket club for a generation or more after that. Their great players, immortalized in '*Nyren*' (*see* 1833), evolved a new and much advanced technique. Cricket being played in Connecticut
1768	Cricket being played at Spa, in the then Austrian Netherlands
1769	First recorded century partnership: 128 for first wicket by T. Sueter and G. Lear for Hampshire *v.* Surrey on Broadhalfpenny Down. First recorded century, 107 by John Minshull, for Duke of Dorset's XI *v.* Wrotham. A stroke-by-stroke score was kept of the match, the first such known. The first reference to cricket in Wiltshire
1771	Sheffield played Nottingham for the first time in a long series of matches. T. White playing for Kent and Surrey against Middlesex and Hampshire made 197 runs in two innings. Two-day matches between important teams by now prevailed: in this season occurred the first known three-day fixture, between the Bourn Club and twenty-two of Dover. The Bourn Club was a leading club of the period, and won by two wickets. First limitation placed on the width of the bat – 4½ in. – at which it remains. First references to cricket in Nottinghamshire and Warwickshire
1772	Picture of boys playing cricket at Harrow School. 15,000 to 20,000 people attended first day of match All England *v.* Hampshire at Bourn Paddock in Kent
1773	The 'best sort of cricket batts' from William Pett now cost 4s or 4s 6d each. The match between Surrey and Hampshire at Laleham Burway in September lasted into five days owing to rain on the second: the first match known to have lasted so long
1774	The first known score of over 300: 307 by Hampshire *v.* England at Chertsey. The weight of the ball established at between 5½ oz and 5¾ oz. From now until 1809, the visiting side had the choice of pitch and innings. The first 'l.b.w.' law. The match between Hampshire *v.* Kent at Broadhalfpenny Down lasted four days August 15 to 18, the first known to last so long which was not interrupted by rain

1775	First reference to cricket in Huntingdonshire
1776	Earliest known score-cards, printed by T. Pratt, scorer, Sevenoaks. About this time the stumps were increased from two to three but it took a few years for the increase to become universal; the third stump did not appear in any edition of the Laws until 1785. First reference to cricket in Leicestershire
1777	First record of the bowler being credited for catches off his own bowling. J. Aylward made 167 for Hampshire *v.* England, the highest score in an important match until 1820. In the same match, Hampshire made 403, the first known total of over 400
1778	Many games of cricket being played in New York at this time and for the next few years
1779	By now, three days was the prevalent duration for a great match. But Kent *v.* Surrey July 21–24 at Bishopsbourn was the first known to be *fixed* for four days. The first recorded single-wicket century, by an un-named Notts player on May 10
c. 1780	W. Harding, and R. Purchase, of Frensham went in to get 228 runs and got 200 without being parted, but the rest of the side only got 20 and so lost
1780	Dukes of Penshurst, established 1760, made the first six-seamed ball and presented it to the Prince of Wales, later George IV. (Faringdon, in his diary of 1811, says that the Duke family had then been making cricket balls for 259 years – not impossible if a distinction is made between family and firm)
1781	First references to cricket in Cheshire and Lancashire
1783	Portrait painted of 'Lumpy' Stevens, the earliest known portrait of a cricketer
1785	French Canadians in Montreal recorded playing cricket on Sundays. The first recorded match in Scotland (*see* however *c.* 1750). (See plate 5.)
1786	The match between White Conduit Club and Kent lasted five days, the first match known to have done so apart from those where weather had interrupted. T. Walker averaged 47·0 in important matches, easily the highest so far ascertained. Earliest known mention of the Sevenoaks Vine Cricket Club (no continuity with the present club)
1787	First match, White Conduit Club *v.* Middlesex, May 21 and following days, on Thomas Lord's first ground, on the site of the present Dorset Square. The name Marylebone Cricket Club first encountered on July 30 playing against Islington C.C. First mention of a county club: Oxfordshire (present club 1921). First instance of the 'follow-on': it was then and for many years later the unofficial custom in some parts of the country for the side which was behind to follow its innings, irrespective of the size of the deficit: sometimes this was insisted on by the team leading, and sometimes by the team behind. First reference to cricket in Dorset

1788	On May 30 occurred the first revision of the Laws by the 'Cricket Club at Marylebone'. The Laws now provided that no run should be scored if the striker were caught: but this had been one of the 1727 Articles of Association. A six-a-side single-wicket match lasted six days, August 29 to September 3, Kent v. Hampshire at Bishopsbourn. Rain did not interfere: 78 runs only were scored. This was the first known six-day match in the history of cricket
1789	First known century in Scotland, 136 by Colonel Lennox, in Aberdeen. The New York Cricket Club still very much in being (see plate 9). First English tour abroad, to Paris, abandoned before it started, owing to the outbreak of the French Revolution
1790	During debates in the Constitutional Convention in Boston, U.S.A., objection was taken to calling the Chief Executive of the United States of America a 'President' since one had a President of a Cricket Club. First reference to cricket in Rutland. First mention of a county club, in Essex (present club 1876)
1791	Publication of the first annual record of match scores, by Samuel Britcher: they subsequently covered matches to 1805. It is of interest that there should have been a demand for such a book at a time when the average number of books of all types published in the whole country was only four hundred a year
1792	The Calcutta Cricket Club in being. The first recorded match in Ireland: Dublin Garrison beat All Ireland by an innings. Sussex and Surrey made 453 v. England at Lord's, the highest total so far, and the highest first-class score until 1862. First reference to cricket in Lincolnshire. First record of a 'second eleven' – of the Nottingham Old Club who beat Beeston.
1793	Mr Hope, a Dutch merchant of Amsterdam, portrayed playing cricket at Rome. First recorded seasonal batting averages. A fixture to last five days was made at Brighton between the Right and Left wing of Officers of the Prince of Wales' Camp at Brighton – the first known five-day fixture
1794	In the only instance of a county giving odds to England, thirteen of England beat Surrey by 3 runs. First reference to cricket in Shropshire. First match between Charterhouse and Westminster, at Lord's. This was the first recorded school match
1795	J. Hammond totalled 800 in important matches, the highest seasonal aggregate until F. Pilch's 811 in 1834. First recorded l.b.w. dismissal
1795–7	Tradition that cricket was played during the first British occupation of the Cape
1796	Match between Eton and Westminster at Hounslow, won by Westminster by 66 runs. The match was played in defiance of Dr Heath, the Eton Headmaster, who flogged the whole XI on their return. R. Robinson attained a seasonal average of 50·00 in important matches. A book published in Hamburg in Germany had a detailed description of cricket

1797 Lord Frederick Beauclerk took a minimum of 66 wickets in important matches, the record for a season until F. W. Lillywhite took 77 in 1813. 'Handled ball' first recorded. Cricket played in Bombay

1798 A revision of the Laws provided for a new ball at the start of each innings – hitherto the same ball had been used throughout the match. The wicket was increased from the 22 × 6 in. of 1740 to 24 × 7 in.

1799 A cricket club formed at Seringapatam, S. India, after the successful siege. First reference to cricket in Devon

1800 Engraving published depicting boy with cricket bat in Philadelphia. A match between Eton and Harrow may have taken place. Nottingham dismissed Leicester for 15 and 8, probably the lowest recorded aggregate for both innings in an important match. First known century in Ireland: 160 by Ensign Beckett for Coldstream Guards *v.* Third Guards at Kinsale

c. 1800 Leg-guards, the precursors of pads, first used by R. Robinson, of Surrey. It was another generation before they began to become usual

1801 Translation into Danish of the 1796 German book on the game, published in Copenhagen. T. Boxall published the first instructional book on cricket in English, *Rules and Instructions for playing at the Game of Cricket*, etc.

1803 William Pitt referred to cricket when introducing his Defence Bill. Cricket was being played regularly in Sydney, New South Wales. Lord Frederick Beauclerk averaged 61·63 in important matches

1804 First known century in India; 102 by R. Vansittart for Old Etonians *v.* Rest of Calcutta at Calcutta. In this year was formed the Islington Albion Club, which first played in White Conduit Fields, but in 1834 moved to Copenhagen House (where, later on, the Middlesex Club played for a few years). The Islington Albion lasted until well into the latter part of the century, and during its middle period was a powerful combination as local clubs go, often being able to hire leading players for its matches. It was in one of its matches that occurred the most remarkable fielding performance known to the history of the game, when a player at slip caught all ten of his opponents in an innings, all at the same end, and all off the same bowler. G. B. Buckley, who recorded this in his unpublished 'More Historical Gleanings' gave no further information about it, but anything of this nature recorded by him is likely to be accurate. The feat cannot have been performed before the 1830s and as it does not occur in Buckley's other material, which extends to 1850, it seems likely it occurred in the latter half of the century

1805 Eton met Harrow at Lord's and won by an innings: Lord Byron was in the losing team. A Harrovian who played in this match recorded, however, that Eton had been beaten the previous year

1806 First Gentlemen *v.* Players match, at Lord's (last 1962). Cricket was played by British prisoners of war in the Argentine. A meeting of the St Anne's Cricket Club in Barbados where the game had evidently been established for some time

1807	First mention of the revival of 'straight-armed' (i.e. round-arm) bowling by John Willes of Kent
1808	Match at Cape Town between officers of the Artillery Mess and the Colony
1809	Lord's second ground opened at 'North Bank', subsequently cut by the Regent Canal. About this time the no-ball was introduced for 'foot over crease' – in 1816 it started to be applied to 'throwing'. The umpires were henceforth to select the pitch: choice of innings was decided by toss. Boston C.C. (U.S.A.) in existence
1810	Lowest score ever recorded in a match of obvious importance: 6 by 'The Bs' v. England at Lord's. Crawfurd's 'Light Division' played cricket at Lisbon. Match played at Green Point Common in Cape Town, still used for cricket matches. An American traveller drew a sharp distinction between cricket as played in England and 'our cricket', and referred to the old long low wicket still used in America
1811	Colonel Maceroni, who had a strong British background, formed a cricket club in Naples during the French occupation under Joachim Murat, King of Naples, with many French and Neapolitan officers as members. The price of Duke's best cricket ball was now 7s.
1813	Cornwall formed a county club: the present club dates from 1894. This was also the first reference to cricket in Cornwall
1814	Lord's third ground opened on its present site, the turf having been successively removed from each of the two earlier ones
1815	June 12, a match played by officers of the Brigade of Guards near Brussels, watched by the Duke of Wellington. Epsom made 476 against Middlesex at Lord's, the highest total in any class of cricket until 1859. In July of this year an eleven of Fakenham, Walsingham and Hempton was dismissed for 0 by an eleven of Litcham, Dunham and Brisley, in Norfolk. This is the first recorded instance of a side being all out for nought
1816	Wide-balls first penalized by the Laws and included with Byes until 1827: no-balls also penalized instead of being treated as 'dead'
1817	In the match between Sussex and Epsom at Lord's, W. Lambert scored 107* and 157, the first time a century had been scored in each innings of a match, and it was not done again until 1867. The aggregate for the match was 1,047 runs for 39 wickets, the first time 1,000 had been exceeded in a match, and this was not done again until 1863. Lambert averaged 63·57 for the season, not beaten until W. G. Grace's 78·25 in 1871. The first mention of cricket in Staffordshire, and further afield, in Tasmania
1818	Cricket being played at Valparaiso in Chile
c. 1818–22	Reference in a poem to cricket at Yale University
c. 1819–24	Two monumental marble statues of a batsman and a bowler, done by Henry Rossi, and exhibited at the Royal Academy: now at Woburn Abbey. (See plates 14 and 15.)

1819   County clubs formed in Cheshire (present club 1908) and Shropshire (present club 1956). The Duke of Richmond, Governor-General of Canada, played cricket at Kingston (Ontario). The wicket raised to 26 × 7 in.

1820   First recorded individual score over 200: 278 by William Ward for MCC *v.* Norfolk – the record for Lord's until 1925 and not exceeded in an important match until 1876. The direct ancestor of the present Northamptonshire Club formed (re-formed 1878): a Leicestershire club in existence (the present club dates from 1879)

c. 1820   Wicket-keeping gloves probably first used by J. Bernard (Eton, and later the West Kent Cricket Club)

1821   First century in Gentlemen *v.* Players; 113* by T. Beagley. A cricket club of evident long standing referred to at Charleston, South Carolina

1822   Gibraltar C.C. played for the first time

1823   H. Bentley issued his *Correct Account of all Matches 1786–1822*: two supplements appeared for season 1823, and 1824–5. The first reference to cricket in Herefordshire, and a county club known to exist in Monmouthshire (present club formed 1962). The wicket again increased to 27 × 8 in.

1824   County club formed in Devon (the present club dates from 1899)

1825   First Harrow *v.* Winchester match, at Lord's, won by Winchester. The night following the match, the Lord's pavilion with many valuable records was destroyed by fire

1826   First recorded century in a school match: 146* by W. Meyrick for Winchester *v.* Harrow. First Eton *v.* Winchester match, won by Winchester. County clubs formed in Warwickshire (the present club dates from 1884) and Perthshire. The first known cricket clubs in Sydney, N.S.W.

1827   First match between Oxford and Cambridge Universities: drawn. Three experimental matches played between Sussex and England to try out the new (round-arm) bowling now perfected by F. W. Lillywhite and James Broadbridge of Sussex. Wides first recorded as such. First reference to cricket in Westmorland (a county club was reported there in 1835). County club formed in Norfolk (the present club dates from 1876). Six-ball overs were used in the Eton *v.* Harrow match at Lord's

1828   Laws amended to allow the bowler to raise his hand level with his elbow. First reference to cricket in Cumberland

1829   An English cricket club in existence near Paris. No-balls were to be scored as such, and debited as one run – the first recorded instance was in 1830. First reference to cricket in Worcestershire. County club formed in Co. Carlow, and in existence in Co. Kilkenny – neither now exists

1830   No-balls first shown separately on score sheet. County club formed for Pembrokeshire (present club 1947)

1831   F. W. Lillywhite took 77 wickets in important matches in the season, the record till 1837. County club formed in Huntingdonshire (present club 1948). The Union Cricket Club in Philadelphia in existence by this date. Buenos Aires C.C. first formed

1832   County club formed in Breconshire (no longer in existence). A cricket club formed in Tasmania, at Hobart: the Colombo Cricket Club formed in Ceylon: mention of cricket in New Zealand though there are reasons to think it had been played much earlier, one being Charles Darwin's reference to Maoris playing at Waiwatc at Christmastime, 1835

1833   Charles Cowden Clarke compiled and wrote, from the recollections of John Nyren, *The Young Cricketer's Tutor* and *The Cricketers of My Time*. The latter is the *locus classicus* for late eighteenth-century cricket personalities, and the book is outstanding as literature

1834   Fuller Pilch achieved an aggregate of 811 runs in important matches: the highest till 1861, and he averaged 45·05. First full bowling analysis kept in the match Yorkshire *v.* Norfolk, including for the first time maiden overs. County club formed for Northumberland (present club 1895) and for Lanarkshire (no longer exists). Cricket was being played at Hamilton and Guelph in Upper Canada (now Ontario) and a cricket club was formed in Toronto. Cricket introduced at Haverford College, Pennsylvania

1835   Revised Code of Laws adopted on May 20. J. H. Kirwan became the first bowler known to have taken all ten wickets in an innings, playing for Eton *v.* MCC at Eton. Length of bat now limited to 38 in., and follow-on now compulsory after deficit of 100 runs, reduced to 80 from 1854 and 60 in a one-day match. County club formed in Co. Wicklow – no longer exists. First mention of cricket in Western Australia

1836   First North *v.* South match: for many years regarded as greatest match of the season. Bats now cost 7s each. Sussex county organization set up, leading to county club in 1839. County club formed for Herefordshire – no longer exists. Cricket being played in Norfolk Island. Upper Canada College, Toronto, known to be playing cricket

1837   F. W. Lillywhite took 120 wickets in important matches, the first time 100 wickets had been exceeded; in 1839 J. Cobbett broke the record by taking 131. A. Adams made 279 in a minor match, the record till 1868. First matches played on the new Trent Bridge ground at Nottingham, opened by William Clarke in September. First recorded match in South Australia. Cricket being played in Singapore

1838   Circumference of ball established at between 9 in. and 9¼ in. A Maidstone newspaper referred to the Kent *v.* Notts match as being for the County Championship. County club formed for Hertfordshire (present club 1876). Formation of Melbourne Cricket Club, and of Launceston Cricket Club in Tasmania. A cricket club in existence in Mexico City

1839   First tied game in important cricket: MCC *v.* Oxford and Cambridge Universities at Lord's. A spring-handled bat now cost 10s 6d and this price was held for many years. About this time practice nets were

271

1839	instituted at Eton. A county club was formed in Queen's County (Co. Leix) – no longer exists. First recorded century in Australia, 120 by F. A. Paulett in Melbourne. Cricket was played in Kabul, Afghanistan. Parsi schoolboys were being instructed in cricket in Bombay
1840	F. W. Lillywhite took 133 wickets in the season and in 1842 beat that by taking 157 wickets. Cricket first played about this time in Georgetown, Guyana. A cricket club formed in Antigua by this time. Cricket club in existence in Rio de Janeiro. First recorded century in Tasmania, 101 by H. Wade in Hobart. The Carleton Cricket Club formed in Ottawa. A match between Toronto Cricket Club and St George's Cricket Club, New York. Cricket being played in Hong Kong. The interval between innings reverted from 15 minutes to 10 minutes but in practice often remained longer till the twentieth century
1841	The Commander-in-Chief of the Army, Lord Hill, issued an order providing for cricket grounds to be made near every barrack-station in the kingdom. County club formed for Nottinghamshire, and one in existence by this date for Berkshire (present club 1895). First publication of the Laws in Tasmania. Cricket being played in the Bay of Islands, New Zealand
1842	The Canterbury Week instituted. County club formed for Kent, direct ancestor of the present club which arose from an amalgamation in 1870: another for Co. Meath (no longer exists). *Punch* first mentioned cricket in July. Wellington Cricket Club in New Zealand already in existence. Trinidad Cricket Club in West Indies already of 'very long standing'. A cricket club formed at University of Pennsylvania (the University C.C. followed five years later). Cricket recorded at Wynberg in South Africa where the first recorded century in that country was made – 110* by B. Taylor
1842–3	Round-arm bowling introduced into Australia
1843	Denison's *Cricketer's Companion* first appeared, issued for four years (in six editions) in all. T. Hunt made the record score in genuine single wicket of 165 *v.* G. Chatterton at Hyde Park, Sheffield. Cricket being played in Maritzburg, Natal. Port Elizabeth Cricket Club formed in Cape Colony
1844	First fully recorded match in New Zealand, at Nelson. Wynberg Cricket Club in Cape Town in existence. St George's Park ground, Port Elizabeth, first used – still used for Test cricket (also called Crusader's Park). First recorded century in North America – 120 by J. Turner. First of series of international matches between Canada and U.S.A., the oldest series of international matches in cricket. County clubs formed in Worcestershire and Cambridgeshire (present clubs 1865 and 1891)
1845	W. Hillyer took 208 wickets in important matches, the first time 200 had been exceeded, and easily the most by a bowler till 1870. The first match at Kennington Oval, and formation of the Surrey Club. County club formed for East Lothian, no longer in existence. First account of cricket

1845 at Auckland, New Zealand, but the game is believed to have been played there at least two years earlier. First recorded century in Sydney, N.S.W., 112* by W. Tunks. *The Laws of Cricket, with Notes and Hints to the Young Cricketer*, by G. A. Barber, published in Toronto, the earliest known Canadian cricket book. Cricket being played in Holland, at Northey. Bermuda Cricket Club in existence by this time. 1845 saw the foundation of the first of the many celebrated amateur touring clubs, I Zingari. In 1851 the Quidnuncs were formed at Cambridge University and the following year the Harlequins at Oxford. In 1856 the Free Foresters were formed, with membership confined to the Midlands until 1891. In 1861, the Incogniti were formed, and in 1862 the Butterflies. A similar wandering club, Na Shuler (The Rovers) was formed in Dublin, in 1863. There has been no such club in Scotland, and overseas the only one with prestige is the Dutch club, 'De Flamingoes' formed in 1926. There are or have been many other wandering clubs whose membership is confined either to former pupils of a particular public school, or to residence in a particular county, and some other more general ones of later date: in these categories could be mentioned Eton Ramblers, Uppingham Wanderers, Hampshire Hogs, Band of Brothers, Emeriti, Nondescripts and Cryptics

1846 The All England XI organized by William Clarke. It toured the country playing local teams of odds and introducing to remote areas the great players of the day. An admirable lithograph of the team, from a drawing by N. Felix the famous Kent batsman was published in 1847. First match played was at Hyde Park, Sheffield, August 31, September 1 and 2, *v.* XX of Sheffield. The Eleven played fewer matches as time went on and the last was in 1879. In opposition to Clarke, J. Dean and J. Wisden formed the United All England XI, who first played at Southampton in August 1852: they lasted until 1869. G. Freeman and R. Iddison then formed the United North of England XI which first played in 1870 and lasted until 1881. Meanwhile in 1865 E. Willsher had formed the United South of England XI which in the 1870s became almost the property of the Grace family and lasted until 1882, having changed its name to United England XI on the demise of the UNEE in 1881. In 1858 T. Sherman formed a New All England XI, and this with changes of management lasted intermittently until 1862: in 1875 and 1876, T. Sherman and W. Caffyn ran a New United South of England XI. A United North and South of England XI, of no great merit, secretary G. Baker, ran from 1866 to 1868. In Ireland, Charles Laurence formed the United Ireland XI in 1856, which ran until 1861, and in Victoria there was a United Victorian XI which lasted two or three years in the early 1860s. There were no other derivatives outside England, but there were several minor teams, which played only one or two matches, with similar titles during the whole period of these much greater Elevens, a period which covered almost forty years.

1846	This year the last match was played for the single wicket championship between A. Mynn and N. Felix. F. P. Fenner opened his ground at Cambridge: it was leased by the University Cricket Club from 1873, and the freehold was purchased in 1892. The telegraph score-board introduced at Lord's, where score-cards were sold for the first time that season. Madras Cricket Club formed in India. International series between Canada and U.S.A. suspended because Canadian batsmen charged down the bowler trying to make a catch (evidently acting on an old eighteenth-century law)
1847	Cricket being played in Karachi. County club for Bedfordshire formed (present club 1899). Cricket club formed at Hamilton, Ontario
1848	William Gilbert Grace born on July 18. E. Hinkly became the first bowler known to have taken all ten wickets in an innings in an important match, Kent v. England at Lord's. Leg-byes first recorded as such. A county club formed by this date in Co. Kildare. Cricket club in existence in Dunedin, New Zealand. Parsis in Bombay form Orient Cricket Club. H. J. Maddock took all 10 for 16 in Toronto – the first time in Canada
1849	First match between Yorkshire and Lancashire. 'Bat' (T. Box) issued his *Cricketer's Manual*: several more issues until 1851. It had some of the contents expected of an annual, including seasonal averages. Fred Lillywhite issued his *Young Cricketer's Treatise* which changed its name to *Guide to Cricketers* in 1850, and became an annual lasting until 1866 and then merged with the *Green Lillywhite*. County clubs formed for Hampshire (present club 1863) and Co. Cork. From now on the pitch could be swept and rolled between innings
1850	Cricket regularly played in Lahore at this time. It was also being played at St George's College, Kingston (Jamaica). The inhabitants of Bloemfontein were challenged to a cricket match

'A wandering club'

Appendix II

DATES IN CRICKET HISTORY
1851-1970

Column *1*	.	England
Column *2*	.	Australia
Column *3*	.	Southern Africa
Column *4*	.	West Indies
Column *5*	.	New Zealand
Column *6*	.	India
Column *7a*	.	Canada and USA to 1946
Column *7b*	.	Pakistan from 1947
Column *8*	.	Other Countries (including Canada and USA from 1946)

Note on Arrangement

From 1851 to 1885 (page 291 the events for Southern Africa (Column 3), West Indies (Column 4), New Zealand (Column 5) and India (Column 6) are gathered together in the third column of each opening. Similarly Canada and the U.S.A. (Column 7a) and Other Countries (Column 8) are given in the fourth column. After 1884 each country is given its column as numbered, Columns 1, 2, 3, 4 appearing on one opening and Columns 5, 6, 7, 8 on the next (except where noted). After 1946, however, Canada and U.S.A. are included under Other Countries and Pakistan is given in Column 7b.

In column 4, Guyana has been used throughout instead of British Guiana, or the earlier Demerara which, when named, refers to the country.

In column 6, highest scores by teams are not shown if below 400. In column 8, generally, only those countries are referred to whose own inhabitants play or have played cricket. Wicket partnerships are stated for Ceylon, and for Denmark and Holland, usually only if over 200. They are only scantily available elsewhere. First matches between countries are also shown. In columns 2-5, first matches between first-class territorial teams are shown but their immense number makes this impracticable both for the U.K. and for India or Pakistan. First matches *by* each county in England are shown as Appendix III.

1. ENGLAND

(including Scotland, Ireland and Wales)

2. AUSTRALIA

1851 Oxford University C.C. rented the Magdalen ground, Cowley, as a University ground: it moved to the Parks in 1881, but now often uses the Christ Church ground when admission has to be charged

1852 The United All England XI formed in rivalry to William Clarke's team: secretaries Wisden and Dean (see 1846 entry). County clubs formed in Carmarthenshire and Renfrewshire (they no longer exist)

1853 The first mention of a Champion County – Nottinghamshire. Cane-handled bats invented about this time. County clubs formed in Lincolnshire (present club 1921) and Kinross-shire (no longer exists)

1854 Last of the public schools weeks involving Eton, Harrow and Winchester at Lord's. William Clarke took 476 wickets in all matches in the season

1850–5 About this time the mowing-machine began to be used on cricket grounds, but sheep continued to be used at Lord's for many years

1855 The Bramall Lane ground was opened at Sheffield. An attempt to institute a county knock-out competition failed. First Marlborough v. Rugby match, at Lord's. County club existed in Dumfriesshire by this date (no longer exists)

1856 A county club formed for Stirlingshire in either this year, or 1862. First Cheltenham v. Marlborough match. Rev. W. Fellows drove a ball 175 yards from hit to pitch on the Christchurch ground at Oxford, the longest authenticated hit

1857 The Cricketers Fund Friendly Society instituted: for ten years the great match between the All England XI and the United XI was played in its support. First match at Old Trafford, Manchester v. Liverpool: the

1850–1 First inter-colonial match, Tasmania v. Victoria at Launceston

1852–3 First century in South Australia, but in a single wicket match: 109 by J. Cocker

1855 Establishment of the Melbourne C.C. on its present ground – the Richmond Paddock

1855–6 First match Victoria v. New South Wales, at Melbourne. A charge for admission was made, for the first time in Australia

1857 First reference to cricket in Queensland (the colony was not separated from New South Wales until 1859). Formation of New South Wales Cricket Association (the date is not finally established and some authorities give

276

3. SOUTHERN AFRICA
4. WEST INDIES
5. NEW ZEALAND
6. INDIA

7a. CANADA
and the U.S.A.

1851 Cricket club formed in Maritzburg, SA: it did not last many years, and the present club dates from 1884
1851 Christchurch Cricket Club, New Zealand, formed and cricket first played in Hagley Park

1853 The Domain first used for cricket in Auckland

1854 Match between Hottentots and Afric-ander [*sic*] Boers in Cape Province: the Hottentots won
1854 First known publication on cricket in India – *Calcutta Cricket Club Matches* 1844–54: it is also the first book of cricket scores known outside the U.K.
1855 Formation of Bloemfontein Cricket Club in the Orange Free State, again with a short existence

1854 Philadelphia Cricket Club and German-town Cricket Club each formed: there had been two earlier Germantown clubs, one form-ed in 1843 which did not last, and one in 1847 which lasted to 1851. (Unless expressly indi-cated otherwise hereafter Philadelphia refers *not* to the club but to the combined team representing the City)
1855 Young American Cricket Club formed: merged with Germantown in 1889
1856 Canada East (Quebec) met Canada West (Ontario) for the first time and won (but Toronto players appeared for Canada East)

8. OTHER COUNTRIES

1857 Vere Cricket Club formed in Kingston, Jamaica. Cricket being played at Codrington College, Barbados. Georgetown Cricket Club known to be in existence and probably formed this year. It became the *de facto* governing body in Guyana and so remained until 1943

1851 Hong Kong Cricket Club formed – still in existence
1852 Cricket first played in the Sandwich Islands, better known now as Hawaii
1856 South African students playing cricket at Utrecht University
1857 First known cricket club formed in Holland, at Northey (no longer in existence)

ground was not purchased by the Lancashire C.C.C. until 1898 when it cost £25,000. First Gentlemen v. Players match at the Oval (last 1934). County club formed in Ayrshire by this date (no longer exists)

1858 First recorded instance of a hat being given to the bowler for taking three wickets with consecutive balls

1859 V. E. Walker became the first cricketer ever to make a century (108) and to take all ten wickets in an innings (10–74) in the same match, for England v. Surrey. In a very minor match, 500 was exceeded for the first time, 546 for 7 wickets by an Oxford XI v. Purton at Purton. G. Parr captained the first English team to tour overseas, to Canada and the U.S.A. Describing it, F. Lillywhite issued the first 'tour book'. A county club in existence in Co. Clare by this date (no longer exists)

1861 R. Carpenter had an aggregate of 989 runs in important matches, the highest so far, but he only averaged 26·02. The first certain partnership of over 200 (but see c. 1780) – 212 by R. Carpenter (100) and T. Hayward (108) for Cambridgeshire v. Surrey, for the third wicket. County organization set up for Yorkshire, became county club in 1863: present club 1891

1861–2 First English tour to Australia, captain H. H. Stephenson. During this tour, the phrase 'test match' was coined but matches were only against odds

1862 England made 503 v. Surrey at the Oval, the highest first-class innings so far. Edgar Willsher was no-balled in this match by umpire John Lillywhite for having his hand higher than his shoulder. Willsher left the field, play was suspended, and resumed the next day with a fresh umpire, Lillywhite refusing to revise his opinion. This episode led to the change in the Laws in 1864.

The first four volumes of *Scores & Biographies* by Arthur Haygarth published. The work recorded all the scores the compiler could discover from 1774 onwards, and eventually down to 1878: the MSS for a further twenty years are in the library at Lord's. J. Wells took 4 wickets in four balls for Kent v. Sussex at Brighton, the first time this had been done in first-class cricket (he was the father of the writer H. G. Wells). The MCC attempted to define county qualifications for the first time, as birth or *bona fide* residence for two years. County clubs formed for Dorset (present club 1896) and Co. Louth (no longer exists)

1859). First cricket annual published: *Australian Cricketer's Guide 1856–7* (Melbourne). Several more such annuals were issued in the next few years and at intervals until 1905 but none was commercially successful

1857–8 T. W. Wills took 181 wickets playing for the Melbourne C.C.: other players also took 100 wickets in the season and the feat is likely to have been performed earlier. G. H. R. Gilbert performed the hat-trick for New South Wales v. Victoria at Melbourne – the first such instance in Australian first-class cricket

1859 First century in Queensland: 118 by J. Bolger in Brisbane

1860–1 Institution of competitive club cricket in Melbourne: first winners Richmond; Hobart followed in 1869–70, first winners Wellington; Sydney in 1871–2, first winners Albert C.C. (of Sydney); Adelaide in 1873–4, first winners Norwood; Brisbane in 1876–7, first winners Albert C.C. (of Brisbane); Perth in 1900–1, first winners Claremont-Cottesloe

1861–2 First visit of English team under H. H. Stephenson and first matches between an English team and Tasmania, Victoria, New South Wales and combined Australia (though all the Australian teams included sixteen or more players). W. J. Hammersley's *Victorian. Cricketer's Guide 1861–2* referred to the five matches against Victoria, New South Wales, and Combined Victoria and New South Wales as 'Test matches': the first known use of these words

1862–3 Over-arm bowling first introduced into Australia

1858 *Canadian Cricketer's Guide* first published – there were two more issues in 1876 and 1877. The National Cricketers' Association formed in New York but had only a short life. M. B. Daly made 106 in a match at Halifax, the first recorded century in Canada

1859 First English tour to Canada and the U.S.A. (captain, G. Parr): won both matches *v.* XXII of U.S.A. and in one of these John Wisden took six wickets in six balls, the North American record, but equalled by F. M. Pellett in Canada in 1890. The tour resulted in the first tour book ever, by Fred Lillywhite. Chadwick's *American Cricket Manual* first issued – two more in 1868 and 1872

1859–60 First N.Z. inter-provincial match: Wellington *v* Auckland. Six-ball overs were used in this match and in the following game between the two provinces, five-ball overs were used

c. **1860** According to J. M. Woodroffe in *Barbados Cricket Annual* (1897–8), Canon E. M. Sealy made a century when at Codrington College. This could not have been after 1860

1860 Victoria (British Columbia) Cricket Club formed

1862 Harvard University Cricket Club formed

1860 First match between Maritzburg and Durban

1861 Cricket played at Potchefstroom in the Transvaal (the capital had only been moved the year before from there to Pretoria)

1862 Annual fixture established between 'Mother-Country' and 'Colonial-Born' in Cape Town: for long the most important fixture there. The series continued into this century

1862–3 G. Mortimer took 15 wickets in the match for Nelson *v.* Wellington at Nelson, a feat equalled in New Zealand first-class cricket five times but never surpassed. Wellington made 13, the lowest first-class score in New Zealand: G. Phillips carried his bat for 8*, the first time this was done in New Zealand first-class cricket

'1862–3, N.Z. G. Phillips carried his bat for 8'*

8 · OTHER COUNTRIES

1858 A cricket club formed in Berlin

1861 First cricket club probably formed in Denmark. First of long series of matches between Oporto C.C. (founded 1855) and Lisbon C.C. (founded 1860)

279

1863 The match between Surrey and Sussex saw 1,062 runs made for 36 wickets, a new record beating the 1817 aggregate. E. M. Grace in all matches made 3,074 runs and took 339 wickets. County clubs formed for Middlesex and West Meath (the last no longer exists) and also for Gloucestershire. The present club was formed between March 14, 1871 (on the demise of its predecessor) and mid-May 1871: the widespread supposition that the present club dates from 1870 has no foundation in fact. In this connection, Gloucestershire's first match was in 1839 and against another county in 1862

1863-4 G. Parr's second team abroad, this time to Australia, became the first to visit New Zealand

1863-4 Second English tour – G. Parr's

1864 Over-arm bowling was legalized on June 10. First Champion County of the regular series – Surrey. From that time, the chief winners have been Yorkshire thirty-one times, with two shared, Surrey seventeen times with two shared, Notts twelve times with five shared. First issue of *John Wisden's Cricketers' Almanack*. First appearance of W. G. Grace in big cricket: four days before his sixteenth birthday he scored 170 and 56* for the South Wales club *v.* Gentlemen of Sussex. In the match between Surrey and Cambridge University a new aggregate record was made of 1,104 runs for 35 wickets. T. Humphrey totalled 1,115 runs in important matches, the first time 1,000 runs had been exceeded. A team from Nottingham visited Paris. County clubs formed as follows: Glamorgan (present club 1888), Lancashire, Somerset (present club 1875), Buckinghamshire (present club 1891), Suffolk (present club 1932), Denbighshire. J. Gilligan made the first recorded double century in Ireland, exactly 200

1864 First match (not eleven-a-side) between Queensland and New South Wales at Brisbane. Formation of first Victorian Cricket Association, dissolved before 1875, re-formed in that year, dissolved 1879, re-formed same year, dissolved 1895, re-formed same year and this is the present body

1865 Practice nets first used at Lord's. *John Lillywhite's Cricketers' Companion* (the *Green Lillywhite*) established and merged with the *Red Lillywhite* from 1886. The All England XI established a new first-class record by making 524 runs against Yorkshire at Sheffield. John Lawrence's *Handbook of Cricket in Ireland* first issued: sixteen issues, last 1887-8. The earliest known printed county annual report with full scores – Shropshire. County clubs formed in Co. Cavan and it is believed King's County (Co. Offaly) by that date – neither still exists

1866 County clubs formed in Co. Waterford and Radnorshire – no longer exist

1866 Formation of Southern Tasmanian Cricket Association (to become, in 1906, the Tasmanian Cricket Association)

1863 First cricket club formed in the Transvaal

1863 (January) Formation of Kingston Cricket Club – oldest surviving club in Jamaica

1864 Cricket being played in the then Red River Colony, now Manitoba

1865 Merion Cricket Club formed

1866 Princeton University Cricket Club formed

1863-4 First visit to New Zealand by an English team – G. Parr's. Dunedin Oval first used for important matches: first match Otago v. Canterbury

1864 Western Province Cricket Club formed in Cape Town

1864 First known match between Madras and Calcutta

1864 First known century in New Zealand: 117 by J. W. A. Marchant for Invercargill against an up-country XI

1865 First matches between Barbados and Guyana in each colony: the home team won in each case. Guyana made 22 in the first match: their lowest score ever. The Barbados match was played on the Garrison Savannah in Bridgetown; the Guyana match on the Parade Ground in Georgetown

1865 Queenstown Cricket Club, in the Border, formed: cricket had been played there at least three years earlier, and Bantu ('Kafirs') had taken part

1866 The Hindus in Bombay form the Union Cricket Club

1866-7 The lowest aggregate in first-class cricket in New Zealand: 151 for 30 wickets in the match Canterbury v. Otago at Hagley Park

8 · OTHER COUNTRIES

1863 Valparaiso Cricket Club thought to have been in existence by this date, and certainly by 1869

1866 Hat-trick first performed in Argentina. First instructional book published originally in Danish. First of a long series of matches between Hong Kong and Shanghai later extending to Singapore (Straits Settlements, Malaya, Malaysia, according to political changes). Hong Kong in this first match made 430, one of the highest scores, if not the highest made outside the U.K. by this time

1867 Culmination of long period of rivalry and ill-feeling between professionals of North and South and of the two All England XIs: these two great matches were abandoned this year. The Gentlemen of Lancashire made 586 against the Gentlemen of Yorkshire at Old Trafford, the then highest for any class of cricket. First MCC tour abroad – to Paris. County clubs formed for Co. Longford by this date (no longer exists), Aberdeenshire, and West Lothian (present club 1929)

1868 Tour of England by a team of Australian Aborigines, managed by Charles Lawrence. The season saw 600 exceeded for the first time by a team, and 300 by an individual: Classical made 630 against Modern at Clifton College, and E. F. S. Tylecote made 404* for Classical. Later in the season, the Cambridge University Long Vacation Club exceeded this total by making 689 against College Servants. E. Pooley, who caught eight and stumped four in the match for Surrey v. Sussex at the Oval, set up a wicket-keeper's record which has twice been equalled but never beaten in first-class cricket. A partnership of 300 probably established for the first time, in one or other of two minor matches. County club formed in Clackmannanshire and also in Co. Galway (the latter no longer exists)

1869 A new match aggregate of 1,136 runs for 21 wickets was established in the game between Gentlemen of the South and Players of the South at the Oval, to be beaten in the same game two years later by 3 runs. The Gentlemen of the South made a new first-class record total of 553 runs

1870 The heavy roller was first used at Lord's: the great general improvement of pitches began with this innovation. Since the 1744 Code a bowler could change ends only once in an innings – he could now do so twice. J. Southerton took 210 wickets in first-class matches in the season, beating Hillyer's twenty-five-year-old record. The 'Varsity match this year known as Cobden's match: Oxford needed 179 to win, and were 176–7 when Cobden did the hat-trick, enabling Cambridge to win by 2 runs. County club for Derbyshire formed. The first certain partnership of over 300 – 305 by T. Hayward (118) v. R. Carpenter (174) for the fifth wicket for All England XI v. XVIII Radcliffe-on-Trent. A county club formed for Peeblesshire.

1867–8 First century in first-class cricket – 110 by R. W. Wardill, Victoria v. New South Wales at Melbourne

1868 Visit by team of Australian aborigines to Great Britain under Charles Lawrence

1868–9 Tasmania made 18 against Victoria (S. Costick 6 wickets for 1 run) at Melbourne, the lowest score in Inter-colonial or Inter-state matches. In the same season, also against Victoria, New South Wales made 37, her lowest score in first-class cricket

1869–70 W. Midwinter scored the first known double century in Australia: 256 for Bendigo v. Sandhurst at Bendigo

1870–1 First inter-university match Melbourne v. Sydney. Six-ball overs used in match between Victoria and Tasmania for the first time in first-class cricket, though they had often been used in minor cricket long before

1867 First known instructional book on cricket in Hindi: the same book was translated into Urdu in 1868. Both were published in Agra, United Provinces (now known as Uttar Pradesh but sharing the same abbreviation – U.P.). Round-arm bowling began to supersede under-arm bowling amongst the Parsis

1868 First recorded tie in India, between the 5th Royal Irish Lancers (114 and 95) and the 102nd Fusiliers (119 and 90) at Lucknow

1868 Cricket first played on the Basin Reserve at Wellington, NZ

1868 Second English tour (captain, Edgar Willsher): matches played against XXII of Canada and XXII of U.S.A., the first drawn, the second won easily by the tourists

1869 Match recorded in San Francisco between California and Victoria (British Columbia)

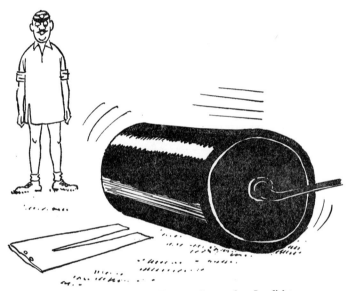

'*1870. The heavy roller was first used at Lord's*'

1869 Cricket played by an Indian team at Tripura in East Bengal

1869 First match Trinidad *v.* Guyana

1870 Cricket first known to have been played in Pretoria

8 · OTHER COUNTRIES

1867 First century in Malaya by L. K. Glass; and in Argentina by T. Jackson (109 for Buenos Aires C.C.)

1868 The first international match in South America – Uruguay lost to Argentina at Montevideo by 33 runs

1870 Amstels Cricket Club formed in Holland, survives after merger in VRA in 1915

1871 W. G. Grace's greatest year. He became the first batsman to make 2,000 runs in a first-class season, totalling 2,739 runs, and establishing a new seasonal record average of 78·25. No other batsman made 2,000 until 1893: Grace's aggregate was not beaten until K. S. Ranjitsinhji did so in 1896 with 2,780 runs, and his average was not beaten until 1887 when A. Shrewsbury averaged 78·71 runs in scoring 1,653 runs. Grace also became the first batsman to score ten centuries in a season, and the first to score 1,000 runs in a month (1,024 runs in August). Percival King's *Scottish Cricketers' Annual* first issued: sixteen issues in all, the last for 1887–8. County clubs formed for Co. Donegal and Co. Limerick (no longer in existence)

1872 First experiment, at Lord's, in covering the pitch before the start of the match. *James Lillywhite's Cricketers' Annual* founded (the *Red Lillywhite*): annually until 1900. County club formed for Staffordshire and by this time too Banffshire (no longer exists)

1873 W. G. Grace became the first to do the 'double' in first-class cricket: 2,139 runs and 106 wickets. He became the first batsman to score a century before lunch in making 134 for Gentlemen of the South *v.* Players of the South at the Oval. Qualifications rules were approved in mid-season for all matches in which a county took part, irrespective of status. A county knock-out competition instituted by the MCC: only two counties participated and the competition lapsed

1874 County club formed in Durham (present club 1882): also in Co. Roscommon, Kincardineshire (they no longer exist) and Nairn

1875 The Royal Engineers made 724 for 8 wickets against I Zingari at Chatham, the first time 700 had been exceeded anywhere. Surrey County Cricket Club instituted annual meetings of county secretaries to arrange fixtures – the meetings were not confined to the leading counties. County clubs formed for Morayshire by this date and in this year for Roxburghshire (neither now exists)

1876 W. G. Grace made the highest first-class score recorded till then in making 344 for MCC *v.* Kent at Canterbury. His next two scores were 177 for Gloucestershire *v.* Nottinghamshire and 318* for Gloucestershire *v.* Yorkshire, and he also made 400* in a minor match in the same season. In all as many as five scores over 300 were made in the season in all classes of cricket, a figure never since

1871 Formation of South Australian Cricket Association

1873–4 First match between South Australia and an English team (captain W. G. Grace) (not eleven-a-side): also first match South Australia *v.* Victoria at Adelaide (also not eleven-a-side) on the Oval, now opened. (Only one other ground has been used in Adelaide for first-class cricket, Unley Oval in 1902–3)

1874–5 First double-century partnership, 218 for first wicket by B. B. Cooper (117) and J. Slight (124) for South Melbourne *v.* East Melbourne on the East Melbourne ground. South Melbourne made 483, the first recorded score in Australia over 400, and the match yielded 1,104 runs for 40 wickets, the first match aggregate of 1,000 runs outside the U.K. First visit by a team from New South Wales (Albert Cricket Club) to Tasmania

1875 First century in Western Australia: 106 by H. Parker for Port *v.* Sapphire

1876 Formation of Queensland Cricket Association. First recorded instance of team being all out for 0 in Australia: Marlborough *v.* Undaunted, in Moore Park, Sydney

1871 First known match in Kimberley, S.A. (then still known as Du Toits Pan)

1871–2 *South African Cricket Guide* 1871–2 issued in Cape Town, the first South African cricket annual

1871 Cricket being played by Indian teams at Benares (U.P.). In a match between Bombay Presidency North and South 975 runs were scored, the highest match aggregate overseas at that time

1872 First recorded double century in India: 228 by Private Sheiring, at Shahjehanpur, who with Colonel Coles (54*) took part in what is both the earliest known century partnership in India and the first recorded last-wicket century partnership of 186

1872 Kingston made 342 (sometimes reported as 356), the first score of over 300 in Jamaica (and perhaps the first in the West Indies). Their opponents, Spanish Town, were then dismissed for 7

1873–4 Wellington tied with Nelson, the only tie in New Zealand first-class cricket. For Wellington *v.* Hawkes Bay, J. W. A. Marchant (*see above*, 1864) took 9 wickets for 21, the first to do so in a first-class match. First known cricket publication in New Zealand: *Auckland Cricketers' Trip to the South in 1873–4*. It covered amongst others the first matches: Otago *v.* Auckland and Canterbury *v.* Auckland

1874 Nelson Cricket Association, N.Z., formed (Only the dates of formation of Provincial Cricket Associations whether major or not, as Nelson, minor, are shown in this table of dates)

1874 Sepoys of a Madras Regiment got up a match at Vizagapatam

1874–5 The first century-partnership in New Zealand first-class cricket: A. M. Ollivier (52) and C. C. Corfe (88) for Canterbury *v.* Otago at Hagley Park – 119 for second wicket

1875 Wellington Cricket Association formed in New Zealand. Maoris known to be playing cricket successfully

1875 A Parsi cricket club in existence at Karachi

1875–6 'Champion Bat' competition, established in Cape Colony: first winners Kingwilliamstown. This competition was the precursor of, and overlapped, the Currie Cup competition and was of similar status

1876 Quartermaster-Sergeant Miller, for Deolali *v.* Igatpuri, took all 10 wickets in an innings, the first record of such a feat in India: he took 18 wickets in the match, the Indian record until 1932–3

1876 Otago Cricket Association, N.Z., formed

1872 Third English tour (captain, R. A. Fitzgerald) – it included W. G. Grace

1873 First University match in Canada, Trinity *v.* Toronto

1874 The first visit to England by a team of American baseballers who also played several cricket matches. Belmont Cricket Club formed, ended 1913. The Halifax Tournament, for a Challenge Cup, took place between the British Military, who were called 'England', Canada, and 'America' (in fact Philadelphia – who won). The cup was used for competition later amongst the leading Philadelphian clubs, and was known as the Halifax Cup. It was played for from 1880 to 1926: Germantown won sixteen times and tied twice, Belmont twelve times and tied once, Merion six times and tied once, Young America three times, Philadelphia C.C. and Frankford each twice, New York (who took part in nine of the later years only) twice. Other competitors were, in the early years Chestnut Hill, Girard, Oxford, in the middle years Radnor, Tioga, and Belfield, and later Moorestown. These clubs were of about the standard each of a good pre-1914 English minor county

8 · OTHER COUNTRIES

1872 Present Rio de Janeiro C.C. formed, re-formed in 1898

1874 First recorded cricket match in Fiji

1875 'Utile Dulci' Cricket Club formed in Deventer, still survives, and the oldest in Holland to do so.

1876 Kjøbenhavns Bold Klub formed, the oldest surviving Danish cricket club attained in English cricket, and only equalled in Australia (three times, 1902–3, 1965–6, 1967–8). No other batsman has ever made three scores of 300 or over in one season. Oxford University made the first score of over 600 in first-class cricket when they made 612 v. Middlesex at Prince's: the match established a new record aggregate of 1,217 runs for 24 wickets.

1876–7 The first Test match played between England and Australia: Australia won

1877 First publication of the oldest surviving county cricket annual, by Kent C.C.C.

1878 Tour by first Australian team to England (captain, D. W. Gregory). Australian cricket established its reputation when the team sensationally defeated a strong MCC XI in a single day and by nine wickets. The match established the lowest match aggregate in first-class cricket of 105 runs for 31 wickets. *Cricket and Football Times* founded, a weekly magazine which lasted until the spring of 1881. The MCC defined amateur status. A county club had been formed by this date in Co. Mayo (no longer exists)

1879 County club formed by this date in Co. Down (no longer exists). Scottish Cricket Union formed, dissolved 1883, reformed March 1908

1876–7 First eleven-a-side match against fourth English team (captain J. Lillywhite): New South Wales v. England at Sydney. First Test match at Melbourne: Australia won this, but lost the second. World's first Test century, 165 by C. Bannerman, for Australia. First recorded century in South Australia, at double wicket: 121* by A. J. Bleechmore

1877–8 First match South Australia v. Tasmania, at Adelaide. Association (or Sydney) Cricket Ground first used. The first tie in an important match in Australia: XV of New South Wales and Victoria 138 and 97 v. 1st Australians 123 and 112. The Commercial Bank made exactly 500 against the Australian Joint Stock Bank on the Association ground in Sydney – the first score of 500 or over in Australia. One month later, it was exceeded on the same ground by the King's School, Parramatta, who made 532 v. Oaklands. J. S. Swift, for Kew Asylum made 1,200 runs (average 92·4) in first eleven club cricket in Melbourne – the first seasonal aggregate of over 1,000

1878 First regular Australian team to England: also visited New Zealand, Canada and U.S.A. (captain, D. W. Gregory). At Lord's, F. R. Spofforth performed the hat-trick v. MCC, the first time by an Australian in English first-class cricket. H. F. Boyle took 6 wickets for 3 runs in the same match, in which only 105 runs were made for 31 wickets, the Australians winning in one day. W. E. Midwinter (16* out of 76) v. Nottinghamshire became the first Australian player (though Gloucestershire-born) to carry out his bat after a completed innings in first-class cricket

1878–9 First visit by team from New Zealand: Canterbury to Victoria and Tasmania. Fifth English team (captain, Lord Harris): lost the only Test. First eleven-a-side match Victoria v. England. F. R. Spofforth performed the hat-trick in the English first innings in the Melbourne Test, the first occasion in a Test match. G. Ulyett took 4 wickets in 4 balls for Lord Harris's XI v. New South Wales, the first of the only two occasions on which this has been done in Australian first-class cricket. W. L. Murdoch became the first Australian to carry out his bat after a completed innings in first-class cricket in Australia (82* out of 177) for New South Wales v. Lord Harris's XI. There was a riot in this match. It also saw the first century opening partnership in Australia of 125 by A. P. Lucas (51) and A. N. Hornby (67)

1876 E. Agostini (75) and G. Wedekind (41) made the first century partnership in West Indian first-class cricket – 110 for the fifth wicket for Trinidad *v.* Guyana on the Parade Ground at Georgetown. First match Guyana *v.* Trinidad

1876–7 Second English team to visit New Zealand – Lillywhite's

1877 Canterbury Cricket Association formed in New Zealand

1877 Formation of the Wanderers Cricket Club in Bridgetown, Barbados – the oldest surviving club in the island

1877–8 First visit to New Zealand by an Australian team (D. W. Gregory's 1st Australians to U.K.): XV of Canterbury beat them by 6 wickets: Canterbury had wanted to play on level terms. Auckland were all out for 13 against Canterbury, equalling the lowest New Zealand first-class score. Dunedin senior competition inaugurated. First match Wellington *v.* Canterbury

1878–9 First tour overseas by a New Zealand team: Canterbury to Victoria and Tasmania (captain, W. F. Neilsen)

1878–9 Proposed Parsi tours to England, and later to Australia, fell through

1879 Aligarh University Cricket Club formed in India: about this time, or shortly after, cricket was widely played at the Punjab University in Lahore. And this year Bombay University played the Parsis

1879 First historical cricket publication in New Zealand: *Cricket Notes* by 'Not Out', being descriptions and scores of Canterbury inter-provincial matches

1879 Cricket in 'Khama's Country' (Botswana)

1877 R. Liesk made 202, the first double century in Canada. *The American Cricketer* founded: for several years issued weekly, later on monthly – lasted till April 1929

1878 United States Cricket Association formed: it lasted many years but it is uncertain whether it survived the First World War – its Challenge Cup was still being played for in the 1930s: at any rate it did not survive the Second World War and a fresh United States Cricket Association was formed in 1961. The first visit to Philadelphia by the Australians (first to England): there was a near riot during the first eleven-a-side match between a North American team and tourists (Philadelphia *v.* Australians) owing to the Australian refusal to accept umpiring decisions (a habit to which they had shown tendencies in England) and the match was left drawn, much in favour of the home team

1879 Lord Harris's team, *en route* home from Australia, played a match in the U.S.A. The fourth English tour (captain, R. Daft), and also the first tour by the Gentlemen of Ireland (captain, N. Hone) who were beaten by Philadelphia, the latter's first victory in eleven-a-side matches. The record ninth-wicket partnership, and the first known of over 200 in North America, of 210 by Boughey (117) and Johnson (100*) in a minor match in Prince Edward Island, Canada

8 · OTHER COUNTRIES

1878 Fijians now regularly playing cricket. Hague Cricket Club formed – perhaps the club with the greatest prestige in Holland

1879 C. H. A. Ross made 105, the first recorded century in Ceylon: G. V. Vanderspar and G. S. Saxton made 250 for the first wicket, the first recorded partnership of over 200 in Ceylon

1880 First Test match in England: Australia beaten by 5 wickets. W. G. Grace made 152, and W. L. Murdoch set himself the task of beating this, which he did by scoring 153*. The first Canadian team toured England but the tour broke up half-way through for financial reasons. A 'very best cane-handled bat' now cost 21s but lesser grades could be had for as little as 8s 6d. Balls now cost from 4s to 7s 6d. County club formed for Forfarshire

1881 W. N. Roe made 415* for Emmanuel Long Vacation Club v. Caius L.V.C. at Cambridge, the highest individual score so far. Uxbridge C.C. became the first team to visit Holland. W. F. Forbes and Lord Throwley put on 404 for the first wicket in a minor match, the first time over 400 had been made for a wicket. Wiltshire formed – present club 1893. Rutland formed – present club 1967

1882 First Australian victory in a Test match in England, by seven runs, at the Oval: a spectator died from excitement. 'The Ashes' tradition established by an 'obituary notice' to English cricket in the *Sporting Times*. The Australians made 643 against Sussex, a new first-class record. The Orleans Club established the English record to the present day for all grades of cricket by scoring 920 against Rickling Green on the latter's ground. For the Orleans Club, A. H. Trevor (338) and G. F. Vernon (259) put on 605 for the second wicket, the first time a partnership had exceeded 600. The first known Saturday start in a three-day English first-class match: England XI v. Australians at Harrogate. Another English record was established when J. Walker took 8 wickets in eight balls. The English third wicket record partnership of 454 established by W. Barnes (226) and W. Midwinter (187) for MCC v. Leicestershire at Lord's. E. Peate took 214 wickets in the first-class season, a new record. The weekly magazine *Cricket* was established, lasted until 1914 with a change of title for the last volume to *The World of Cricket*. County clubs formed in Caernarvonshire and Flintshire, and first mentioned for Montgomeryshire (the present club there dates from 1898)

1879–80 First total of over 600 in Australia – 742 by East Melbourne v. Tasmania at Melbourne

1880 First Test in England: England won, at the Oval: the 2nd Australians were captained by W. L. Murdoch

1880–1 First eleven-a-side match Victoria v. South Australia, at Melbourne. The 'D. Long Trophy' donated for competition between Victoria and New South Wales: in December 1881, Victoria having won three matches in succession, won the trophy outright. The trophy was thus the precursor of the 'Sheffield Shield'. A. Denius, in a minor match in New South Wales, playing against an XVIII, took all 17 wickets for 32. W. Vint (110*) and R. P. Dixon (60*) made the first recorded last wicket partnership in Australia (136*) playing in Melbourne senior cricket

1881–2 F. R. Spofforth took all 20 wickets for 48 runs (all bowled) in a minor match at Bendigo (done four other times in Australia). First double century ever scored by a coloured cricketer: 280 by S. Morris (from Jamaica) in Melbourne. First treble century in Australia: 321 by W. L. Murdoch for New South Wales v. Victoria, at Sydney. W. L. Murdoch and S. P. Jones (109) made 245 for the fourth wicket – the first partnership of over 200 in Australian first-class cricket. New South Wales made the then world record first-class score of 775, and 1,412 runs were scored in the match. For Victoria's last wicket, G. E. Palmer (76*) and W. H. Cooper (29) made 100, the first time this had been done in Australian first-class cricket. Less than two months earlier, over 1,000 runs had been scored in a first-class match in Australia for the first time – 1,049 runs for 33 wickets, Shaw's team v. Australia at Melbourne. Shaw's team was the sixth: lost two Tests and drew one. First Test played at Sydney, on the existing ground. C. T. B. Turner took all 10 wickets in one innings and 17 for 69 in the match for Bathurst XXII against Shaw's team. Two centuries in a match by a batsman for the first time in Australia – A. C. Bannerman 111 and 104* for Carlton v. Albert at Sydney – the feat had only been performed six times before in England and there had been no other such occurrences outside England

1882 First victory by 3rd Australians (captain, W. L. Murdoch) in a Test in England, by 7 runs at the Oval (the only Test that season), thus giving rise to the 'Ashes' tradition. F. R.

1880 Bolan Pass XI made 678 *v.* Subordinates at Peshawar, the first total over 600 in India

1880 Sabina Park occupied by Kingston Cricket Club, Jamaica

1880–1 Second Australian tour to New Zealand (2nd Australians to U.K.): G. Watson made 175 for Canterbury *v.* Otago at Hagley Park: he thus scored the first century in New Zealand first-class cricket on his initial appearance. Canterbury's score of 381 was also the record first-class score at that time

1881 Cricket in Maseru (Lesotho)

1881–2 Third English team to tour New Zealand: Shaw's, which became also the first team to play at Lancaster Park, Christchurch

1881–2 First double century by a West Indian in Australia (q.v.)

1880 The first Canadian team to the U.K. (captain (later, the Rev.) T. D. Phillips): it was not representative and the tour was abandoned half-way through. The Ontario Cricket Association formed: no continuity with the present organization which was reconstituted in 1949 from another which had been formed in 1933

1881 Shaw's team to Australia played five matches in the U.S.A. *en route*. C. J. Logan took 178 wickets in the season, the first time a bowler is known to have taken more than a hundred wickets in Canada

1882 A. G. Brown (64) and G. N. Morrison (133*) made 198 runs for the eleventh wicket in a twelve-a-side game in Canada. The 3rd Australians to England played two matches in the U.S.A. on their way home. *Canadian Cricket Field* instituted: a weekly magazine, lasted the season only

8 · OTHER COUNTRIES

1882 First century in West Indies first-class match: 123 by E. F. Wright for Guyana *v.* Trinidad on Parade Ground, Georgetown. Formation of Pickwick Cricket Club in Bridgetown and its occupancy of the Kensington ground

1881 First instructional book in Spanish: *La Tranca* by J. W. Williams, published in Buenos Aires. The first of very many interchanges of visits between Holland and England when the Uxbridge Cricket Club visited Holland. The first century in Fiji, 101 by W. A. Groom

K

1882–3 On their way to Australia to recover 'the Ashes' (q.v. Australia) the Hon. Ivo Bligh's team played two matches in Ceylon, the first English team to do so

1883 Surrey made 650 against Hampshire at the Oval, a new record for important matches. J. Martin took all twenty of his opponents' wickets when playing for Stockbridge *v.* Abbots Ann, the first of two occasions (the second by one White in 1921 at Bristol) on which this feat is known to have been performed in England. County club formed for Ross-shire still exists

1884 After wide circulation to many overseas authorities, a completely new code of Laws was adopted by the MCC on April 21. The new Laws mentioned boundaries for the first time, though operative with varying allowances long before: five- or six-ball overs were legalized for one-day cricket, but, as has been seen, were widely used, before. First Tests played at Lord's and at Old Trafford. The Gentlemen of Philadelphia undertook their first tour to the U.K. H. N. Dumbleton (325) and C. L. Young (204) made the English record fourth-wicket partnership of 464 for Royal Engineers *v.* Royal Marines. W. F. Holms made 303* in a minor match in Scotland, the Scottish record. County club formed for Cumberland (present club 1948)

1884–5 Irish Cricket Union formed in Dublin – present organization dates, however, from 1923

Spofforth took 14 wickets for 90 in the match: no Australian has bettered this in Tests and only C. V. Grimmett has equalled it, against South Africa in 1931–2. W. L. Murdoch, H. H. Massie and A. C. Bannerman each made 1,000 runs in matches against first-class teams, the first Australians to do so. W. L. Murdoch did so before any Englishman that season, a feat equalled only by C. G. Macartney and D. G. Bradman

1882–3 The seventh English team was the first to play Queensland (not eleven-a-side). The captain was the Hon. Ivo Bligh. The eventual programme for this tour provided for three matches against Murdoch's 1882 team and for two (only one played) against a Combined Australia eleven (inevitably a stronger combination than Murdoch's XI). Bligh's team had the best of the three matches against Murdoch's team and was therefore said to have regained the Ashes. The later match lost against Combined Australia was not relevant to the Ashes theme. J. Slight (279) and J. Rosser (192) made 395 for the first wicket for South Melbourne *v.* St Kilda, the first partnership of over 300 in Australia

1883 S. M. J. Woods, at Royston College, Sydney, took seven wickets in seven consecutive balls, the Australian record, though equalled four times since

1883–4 Tasmania toured New Zealand. G. Giffen took ten for 66 for the 4th Australians *v.* Rest at Sydney, the first of the four occasions on which this feat has been performed in first-class cricket in Australia. W. Bruce made 328* for Melbourne *v.* Hotham, the Australian record until 1892–3

1884 First visit by an Australian team (4th Australians) to Ceylon. They were captained by W. L. Murdoch and in England lost one and drew two Tests. During the English tour, G. Giffen scored a century and took the hat-trick against Lancashire, a feat not performed by any other Australian in first-class cricket. W. L. Murdoch made 211 in the Oval Test – highest score by an Australian captain in England until 1964, in Tests. In first-class matches, F. R. Spofforth took 207 wickets, average 13·25, the first of only two touring Australians to take over 200 wickets in an English season. He took seven wickets for 3 *v.* an England XI at Birmingham

1884–5 First series of five Tests in Australia – England won three and lost two (the eighth team; captain, A. Shrewsbury) (up to and

1882-3 Winburg made 505 for 5 wickets *v*, Brandfort in the Orange Free State, the first known score of over 500 in South Africa. Century partnerships made for the first time in South African cricket, for the second and for the third wickets

1882-3 C. Cox hit the ball 156 yards in a match at Wanganui, probably the longest hit in New Zealand. (W. J. Ford of Middlesex once hit the ball 'far out of the ground into the sea' at Nelson but there is no estimate of distance known: he did this between 1886 and 1889.) Hawkes Bay Cricket Association formed: also Auckland Cricket Association (though an earlier association had been formed in 1881 which had not survived)

1883 The Muslims in Bombay form the Mohammedan Cricket Club (which became the Muslim Gymkhana in 1893)

1883-4 Tasmania (captain, J. G. Davis) became the first Australian colony to send a team to New Zealand, and was thus the first Australian team to play first-class matches in New Zealand. They were beaten once by Otago and twice by Canterbury. First recorded double century in New Zealand: 220 by C. Strange for Banks *v.* Insurance in Christchurch. Carisbrook first brought into use for first-class cricket in Dunedin

1884 Bourda ground occupied by Georgetown Cricket Club: first match December 1885

1884 First match between Bombay Gymkhana (Europeans) and Parsi Gymkhana, won by Bombay by an innings and 38 runs. From this encounter developed the Bombay Presidency matches and later tournaments (there had been an earlier match between Bombay Gymkhana and a Parsi team in 1877). Lieut C. Mackenzie (259) and Lieut Taylor (160) made 321 for first wicket for Simla *v.* Queen's Royal West Surrey Regiment at Simla, the first recorded partnership of over 200, let alone over 300, in India and also the first known century first-wicket partnership. An individual surnamed Bone playing for S.R.A. *v.* 'A' Troop 12th Royal Lancers at Bangalore took 7 wickets in seven balls, which remains the Indian record. A Ceylon team visited Calcutta, the first of a long and very numerous interchange of visits between teams of the two countries at all levels of cricket

1884-5 C. Frith took the first hat-trick in New Zealand first-class cricket for Otago *v.* Canterbury at Carisbrook. A project to send a combined New Zealand team to Australia was

1884 First tour by Gentlemen of Philadelphia to U.K. (captain, R. S. Newhall): W. C. Loury took 121 wickets in the season, the first time it had been done in the U.S.A. J. A. Scott made 1,054 runs in the season, also for the first time in the U.S.A. Cricket first mentioned in Alberta

Continued on page 295 as column 7(a) until 1947

8 · OTHER COUNTRIES

1883 Dutch Cricket Association (Nederlandsche Cricket Bond) formed, the oldest surviving of all national cricket bodies. It was awarded the title 'Royal' ('Koninklijke') in 1958 by Queen Juliana

1884 Cricket first played in Samoa: it became something like a fever and had to be prohibited by law in 1890: the prohibition was soon relaxed but has had to be reimposed from time to time after natural disasters, the people preferring to play cricket than to rebuild ruined homes. First inter-state match in Malaya, Perak-Penang

Continued on page 295 as column 8   291

1885 J. S. Carrick made 419*, a fresh individual record, for West of Scotland against Priory Park in Chichester. L. Hall and G. Ulyett became the first opening pair to make a century partnership in each innings (123 and 108) for Yorkshire v. Sussex at Hove. The second-class counties met together, thus effectively defining who were first-class at that time. Norfolk in making her record score of 695 v. MCC at Lord's is the only minor county (other than those later promoted) ever to have exceeded 600

1886 Four centuries were scored in one innings for I Zingari v. Bullingdon at Oxford, the first occasion on which this had been done. A. E. Stoddart made 485 for Hampstead v. Stoics at Hampstead, a new individual record. The first Indian team, the Parsi Gentlemen, toured England. Edgbaston brought into use for Warwickshire v. MCC: the ground had been bought the previous year. J. Dunn made 2,968 runs in Ireland, the record for an Irish season

1887 The White Heather C.C. formed, the first women's cricket club: it lasted until the 1950s. Derbyshire ceased to be reckoned a first-class county. The Cricket Council was established, to control county cricket, to advise about tours and to make proposals about Laws to the MCC

1888 The MCC made its record score (apart from overseas touring team) of 735 for 9 wickets v. Wiltshire at Lord's. Surrey made 698 against Sussex at the Oval making a new first-class record. In this year and the next, the present Lord's pavilion was built. C. T. B. Turner took 283 wickets during the season, the record for any overseas player to this day, and the then record for a bowler in England. The *Athletic News Cricket Annual* established: it lasted with breaks during two World Wars, and with a change of name in 1947 to the *Sunday Chronicle Cricket Annual* until 1955. Birmingham League formed (December 1888) – the first cricket league in England. R. A. A. Beresford made 102* and 307* in a House match at Oundle School, the first of only two occasions that 300 has been scored in performing this feat (*see* India, 1962–3)

including the 1936–7 series, all Test matches in Australia were played to a finish). First Test played at the Adelaide Oval. Australia used four captains (only equalled by the West Indies in 1929–30 and India in 1958–9). F. Howlett took 7 wickets in seven balls in a minor match, in South Australia. In the first match played by a South Australian team (Adelaide Federal XI) in New South Wales (at Wentworth v. a local XV), the visitors made 192 against which the local XV had *three* innings totalling 36, 24 and 27. In the first two, G. Giffen took 17 wickets for 37 runs: in the third, J. F. Traynor took all 14 in one innings for 17

1885 Formation of Western Australian Cricket Association

1885–6 G. Giffen took 17 wickets for 201 runs for South Australia v. Victoria at Adelaide – the only occasion on which this has been done in a first-class match in Australia. J. Darling (252 – the record at that time in South Australia) and A. S. J. Fry (125) made 278 for the second wicket (the Australian record until 1890–1) for Prince Alfred College who made 500 in all (the then record in South Australia), against St Peter's College

1886 Formation of Northern Tasmanian Cricket Association. The 5th Australians (captain, H. J. H. Scott) toured Great Britain that season: they lost all three Tests. It was the first tour which was not arranged as a speculation by the players but organized by the Melbourne Cricket Club

1886–7 Ninth English team: Captain, A. Shrewsbury: won both Tests. The then world first-class record of 803 for nine wickets set up by Non-Smokers v. Smokers in Melbourne. A. Shrewsbury (236) and W. Gunn (150) made 310 for the third wicket – the first time a partnership of over 300 had been made in Australian first-class cricket

1887–8 Two English teams visited Australia: one Shrewsbury's (but captained by C. Aubrey Smith) the other G. F. Vernon's. They joined forces to play one Test (captain, W. W. Read) which was won. First eleven-a-side match South Australia v. England. C. T. B. Turner took 106 wickets in the first-class season, the only occasion on which 100 wickets has been exceeded. This was a highly meritorious performance for Turner collected his wickets in 12 matches. In 1894–5, Giffen needed 11 matches for 93 wickets, and the same number were needed by Grimmett for his 82 in 1929–30, by Mailey for his 81 in 1920–1 whilst Benaud needed 13 matches for his 82 in abandoned. Wellington senior competition inaugurated: Auckland followed in the next season. The first century opening partnership in New Zealand – 100 by J. P. Firth (54) and W. J. Salmon (50) for Wellington *v.* Nelson (then first-class) at Basin Reserve

From this point on column 3 is devoted to Southern Africa, column 4 to the West Indies, column 5 to New Zealand and column 6 to India

1885 Issue of a further cricket annual in South Africa – the *Natal Cricket Annual*; in 1888–9 it became the *South African Cricket Annual*, was last issued for 1891–2, but was revived for two more issues in 1906–7. Except for the first issue, and the 1891-2 issue, it was edited by J. T. Henderson (W. W. Edwards was the 'Cover Point' who edited the first issue)

1886 West Indian team toured Canada and U.S.A. (captain, L. R. Fife): played thirteen matches (none first-class). The first West Indian cricket book, describing the tour in detail, was issued in Georgetown the following year

1886–7 Cricket first played in Johannesburg. In Natal, F. F. Crawford made 1,364 runs in the season, in all matches the first aggregate of over 1,000 in South Africa. A century partnership for the first wicket recorded for the first time, 190 by F. F. Crawford (136) and R. McComb (90) in a club match in Natal

1887 Albert Park Oval, Durban, formed. Early in the 1900s Lord's was taken into use but this ground was taken over by the Railways: therefore Kingsmead was brought into use in 1922–3. Wanderers Cricket Club first formed in Johannesburg and a ground first granted. The Cricket Club only lasted a short time

1887 U.S.A. team (captain, C. L. Bixby) toured West Indies and beat West Indies in the one representative match; West Indies were all out for 19. E. F. Wright made 1,084 runs (average 40·40) for Georgetown Cricket Club: this figure includes all matches and it is the first time 1,000 runs were made in a West Indian season

1887–8 W. Long, for Potchefstroom against Moss Valley, Transvaal, took all 10 wickets for 6 runs, believed to be the first such occurrence in South Africa. H. L. Allen, for Kroonstad *v.* Heilbron (O.F.S.) took 17 wickets in the match (for 26), the first instance in South Africa

1888 Newlands ground formed in Cape Town. Wanderers Club now formed in Johannesburg on a permanent basis, covering all sports

1888 Unsuccessful attempts to organize both a West Indian tour to England and matches between Jamaica and Barbados

293

Continued from page 293, last reference 1884–5   *Continued from page 291, last reference 1884*

1885 E. G. Wynyard made 123 and 106 for Visitors *v.* Residents at Naini Tal, the first time this feat was performed in India. Dr M. E. Pavri became the first Indian to perform the hat-trick

1886–7 Third tour by Australians (5th team to U.K.). Against a Wellington XXII, they made 475, the highest score at that time in New Zealand. The first double-century partnership in New Zealand – 202 for the first wicket – was made by S. P. Jones (159) and G. E. Palmer (76) in this match
1887–8 Fourth English team to New Zealand (captain, C. Aubrey Smith)

1886 The first Indian team to tour overseas – Parsi Gentlemen to U.K. (captain, Dr D. H. Patel), followed by another such team in 1888 (captain, P. D. Kanga)

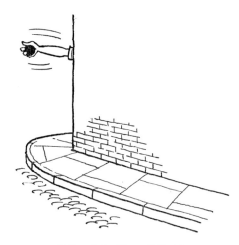

"Round-the-Corner" Smith

Continued from top page 291, last reference 1884

Continued from bottom page 291, last reference 1884

1885 Six-ball overs (or longer) introduced officially in Philadelphian cricket, although they had often been used earlier. Fifth English tour (captain, the Rev. R. T. Thornton): won one and lost one *v.* Philadelphia. The first recorded Gentlemen *v.* Players match in Philadelphia (the match was never less than two-days duration and was more than once won by the Players, who were mostly English professionals on contract). The Eastern Canada Cricket Association in existence by this date: it would equate with the modern Quebec Cricket Association with which, however, it has no continuity

1886 A team from the West Indies toured Canada and the U.S.A. for the first time. The sixth English tour (captain, W. E. Roller): won two matches *v.* Philadelphia. B. T. A. Bell made 1,036 runs for the first time in a Canadian season. Cricket first played in Vancouver

1887 U.S.A. team toured the West Indies (q.v.). Second Canadian tour to U.K. (captain, Dr E. R. Ogden). Negotiations with the Melbourne C.C. for a Philadelphian tour to Australia broke down. W. M. Massie made 264* in a minor match in Florida, the first time 200 or over had been scored in the U.S.A.

1887 A. J. Denison took 10 wickets in an innings in a twelve-a-side match in Ceylon

1888 Second tour by Gentlemen of Ireland to U.S.A. and Canada (captain, D. Cronin). Philadelphia won both matches against them. Six-ball overs adopted officially by the U.S.C.A., who also adopted an 'l.b.w.' law somewhat different from the MCC Law (it was rescinded in 1896 owing to the undesirability of differences between two countries on a law of this importance). J. Cuddahy became the first to take all 10 wickets in an innings, in a New York club match, in the U.S.A.

1888 Boys playing cricket in Gold Coast (now Ghana) villages 'as vigorously as in England', according to the then Governor. Eighteen from Brazil visited Argentina

1958–9. Umpires wore white coats for the first time in Australia in the match between Victoria and G. F. Vernon's XI. L. O. S. Poidevin, then aged eleven, made 271* and took 19 of his opponents 20 wickets, a feat without parallel

1888 C. T. B. Turner took 283 wickets in first-class matches during the 6th Australians' tour of Great Britain, a total not approached by any other overseas cricketer and only exceeded by two Englishmen. They were captained by P. S. McDonnell and won one and lost two Tests. During the tour Turner took 17 wickets for 50 in a match (including 8 for 13) v. an England XI at Hastings. In another match against an England XI, at Stoke, he took 9 for 15

1888–9 Cricket first played by visiting American team in Australia (Spalding's Baseballers)

1889–90 First eleven-a-side match New South Wales v. South Australia, at Sydney

1890 Proposals made and guarantees provided for a ten-match tour of South Africa by the 7th Australians after their tour of England. This would have been the first tour of South Africa by an Australian team, but the negotiations broke down. Seventh Australians to England (captain, W. L. Murdoch) lost two Tests, the Manchester Test being abandoned without a ball being bowled

1890–1 442 for the eighth wicket for Sydney v. Warwick, by E. G. Noble (227) and S. E. Gregory (235) – the record Australian partnership for any wicket until 1913–14: still the world's record for that wicket, and the first time a partnership of over 400 had been made in Australia. The first inter-colonial women's match, Victoria v. New South Wales. Miss Rosalie Deane became the first woman in the world to make a century in each innings: 195 and 104 for Inter-colonial Ladies v. Sydney Ladies Club, at Sydney

1891–2 12th English team (Lord Sheffield's, captain W. G. Grace) – won one and lost two Tests. Australasian Cricket Council established: a weak body, dissolved in January 1900. 828 scored by Melbourne v. Essendon – the Australian record, until 1895–6. G. Giffen scored 271 and took 16 wickets for 166 (9–96 and 7–70) for South Australia v. Victoria at Adelaide, an unparalleled feat. In doing it, he completed 1,101 runs (average 84·69) and 102 wickets (average 13·5) in eight matches against Victoria in consecutive seasons from 1884–5

1888–9 First English team to tour South Africa, Major Warton's (captain, C. Aubrey Smith). It played two eleven-a-side games against South Africa: the other games all being against odds

1889 A new match aggregate of 1,295 runs for 36 wickets set up between Middlesex and Yorkshire at Lord's, beaten in 1890 by 1,339 for 39 wickets in the Sussex v. Cambridge University match at Hove, and in 1891 in the same match at Hove, with 1,402 runs for 40 wickets. Headingley Cricket Ground opened (first county match there in 1891). Five-ball overs legalized for all cricket. Declaration permitted but limited to one-day matches or the third day of a three-day match. The limit was gradually lessened and abolished in 1957. From now on a bowler could no longer bowl two overs in succession but otherwise could change ends whenever he pleased

1889–90 First English team to tour India and Ceylon: G. F. Vernon's

1890 Cambridge University became the first first-class team to make over 700 when they made 703 for 9 wickets declared against Sussex at Hove: it is also to this day the largest second innings total in England as well as the English University record. G. A. Lohmann took 220 wickets in the season. The Lancashire League formed under the name of North East Lancashire League (name changed in 1892)

1891 Somerset joined the first-class counties

1888-9 Kimberley made 569 against De Beers, establishing a new South African record total. First visit by an English team (captain, C. Aubrey Smith). First matches against a representative South African team, which lost both. R. Abel made 120 in the second match, the first first-class century in South Africa

1889-90 Currie Cup Tournament established: first winners Transvaal. Winners since the start of the competition are as follows: Transvaal fourteen, and four jointly; Natal fourteen, and three jointly; Western Province nine, and two jointly; Griqualand West one. E. Beech became the first South African to make two centuries in the same match, 117* and 132 for Pirates v. Kimberley at Kimberley. Kimberley made 445 v. Natal, the first score of over 400 in South African first-class cricket. Kimberley made 682 v. Arabs: the highest score until 1955-6 in any grade of cricket in South Africa. C. Mills, in this match, made 297, the first score of over 200 in South Africa. He was assisted by J. H. Chapman (97) in making the first recorded partnership of over 200 in South African cricket: 202 for the fifth wicket. A tournament for Malay teams organized at Newlands, with teams from Cape Town, Port Elizabeth, Johannesburg, and Claremont. P. H. de Villiers took 152 wickets in the season. The first recorded last-wicket century partnership in South Africa of 100 made by A. Richards (123*) and G. Cloete (42*) in a club match in Newlands. First matches Natal v. Western Province, v. Eastern Province and v. Griqualand West, and Transvaal v. Griqualand West

1890 South African Cricket Association, the governing body of white cricket in South Africa, formed April 8. Cricket Unions formed this year for Western Province, Eastern Province, Griqualand West, and Natal (which became the Natal Cricket Association in 1908--9). The Orange Free State Cricket Union probably dates from this period, though it has not been possible to establish this certainly. These Unions were the controlling authorities for white cricket in their areas

1890-1 In the match between Transvaal and Griqualand West, 1,402 runs were scored for 40 wickets, the then second highest match aggregate in the world. It was the highest match aggregate in South Africa until 1925-6. The match lasted seven days and was the first first-class match in the world to last longer than five days. Guarantees were provided for a ten-match tour by the 7th Australians after their

1889 First century by a West Indian in England: G. Elliott 117* for West Indies v. Tufnell Park (this was a scratch team of West Indians in England, not a tour)

1891 First inter-colonial tournament between Barbados, Trinidad and Guyana: played on the Wanderers ground, it was won by Barbados

1889–90 An unofficial New South Wales team (captain, J. Davis) toured New Zealand. A. E. Moss took 10 wickets for 28 runs for Canterbury against Wellington at Hagley Park, the only player to perform this feat in New Zealand first-class cricket

1889 First known instructional book on cricket in Marathi, published in Baroda

1889–90 First known tour by an English team: G. F. Vernon's (who were beaten by the Parsis by 4 wickets)

1890 F. C. Brittain produced the *Record of the Past Season 1889–90*, the first New Zealand cricket annual. It was devoted largely to cricket in Wellington: two subsequent issues appeared in 1891 and 1893 (covering two seasons) and ranging more widely. 'Trundler' (W. H. Newton) produced another annual for four years from 1895 to 1898 covering all New Zealand cricket. No more such annuals were issued until 1931

1890 A Parsi Cricket Club formed in Shanghai, probably the first Indian cricket club to be established outside India

1890–1 W. T. Wynyard, who played for Wellington against Canterbury at the Basin Reserve, became the first Maori to play in first-class cricket

1891 H. H. Maharao Umedsinhji of Kotah became the first Indian known to have taken all 10 wickets in an innings, at Mayo College. A proposal for another extended tour of the U.K. by the Parsis fell through

 Continued on page 304

Continued on page 304

1889 Second Philadelphian tour to the U.K. (captain, D. S. Newhall) and the first to play first-class matches in England. The U.S.C.A. adopted the principle of declarations at any time during a match – sixty years before it became part of the MCC Laws. Two hundred was exceeded for the first time in a first-wicket partnership in Canada when F. A. Kaiser (125*) and F. A. W. Taylor (111*) made 252 unbroken in a club match at Halifax

1890 Eight- or ten-ball overs adopted in Philadelphian cricket. Jerome Flannery issued the first regular *American Cricket Annual*, taken over after his death by F. Fitzmaurice Kelly (second only, if at all, to F. S. Ashley-Cooper, as an historian and statistician of the game, in his time): after a slight intermission, publication was taken over by Spaldings, the well-known sports goods firm: it ran till 1914. A tour by Parsis to the U.S.A. and Canada was mooted but fell through

1891 Seventh English tour (captain, Lord Hawke): won one and lost one *v.* Philadelphia. A Philadelphian club team visited Bermuda, the first of a long interchange of visits in which Canada later joined and which continues to the present time. G. S. Patterson made 1,000 runs and took 100 wickets for the first time in Philadelphian cricket. Germantown made 631 *v.* Rosedale (an old Toronto club): the first time 600 had been exceeded in North America. A visit by an all-American team to the U.K. (as distinct from a Philadelphian team) fell through after twenty-three fixtures had been arranged

1889 The Danish Ball-Games Union (Dansk Boldspil Union) formed, originally to look after cricket: over the years it paid less and less attention to cricket and more and more to football, so, in 1953, the Danish Cricket Association (Dansk Cricket Forbund) was formed

1890 First mention of cricket in Zanzibar. First cricket club formed in Siam (now Thailand). First tour by a Danish team outside Denmark, to Berlin. First competitive cricket played in Denmark. Colonel Churchill took 18 wickets for 52 in a club match in Ceylon, the Ceylon record

1890–1 First tour from Ceylon to Malaya

1891 First representative match by a Dutch team, *v.* Rambling Britons. Inauguration of the Dutch Cricket League

Continued on page 305

Continued on page 305

1892 The first Dutch team toured England – Gentlemen of Holland. The tea interval first mentioned in a match in Glasgow between Scotland and Yorkshire

'*1892. The tea interval first mentioned in a match in Glasgow . . .*'

1893 Over 800 attained for the first time in a first-class match in England, by the Australians in making 843 against Oxford and Cambridge Universities Past and Present at Portsmouth. South London Cricket Association formed, the ultimate ancestor of the Club Cricket Conference: its secretary was E. A. C. Thomson (*see* 1910). Leicester Schools Cricket Association formed – the first such body
1894 First South African team toured England, captain H. H. Castens. The tour was not first-class. The MCC approved the recognition of Derbyshire, Essex, Leicestershire and Warwickshire as first-class counties for season 1894, and Hampshire at the end of the season: they all entered the Championship in 1895. The follow-on now compulsory after deficit of 120 runs in a three-day match. County club formed for Bute (no longer exists)

1892–3 Sheffield Shield instituted for competition between New South Wales, South Australia and Victoria. All matches were played to a finish up to the end of the 1926–7 season: Queensland was admitted to the competition in 1926–7, and in the following season matches were limited to four days and a pre-lunch session (reduced to four days from 1930–1): Western Australia was admitted in 1947–8. New South Wales has won thirty-six times, Victoria twenty-one times, South Australia nine times and Western Australia twice. First eleven-a-side matches South Australia *v.* Western Australia at Adelaide. Victoria *v.* Western Australia at Melbourne and Queensland *v.* New South Wales at Brisbane. F. Laver made 352* for East Melbourne *v.* St Kilda, the record for only ten months. G. Giffen playing for Norwood against Adelaide went in first and carried out his bat for 172*, having taken all 10 wickets for 149 in the Adelaide innings. It is believed that this is the only occasion that the very rare feat of scoring a century in one innings and taking all 10 of the opponents' wickets in one innings in a good-class match has been achieved in Australia. G. Neale in a minor country match in New South Wales performed the hat-trick three times in three overs in one innings, taking 4 wickets in four balls in one of them and 10 wickets in all for 5 runs. Sotala and Wattle Flat, in a minor New South Wales country game, each made 49 and 37 in their first and second innings, the first recorded instance of a double-tie match in Australia
1893 The then world first-class record of 843 set up by the 8th Australians (captain, J. McC. Blackham) *v.* Oxford and Cambridge Past and Present. England won one and drew two Tests. The 8th Australians were beaten by an innings by Philadelphia (who did the same to the 9th Australians in 1896). Of the eleven matches altogether, played on even terms between Philadelphia and Australian teams, Philadelphia won three and Australians six, the first match (in 1878) being drawn in Philadelphia's favour' and the last (in 1913) in Australians' favour
1893–4 District cricket introduced in Sydney, first winners East Sydney; Adelaide followed in 1897–8, first winners East Torrens and Brisbane in the same season, first winners Woolloongabba; Hobart in 1905–6, first winners North Hobart; Melbourne in 1906–7, first winners East Melbourne. District cricket

U.K. tour, but the project fell through. C. E. Finlayson made 1,823 runs in the season, the then record aggregate. Kimberley made 475 *v.* Transvaal at Johannesburg, establishing a new first-class record. A second Malay tournament was played at Kimberley, three teams from Cape Colony taking part. A Natives (presumably Bantu) cricket tournament took place at Port Elizabeth; four teams from Cape Colony took part. A match played at Kroonstad (O.F.S.) between Natives (? Bantu) of Potchefstroom (Transvaal) and the Native Cricket Club of Kroonstad. First matches Western Province *v.* Eastern Province and *v.* Griqualand West, and Eastern Province *v.* Griqualand West

1891 Transvaal Cricket Union formed. First match in Rhodesia, Police *v.* Civilians at Fort Salisbury

1891–2 Second tour by an English team (captain, W. W. Read): South African team lost only representative match. Read's team played XVIII Malays, whom they beat by 10 wickets, the only occasion on which an English team has met a non-white team in South Africa. A. E. Halliwell (139*) and T. Routledge (147*) made 289* for the first wicket in Johannesburg the first time an opening partnership of over 200 had been made in South Africa

1892–3 First match Western Province *v.* Transvaal

1893–4 First match Transvaal *v.* Eastern Province and *v.* Natal

1894 First visit by a South African team to England (captain, H. H. Castens): the tour was not first-class. The *Cricket Field* in its issue March 31 noted that the South African team would regret before the season was out that they were so particular about the colour of their men, in a comment about the omission of their fast bowler T. Hendricks, a Malay. He had been omitted as a result of 'the greatest pressure by those in high authority in Cape Colony' (ibid., 4, viii, 94)

1892 H. C. Clarke took all 10 wickets for 30 runs for Harrisonians against Codrington College, believed to be the first time this was done in West Indian cricket

1893 Cup subscribed for by competing colonies for inter-colonial tournament: hence numbering of these tournaments is sometimes reckoned from this year. Guyana did not take part on this occasion, and Barbados won. The Cup was last played for in 1939. With one exception (in 1921) all matches were played out and many lasted five days and more. First match Trinidad *v.* Barbados

1894 First match between St Lucia and St Vincent: latter won. First match between St Lucia and Dominica – former won

Continued on next opening

was introduced in 1907–8 in North Tasmania but was not a success: and in Perth in 1959–60, first winners South Perth. C. Hill, then aged sixteen, made 360* for Prince Alfred College v. St Peter's College, the Australian record until 1895–6, and the world inter-school record until 1904–5

1894–5 First English team to tour West Indies, R. S. Lucas's
1895 W. G. Grace at the age of forty-six made 1,000 runs in May, the first time this had been done. He also completed his hundredth century in first-class cricket. Lancashire made 801 against Somerset at Taunton, a new first-class record for an English team (and their record to this day), and A. C. MacLaren in the same match made the record first-class score for an Englishman to this day of 424. Oxford University made their record score of 651 v. Sussex at Hove. Essex made their record score of 692 v. Somerset at Taunton. A fresh match aggregate of 1,410 runs for 28 wickets established in the game between Sussex and Oxford University at Hove. T. Richardson took 290 wickets in the season, a remarkable feat for a fast bowler, and the record until 1928. T. Westray took the first English team to Portugal. The world record in any class of cricket of 623* for the second wicket was established by Captain W. C. Oates (313*) and Private F. Fitzgerald (287*) for the Royal Munster Fusiliers against the Army Service Corps at the Curragh; Captain Oates's score is the Irish individual record. The great Irish player R. J. H. Lambert made 2,040 runs and took 209 wickets in the Irish Season, the record, and repeated it the following year. The Minor Counties Cricket Association formed, and the Minor Counties championship instituted – the leading winners are Lancashire Second Eleven and Buckinghamshire each seven times, and Staffordshire six. Buckinghamshire have also shared once

1894–5 13th English team (captain A. E. Stoddart) won three, lost two Tests. First eleven-a-side match Queensland v. England. C. J. Eady (116 and 112*) scored a century in each innings for Tasmania v. Victoria, the first time this was done in Australian first-class cricket. They were also his maiden centuries; 1,665 runs were scored for 39 wickets in the match between Melbourne University and North Melbourne, the world record match aggregate until 1897–8. In the first Test at Sydney, 1,514 runs were scored for 40 wickets, the record first-class aggregate until 1897–8. A. Coningham, by having A. C. MacLaren caught off him by Trott for o, in the second Test at Melbourne, became the first cricketer to take a wicket with his first ball in a Test. Though five others have since done so, he remains the only Australian to have been so successful
1895–6 First visit by an official New South Wales team to New Zealand (it had been preceded by two unofficial tours). J. Worrall made 417* – the first score in Australia of over 400 – for Carlton, who thus were able to compile the then world record total of 922 against Melbourne University. (On the *same day* East Melbourne completed 876 against Richmond, and Melbourne 683 v. St Kilda). Score-board with full details of bowling as well as batting first brought into use at the Sydney Cricket Ground, the design of Ned Gregory (extended batting details had been shown for many years before on Australian score-boards). Five centuries were made in one innings for the first time in the world: Paddington v. Burwood, Sydney. New South Wales equalled this and set up the world first-class record in 1900–1 v. South Australia, not beaten until 1945–6 in India. K. E. Burn, 117* and 162* for Wellington v. Break O'Day became the first Australian batsman, and only the second in all cricket history, to make an undefeated century in each innings. Later in the same season, H. Pellew did even better when he scored 102* and 104* in a South Australian country match, and established a record by actually carrying his bat through each completed innings. In a second-

1894–5 First issue of *Barbados Cricket Annual* (editor, J. Wynfred Gibbons): annually till 1913–14

1895 First visit by English team to West Indies (captain, R. Slade Lucas). Lucas (64) and R. P. Sewell (51) made the first first-wicket century partnership in the West Indies of 105 *v.* Barbados at Kensington. H. R. Bromley-Davenport did the hat-trick for first time in West Indian first-class cricket *v.* Guyana at Bourda. In the second match *v.* Barbados, Barbados scored 517 runs, the first time over 500 had been made in the West Indies: in the match 1,373 runs were scored for 39 wickets, the first time an aggregate of over 1,000 runs had been made in a West Indian match

1895–6 Third visit by English team (captain, Lord Hawke): South African team lost all three representative matches. First eleven-a-side match by an English team *v.* Western Province. Lord Hawke's team made 482 *v.* South Africa, at Johannesburg, beating the 1890–1 first-class record. J. H. Sinclair scored 157* and took all 10 wickets for 103 in a minor match, the first time this remarkable feat was done in South Africa. Eleven members of the Hofmeyr family (including Jan Hendrick Hofmeyr, senior) played as a team in a match at Stellenbosch

1892 Southland and Westland Cricket Associations formed. Westland was never first-class, and the association has long ceased to exist. Southland had played cricket for many years and one of the oldest series of matches in New Zealand was Otago v. Southland dating from 1863–4

1892–3 Projected tour by Fiji to New Zealand fell through after many arrangements had been made. First match Wellington v. Otago

1893 Marlborough Cricket Association formed: has never been first-class

1893–4 A. D. Downes took 4 wickets in four balls for Otago v. Auckland, the only time this has been done in New Zealand first-class cricket. Second visit by unofficial New South Wales team (captain, J. Davis): though they lost to Canterbury by an innings, they beat New Zealand in the first representative match ever played by New Zealand. The match against Hawke's Bay was unique in that it was arranged to, and did in fact, take place on two different grounds, the Napier Recreation ground for the first day, and Farndon Park for the second: such an event is believed never to have occurred elsewhere in first-class cricket. Canterbury made 400 for 5 wickets against Auckland at Lancaster Park, the then record first-class score: in this match L. A. Cuff (176) and J. D. Lawrence (167) made the first treble-century partnership in New Zealand – 306 for the first wicket

1894 Establishment of the New Zealand Cricket Council, the governing body of cricket in New Zealand. Taranaki Cricket Association formed (not first-class after 1897–8) and all ten provinces now had cricket associations. Dates of the non-first-class minor associations are not given here owing to their large number

1894–5 First visit by a team from Fiji (captain, J. S. Udal): two matches lost v. Auckland and Canterbury, and four won v. Southland, Nelson, Hawke's Bay and Taranaki

1895–6 First visit by an official New South Wales team (captain, L. T. Cobcroft): lost to an official New Zealand team. W. F. Raphael made 299* in a minor match in Christchurch, the record score in New Zealand until 1905–6. Carisbrook made 458 v. Excelsior in Dunedin the then record score by a New Zealand team. This was beaten by Midland who made 510 v. Rivals at Wellington

1892 First Presidency match in Bombay – Europeans v. Parsis

1892–3 Second tour by an English team: Lord Hawke's, who won the only representative match, but against the Parsis lost to them once by 109 runs and in the return won by only 7 runs

1893 K. S. Ranjitsinhji became the first of eleven Indian cricket Blues at Cambridge University (it would be inappropriate to list all his, and his nephew's – K. S. Duleepsinhji's – remarkable feats as they belong rather to English than Indian cricket, but a few of Ranji's are noted where relevant to other fine performances by Indians)

1894 The Hindu Gymkhana formed in Bombay

1894–5 Colonel J. G. Greig carried out his bat for 79* for Europeans v. Parsis at Bombay, the first time this was done in Indian first-class cricket

1895–6 H. E. Browne performed the hat-trick for Europeans v. Parsis at Poona, the first time in Indian first-class cricket

1892 Third tour by the Gentlemen of Ireland (captain, J. M. Meldon): they won one, lost one and drew one of the matches *v.* Philadelphia. The Canadian Cricket Association formed on a Dominion-wide basis. It lapsed during the First World War and attempts to revive it in 1922 and 1928 failed. In 1934 a Dominion Advisory Cricket Board was established which led to the formation of the present Canadian Cricket Association in 1940: its constitution was revised in 1949. G. S. Patterson made 1,748 runs in the season, the U.S.A. record. The North American third-wicket record of 267 established by A. M. Wood (182) and G. S. Patterson (132) for Gentlemen *v.* Players in Philadelphia

1893 The 8th Australians on the way home won one and lost one *v.* Philadelphia but won the first match between Australia and Canada. The first partnership of over 300 in North America – 305 unbroken by M. R. Cobb (126*) and H. Tyers (170*) in a match in New York

1894 Eighth English team (captain, Lord Hawke): won two *v.* Philadelphia. E. Attewell took 190 wickets in the season, the Canadian record. G. S. Patterson's XI made 689 *v.* A. M. Wood's XI in Philadelphia – still the North American record. The North American first-wicket record partnership of 340 unbroken was made by W. R. Robertson (206*) and A. G. Sheath (118*) in San Francisco. The North American sixth-wicket record of 219 was made by H. I. Brown (153) and E. W. Clarke, jun. (106) in Philadelphia

1895 Ninth English team (captain, F. Mitchell): won one and lost one *v.* Philadelphia. An organization called the Associated Cricket Clubs of Philadelphia to control club and international cricket in the city came into being. The Manitoba Cricket Association was in existence about this time: though moribund between 1906–10 it was then revived and continues

1892 First Dutch tour to England, Gentlemen of Holland

1893 First tour from Malaya to Ceylon. First double century in Argentine: 249 by R. W. Rudd

1893–4 First known double-century partnership in Argentina: 264 for the first wicket by J. R. Garrod (116) and P. M. Rath (138) in Buenos Aires. J. R. Garrod this season also made the record seasonal aggregate to this day of 1,436 runs. P. M. Rath is reported, without confirmation, to have taken 6 wickets in six balls (in one over, that is: if so, this would confirm that six-ball overs were then in use in Argentina – always likely)

1894 First recorded century in Holland – 120* by C. J. Posthuma

1894–5 J. R. Garrod became the first to take all 10 wickets in an innings in Argentina

1895 Dimbula made 518, the first score of over 500 in Ceylon

1896 Yorkshire made 887 against Warwickshire at Edgbaston, the first-class record in England until 1938 and still the county record. R. Peel (210*) and Lord Hawke (166) made 292 for the eighth wicket in the game, the English record. Cambridge University made the English record fourth innings total of 507 for 7 wickets to beat MCC at Lord's
1898 A Board of Control set up to administer Test matches played in England. It was absorbed into the Test and County Board in 1969. J. T. Brown (300) and J. Tunnicliffe (243) made 554 for the first wicket for Yorkshire v. Derbyshire, the first time a partnership had exceeded 500 in first-class cricket. Derbyshire made their record score of 645 v. Hampshire at Derby. Worcestershire by winning the Minor Counties Championship three times in succession established a record that has still to be emulated by any other team
1899 Worcestershire entered the first-class championship. The first five-match series of Tests played in England: Australia won the only finished game, at Lord's. First Tests played at Trent Bridge and Headingley. A single Selection Committee was set up by the Board to choose teams for all five Tests, a task hitherto performed by the ground authority. K. S. Ranjitsinhji exceeded 3,000 runs in first-class season, making 3,159 runs for an average of 63·18. The following year he made 3,065 runs for an average of 87·57. 1899 was the year when R. M. Poore averaged 91·23. A. E. J. Collins made the world record individual score in any class of cricket of 628* for Clarke's House v. North Town, a junior house-match at Clifton College. Warwickshire made their record score of 657 for 6 wickets declared v. Hampshire at Edgbaston. Surrey made their record score of 811 v. Somerset at the Oval. R. Abel (193) and T. Hayward (273) made 448 for the fourth wicket for Surrey v. Yorkshire at the Oval, the English first-class record for that wicket. The English record for the sixth wicket of 411 was made by R. M. Poore (304) and E. G. Wynyard (225) for Hampshire v. Somerset at Taunton. In this match Hampshire made their record score of 672 for 7 wickets declared. A. T. Kemble took the first English team to tour the Canary Islands

eleven match between Melbourne and East Melbourne, four of the latter were stumped off successive balls. A. Mather, playing A. Foster at single wicket in Singleton, New South Wales, made 152, the highest score at single wicket in Australia, and the second highest in the world
1896 The lowest score – 18 – made by an Australian team in England v. MCC at Lord's. This was the first Australian team to come to England on an official basis, the MCC having concerned itself with the tour arrangements, and the Australasian Cricket Council with its selection. They were the 9th Australians (captain, G. H. S. Trott) and lost two and won one Test
1896–7 Follow-on established at 200 runs in Sheffield Shield (and certain other) matches. Queensland toured New Zealand: on return played South Tasmania at Hobart – this being the first encounter between Queensland and a Tasmanian representative team: the next occurred almost seventy years later, in 1965–6. First match on Brisbane Cricket Ground (Woolloongabba). First issue of weekly magazine *Australian Cricket* (lasted eighteen weeks). L. W. Pye made 2,333 runs in the season (average 66·65), the first to make 2,000 in an Australian season
1897–8 14th English team (captain, A. E. Stoddart) won one and lost four Tests. 1,000 runs in a first-class season exceeded for the first time by K. S. Ranjitsinhji, A. C. MacLaren and C. Hill. Melbourne University established the then world record score of 1,094 (including five centuries) against Essendon on the University ground. C. J. Eady scored 205 and 120* for Break O'Day v. Wellington, the first time a century and a double century had been scored in one match in Australia, and only the second time in the world. A. Campbell became the first schoolboy in the world to make a century in each innings in an inter-school match when he made 117* and 118 at Sydney. 1,739 runs were scored for 40 wickets in the match between New South Wales and A. E. Stoddart's XI, the world record aggregate until 1908–9
1898–9 First visit by an official New Zealand team to Australia, captain L. T. Cobcroft. First eleven-a-side matches, New South Wales v. Tasmania at Sydney and Queensland v. South Australia at Brisbane. New South Wales established the then Australian first-class record of 839 against Tasmania

1896 Border Cricket Union formed. Ramblers Cricket Club, Bloemfontein, formed: their ground had been used from 1888 on, and they improved it. It is now (1970) about to be taken over for other uses. Transvaal Indian Cricket Union first formed

1896–7 J. H. Sinclair made 301* for G. Beves's XI v. Roodeport, the first score of over 300 in South Africa. Western Province made 483 v. Griqualand West at Johannesburg, beating the previous season's first-class record. G. A. Lohmann (9 for 88) and G. A. Rowe (10 for 48) bowled unchanged in this match, the first of three occasions this has happened in South African first-class cricket

1897 Barnato trophy presented for inter-provincial competition between Coloured teams. First establishment of South African Coloured Cricket Board

1897–8 The first partnership of over 300 in South Africa: 303 for first wicket by Captain Mainwaring (193) and Mr Lowndes (117) for Royal Dublin Fusiliers v. Civilians at Maritzburg. First matches Border v. Griqualand West, v. Transvaal and v. Natal

1898 Rhodesian Cricket Union formed. Six-ball overs widely used in South Africa

1898–9 Fourth visit by an English team (captain, Lord Hawke): South Africa lost both representative matches. First visit (by Lord Hawke's team) of an English team to Rhodesia. Lord Hawke's XI made 537 for 6 wickets declared v. Transvaal at Johannesburg, the first score of over 500 in first-class cricket in South Africa, in the first eleven-a-side match by an English team v. Transvaal. First inter-provincial tournament for Coloured Cricketers, winners Western Province. A. E. Goldman took 7 wickets in seven balls, the South African record for many years

1896 First matches Guyana v. Jamaica and Barbados v. Jamaica. Occupation by Queen's Park Cricket Club of their present ground, the St Clair Oval in Port of Spain. The precise date of formation of this club is not known: it had certainly played on the Savannah some years before this. It became the recognized *de facto* controlling authority in Trinidad and so remains. C. R. W. Chandler took 126 wickets in the season in Jamaican club cricket, the first time over 100 wickets had been taken in a West Indian season

1897 Two English teams toured West Indies, under Lord Hawke and A. Priestley. The latter's team played combined West Indies (who won) which was thus the first representative match between West Indies and an English team. A. J. Somers-Cocks did the hat-trick for Barbados v. Priestley's XI, and in all matches took 137 wickets, average 10·88. L. S. d'Ade (140*) and S. A. Rudder (53) added 103 for the last wicket for Trinidad v. Priestley's XI, the first time a three-figure last-wicket partnership had been made in West Indian cricket. C. E. Goodman took 57 wickets in first-class matches in the season (average 11·85), still a record for a West Indian: in all matches he took 130 wickets (average 8·86). First and only issue of *Jamaica Cricket Annual*. Six-ball overs in use in Jamaica, and adopted in Barbados. Six-ball overs had occasionally been used long before, and the first colonial matches in 1865 had seen both five- and six-ball overs. G. B. Y. Cox (161) and H. B. G. Austin (129) scored 263 for the second wicket for Barbados v. Trinidad, the first time a partnership had made over 200 in first-class cricket in the West Indies

1896–7 The fourth visit by a representative Australian team (9th to U.K.): all matches were against odds. Queensland (captain, O. Hitchcock) also toured, and lost the representative match against New Zealand. H. B. Lusk made 1,000 runs in representative and senior cricket – the first player to do so. Wellington made 401 for 8 wickets v. Canterbury, at Lancaster Park, the then record first-class score by a New Zealand Team. Queensland made 492 v. Hawkes Bay, the then record first-class score in New Zealand. In a minor match Midland made 556 v. Rivals, at Wellington, exceeding their own record made against the same team the previous season

1897–8 A. B. Williams scored 114 and 105 for Midland v. Wellington, the first player to make a century in each innings of a match in New Zealand. Wellington made 404 v. Canterbury, at Basin Reserve, beating their own record the previous season against the same opponents

1898–9 First visit by a representative New Zealand team (captain, L. T. Cobcroft, see also 1895–6) to Australia: no first-class matches won. Napier United 'A' made 609 v. Napier United 'B', the first score in New Zealand of over 600; in this match the record New Zealand sixth-wicket partnership of 360 was made by H. C. Wilson (200) and G. Marshall (252★)

1899–90 First visit by Melbourne Cricket Club (captain, C. H. Ross): won six matches out of seven, including the representative match against New Zealand. Wellington made 464 v. Otago, the then record first-class score by a New Zealand team

1896 Badeshi Ram became the first Indian to score a double century (219) in India, K. S. Ranjitsinhji became the first Indian to score a century in each innings, for Sussex v. Yorkshire. In the following year he made the first of his fourteen double-centuries in first-class cricket: amongst Indians, V. M. Merchant comes next with eleven

1898 K. S. Ranjitsinhji (257) and Colonel K. M. Mistri (255) became the first Indians to make a partnership of over 300: 376 for the third wicket for Patiala v. Ambala at Ambala

 Continued on page 314

Continued on page 314

1896 First visit by Haverford College to the U.K. to play English public schools: there were five more such visits, the last in 1925. The 9th Australians played three matches *v.* Philadelphia on the way home, winning two and losing one. W. H. Cooper became the first to do the double in Canadian cricket
1897 The tenth English team (captain, P. F. Warner): won one and lost one *v.* Philadelphia. Another cricket magazine founded in Philadelphia, *Cricket Club Life*, which lasted until 1901. The third tour by Philadelphia to England (captain, G. S. Patterson): all eleven wickets taken in a minor twelve-a-side match in Canada by A. T. Goward

1896 Ch. Buchwald made the first recorded century in Denmark while still at school – 102
1897 The first historical and instructional book in Dutch, by W. P. Mulier. Lieut F. J. Bowen took over 200 wickets in the season in Ceylon, the first time this had been done

1898 Eleventh English tour (captain, P. F. Warner): won two *v.* Philadelphia
1899 Twelfth English tour (captain, K. S. Ranjitsinhji): won two *v.* Philadelphia. J. B. King did the double on the first of four occasions in his career, in Philadelphian cricket

1898 The first double century in Malaya, 212 by Dr Lucy at Kuala Lumpur. Private Whaley made two centuries in a match in Gibraltar, the only time the feat has been performed there
1899 The first important match in Kenya. T. W. Wright made the first double century in Ceylon, 202*. *Ceylon Cricket Annual* first issued: many such annuals have issued over the years under varying titles. Argentine Cricket Championship Committee formed, developed into the Argentina Cricket Association in 1913. W. Lacey and W. A. Forbes made the Argentine last wicket record of 141

Continued on page 315

Continued on page 315

won the only completed match of the first series of five Tests in England. First score of 300 by an Australian in England: 300* by V. T. Trumper v. Sussex at Hove. W. P. Howell took all 10 Surrey first innings wickets for 28 during his first match in England, an unparalleled performance. In November the New South Wales Cricket Association made the first inquiries towards forming an Australian Cricket Board of Control

1900 R. Abel scored twelve centuries in the season, beating W. G. Grace's twenty-nine-year-old record. The first West Indian tour to this country, not first-class: captain R. S. A. Warner. E. A. C. Druce (201*) and V. P. Johnstone (120) made 293 for the ninth wicket in a club match at Eastbourne, the world record to this day. Six-ball overs now legalized for all matches. The follow-on now optional after 150 runs in a three-day match, 100 in a two-day and 75 runs in a one-day match

1899–1900 Melbourne Cricket Club toured New Zealand. By scoring 123* and 213* for Wellington v. Break O'Day, K. E. Burn joined his fellow Tasmanian C. J. Eady in performing this feat, for only the third time in the world; nor did any other Australian do so for twenty years

1901 R. Abel beat Ranji's aggregate by scoring 3,309 runs, but averaged only 55·15. C. B. Fry made thirteen centuries in the season, equalled by T. Hayward in 1906 and E. Hendren in 1923 but beaten by J. B. Hobbs in 1925. Fry made six of his centuries in successive innings, establishing a world record only equalled by D. G. Bradman in 1938–9

1900–1 C. Hill made 365* for South Australia v. New South Wales at Adelaide, thus beating Murdoch's 1882 record. In doing so, he and E. Walkley (53) made 232 for the ninth wicket, the Australian record. In the Sydney match between the two teams New South Wales made 918, the record total in that State, and new world first-class record which was not surpassed until 1922–3. Five players scored centuries. G. H. Gatehouse (247) and O. Douglas (200*) made 370 for the sixth wicket in a Hobart club match – the Australian record in Australia. J. J. Dowd in a minor school match at Bathurst, New South Wales, took the last seven wickets of his opponents' innings with consecutive balls

1902 First Tests played at Edgbaston and at Bramall Lane, the latter being the only Test ever played in Sheffield. A new match aggregate of 1,427 runs for 34 wickets set up in the game between Sussex and Surrey at Hastings. The first MCC tour to Holland, captain A. H. Hornby. *Ayres' Cricket Companion* first appeared, annually until 1932. W. H. Hyman scored the then record number of sixes – thirty-two in his innings of 359* for Bath Association v. Thornbury at Thornbury; the record for many years. The record sixth-wicket partnership in England of 428 made by W. W. Armstrong (172*) and M. A. Noble (284) for Australians v. Sussex at Hove. K. S. Ranjitsinhji (230) and W. Newham (153) made 344 for the seventh wicket, the English first-class record, for Sussex v. Essex at Leyton. Sussex made their record score of 705 for 8 wickets declared v. Surrey at Hastings. Scottish County Championship inaugurated

1901–2 15th English team (captain, A. C. MacLaren) won one, lost four Tests. MacLaren's team made the record score for an English team in Australian first-class cricket of 769 v. New South Wales at Sydney. First draw in inter-colonial or inter-state cricket – Queensland v. New South Wales. First individual score of over 500: 566 by C. J. Eady in Hobart. This remains the record score in Australia and it is regrettable that the circumstances of its compilation were not above criticism. In this match Break O'Day made 911, the record Tasmanian total; and 429 was made for the seventh wicket by Eady and W. Abbott (143), the world record for this wicket

1902 11th Australians (captain, J. Darling) won two, lost one and drew two Tests. V. T. Trumper made 2,570 runs in the English season, the first Australian to do so: the feat was remarkable as it was a very wet summer and only two Englishmen were able to top the

Continued on next opening

1900 But for the South African War, which forced the cancellation of the tour, a South African team would have met the West Indians at Lord's

1901 Second visit by South African team to England (captain, M. Bisset). South Africans made 692 v. Cambridge University at Fenner's, the highest score to this day by a South African team overseas, and the highest in first-class cricket. Match played in Colombo, Ceylon, between Boer Prisoners of War and Colts Cricket Club (who included cricketers of all races)

1901–2 In becoming the third batsman to hit two centuries in a match in South Africa, Captain A. C. Richards actually hit 286 (101* and 185) out of 311 from the bat, the next highest scores being 2 in the first innings and 6 in the second

1900 First tour by West Indies to England (captain, R. S. A. Warner): matches not reckoned first-class. L. S. Constantine (113) and W. J. Burton (64*) made 162 for the ninth wicket v. MCC at Lord's, the record for that wicket by West Indians. Against Leicestershire, P. F. Warner (113) and C. A. Ollivierre (159) put on 238 for the first wicket, the first double century opening partnership by West Indians

1901 F. Hinds (a professional) took 10 wickets for 36 for A. B. St Hill's XII v. Trinidad XII, the only occasion on which 10 wickets in an innings have been taken in West Indian first-class cricket. (Professionals were not allowed to take part in matches for the inter-colonial cup – though they could and did play in other colony matches until the 1930s)

1902 H. D. G. Leveson-Gower's XI (more commonly called R. A. Bennett's XI) toured West Indies, and was the first team to play a series of matches v. West Indies – latter won two out of three. S. G. Smith took 16 for 85 for West Indies v. R. A. Bennett's XI and E. M. Dowson took 16 for 58 for Bennett's XI v. Jamaica: the figure has not since been exceeded in a first-class match. Dowson took 80 wickets, average 12·46, the record number of wickets in a first-class season

Continued on next opening

'*1903. An abortive agitation for wider cricket wickets*'

1903 An abortive agitation for wider cricket wickets and play-to-a-finish Tests in England: the latter partly conceded from 1905, when in certain circumstances the last Test could be played to a finish; and was in 1912. First representative Public Schools team played at Lord's. Kent became the first county to tour abroad when they visited U.S.A. (q.v.). Nottinghamshire made their record score of 739 for 7 wickets declared v. Leicestershire at Trent Bridge

1903–4 First MCC tour to Australia (q.v.), captain P. F. Warner. R. E. Foster (287) and W. Rhodes (40*) made the world record Test last-wicket partnership of 130 at Sydney

1904 Advisory County Cricket Committee set up by the MCC: it was absorbed into the Test and County Board from 1969. A new aggregate of 1,492 for 33 wickets set up in the match between Worcestershire and Oxford University, the record until 1927. The English seventh-wicket partnership record of 367* established by H. A. Bates (259*) and V. F. Critchley (104*) for Honor Oak II v. Brunswick at Beckham

312

2,000 aggregate, but their averages did not compare with Trumper's. Trumper also made the then record number of centuries in an English season for a tourist – eleven. Australians all out for 23 against Yorkshire at Leeds – the lowest total against an English county by any overseas first-class touring team (*see also* England)

1902–3 Darling's became the first Australian team to visit South Africa; three matches were played against combined South Africa of which the Australians won two and drew the other: though these have subsequently come to be regarded as the first Test matches between the two countries they were not so reckoned or described at the time, either officially or unofficially by either country. During the tour, W. P. Howell took 17 wickets for 54 in the match v. Western Province – only the third Australian to do so, and none have done so since. First eleven-a-side match Queensland v. Victoria, at Brisbane. Queensland made 40, her lowest score in first-class matches. T. Hastings making 106* made the then highest score for a number eleven batsman in first-class cricket, when he assisted M. Ellis (118) to add 211 for Victoria v. South Australia. 16th England team, Lord Hawke's (captain, P. F. Warner): played no Tests

1903–4 First visit by MCC team to Australia (captain, P. F. Warner): England won three and Australia two Tests, this was the seventeenth English team. First eleven-a-side match Tasmania v. England. Victoria were all out for 15 against MCC – the lowest first-class score in Australia. R. E. Foster made 287 in the first Test at Sydney – the highest score by an Englishman in Australia in this series. The first declaration in first-class cricket in Australia, by MCC v. South Australia at Adelaide, November 1903. In each making a double century in the same innings R. A. Duff (271) and M. A. Noble (230) did this for the first time in Australian first-class cricket, for New South Wales v. South Australia. V. T. Trumper and R. A. Duff became the first Australian opening pair to put on 100 for the first wicket in each innings of a match when they added 113 and 119* for New South Wales v. Victoria. W. W. Armstrong (438) and E. Monfries (123) made 433 for the fifth wicket for Melbourne v. University, the record for that wicket

1904 The Sydney High Court decided that cricket was to have priority over all other activities on the Sydney Cricket Ground

1902–3 First visit by Australians (11th to England) to South Africa (captain, J. Darling): South Africa lost two of the three unofficial representative matches. W. P. Howell for Australians *v.* Western Province took 17 wickets for 54, the first time this had been done in a first-class match in South Africa (the first eleven-a-side match by Australians against a Province). J. J. Kotze for Transvaal *v.* Griqualand West at Port Elizabeth became the first South African cricketer to do the hat-trick in first-class cricket. First match Border *v.* Eastern Province

1903–4 Formation of South Western Districts Cricket Union: it did not have a separate existence for long. Transvaal made 501 *v.* Orange River Colony as it was then called, at Bloemfontein, the first score of over 500 by a South African team in first-class cricket in South Africa: this was the first match by Orange River Colony *v.* Transvaal. The season also saw the first match Border *v.* Western Province

1904 Third visit by South African team to England (captain, F. Mitchell). But for the cancellation of their tour, the Indian team would have played them at Lord's

1903 First known double century: 207* by L. D. Samuel for Kingston Cricket Club *v.* Melbourne Cricket Club. (The Melbourne Club had a fine ground in the centre of Kingston on which many first-class matches were played. It was sold for building early in the 1960s.) A. H. Brebner made 140 and 104* for Georgetown Second XI *v.* Guyana Second XI at Bourda, the first player to make two centuries in a match in the West Indies

1902–3 Fifth English team to tour New Zealand – Lord Hawke's (captain, P. F. Warner): won every match of eighteen, including both representative matches. Warner in making 211 v. Otago at Carisbrook made the then highest score in New Zealand first-class cricket. G. T. Thompson took 57 wickets in the seven first-class matches in the tour – the record aggregate for a bowler in first-class cricket in a New Zealand season

1903–4 In the match between Otago and Southland, G. C. Austin for Otago and C. G. Wilson for Southland each carried their bats, for 182* and 117* respectively: an unusual occurrence. S. T. Callaway took 54 wickets in the first-class season, the record for a New Zealand cricketer. The first match played between North Island and South Island, won by the latter by 2 wickets. Eight more such matches have been played, the last in 1968–9; South Island has won four, North three and two have been drawn. District cricket was inaugurated, following the Australian pattern, in Auckland. It ceased after 1919–20: was started again for 1952–3 and discarded once again after the 1966–7 season. District cricket was inaugurated in Christchurch in 1905–6, but abandoned after the 1919–20 season. In Wellington, district cricket was started in 1909–10, but abandoned after the 1919–20 season. It has never been known in Dunedin

1904–5 Fifth visit by a representative Australian team (12th to U.K.): won one, and had easily the best of the draw in the other of the two representative matches. In two successive matches against New Zealand, Australia established new first-class records: 533 and 593 for 9 wickets declared

1902–3 The third tour by an English team: Oxford University Authentics (captain, K. J. Key): established a new Indian record of 696 v. Peshawar. Madras made 537 v. Ceylon, not exceeded by *any* Indian team against tourists until 1960–1 and then only by 2 runs when India made 539 for 9 wickets declared v. Pakistan (the present record): 537 remains the Madras record

1903–4 In the course of ten days, L. P. Collins three times made a century in each innings when playing for the Gurkha Brigade. Elphinstone College became the first Indian school to tour outside India when they visited Ceylon. Jehangir H. Elchidana became the first to take all 11 wickets in a twelve-a-side match when he took 11 wickets for 21 runs in an inter-school match in Bombay

1904 A proposed All-India tour to England fell through for financial reasons after all fixtures had been agreed

1904–5 A. H. Mehta, 9 for 36, and M. D. Bulsara, 8 for 43, bowled unchanged for Parsis v. Europeans at Bombay, the first time this was done in Indian first-class cricket

1901 The thirteenth English tour (captain, B. J. T. Bosanquet): won one and lost one *v.* Philadelphia

1902 Lord Hawke's team *en route* to New Zealand and Australia, played one match in the U.S.A. The North American eighth-wicket of 224 made by A. G. Priestman (100*) and R. Krause (100) in Philadelphia. The Quebec Cricket Association in existence about this time

1903 The fourth tour by Philadelphia to the U.K. (captain, J. A. Lester). Kent (captain, C. J. Burnup), toured the U.S.A. and won two matches *v.* Philadelphia. The North American fourth-wicket record of 313 runs was made by J. M. Laing (249) and J. G. Davis (103*) in Chicago

1900 C. J. Posthuma became the first to take over 100 wickets in the season in Holland. A. Nijland became the first to take all 10 wickets in an innings in Holland. First tour from U.K. to Denmark by Royal High School F.P., Edinburgh, who also visited Berlin and played the Preussen C.C. in a match billed as 'Deutschland gegen Schottland'

1901 Entebbe Sports Club in existence by this time: it was the principal cricket club in Uganda for many years

1902 The first MCC tour to Holland. E. Weerasuriya made 140 and 106 for Prince of Wales School (Masters) *v.* Prince of Wales College, the first time two centuries in a match had been made in Ceylon

1904 The first inter-colonial match in West Africa, between Lagos (Southern Nigeria) and the Gold Coast

1904–5 First unofficial eleven-a-side Test between New Zealand and an official Australian team (12th to England). O. H. Dean made 412 in 210 minutes for Sydney Church of England Grammar School v. Newington College, the world record for inter-school cricket until 1908–9. His innings included one five and 76 fours

1905 As stated, from this season the last Test could be played to a finish in certain circumstances: the possibility existed for all Test series up to and including 1939 except 1907 v. South Africa and the (originally planned) one-match series v. New Zealand in 1931 and India in 1932. It also existed for the 1946–7, 1948 and 1950–1 series against Australia. Northamptonshire entered the first-class championship. First MCC tour to U.S.A. and Canada (q.v.), captain E. W. Mann

1905–6 First MCC tour to South Africa (q.v.), captain P. F. Warner: the team played the first Tests against South Africa who won the rubber

1906 T. Hayward made 3,518 runs in the season, the record until 1947: he averaged 66·37. G. H. Hirst established a first-class record not since equalled when making 2,385 runs and taking 208 wickets. The Queenslander, Alan Marshal in all matches made 4,350 runs and took 210 wickets. Leicestershire made their record score of 701 for 4 wickets declared v. Worcestershire at Worcester. Worcestershire made their record score of 633 v. Warwickshire at Worcester. Responsibility for Fifeshire county team taken over by Dunfermline C.C. (formed 1857)

1906–7 First MCC team to New Zealand (q.v.), captain E. G. Wynyard

1907 Fourth South African team to England (captain P. W. Sherwell) played the first official South African Tests in England. North Wales county championship inaugurated about this time. To clarify 'ambiguity' a new ball was permitted after 200 runs. Hitherto it had been the custom to take one if the old ball was damaged. The limit of 200 runs remained until 1946, when the first of what have seemed like an endless series of changes was made, the limit now being reckoned by overs (85 six-ball)

1905 12th Australians (captain, J. Darling) lost two and drew three Tests. Australian Board of Control established. After a continuous existence of seventy years, the oldest surviving Australian cricket club, the Derwent, of Hobart, was disbanded to make way for District cricket

1905–6 First declaration in domestic first-class cricket by South Australia v. Western Australia at Fremantle, February 1906

1906–7 Highest score ever made in Queensland – 383 by C. W. Gregory for New South Wales v. Queensland at Brisbane (it remained also the Australian first-class record until 1922–3). 318 of these runs were made in one day, a record in first-class cricket anywhere until Macartney's innings in 1921. New South Wales made 763 which remains the record first-class total in Queensland. After this season, the follow-on ceased to be compulsory in Australian domestic first-class cricket. E. P. Barbour aged fifteen, made 1,726 runs (average 53·94) and took 142 wickets (average 12·00) for Sydney Church of England Grammar School. The following three seasons he repeated the feat, making 1,767 runs (average 60·9) and taking 105 wickets (average 14·86) in 1907–8; 2,146 runs (average 63·11) and 142 wickets (average 11·16) in 1908–9; 1,516 runs (average 65·91) and 122 wickets (average 9·90) in 1909–10, thus completing a school cricket career quite without parallel

1907–8 2nd MCC tour (captain, A. O. Jones): won one and lost four Tests. First tour by Fijian team to Australia: matches played against all States except Western Australia. First eleven-a-side matches Western Australia v. New South Wales and Western Australia v. MCC, both at Perth. New South Wales, in making 572 (set 593) against South Australia made the highest fourth innings total in Australia. M. A. Noble (176) and S. E. Gregory (201) in making 315 for the fourth wicket for New South Wales v. Victoria at Sydney were the first Australians to share in a partnership of over 300 in first-class cricket in Australia

1904–5 Rhodesia participated in the Currie Cup, but did not do so again until 1929–30. First match Transvaal *v.* Rhodesia

Between **1901** *and* **1906** C. G. Fichardt (229) and L. Richardson (113) made 401 for the second wicket at Bloemfontein, the first partnership over 400 in South Africa and still the South African record for that wicket

1905–6 Fifth visit by an English team, and first by the MCC (captain, P. F. Warner): first unofficial Tests played: South Africa won four and lost one. First eleven-a-side matches by MCC *v.* Natal and *v.* Eastern Province. First Tests played at Old Wanderers in Johannesburg and Newlands in Cape Town. A proposal for the 12th Australians to visit South Africa after their English tour was turned down. An annual Ladies' match between Durban and Maritzburg was in existence at that time. E. W. Elliott, in scoring 332 for Borderers *v.* Newcastle Garrison in Natal, made a fresh South African individual record. P. Eland (251) and T. Eden (153) made 356 for the fourth wicket, the record for that wicket in South Africa, in a club match at Johannesburg

1906–7 *South African Cricket Annual* revived: one more issue in 1908, and then no others until after the Second World War. Western Province made 509 *v.* Griqualand West, at Johannesburg, beating the 1903–4 South African record. A. E. E. Vogler took 10 for 26 for Eastern Province *v.* Griqualand West, the only time a bowler has taken all 10 wickets in a South African first-class match: he took 16 for 38 in the match, the best by a South African bowler, and took them all in one day. *En route* to New Zealand, the MCC team (captain, E. G. Wynyard) played a match at Cape Town. First matches by Orange River Colony *v.* Western Province, *v.* Eastern Province, *v.* Griqualand West and *v.* Natal

1907 Fourth South African tour to England (captain, P. W. Sherwell): South Africa lost one and drew two of the three official Tests now played for the first time. A project for the team to visit Philadelphia after the English tour fell through

1905 First visit by English team (Lord Brackley's) to include professionals. It was also the first, but, unhappily, not the last team to cause unpleasantness by its attitude. those responsible being all amateurs. When Jamaica played Lord Brackley's XI it was the first time a three-day match was played in Jamaica. First matches Jamaica *v.* Trinidad

1906 First tour by West Indies to England reckoned first-class (captain, H. B. G. Austin). S. G. Smith did the double in *all* matches

1905–6 Second visit by Melbourne Cricket Club (captain, W. W. Armstrong) who won eight and drew two matches including the only representative match. W. W. Armstrong made the first recorded treble century in New Zealand, 335 against Southland. Eden Park, in Auckland, was formed into a cricket ground, but did not see its first first-class match until A. Sims's Australians played there in 1913–14. 299 made for the eleventh wicket in a twelve-a-side club match by E. V. Sale and a Mr Robinson – the world record

1906–7 Sixth English team to tour New Zealand, the first by the Marylebone Cricket Club (captain, E. G. Wynyard): won ten matches including one representative match, and lost two, against Canterbury and against New Zealand in the other representative match. The Plunket Shield was instituted for competition amongst the major associations, the first winners being Canterbury. The competition was under the challenge system until 1921–2 when the present competitive system was adopted. In the challenge period, Canterbury won sixteen matches, Auckland fourteen, and Wellington two: Otago and Hawke's Bay each challenged without success. Southland, though eligible from 1914–15 to 1920–1, never challenged. Since 1921–2, Wellington and Auckland have each won twelve times, Canterbury nine and Otago six. Central Districts (consisting of minor associations from the Wellington major association area), admitted in 1950–1, have won three times, and Northern Districts (formed from the Auckland minor associations), admitted 1956–7, once. Plunket Shield matches were all to be played out until the end of the 1927–8 season (there were in fact two draws in the period, one owing to a programme muddle and the other owing to incessant rain). The first inter-university match, between Canterbury University College and Victoria College, Wellington

1907–8 Canterbury made 623 against South Canterbury at Hagley Park, the then record New Zealand score and still the Canterbury record. Auckland made 539 v. Canterbury on the same ground, establishing a fresh New Zealand first-class record

1905 G. H. S. Fowke became the first to make over 300 in India, 309 in a regimental match in Peshawar

1906 The first representative match between Hindus and Europeans at Bombay: Hindus won

1907 The Bombay Tournament became Triangular with the admission of the Hindus. Colonel K. M. Mistri became the first Indian to score a century in each innings in India when he made 123 and 158 for Chail v. Simla

1908 The first Presidency match in Madras: Europeans v. Indians. The match was revived in 1915 and played regularly until 1946

1905 The peak of interest in cricket was reached in Philadelphia with 375 matches recorded in that season. The first MCC (and fifteenth English) tour to the U.S.A. and Canada (captain, E. W. Mann): won one and lost one *v.* Philadelphia. J. B. King made 315, the first individual score of over 300 in North America. He took part with A. M. Wood (106) in making the North American second-wicket record of 339 for Belmont *v.* Germantown in the same match. The first tour from Bermuda to the U.S.A. (*see also* 1891) by the Hamilton Cricket Club. A Canadian player, T. W. Dyson, took 20 wickets for 43 runs, in a twelve-a-side game in Canada, including all 11 wickets in the second innings

1906 J. B. King again made over 300 when he established the North American record to this day of 344*, for Belmont *v.* Merion

1905 Lieut F. O. Faviell did the double in Ceylon cricket, for the first time. First match between Holland and Belgium

1907 The University of Pennsylvania became the first university to tour overseas when it visited England. The second MCC (and sixteenth English) tour (captain, H. Hesketh-Pritchard): drew two *v.* Philadelphia. H. V. Hordern, the well-known Australian googly bowler then studying in Philadelphia, took 213 wickets in the season, the North American record

1908 The fifth, and last, full Philadelphian tour to the U.K. (captain, J. A. Lester): J. B. King took 120 wickets in all matches on the tour, but only 87 in first-class cricket: nevertheless he averaged 11·01 per wicket, and headed the English bowling averages, not to be excelled till 1958 by H. L. Jackson of Derbyshire. It is of interest that eight of this team were still alive fifty years later

1907 C. Feith made 209, the first double century scored in Holland. R. T. Reid made 234*, the Malayan record

1908 The Portuguese Ambassador to Brazil, the Conde Selir, presented a trophy named after him, for inter-state competition in Brazil: it is still contended for

319

1909 After much lobbying in the preceding two years or so, the Imperial Cricket Conference was formed with the MCC, Australia and South Africa as founder members. Surrey scored 645 for 4 wickets *v.* Hampshire at the Oval, all in one day, the record for an English team. The record English partnership of 393 for the fifth wicket made by E. G. Arnold (200*) and W. B. Burns (196) for Worcestershire *v.* Warwickshire. The record last-wicket partnership by English cricketers of 235 made by F. E. Woolley (185) and A. Fielder (112*) for Kent *v.* Worcestershire. The first MCC tour to Egypt (captain G. H. Simpson-Hayward)

1910 Canadian Zingari became the first club team from outside Europe to tour England. Eton *v.* Harrow match became famous as 'Fowler's match' after he had been largely responsible with his innings of 64 for setting Harrow any target to win at all. That target was only 55 but Harrow could only make 45, Fowler taking 8 wickets for 23. J. Chapman (165) and A. R. Warren (123) made 283 for the ninth wicket for Derbyshire *v.* Warwickshire, the world first-class record for that wicket. E. A. C. Thomson (*see* 1893) now set up the Club Cricketer's Charity Fund and from this in 1915 came the London and Southern Club Cricket Conference, whose name became simply Club Cricket Conference in 1926, the earliest of the major geographical associations of cricket clubs. Six runs were henceforth allowed for hits over the boundary (hitherto allowed only for hits out of the ground). In winning the county championship by August 12, Kent did so on the earliest recorded date

1910–11 The first MCC team to tour West Indies (q.v.), captain A. W. F. Somerset

1911 Warwickshire became champions, the first of the counties outside the original contenders to do so. The first tour by All India to England (captain, the Maharajah of Patiala): some first-class matches played. C. B. Fry scored seven centuries in successive innings in first-class and minor cricket, the world record. The Somerset Clergy, in a one-day match made 453 for 9 wickets in 215 minutes, and declared leaving their opponents, the Somerset Stragglers, two and a half hours to win: the latter did so for one wicket in 122 minutes. Thus 911 runs were scored in under 5¾ hours, the greatest sustained rate of scoring known in one day. A team from Leicester became the first to visit Germany

1911–12 The first MCC tour to South America (captain, Lord Hawke)

1908–9 In the match between New South Wales and Victoria at Sydney, 1,911 runs were scored for 34 wickets, the then world record match aggregate. H. Donnan (353) and A. Cooper (228) made 426 for the fourth wicket, still the Australian record for that wicket, in a club match in Sydney. J. A. Prout made 459 for Wesley College *v.* Geelong College, the record inter-school score until 1914–15. In the same match Wesley College made 710, the record inter-school total for one week when it was beaten by Sydney Grammar School who made 916 against Sydney Church of England Grammar School, the record until 1914–15. Brisbane made 828 *v.* Richmond River, the record total in Queensland. For Mosman's Preparatory School *v.* Sydney Church of England Grammar School 2nd XI, one of the Mosman boys equalled the Australian record by taking seven wickets in seven consecutive balls. A. C. Newton (213*) and J. Barnett (185*) made an unbroken 400 for the first wicket for Queen's College, Hobart *v.* Hutchins School, probably the largest opening partnership ever made in inter-school cricket

1909 First team to Great Britain under the auspices of the Board of Control – 13th Australians (captain, M. A. Noble), won two, lost one and drew two Tests.

1909–10 A minor association in New South Wales experimented with eight-ball overs. E. J. Long for North Sydney *v.* Burwood in a Sydney first-grade match established an Australian record by stumping seven and catching one in one innings, thus equalling world record. In a minor match in Sydney, H. Gray scored 108 and then took 5 wickets in five consecutive balls

1910–11 First visit by South African team to Australia (captain, P. W. Sherwell), won one and lost four of the five Tests. Matches played against all States except Western Australia. In the return match New South Wales *v.* South Africans each side scored over 400 runs in each of the four innings, the first time this had ever been done. G. A. Faulkner made 1,534 runs, the record first-class aggregate in Australia at that time, and still the record for a South African batsman in Australia.

1911–12 3rd MCC tour (captain, P. F. Warner, who fell ill and was succeeded by J. W. H. T. Douglas): won four Tests, lost one. F. E. Woolley in making 305* against Tasmania made the first 300 by an Englishman in Australia: it remained the highest score by any non-Australian in Australia until 1962–3. C. Hill became the first to aggregate 10,000 runs

1909 Visit by Philadelphians to Jamaica. H. V. Hordern took 16 wickets for 86 v. Jamaica. Guyana scored 529 in match v. W. Shepherd's XI – the highest score till then in the West Indies

1909–10 Second MCC tour to South Africa (captain, H. D. G. Leveson-Gower): South Africa won three and lost two Tests. First Test played at Lord's, Durban. First eleven-a-side match MCC v. Border. D. Denton in making 139 and 138 for MCC v. Transvaal became the first cricketer to make two centuries in a South African first-class match. J. B. Hobbs in making 1,194 runs became the first cricketer to make over 1,000 runs in a South African first-class season: he did it again in 1913–14, and only he, L. Hutton, W. R. Hammond, J. R. Reid (New Zealand) and R. G. Pollock have performed this feat twice

1910–11 First tour to Australia (q.v.) by South Africans; negotiations for the team to tour New Zealand fell through. G. A. Faulkner made 1,534 runs in the Australian season, the first of six South Africans to make over 1,000 runs in Australia, none of whom have exceeded his aggregate. First match Border v. Orange Free State

1910 Cork Cup presented for competition by the Administrator, the Hon. P. C. Cork, amongst the Windward Islands: first winners, St Vincent. The competition was on a knock-out basis

1911 First visit by MCC team (captain A. W. F. Somerset): won two and drew one of the representative matches. The match v. Jamaica was tied – the only tie in first-class cricket in the West Indies

1908–9 The Heathcote Williams Shield presented for competition amongst New Zealand secondary schools: first winners were Christchurch Boys' High School, who have won the Shield nine times. Auckland Grammar School have won eight times, and Palmerston North Boys' High School three times. Competition for the Shield was discontinued between 1929–30 and 1952–3 when the last match for it was played

1909–10 Sixth visit by a representative Australian team (captain, W. W. Armstrong) who won both representative matches. New Zealand opened negotiations for the South African team to Australia in 1910–11 to come on to New Zealand, but they were unsuccessful. Havelock were all out for 0 *v.* Whareti, the first time this had been recorded in New Zealand. Auckland made 579 *v.* Otago at the Domain, a new record first-class score by a New Zealand team. A women's inter-provincial match took place between Canterbury and Wellington: it is believed there had been a match some four or five years earlier.

1910–11 Negotiations for MCC to visit New Zealand after 1911–12 tour to Australia unsuccessful. Hawke Cup instituted for competition amongst the minor associations. The competition was on a tournament basis in the first season (won by Southland) and in the third season (won by South Auckland – now Waikato): otherwise it has always been conducted on the challenge system. Nelson has resisted forty-five challenges, and has held the trophy for the longest period (excluding war years) from December 1958 to February 1965. Manawatu has resisted forty-two challenges, Wanganui and Waikato thirty each, Hutt Valley eight, Hawke's Bay seven, Taranaki six, Poverty Bay four, Wairarapa and Southland two each and Marlborough one. Other teams to have won the Hawke Cup, though without being able to resist any challenge, have been Rangitikei (twice), Northland and North Canterbury. L. Dacre, elder brother of C. C. Dacre, made two centuries in different matches on the same day. The record New Zealand partnership – 518 for the second wicket – made by A. Young (275) and L. MacMahon (226*) in a minor match at Gisborne

1911–12 T. M. McFarlane took five wickets in five balls in a senior club match in Dunedin, but his side still lost by 10 wickets. He was an all-rounder: within two months he had made 211 which included eleven sixes and twenty-

1911 First All India tour to the U.K. (captain, the Maharajah of Patiala (the second of three successive celebrated cricketers in that title)

1909 Fourth and last tour by the Gentlemen of Ireland (captain, F. H. Browning): lost both matches *v.* Philadelphia. J. B. King took all 10 wickets for 33 runs against them in one, all clean bowled, including also the not-out batsman whose stumps had been hit by a no-ball. He achieved all 10 wickets for the third time in his career. The Philadelphians toured Jamaica (captain, H. G. Pearce): they won two and lost one *v.* All Jamaica

1910 An Alberta Cricket Association formed: also a Saskatchewan Cricket Association – the present body, however, dates from 1959. The Canadian Zingari, a wandering club of many years standing and modelled after the English I Zingari (except that it had rules!) became the first Canadian club to tour the U.K. (captain, W. J. Fleury). L. Thomas (182) and P. Lee (124) established the North American fifth-wicket record of 264 in Philadelphia. The Western Canada Tournament was organized for competition among the four Western Canadian provinces: in all, British Columbia won six times, Alberta four and each shared once

1911 The first All Bermuda team to visit Philadelphia. The first American club tour to the U.K. – Germantown C.C. (captain, Dr J. N. Henry). The North American tenth-wicket record of 124 unbroken made by Dr D. Macfarlane (62*) and U. G. S. Grant (57*) in Philadelphia. *Canadian Cricket* instituted – a monthly magazine which ran for two years. Ten-ball overs were adopted for the Halifax Cup competition

1910 In a regimental match in Malta, 1,683 runs were scored for 39 wickets, a remarkably high aggregate in a minor match at this or any other period (though not the record)

1911 W. T. Greswell took 232 wickets in Ceylon, the record. The record Ceylon last-wicket partnership of 141 unbroken established by C. A. Pereira (84*) and A. de Alwis (128*). The first century recorded in East Africa, 117 by H. Pickwood in Nairobi

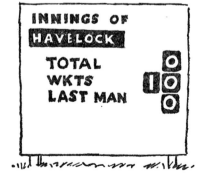

'*1909–10. N.Z. Havelock were all out for 0*'

1912 The first and only Triangular tournament, held in England and won by England from Australia and South Africa. This season the first 'Trial' matches for Test selection were held. W. Clarke, a schoolboy in a minor match in Kent obtained three hat-tricks in the first innings and two in the second

1913 The Incogniti became the first private club to tour outside Europe when they visited the U.S.A. In the U.K., C. H. Titchmarsh in all matches scored twenty-one centuries and made 4,016 runs
1914 Northamptonshire made their record score of 557 for 6 wickets declared, v. Sussex at Hove. The outbreak of war curtailed all grades of cricket, including the county championship. No first-class cricket was played again in England until 1919, but several of the northern leagues continued in being, employing some of the best known English professionals

in first-class cricket in Australia only. Industrial action was threatened by Australian Trade Unions against the fourth Test at Melbourne if J. N. McLaren (who had acted as a special constable in a strike earlier that year) played: though in the twelve named, he was omitted but played in the fifth Test
1912 Triangular Test series in England. 14th Australians (captain, S. E. Gregory) gravely weakened by dispute between Board and players. The third Test at the Oval, between England and Australia, was played to a finish, the first time it had happened in England though provision had been made for it if circumstances required from 1905 onwards. The two earlier Tests had been drawn. King George V visited Lord's while Australia played South Africa: the first visit by a reigning sovereign to a Test match. Australia won two Tests v. South Africa. In the match between Australia and South Africa at Old Trafford, T. J. Matthews performed the hat-trick in each innings, done on only three other occasions in first-class cricket and never again in a Test. C. G. Macartney became the second Australian to complete 1,000 runs in an English season before any Englishman, when he did so on June 19. First visit by Australian team to Bermuda and Fiji
1913 The first extended tour by an Australian team containing first-class players to North America: forty-eight matches played
1913–14 First eleven-a-side match South Australia v. New Zealand, at Adelaide. Second New Zealand team to Australia (captain, D. Reese). A. Sims's Australian XI touring New Zealand made 922 for nine wickets v. South Canterbury XV, the largest total ever made by any touring team (see also New Zealand). In making 641 for the third wicket for Buffalo River v. Whorouly at Gapsted in Victoria, T. Patton (408) and N. Rippon (321) established the world record partnership for any wicket
1914 Projected tour by Tasmania to England fell through despite promises of substantial guarantees: no Australian State has ever toured outside Australasia
1914–15 Highest score ever made in Victoria, and also the world highest in inter-school cricket: 506* by J. C. Sharpe for Melbourne Church of England Grammar School v. Geelong College. His team made 961, the world record total in an inter-school match
1915–16 Eight-ball overs first tried out in first-grade cricket in New South Wales

1912 Triangular Tests: fifth South African tour to England (captain, F. Mitchell): of six Tests played South Africa lost all three to England, and lost two and drew one against Australia. S. J. Pegler took 189 wickets on the tour, the record number of wickets taken by a South African in first-class cricket in England
1912–13 A South African team visited Rhodesia and Portuguese East Africa for the first time

1913–14 Third MCC tour to South Africa (captain, J. W. H. T. Douglas). England won four Tests, the other being drawn. First Test played at Crusader's Park, Port Elizabeth. S. F. Barnes took 17 wickets for 159 for England v. South Africa in Johannesburg, the second and last occasion on which this feat has been performed in South African first-class cricket. He took 104 wickets on the tour, the first time 100 wickets had been taken in a South African first-class season. MCC established a new South African record by making 565 for 8 wickets declared v. Orange Free State at Bloemfontein (the first eleven-a-side match between the two teams. MCC also played on equal terms v. Griqualand West for the first time)

1912 Wanderers made 673 v. Pickwick in the Barbados Challenge Cup competition: the first score over 600 in the West Indies, and the record until beaten by Barbados in 1926–7

1913 Second tour by MCC (captain, A. W. F. Somerset): won two and lost one of the representative matches. In the match against Barbados, A. W. F. Somerset (55*) and W. C. Smith (126) added 167 for MCC's last wicket (the West Indian record for that wicket), the Barbados pair, P. H. Tarilton (157) and H. W. Ince (57*) having already made 100 for the Barbados last wicket in the same match, a most unusual occurrence in any class of cricket. P. H. Tarilton made 1,084 runs, average 83·38, in all matches in the Barbados season, the first time it had been done in that island. Sir Hesketh Bell presented a cup for competition on a knock-out basis amongst the Leeward Islands, of which he was then Governor. The first winners were Antigua. E. R. D. Moulder carried his bat for 104* for West Indies v. MCC at Bourda the first time anyone had carried his bat for a century in first-class cricket five fours. In 1908–9 he had made two centuries in the same match in Dunedin senior cricket, only the second New Zealander to have done so. R. G. Hickmott, aged eighteen in March 1912, made 1,694 runs, average 67·76 and took 112 wickets, average 13·42, in school and senior club cricket in Christchurch. The Otago–Canterbury match lasted five days, the first of three in the Plunket Shield to do so

1912–13 C. C. Dacre, then under fourteen, scored 1,817 runs and took 149 wickets of which 924 runs and 100 wickets were for his school

1913–14 Second tour by New Zealand to Australia: though they lost two of the four first-class matches they beat Queensland, the first victory by a New Zealand team in first-class cricket in Australia. First match between North and South Island Universities. Visit by A. Sims's unofficial but very powerful Australian team, who won both the representative matches. In the second of these, four centuries were made for the Australians, a record in New Zealand first-class cricket. J. N. Crawford made 354 for the Australians against South Canterbury XV, the record for New Zealand until 1949–50. It is the highest score by an Englishman (he was of course the Surrey amateur) or any other batsman outside his own country in any class of cricket. The team made 922 for nine wickets, the record score in New Zealand cricket. V. T. Trumper made 293 against Canterbury and set up a fresh New Zealand first-class record. With A. Sims (184*) he made 433 for the eighth wicket, the world first-class record. The Australians score of 658 against Auckland at Eden Park, the first first-class match on that ground, was the then record New Zealand first-class score

1914–15 A Fiji team was to have toured New Zealand, but the project was abandoned owing to the outbreak of war. H. M. Butterworth made 911 in four consecutive innings (194, 296, 311 and 110*) in minor matches at Wanganui

1915–16 First treble century by a New Zealander: 334* by H. B. Lusk for West Christchurch v. St Albans in Christchurch

1912 The Bombay Tournament became Quadrangular with the admission of the Muslims

1912–13 M. D. Parekh performed the hat-trick for Parsis v. Hindus at Bombay, the first Indian to do so in Indian first-class cricket

1913–14 The first Inter-University match in India, between Madras University and Bombay University, won by the latter by 7 wickets
1914 P. N. Polishwalla published the first of his many works on cricket, some of which partook of the nature of cricket annuals, and some of which were indeed so entitled: the last appeared in 1934

1915 The Muslims made 21 v. Europeans at Poona, the lowest score in Indian first-class cricket
1916 The Sind Tournament was first played: Parsis beat Hindus. Revived in 1919, it was played in most years up to 1946–7 and was revived again after Partition in Pakistan. In 1919 a permanent Committee was set up and this led, in 1924, to the formation of the Karachi Cricket Association, the name being changed to Sind Cricket Association in 1928. The tournament, though important, was not first-class, being restricted to Karachi residents or Karachi-born

1912 The 14th Australians (to U.K.) toured North America on their way home: won one and lost one v. Philadelphia. The North American seventh-wicket record of 213 unbroken was made by O. D. Rasmussen (106*) – well-known in cricket in Shanghai – and W. D. Cochrane (101*) in Los Angeles. The Canadian partnership record of 265 unbroken was made by F. F. Burnett (158*) and F. W. Johnson (100*) in Calgary, for the first wicket

1913 The Incogniti became the first private club (and the seventeenth English team) to tour North America (captain, E. J. Metcalfe): they won one and lost one v. Philadelphia. Austin Diamond's Australians made an extensive tour of North America, beating Combined U.S.A. and Canada twice, Philadelphia twice (and drawing once) but losing to Germantown C.C. by four wickets. They established the Canadian record total of 633 for eight wickets declared v. a Vancouver XV. R. J. Beecham scored 249 in British Columbia, the record by a Canadian to this day

1912 A. van Gogh (203) with F. H. J. Holder (87) established the record Dutch second-wicket partnership of 256. First tour to South America from outside the continent, the MCC led by Lord Hawke: won two and lost one representative match v. Argentina. During this tour A. C. MacLaren (172) and N. C. Tufnell (163*) established the Argentine third-wicket record of 314, for MCC v. Argentine. Born at Hurlingham (K. Henderson (217), and G. W. Ferguson (90), got within three of it in 1938–9). In an all-day match in Ceylon 905 runs were scored. E. J. Melder scored 1,548 runs in the season, the Ceylon record

1913 1,319 runs were scored for 32 wickets in a club match in Ceylon, the record match aggregate there. Hague C.C. established the Dutch record total when making 580 for 8 wickets v. Hilversum

1914 First visit by a Kenya team to Uganda

1916 The record Dutch fourth-wicket partnership of 242 unbroken made by J. Billeveld (127*) and B. Thomas (101*). The first Dutch cricket annual appeared: one further issue the following year. Cricket now being played regularly in Tanganyika. The Samoa Cricket Association formed in Apia. Dr E. P. Barbour made two centuries in a match in Egypt, the first time it was done there

Eight-ball overs adopted for all domestic first-class cricket in Australia. In a minor match in New South Wales, Dr L. O. S. Poidevin became the first Australian to complete a hundred centuries in all cricket

1919 The Australian Imperial Forces undertook an extensive tour in England: its captain was C. E. Kelleway who however had to return home in June and handed over to H. L. Collins

1919 County championship matches restricted to two days, with long playing hours, as an experiment: it was not successful. The Australian Imperial Forces conducted an extensive tour with their first XI

1920 The County Championship reverted to three-day cricket, with the Saturday start now general

1919–20 The AIF also visited South Africa (q.v.)

1920–1 4th MCC tour (captain J. W. H. T. Douglas) lost all five Tests against Australia, a unique failing in this series of matches. W. W. Armstrong (157* and 245) for Victoria v. South Australia became the first Australian to make a century and a double century in a first-class match. Victoria, in making 724 in their second innings against South Australia established the world record second innings total. Within six weeks it had been beaten by New South Wales who made 770, also against South Australia. In the only innings of their other matches against South Australia, Victoria had made 639 and New South Wales 802! This last match was abandoned as a draw as rain had poured down for three days – the only draw in Sheffield Shield cricket before 1927–8.) W. Bardsley (235) and C. E. Kelleway (168) made 397 for the fifth wicket for New South Wales v. South Australia – still the Sheffield Shield record for any wicket. The Australian record second wicket partnership of 525* made by G. Conran (295*) and P. Watsford (214*) in a country match in New South Wales.

1921 Glamorgan admitted to the County Championship: no other counties have been admitted since then. Foundation of *The Cricketer* (first editor, P. F. Warner) the oldest surviving cricket magazine

1921 15th Australians (captain, W. W. Armstrong) won three and drew two Tests. C. G. Macartney scored 345 runs in a day, the world record in first-class cricket, in the match between the Australians and Nottinghamshire. It is to this day the record first-class score made by an Australian or any other batsman outside his own country.

1921–2 Third tour by Australians to South Africa (q.v.)

1922 First MCC tour to Denmark (captain, R. P. Keigwin). Lancashire School Cricket Association formed, the first county-wide organization for secondary schools cricket

1922–3 First score in an Australian first-class match of over 400: 429 by W. H. Ponsford for Victoria v. Tasmania, the then world first-class record. Victoria made 1,059, the then world record for first-class cricket and beat Tasmania by an innings and 666 runs, the greatest margin in any first-class (or probably any other) match until 1964–5 when it was beaten in a match in Pakistan. This was Pons-

1923 Middlesex made their record score of 642 for 3 wickets declared v. Hampshire at Southampton

1919–20 Second visit by an Australian team to South Africa: the Australian Imperial Forces (captain, H. L. Collins): won both representative matches. C. N. Frank in making 108 for Transvaal v. A.I.F. became the first South African to make a century on debut in first-class cricket. This game and that v. Natal were the first eleven-a-side matches by Australians against these teams. A. D. Nourse (sen.) made 304* for Natal v. Transvaal, the first score of over 300 in first-class cricket. J. W. Zulch in making 185 and 125 for Transvaal v. Orange Free State at Bloemfontein became the first South African to make two centuries in a first-class match

1920–1 720 runs scored in one day for 15 wickets in the match between Orange Free State and Border, the South African record for one day's play. J. W. Zulch made a century before lunch for Transvaal v. Orange Free State in Bloemfontein, the first South African ever to do so in first-class cricket

1921–2 Third tour by Australians (15th) (captain, H. L. Collins). South Africa lost one and drew two Tests. First Test played on the Kingsmead ground, Durban. These were the first officially recognized Tests between the two countries in South Africa. From this season, Currie Cup matches were of three days' duration totalling 21 hours play except in 1923–4 and 1931–2: some other first-class matches in South Africa continued to be of two days' duration, however

1922 First visit by a South African Indian team to India

1922–3 Fourth MCC tour to South Africa (captain, F. T. Mann) South Africa won one, lost two and drew two Tests. N. V. Lindsay (160*) and G. R. McCubbin (97), for Transvaal v. Rhodesia at Bulawayo made the record South African ninth-wicket partnership of 221

1920 P. H. Tarilton made the first score of over 200 in a West Indian first-class match when he made 304* for Barbados v. Trinidad: Barbados made 623 runs, the first total of over 600 in first-class cricket

1921 1,799 runs were made for 39 wickets in the match between Wanderers and Pickwick on the Pickwick ground, thus breaking the previous record match aggregate made in 1895: it remains the record in domestic West Indian matches. The match lasted seven days. G. Challenor scored 206 and 133 – the first time this rare feat was performed in the West Indies.

1922–3 K. I. R. Kirkpatrick (185) and J. E. Chabroll (156) in scoring 320 for the third wicket for Guyana v. Georgetown made the first partnership of over 300 runs in the West Indies

1923 Third West Indian tour to England (captain, H. B. G. Austin). G. Challenor became the first West Indian tourist to make 1,000 runs in a first-class season. There were two remarkable matches: against Surrey, G. Challenor carried his bat for 155* having added with G. N. Francis (41) 136 for the last wicket; in the second innings he and P. H. Tarilton opening made 121 without being parted, to win the match. At Scarborough what was virtually an England XI was set 28 to win and lost 6 wickets for 19 in doing so

L*

1917–18 North made 633 for seven wickets against Returned Soldiers at Wellington, the then record by a New Zealand team. W. S. Brice took 93 wickets in senior club cricket in Wellington and 117 in senior and first-class cricket: both records for that centre. Over 100 wickets in such cricket have been taken there by J. N. Crawford, R. W. Blair (three times) and J. R. Reid. J. Grey made 343 in senior cricket in Christchurch, the record score by a New Zealander until 1949–50. His team, Sydenham, made 599 for 4 wickets declared, the record for senior cricket in Christchurch

1918–19 Eight-ball overs first used in New Zealand first-class cricket. They became regularly so used in 1919–20, but occasional matches were played with six-ball overs (notably by Canterbury) until 1923–4: in 1926–7 New Zealand reverted to six-ball overs for first-class cricket, but returned to eight-ball overs in 1937–8. These were retained until 1944–5 for first-class cricket, and continued to be used in some minor competitions in New Zealand and were adopted again for all cricket from 1968–9

1919–20 Auckland made 643 v. Canterbury at Eden Park, the then record first-class score by a New Zealand team. Murphy's Pipe Works in successive matches made 701 for six wickets declared on the Basin Reserve and 741 in Anderson Park at Wellington, both being records by New Zealand teams

1920–1 Seventh official visit by an Australian team (captain, V. S. Ransford): won one and drew the second representative match. Australia made 663 against New Zealand at Eden Park, a new record in New Zealand first-class cricket

1922–3 Second tour by MCC to New Zealand (captain, A. C. MacLaren): New Zealand drew one and lost two of the representative matches

1923–4 Second official tour by a New South Wales team (captain, C. G. Macartney): won both representative matches. In the course of their match against Otago, New South Wales scored 649 runs for the loss of 7 wickets in one day and went on to make 752 for 8 wickets declared, the record first-class score in New Zealand. C. G. Macartney for New South Wales against Wellington became the first player to make a century before lunch in New Zealand: he did it again v. Otago. In the match between Otago and Wellington, 1,905 runs were scored for 40 wickets, the record New

1918 F. A. Tarrant took all 10 wickets in an innings and made 182* in an innings in the same match for Lord Willingdon's team v. Maharajah of Cooch Behar's team, one of the few occasions on which this feat has been performed in first-class cricket, the only time in Indian cricket, and the first time all 10 wickets had been taken in an innings in Indian first-class cricket

1922 First visit to India of a team of South African Indians, to Calcutta to play cricket and football against the well-known Mohan Bagan Club. Gwalior Sports Association was formed: it took part in the Ranji Trophy from 1943 to 1947 but was later absorbed by Holkar C. A. (or Central India). The first All India cricket tournament in New Delhi, won by the Maharajah of Patiala's XI: the tournament was played in most years until the early 1930s

1922–3 The Lahore Tournament instituted: first winners Europeans. Subsequent tournaments were played only in 1924, 1925, 1926, 1928 and 1939

1917 The record eighth-wicket partnership in Ceylon of 230 by A. P. Wijetange (263 retired) and W. Fernando (80)

1918 Ch. Buchwald made 205*, the first double century scored in Denmark. The record Dutch sixth-wicket partnership of 211 made by Captain A. D. Gaye (146*) and M. C. Platt (82) – they were playing for British Prisoners of War and Civilian Internees in Holland

'*1922. In Philadelphia ten-ball overs were adopted*'

1918–19 C. Holland made two centuries in a match (146 and 100*) in Argentina, the first time this had been done. About this time. A. G. Lawrie made 300* in an *afternoon* match in Valparaiso

1919 B. J. Kortlang, who played in many different parts of the world, made 1,690 runs in the season, the Canadian record

1920 The Incogniti paid their second visit (captain, E. J. Metcalfe): won two *v*. Philadelphia. A proposed Australian tour to Canada was postponed until 1921 but never took place

1921 The last extended tour by a Philadelphian team to the U.K. – the Philadelphian Pilgrims, a club whose members all had to be Philadelphian internationals. *Canadian Cricket Annual* first issued – two more issues

1922 Third Canadian tour to the U.K. (captain, Norman Seagram). In Philadelphia ten-ball overs were adopted for half-day matches and eight-ball overs for all others. The British Columbia Cricket Association formed

1923 The Free Foresters paid their first visit (the nineteenth English tour) (captain, E. G. Wynyard): won one and drew one *v*. Philadelphia. Canada officially adopted six-ball overs but eight-ball overs were in frequent use again by 1929

1919–20 First issue of the *Yearbook of Argentine Cricket*: eight more followed, all edited by J. McGough, the leading authority on Argentine cricket

1920–1 First of a regular series of international matches in South America, this being Chile *v*. Argentina. In fifty matches played, Argentina has won twenty-seven (eleven *v*. Chile, sixteen *v*. Brazil), Chile six (*v*. Argentina) and Brazil four (all against Argentina): the others have been drawn. Brazil has not yet played Chile and Peru has beaten Chile once

1921 The MCC visited B.A.O.R. in Germany

1921–2 B. H. Smyth (158*) and H. D. Williams (133*) made the Argentine second-wicket record partnership of 292 unbroken. First matches between Argentina and Brazil

1922 The Brazil Cricket Association formed. The Ceylon Cricket Association formed, merged in the Ceylon Cricket Board of Control (first formed in 1948) in 1965. The first double century in East Africa, 201* by C. A. Turpin in Kampala

1924 First tour to England by a team from the Argentine, E. W. S. Thomson's XI. Somerset made their record score of 675 for 9 wickets declared *v.* Hampshire at Bath. Hours of play in county championship matches now standardized at 18 hours, excluding luncheon and tea intervals but including an extra half-hour to obtain a result if claimed and intervals between innings. Some county matches hitherto had as many as 21 playing hours

1925 J. B. Hobbs equalled and then beat W. G. Grace's record of 126 first-class centuries: he went on to make 199 centuries by the time he retired in 1934. He also made sixteen centuries in the season, the record until 1947. County club formed for Anglesey (present club 1951)

1926 India, New Zealand and the West Indies admitted to the Imperial Cricket Conference. First tour to England from Denmark: Gentlemen of Denmark. Formation of Women's Cricket Association

1926–7 First MCC tour to India and Ceylon (captain, A. E. R. Gilligan)

1927 First New Zealand tour to England (captain, T. C. Lowry). In the match between MCC and the New Zealanders at Lord's, the record match aggregate for a three-day game in England was established of 1,502 runs for 28 wickets. During the New Zealand tour, a wireless commentary was broadcast in England for the first time, during their match against Essex. First tour to Gibraltar – Cryptics C.C. Ball reduced in circumference to between $8\frac{13}{16}$ in. and 9 in. (these being the dimensions which had in fact prevailed for some years without anyone noticing!)

ford's fourth innings in first-class cricket: in his first eight he totalled 1,051 runs. A. J. Richardson made 280 for South Australia *v.* MCC, the then highest score in Australia against an English team. First wireless commentary on a cricket match in the world – New South Wales trial match, played as a Testimonial match for C. Bannerman, November 1922. 5th MCC tour (captain, A. C. MacLaren) played no Tests

1923–4 W. H. Ponsford (248) and E. R. Mayne (209) made 456 for the first wicket for Victoria *v.* Queensland at Melbourne, the record for that or any other wicket in Australian first-class cricket. The follow-on was reduced to 150 runs in three-day first-class matches other than Inter-state matches. Dr E. P. Barbour made 1,154 runs (average 88·2) and took 111 wickets (average 9·9) in Newcastle first-grade cricket, the only occasion, it is believed, on which the double has been performed in this class of cricket in Australia. C. Sheriff, aged sixteen, of Melbourne, established a unique record by scoring 1,004 runs in the season in seven innings *without once being out*

1924–5 6th MCC tour (captain, A. E. R. Gilligan) lost four Tests, won one. Eight-ball overs first used in Test matches (they were *not*, however, used in the series played from 1928–9 to 1932–3). The first wireless commentary on a Test match took place in this series. Another cricket magazine instituted, the *Australian Cricketer* – seven monthly issues only

1925–6 Third New Zealand tour to Australia, captain W. R. Patrick. In the New South Wales *v.* South Australia match at Sydney, 1,929 runs were made for 39 wickets; the world record aggregate until 1938–9. It remains the record Australian aggregate. This was the first first-class match in the world to last eight days. A. O. Burrows sent a bail 83 yds 1 ft 9 in. in a club match in South Tasmania

1926 16th Australians (captain, H. L. Collins) drew four but lost the fifth Test

1926–7 Declaration permitted after second day's play in Sheffield Shield matches; the first did not take place until the following season. Victoria made 1,107 against New South Wales at Melbourne. The score, which remains the world record, was made in two days. New South Wales were beaten by an innings and 656 runs. W. H. Ponsford and A. F. Kippax each made 1,000 runs in the season, the first time it had been done in a purely domestic season

1923–4 Transvaal had a remarkable record in this season's Currie Cup Tournament in that they won each of their five matches by an innings. The same season saw J. M. M. Commaille (132*) and A. W. Palm (106*) make the record South African sixth-wicket partnership, 244* for Western Province v. Griqualand West at Johannesburg

1924 Sixth South African tour to England (captain, H. W. Taylor): South Africa lost three and drew two Tests: in the first Test at Edgbaston, South Africa were all out for 30, the lowest score in Tests by South Africa

1924–5 Ninth tour by an English team, S. B. Joel's (captain, the Hon. L. H. Tennyson): South Africa won two, lost two and drew one of the five unofficial Tests. First eleven-a-side match by an English team v. Rhodesia

1925–6 1,456 runs were scored for 38 wickets, the record aggregate for a Currie Cup match, between Griqualand West and Natal at Kimberley. The match between Orange Free State and Eastern Province ended in a tie, the only South African first-class match ever to have done so. In the match between Orange Free State and Western Province at Bloemfontein the Orange Free State last wicket pair (L. R. Tuckett and L. G. Fuller in the first innings, L. R. Tuckett and F. Caulfield in the second innings) put on over 100 in each innings, a feat unparalleled in first-class cricket anywhere

1926 South African Independent Cricket Board established for coloured cricketers: the name was changed in 1948 to make this clear

1926–7 Currie Cup first played on turf wickets. Orange Free State made 552 v. Natal at Bloemfontein, establishing a fresh South African first-class record by a South African team in South Africa (it remains the Orange Free State record). In that match S. K. Coen (165) and J. M. M. Commaille (186) made 305 for Orange Free State, the record first-class second-wicket partnership in South Africa by South Africans. Transvaal made 583 against Eastern Province at Johannesburg, and this beat the Orange Free State record and the MCC score of 1913–14. For Natal v. Orange Free State at Bloemfontein J. F. W. Nicolson (252*) and I. J. Siedle (174) made 424 for the first wicket, the South African record wicket partnership. A. F. Borland took 4 wickets in four balls for Natal v. Griqualand West, the first time in South African first-class cricket by a South African. The feat had earlier been done by S. Haigh for MCC v. Army in 1905–6, in a match the status of which is doubtful, although generally accepted

1924 First match Trinidad v. Windward Islands

1925 Formation of the Jamaican Cricket Association, the controlling authority for all cricket in Jamaica

1926 Third MCC and eighth English tour to West Indies (captain, Hon. F. S. G. Calthorpe) won one, drew two representative matches. P. Holmes (244) and W. E. Astill (156) made 327 for the fifth wicket for MCC v. Jamaica, the record for that wicket in the West Indies, and the first partnership of over 300 in West Indian first-class cricket. L. G. Crawley (85) and F. Watson (103*) made 168 for the ninth wicket for MCC v. Jamaica at Melbourne Park – the record for that wicket in the West Indies. Mr R. Beaumont (chairman, Trinidad Leaseholds Ltd, and a member of the 1912 South African team to England) donated a cup for competition between North and South Trinidad. The first match was a draw but South, having won an earlier match the previous year were deemed the holders. The match became first-class from 1959. First match between Leeward Islands and Barbados

1927 Barbados established new West Indian records for team totals in successive matches: 715 for 9 wickets declared v. Guyana, followed by 726 for 7 wickets declared v. Trinidad. They were the first scores of over 700 in the West Indies. The match v. Trinidad lasted nine days (of which two rained off) and provided the domestic West Indian first-class aggregate record of 1,677 runs for 37 wickets. Formation of West Indies Cricket Board of Control on January 22, 1927

Zealand match aggregate. Otago were set 641 to win and made 495, the record fourth innings total in New Zealand. J. S. Shepherd and R. V. de R. Worker made 154 and 155 for the first wicket in each innings for Otago, the first time this had been done in New Zealand

1924–5 First visit by an official team from Victoria (captain, E. R. Mayne): lost to Wellington but won one and drew the other representative match. C. C. Dacre made 127* and 101* for Auckland *v.* Victoria, the first occasion on which this feat had been performed in New Zealand first-class cricket, and the only occasion in which both innings were not out. The record first-wicket partnership in New Zealand of 441 made by J. W. E. Mills (236*) and H. Gillespie (234) in a club match in Auckland

1925–6 Third official visit by a New Zealand team to Australia: won no first-class matches. In the match *v.* Northern New South Wales Country Districts at West Maitland, New Zealand made 681, the record score by a New Zealand team outside New Zealand. A. Rimmer, aged fourteen, took all 20 of his opponents' wickets in a junior school match for 16 runs, the only occasion on which the feat had been performed in New Zealand. J. S. Hiddleston made a century before lunch for Wellington *v.* Canterbury, the first New Zealander to do so in first-class cricket

1926 New Zealand admitted to the Imperial Cricket Conference

1926–7 Third tour by Melbourne Cricket Club (the tour was arranged at the last moment to take the place of South Australia): though no matches were lost, three of the five victories were against minor associations and both representative matches were drawn. In one of these at Lancaster Park, New Zealand made 602 for 9 wickets declared – the only occasion a New Zealand representative team has exceeded 600 in New Zealand. During the tour W. W. Armstrong (166) and his brother T. G. (89*) made 226 for the last wicket against Waikato at Seddon Park, Hamilton, the New Zealand record for this wicket

1927 First New Zealand tour to England (captain, T. C. Lowry): the team also visited Ceylon and Australia. No Test matches were played; in the match *v.* MCC 1,502 runs were scored for 28 wickets, the highest match aggregate in England apart from Test matches, and the third highest including Test matches

1924 Southern Punjab Cricket Association formed, a later contender in the Ranji Trophy: the name was changed to Patiala from 1953 and back again in 1958

1926 India admitted to the Imperial Cricket Conference

1926–7 The first visit by the MCC, fourth by an English team (captain, A. E. R. Gilligan): MCC beat All India, but could only draw with All India (Indians). C. K. Nayudu, for Hindus *v.* MCC at Bombay, hit eleven sixes in his innings of 153, the record for first-class cricket in India. M. W. Tate took 92 wickets in all matches allegedly first-class in India but many of them were suspect as to status. However, even after taking a properly restrictive attitude to some matches, R. E. S. Wyatt undoubtedly topped the thousand runs and may therefore have been the first to do so in the Indian season

1927 The Board of Control for Cricket in India formed in April. Azim Khan of Alwar took all 10 wickets in an innings for the ninth time in his career, the first in 1914, all in good-class cricket. The Northern India Cricket Association was formed shortly before the Board of Control was formed: after Partition, that part in Pakistan became the Punjab Cricket Association, and the Indian part became the East Punjab C.A. The North-West Frontier Province Cricket Association was formed from N.I.C.A. in 1936

1924 The Incogniti paid their third visit (again captained by E. J. Metcalfe): drew two v. Philadelphia

1924 E. W. S. Thomson's Argentine XI became the first from South America to tour the U.K. The first double century in Fiji, 214* by W. Tuinaceva, who also established the Fijian seasonal record of 1,106 runs

1925–6. N.Z. J. S. Hiddleston made a century before lunch'

1925 Denmark was using eight-ball overs about this time. The record Dutch partnership for any wicket established by J. H. H. Kessler (227) and W. G. L. van Spengler (127): 351 for the first wicket

1926 First Danish tour to the U.K.: Gentlemen of Denmark

1926–7 Second MCC tour to South America (captain, P. F. Warner): won two, lost one, and drew one v. Argentina. The team also visited Chile, Uruguay and Peru. First three-day match between Ceylon and an English team, MCC, who won. Other such matches were played in 1933–4, 1936–7, 1951–2 and 1968–9

1927 The first match between Sierra Leone and the Gambia. The highest score in Brazil – 534 v. Argentina

335

First (unofficial) visit by Australian team to Malaya: they played nine matches, of which two were three-day matches against Malaya. Malaya won one, Australians the other

1927–8 First overseas tour by an Australian school: St Peter's College, Adelaide to Ceylon. W. H. Ponsford scored 437 runs for Victoria *v.* Queensland, again breaking the first-class record. He also became the first batsman in Australia to make 1,000 runs by the end of December: and the first batsman in the world to make 1,000 runs in a calendar month overseas – he actually made 1,146 runs between December 2nd and 31st, of which over 1,000 (1,013) were in four consecutive innings, a feat without parallel in first-class cricket. In this season he became the first batsman first to equal and then to surpass W. G. Grace's career record of three innings over 300. No one else has made over 400 on two occasions. Sheffield Shield matches hitherto played out were now limited to four days each of 5½ hours play, and one day of 2½ hours playing-time

1928–9 7th MCC tour (captain, A. P. F. Chapman), won four Tests, lost one. Follow-on reduced to 150 runs in Sheffield Shield matches. Declaration permitted after first day's play. Test match played for the first time at Brisbane, on the Exhibition ground. D. G. Bradman established the record first-class aggregate for a season of 1,690 runs. W. R. Hammond established the record first-class aggregate for a tourist of 1,553 runs, A. F. Kippax (260*) and H. Hooker (62) added 307 for the last wicket for New South Wales *v.* Victoria, beating the 1901–2 world record, also made in Australia. In the return match Hooker took 4 wickets in four balls, the only Australian to have done so in first-class cricket in Australia

1928 First Test matches played in England by the West Indies (captain, R. K. Nunes). England won the rubber, Gloucestershire made their record score of 653 for 6 wickets declared *v.* Glamorgan at Bristol. A. P. Freeman took 304 wickets in the season, the first-class record. W. R. Hammond caught 78, the record for a fielder. L. E. G. Ames became the first to do the wicket-keeper's double, making 1,919 runs and taking 121 wickets. He did it again the following year, this time taking 127 wickets (caught 79), the record for a wicket-keeper. J. H. Rogers, at Birkenhead School, became the first schoolboy cricketer in England to do the double: he did it again in 1929. The record number of first-class centuries in a season was scored – 414

1929–30 First Test matches by New Zealand against England (England captain, A. H. H. Gilligan). England won the series. England made the highest recorded first-class score in the West Indies, when they made 849 at Kingston in the fourth test. E. Hendren made the record number of runs for a West Indian season of 1,765

1929–30 8th MCC tour (captain, A. H. H. Gilligan) played no Tests. First match Tasmania *v.* Western Australia, at Hobart. D. G. Bradman scored 452* for New South Wales *v.* Queensland at Sydney, the then world first-class record. It remains the Australian first-class record, and the New South Wales record for any class of cricket. Bradman became the first batsman to make 3,000 runs in an Australian season in all matches (3,619, average 109·66). Miss F. Tamsett playing in a women's cricket competition in Goulburn, New South Wales, made 1,009 runs and took 159 wickets, the first woman in the world to do the double. It was twenty-five years before any other woman did this

1927–8 Fifth MCC tour to South Africa (captain, R. T. Stanyforth): South Africa won two, lost two and drew one Test. MCC made 592 for 7 wickets declared against Orange Free State at Bloemfontein, beating the 1926–7 first-class record

1928 Western Province Bantu Cricket Union established
1929 Seventh South Africans to England (captain, H. G. Deane): South Africa lost two and drew three Tests

1928 First official Test matches during fourth West Indian tour to England (captain, R. K. Nunes): all three won by England. L. N. Constantine became the first and so far only West Indian to do the double in England: 1,381 runs average 34·52 and 107 wickets average 22·95 and against Northamptonshire he made 107 in one innings and did the hat-trick in the same match, the only West Indian to perform that feat also

1929–30 Rhodesia decided to re-enter the Currie Cup: stayed in for this season and 1931–2. The season saw the first matches by Rhodesia v. Griqualand West, v. Orange Free State, v. Border and v. Eastern Province. In this extraordinary season, Western Province made the then record first-class score in South Africa (and still her own record) of 601 against Border. Within a fortnight Griqualand West made 602 against Rhodesia, and six weeks later topped this by making 603 (still her own record) against Western Province, both matches at Kimberley. S. S. L. Steyn (261*) and D. P. B. Morkel (114) for Western Province v. Border at Cape Town made the South African record eighth-wicket partnership of 222

1929 The Guyana v. Barbados match lasted seven days, without rain interrupting

1927–8 Eighth official visit by an Australian team (captain, V. Y. Richardson): won one and drew the other representative match. Wellington made their record score of 595 *v.* Auckland at Basin Reserve

1928–9 W. E. Merritt took 98 wickets in senior club cricket in Christchurch, the record for that centre. Including first-class and other matches for Canterbury he took 125 wickets. Otago made her record score of 602 for 8 wickets declared *v.* Canterbury at Carisbrook. Plunket Shield matches were limited from this season to four days of six hours playing-time each

1929–30 Third tour by MCC to New Zealand (captain, A. H. H. Gilligan): four official Tests played – New Zealand drew three and lost one. These were the first Tests to be played at Eden Park, Auckland; Lancaster Park, Christchurch; and Basin Reserve, Wellington. They and Carisbrook remain so far the only grounds on which official Tests have been played in New Zealand; other grounds have been used for unofficial representative matches. The record seventh-wicket partnership in New Zealand of 265 made by J. L. Powell (164) and N. Dorreen (105*) for Canterbury *v.* Otago at Lancaster Park

1928 The Cricket Association of Bengal and Assam formed: in 1939, the Assam C.A. was formed from it, but was disaffiliated from 1942 and reformed in 1947

1929 The first score of over 700 in India – 726 by the 4/7th Dragoon Guards. The Delhi and District Cricket Association formed

1927–8 The East African individual record of 252* made by M. Walter in a club match in Nairobi

1928 West Indies undertook an extensive tour in the eastern United States. Against a visiting Bermuda team, Philadelphia played for the last time – a draw

1928 In Germany, in a garrison game in the B.A.O.R., the 2nd Royal Fusiliers made 612 v. the 2nd Berkshires, the highest total in Europe

1928–9 T. A. Cairns achieved the remarkable personal feat of being not only the first to take over 100 wickets in the Kenya season (125) but also the first to make over a thousand runs (1,397)

1929 V. T. Logavatu took all 10 wickets in an innings for the first time in Fiji. The first of many visits to the U.K. by teams from East Africa, this time by the Kenya Kongonis, and followed by the Tanganyika Twigas and the Uganda Kobs. The record Ceylon partnership for the fourth wicket of 301 was established by D. Le Merrier (197) and J. F. Burrows (151)

1929–30 Third English tour to South America, Sir Julien Cahn's: won one and drew two representative matches v. Argentina

1930 Four-day Tests approved for England v. Australia matches in England. In the Lord's Test, a record match aggregate for four-day matches in England was set up of 1,601 runs for 29 wickets. D. G. Bradman scored six double centuries in the season, beating K. S. Ranjitsinhji's record of five in 1900. A German team (chosen from the four clubs of the Berlin League), toured England for the first time. Foundation of *Women's Cricket*: lasted until 1967. H. W. P. Middleton caught one and stumped eight in one innings in a Repton House match, the world record for the number of stumpings, and the English record for total victims

1931 First Test matches by New Zealand in England (captain, T. C. Lowry). England won the series. H. Sutcliffe in making 3,006 runs for the season averaged 96·96 runs, the record for an English batsman. L. E. G. Ames (137) and G. O. B. Allen (122) made 246 for the eighth wicket for England v. New Zealand at Lord's, the world record eighth-wicket Test partnership

1932 First Test match by an Indian team, captained for the tour by the Maharajah of Porbandar, but for the Test by C. K. Nayudu: England won. First tour by a combined South American team (captain, C. H. Gibson): some first-class matches played. L. E. G. Ames completed the wicket-keeper's double for the third time, making 2,482 runs and taking 100 wickets. P. Holmes (224*) and H. Sutcliffe (313) by making 555 for the first wicket for Yorkshire v. Essex established a new record for any class of cricket

1930 17th Australians (captain, W. M. Woodfull) won two, lost one and drew two Tests. D. G. Bradman scored 334 for Australia v. England at Leeds, the highest Test score by an Australian batsman: 309 of these were made in one day, a record for a Test match. He scored 974 runs in the five Tests, the world record aggregate for a series. By the end of the tour in England, Bradman had scored 6,829 runs in under twelve months for an average of 106·70, an extraordinary feat. In scoring 1,000 runs by the end of May, Bradman became the first Australian to do so and joined the small company of Australians who have reached 1,000 runs for the season in advance of any English batsman. J. E. C. Moore in a minor match at Griffith, New South Wales, hit the ball a measured 170 yds 1 ft 5 in., the longest hit in Australia and the second longest authenticated hit in the world

1930–1 First visit by West Indian team to Australia (captain, G. C. Grant): won one of five Tests. Matches played against all States except Western Australia. Sheffield Shield matches henceforth limited to four days of 5½ hours playing-time. Queensland made 687 v. New South Wales at Woolloongabba, Brisbane, the record by Queensland. Larger wicket adopted for use in Sheffield Shield matches. Formation of Australian Women's Cricket Council. Third Australian cricket magazine founded – the *Australian Cricketer*, which was issued monthly, and later weekly, until early July 1934

1931–2 Second tour by South Africa (captain, H. B. Cameron). First match between Western Australia and South Africans. D. G. Bradman scored 299* v. South Africa at Adelaide, the then highest Test score in Australia. South Africa lost all five Tests, the second time Australia has been completely successful in a five-match series. The Brisbane Test was played for the first time on the Woolloongabba ground. Australian-made cricket balls sanctioned for use in the Sheffield Shield. They were not, however, used in Test matches until 1946–7. In a minor match at Geraldton R. V. Sewell made 250, the record individual score in Western Australia

1932 A. A. Mailey took an unofficial team of first-class cricketers in the second extended tour of North America, playing fifty-two matches in all. D. G. Bradman scored 260* v. Western Ontario XVIII, and thus established the Canadian record individual score. In all matches on the tour he scored 3,782 runs, average 102·21, and in the twelve months including the previous Australian season, at least 5,970 runs, for an average of 106·60

1930 First official Tests in West Indies during fourth MCC tour (captain, Hon. F. S. G. Calthorpe): West Indies won one, lost one and drew two. These were the first Tests to be played on the Kensington Oval, Bridgetown, the Bourda ground at Georgetown, Sabina Park in Kingston, and Queen's Park (St Clair) Oval in Port-of-Spain and they remain so far the only grounds used in the West Indies for Tests. England scored 849 in the Fourth Test – the highest total in the West Indies and the highest by an English team overseas. In the match, 1,815 runs were scored for 34 wickets, the record first-class match aggregate in the West Indies. E. Hendren (1,765) runs and A. Sandham (1,281 runs) became the first players to make over 1,000 runs in first-class cricket in a West Indian season. E. Hendren scored 886 runs in February, perhaps the largest number of runs scored in a calendar month overseas outside Australia. O. A. Viveiros caught six and stumped two in one innings in a club match in Guyana

1930–1 Sixth MCC tour to South Africa (captain, A. P. F. Chapman): South Africa won one and drew four Tests. The Tests at Durban and Cape Town were played on turf for the first time. On this tour MCC played the first international match in what is now Zambia: Northern Rhodesia *v.* MCC at Livingstone (not first-class). P. Hugo for Smithfield *v.* Aliwal North took 9 wickets in nine balls, the world record, since equalled in New Zealand

1930–1 First West Indies tour to Australia (captain, G. C. Grant): Australia won four Tests and lost one. G. A. Headley scored 1,066 runs in the season, the first West Indian to score 1,000 runs in a first-class season outside U.K.

1931–2 Second South African tour to Australia and first to New Zealand (q.v. both countries). E. P. Nupen, for Transvaal *v.* Griqualand West equalled Vogler's record of 1906–7, by taking 16 wickets for 136 runs

1932 South African Bantu Cricket Board formed

1932 G. A. Headley (344*) and C. C. Passailaigue (261*) scored 487* for Jamaica *v.* Hon. L. H. Tennyson's XI, the world record first-class sixth-wicket partnership, the first partnership over 400 in the West Indies, and the first over 300 by West Indians in first-class cricket. Jamaica made 702 for 5 wickets declared, the highest by Jamaica. G. A. Headley in making 344* made the highest score for Jamaica. (Passailaigue's name is sometimes spelt other ways but this is how he spells it.)

1930 New Zealand Cricket Annual for 1930–1 produced: one issue only

1930–1 First visit by West Indies to New Zealand (captain, G. C. Grant) *en route* to Australia: one match played, not first-class, *v.* Wellington was set down for two days but rain curtailed it to one

1931 Second tour by New Zealand to England (captain, T. C. Lowry): drew two Tests but lost the third

1931–2 First treble century in first-class cricket in New Zealand, 338* by R. C. Blunt for Otago *v.* Canterbury at Lancaster Park. Of these he made 315* in one day, the record by a New Zealander or in New Zealand first-class cricket. He and W. Hawkesworth (21) made 184 for the last wicket, the New Zealand first-class record for that wicket. First visit by South Africa to New Zealand (captain, H. B. Cameron): New Zealand lost both Tests

1930 The Bombay Cricket Association formed. In 1934 the Gujarat Cricket Association was formed, taking in part of the Bombay area: in the same year the Maharashtra C.A. was also formed out of the Bombay area. The Madras Cricket Association was formed, and re-formed in 1935: in 1953 the Andhra C.A. was formed out of its area. Playing in England for the Indian Gymkhana, S. Nazir Ali scored 3,900 runs and took 210 wickets in the season, a feat only short of that of Alan Marshal, the Australian, in 1906

1930–1 The Moin-ud-Dowlah Gold Cup Tournament instituted: first-class at the start, it came to be held irregularly and later deteriorated in status. It was successfully revived in 1962. A tour by the MCC was postponed for a year, for political reasons, and then cancelled

1931 First issue in April of the *Illustrated Cricket and Sporting News*: the first cricket magazine in India. The name was changed in 1932 to *Indian Cricketer* but the magazine did not survive 1933. The Rajputana C.A. was formed: it changed its name to Rajasthan C.A. in 1957

1932 The second All India tour to England (captain, the Maharajah of Porbander, but C. K. Nayudu captained in the only Test, which was lost). The Western India States Cricket Association formed; it became the Kathiawar C.A. from 1946. The Nawanagar C.A. was formed out of W.I.S.C.A. in 1936. Both Nawanagar and Kathiawar were merged in the Saurashtra C.A. from 1950

1930 A further West Indian tour in the eastern United States, and a tour by a Jamaican team

1930 The highest total in South America – 612 for 6 wickets declared by Argentina *v.* Chile. H. van Manen became the first Dutch cricketer to make 1,000 runs in the season. The first (monthly) issue of the Danish magazine *Kricket* (from 1935 called *Cricket*) appeared: has run regularly since then including during the German occupation

1931 Ridley College became the first Canadian school to tour outside North America when they visited Bermuda. *Songs of the Cricket Field* by F. C. Benson, a book of poems, issued privately in Philadelphia

1931 H. M. Martineau's XI made 531 *v.* All Egypt, the Egyptian record total. The first (weekly) issue of the Dutch magazine *Cricket* appeared: has run regularly since then, including during the German occupation but had to be suspended at the time of the Liberation owing to paper shortage. The first inter-University match in Holland, between Leiden University and Utrecht University

1932 A. A. Mailey's Australian team conducted an extensive tour of the U.S.A. and Canada, but did *not* visit Philadelphia. They beat Canada in the only eleven-a-side match. D. G. Bradman established the Canadian record of 260 runs *v.* Western Ontario XVIII.

1932 Combined South American team (captain, C. H. Gibson) made a tour, recognized as first-class, to the U.K. The first match by a representative Danish XI, *v.* Sir Julien Cahn's XI. Formation of the Nigerian Cricket Association (Europeans only) followed in 1933 by the formation of a body with the same name for Africans only: the two merged in 1956

1932–3 The 'bodyline' controversy during the MCC tour of Australia. W. R. Hammond made 336* *v.* New Zealand at Eden Park, Auckland, the highest first-class score by an Englishman outside England.

1933 (autumn) First tour by an English team to include Bermuda – Sir Julien Cahn's
1934 The record second-wicket first-class partnership in England of 451 by W. H. Ponsford (266) and D. G. Bradman (244) for Australia *v.* England at the Oval. Kent made their record score of 803 for 4 wickets declared *v.* Essex at Brentwood. The MCC condemned 'bodyline' and issued instructions to umpires against its future practice

1934–5 First English women's tour abroad, to Australia and New Zealand

1935 L. W. Newman scored 4,138 runs in club cricket, the world record for this class of cricket. Playing for Somerset Stragglers against United Services at Devonport, H. N. E. Alston (128 and 101*) and H. G. M. Rem (105 and 102*) opening the innings in each case each made two centuries in the match, a unique record and the first opening pair to put on over 200 in each innings (223 and 209)
1936–7 First tour by an English team to Malaya – Sir Julien Cahn's

1932–3 9th MCC tour (captain D. R. Jardine): the 'body-line' controversy. England won four Tests and lost one. H. Sutcliffe became the only non-Australian to make 1,000 runs by end of December. T. W. Wall (South Australia) took all 10 wickets in the first innings of New South Wales at Sydney – the first time this had been done in the Sheffield Shield. The first tie in Australian first-class cricket: MCC, 321 and 183 for 9 wickets declared *v.* Victoria, 327 and 177 for 3 wickets. C. L. Badcock, then aged just under nineteen, made the record aggregate for a season in Tasmanian cricket of 1,566 runs. In the following season he exceeded this aggregate by making 1,970 runs, and also made 274 for Tasmania *v.* Victoria, the highest individual score for Tasmania
1933–4 D. G. Bradman completed 1,000 runs in a first-class season for the sixth successive year, a feat unapproached by any other batsman. I. S. Lee (258) and S. O. Quin (210) made 424 for the fourth wicket for Victoria *v.* Tasmania, the Australian first-class record
1934 18th Australians (captain, W. M. Woodfull) won two, lost one and drew two Tests. W. H. Ponsford (266) and D. G. Bradman (244) made 451 for the second wicket for Australia *v.* England at the Oval, the record Australian Test partnership for any wicket
1934–5 First visit by English women to Australia: Australia drew one and lost two Tests. In a minor match in New South Wales, C. Forbes made 46 runs in an eight-ball over, the then world record, beaten in 1952–3. C. W. Andrews (253) and E. C. Bensted (155) made 335 for the seventh wicket for Queensland *v.* New South Wales – the Australian first-class record
1935–6 First (unofficial) visit by an Australian team to India (q.v.). The first visit by a schools team from overseas (Royal College, Colombo). Fourth tour to South Africa (q.v.). Highest score ever made in South Africa: 369 by D. G. Bradman for South Australia *v.* Tasmania at Adelaide. Bradman surpassed Ponsford's first-class career record of scoring over 300 on four separate occasions. 10th MCC tour (captain, E. R. T. Holmes) played no Tests
1936–7 11th MCC tour (captain, G. O. B. Allen), lost the series after winning first two Tests. D. G. Bradman made 270 *v.* England at Melbourne, the highest score then by an Australian or an Australian captain in a Test match against England in Australia. With J. H.

1933 First Bantu inter-provincial tournament
1933–4 R. J. Crisp took 4 wickets in four balls (in the match Western Province v. Natal at Kingsmead) for the second time in his career. No other bowler has performed this feat twice in first-class cricket
1934–5 Transvaal made 609 v. Orange Free State at the Wanderers, the record Transvaal total. H. B. Cameron (182) and A. W. Briscoe (191) made 327 for the fifth wicket for Transvaal v. Griqualand West at Johannesburg, the South African record for that wicket
1935 Eighth South Africans to England (captain, H. F. Wade): South Africa won one and drew four Tests: the tour thus included the first South African Test victory in England
1935–6 Fourth tour by Australians to South Africa (captain, V. Y. Richardson): South Africa lost four Tests and drew one – all were played on turf. In this tour, the Australians first met Eastern Province, Border, Griqualand West, Rhodesia and Orange Free State on level terms. A. D. Nourse (sen.) played in his last first-class season at the age of fifty-eight. No other South African cricketer has played first-class cricket after reaching the age of fifty
1936–7 Eight-ball overs were first tried in first-class cricket in South Africa (they had been used at least fourteen years earlier in Transvaal club cricket); they were adopted for all first-class cricket the following season and were used until the 1959–60 season. M. I. Yusuf made the highest individual score in Southern Africa (412*) for Schools Cricket Club v. Star Cricket Club at Bulawayo. Natal made 664 for 6 wickets declared v. Western Province at Durban, the record South African first-class score in South Africa

1933 E. L. G. Hoad (149*) and H. C. Griffith (84) made 138 v. Sussex at Hove, for the 5th West Indian touring team (captain, G. C. Grant) – the record by West Indians for the last wicket. G. A. Headley (2,320 runs) became the first of only two West Indian tourists to make 2,000 runs in the season. West Indies lost two Tests and drew one. Formation of Barbados Cricket Association, the governing body of cricket in that island

1935 West Indies won a Test rubber for first time against England, winning two, losing one and drawing the fourth match against the fifth MCC touring team (captain, R. E. S. Wyatt). The first Test was remarkable – on a rain-wrecked wicket at Kensington, each team batted twice, only one innings was completed, and England won by 4 wickets, in a match aggregate of 309 runs for 29 wickets: West Indies, 102 and 51 for 6 wickets declared v. England, 81 for seven wickets declared and 75 for 6 wickets (after being 48 for 6)
1936 Yorkshire became the second County to tour overseas, in visiting Jamaica. They won one and drew two matches against the island. Two matches were five-day fixtures – possibly the only matches of this length played by a county in modern times. E. A. V. Williams (131*) and E. A. Martindale (134) made 255 for the eighth wicket for Barbados v. Trinidad at Kensington, the West Indian record for that wicket

1932–3 Fourth tour by MCC to New Zealand (captain, D. R. Jardine): both Tests drawn. The match against Wellington, though only two days, was ruled first-class

1934 Formation of New Zealand Women's Cricket Council
1934–5 First tour of New Zealand by English women's team. England won the only Test
1935–6 Fifth tour by MCC to New Zealand (captain, E. R. T. Holmes): four unofficial Tests drawn. C. K. Jackman stumped seven in the match and four in one innings for Canterbury *v.* Wellington, the New Zealand record
1936–7 Sixth MCC tour to New Zealand (captain, G. O. B. Allen): one unofficial Test drawn. A projected tour by an Indian team led by the Jamsaheb of Nawanager was abandoned at the last moment. The world record first-class partnership for the third wicket of 445 was made by P. E. Whitelaw (195) and W. N. Carson (290) for Auckland *v.* Otago at Carisbrook

1932–3 The first tour by All Ceylon to India (captain, C. H. Gunasekara): both unofficial Tests were drawn. Y. S. Ramaswami took all 20 wickets for 21, in an inter-schools match, the only time this has been done in India: his feat included the hat-trick
1933 The Mysore Cricket Association formed. The Central India C.A. also formed: it closed down in 1940 and was succeeded by the Holkar C.A. (also occasionally called Indore) from 1941. Holkar in turn became Madhya Bharat (which is Hindi for Central India) in 1955. But when Madhya Pradesh C.A. became Vidharba C.A. in 1957, Madhya Bharat, confusingly adopted the name of Madhya Pradesh C.A. (these changes were consequent upon political changes, and were not avoidable by the cricket authorities). (*See* Central Provinces under 1934.)
1933–4 D. R. Havewalla scored 515, including 55 fours and 32 sixes (equalling the then world record), the record for all grades of Indian cricket. He was playing for the Bombay Baroda and Central India Railway Sports Club against Xavier College. His team made 721 (the then highest by an Indian team) after facing a total of 446, and won by an innings. The second MCC tour (captain, D. R. Jardine) won two Tests and drew the other. The first Tests played at Bombay, on the Gymkhana ground, Eden Gardens in Calcutta, and the Chepauk ground in Madras. The Cricket Club of India founded in New Delhi, and later moved to Bombay
1934 The Baroda Cricket Association formed, under the original title of 'Central Board of Cricket, Baroda', The Central Provinces and Berar C.A. formed: from 1948 the name was changed to the Hindi equivalent, Madhya Pradesh, and to Vidharba C.A. from 1957. The Hyderabad C.A. formed about this time (this was Hyderabad in the Deccan, not in Sind). First issue of another cricket magazine, *Indian Cricket*, a monthly of high quality which lasted until January 1940
1934–5 The Ranji Trophy instituted. Hours of play could vary from 5 to 6 hours per day until 1942, but from then to 1948 from 5 to 5½ hours per day: from 1948 they were standardized at 5½ hours per day. The number of days' play varies according to the stage in the competition, preliminary matches being three days, quarter and semi-finals four days, and finals five days. The first winners were Bombay who have won twenty-one times in all: Baroda and Holkar being next with four each. Southern

1932–3 E. H. Crickmay became the first to take all ten wickets in an innings in Kenya, 10 for 20 at Mombasa

1933 The twenty-first and twenty-second English tours: Cambridge University Vandals (captain, P. M. Heywood), and Sir Julien Cahn's – the latter became the first English team to visit Bermuda. A Nova Scotia Cricket Association formed: did not last long, and the present body dates from 1967

1934 Another Canadian cricket magazine started, *Cricket*: had only a few monthly issues

1935 The first of many tours by teams from Canadian schools, and also of Canadian Colts, to the U.K.

1936 The fourth Canadian tour to the U.K. (captain R. C. Matthews). The Lord Atholstan Trophy inaugurated for competition between Ontario and Quebec

1934 The record Dutch third-wicket partnership of 191 made by Jhr. W.v.d. Bosch (119) and Dr M. Jansen (93). Dutch Women's Cricket Association formed. H. A. G. Nielsen became the first to take all 10 wickets in an innings in Denmark, 10 for 11. The record Danish sixth-wicket partnership of 240 made by H. Andreasen and M. Worm. The record ninth-wicket partnership in Ceylon of 219 made by F. Pereira (114*) and D. Arndt (110)

1935 The South Africans who toured England that season became the first overseas touring team to England also to visit Holland: a further visit was paid in 1951 by the South Africans. J. Offerman made 240*, for Hermes-D.V.S., the Dutch record. H. W. Glerum made 1,270 runs in the season, the Dutch record. An Egyptian cricket club for Egyptians only formed, and played H. M. Martineau's XI. The record sixth-wicket partnership in Ceylon of 299 made by D. W. L. Lieversz (211*) and J. Murray (163)

1935–6 First three-day match between Australians and Ceylon – Australia won

1936 Hjørring made 562, *v.* Viborg, the Danish record. The *Malacca Sports Annual* issued, with a large section on cricket: no other issue known

1937 First Australian women's tour to England

1938 First Television of a Test, England v. Australia at Lord's. At the Oval, England made 903 runs for 7 wickets declared, the record Test score and the record first-class score by an English team. In this innings, L. Hutton made 364, then the world record for a Test. D. G. Bradman averaged 115·66 for the season, easily the record. First tour outside Europe by an English school – Taunton School, to Jamaica. A. E. Fagg performed the unique feat in first-class cricket of scoring a double century in each innings – 244 and 202* for Kent v. Essex at Colchester

1939 The West Indian tour cut short before its end owing to the imminence of hostilities. H. M. Martineau's team to Egypt became the first touring team to travel by air. Though first-class cricket in England was suspended during the Second World War, much other good class cricket continued to be played. Eight-ball overs used in England up to and including 1945 (though not in the 'Victory' Tests)

1945 Australian Services XI toured England: played five 'Victory' Tests, among the first first-class matches since 1939. Formation of the Society of Cricket Statisticians now known as the Cricket Society, the oldest surviving organization of cricket enthusiasts

1946 The tenth-wicket record in England of 249 made by C. T. Sarwate and S. N. Bannerjee (q.v. under India). County club formed in Merioneth

Fingleton (136) he helped to compile the record Test sixth-wicket partnership of 346

1937 First visit by an Australian women's cricket team to England, won one, lost one, and drew one Test

1938 19th Australians (captain, D. G. Bradman) won one, lost one and drew two Tests. The Manchester Test was abandoned without a ball being bowled. D. G. Bradman became the only *batsman* to average over one hundred in an English season (minimum twelve innings) – 2,429 runs, average 115·66. (In 1953 W. A. Johnston, not out sixteen times out of seventeen innings, averaged 102·09.) By completing 1,000 runs on May 27, Bradman did so at the earliest date on record in an English season: he also made his 1,000 runs before the end of May for the second time.

1938–9 D. Tallon, playing for Queensland v. New South Wales, took 12 wickets in the match (caught 9, stumped 3) thus equalling the world record established in 1868. D. G. Bradman made six centuries in consecutive innings, equal to the world first-class record

1939–40 South Australia made 821 for 7 wickets v. Queensland at Adelaide, the record total in or by South Australia

1940–1 A. R. Morris became the first batsman in the world to make a century in each innings of a first-class match on debut: 148 and 111 for New South Wales v. Queensland at Sydney

1941–2 L. Fallowfield scored five consecutive centuries in Sydney first-grade cricket but failed by 4 runs to beat V. T. Trumper's record when in his sixth innings he made 96*

1945–6 First (and so far only) official Test between Australia and New Zealand: Australia won

 Continued on page 354   *Continued on page 354*

1937–8 North-East Transvaal Cricket Union formed and entered Currie Cup: first matches accordingly by this team against Western Province. Transvaal, Orange Free State and Griqualand West

1938–9 Seventh MCC tour to South Africa (captain, W. R. Hammond). All matches except one in Rhodesia played on turf. South Africa lost one and drew four Tests. The fifth Test went to the record length of ten days, due chiefly to loss of time through rain. 1,981 runs were scored in it, for 35 wickets, the record Test and South African match aggregate. England made 654 for 5 wickets (set 696 to win), the world record fourth innings total. MCC made 676 against Griqualand West at Kimberley, the record first-class score in South Africa. In this match, four players each made centuries for MCC, the first such occurrence in South African first-class cricket. First eleven-a-side match MCC v. North-East Transvaal. Turf wickets were brought into use during the season in Rhodesia

1939–40 E. A. B. Rowan made the record first-class South African score of 306* for Transvaal v. Natal. Inauguration of 'Nuffield' tournament – inter-provincial matches between representative teams of schoolboys. D. Hope in a club match in Durban made 253* which included 36 sixes – the world record

1940 South African Indian Cricket Union formed

1942 F. Roro made 304 for Crown Mines v. Main Reef at Johannesburg, the highest score by a Bantu cricketer. He was the first South African known to have made over 100 centuries in his career

1942–3 A. D. Nourse (jun.) for a South African XI v. Military Police in Cairo hit nine successive sixes (equal to the world record), six in one over, and eleven sixes in twelve balls (the world record)

1946 Last matches played on old 'Wanderers' ground, Johannesburg: Ellis Park used for Test and first-class matches from 1946–7 to 1955–6

1938 K. H. Weekes (Lucas C.C.) made 1,018 runs in the Jamaican season, average 169·66. Eight-ball overs adopted for West Indies first-class, and probably other cricket, and used until the autumn of 1946

1939 The first matches between Trinidad and Jamaica in Trinidad (they were trials for the team to England whose tour was cut short by the outbreak of war). 6th West Indians (captain, R. S. Grant): lost one and drew two Tests

1942 Trinidad made 16 v. Barbados at Kensington, the lowest total in West Indian first-class cricket. No total less than 40 has been made since, and indeed not otherwise since 1902. In a match between Georgetown and Guyana at Bourda 1,668 runs were scored for 35 wickets (the Guyana record)

1943 Formation of Guyana Cricket Board of Control which took over control of cricket from the Georgetown Cricket Club

1944 F. M. M. Worrell (308*) and J. D. C. Goddard (218*), in scoring 502* for the fourth wicket for Barbados v. Trinidad, made the first partnership of over 500 in the West Indies

1946 C. L. Walcott (314*) and F. M. M. Worrell (255*) made 574* for the fourth wicket for Barbados v. Trinidad – the record partnership in West Indian cricket for this or any other wicket. C. L. Walcott's 314* is the highest ever for Barbados. A. M. Taylor (110*) and E. A. V. Williams (58) made 125 for the ninth wicket for Barbados v. Guyana at Bourda – the record for that wicket by West Indians in the West Indies.

Continued on page 355   *Continued on page 355*

Punjab made 22 *v.* Northern India at Amritsar, the lowest score in the Ranji Trophy. Baqa Jilani took the hat-trick for the first time in the Ranji Trophy and only the fifth time in Indian first-class cricket

1935–6 The Maharajah of Patiala sponsored the first (unofficial) tour by Australians to India (captain, J. S. Ryder): they won two and lost two of the unofficial Tests. S. M. Kadri made a century in each innings (105 and 114) for Bombay *v* W.I.S.C.A. at Poona, the first time the feat had been performed in Indian first-class cricket. The Rohinton Baria Trophy for Inter-University competition first competed for. Bombay University has won twenty-two times, Punjab University four times and Mysore and Delhi Universities each three times

1936 The Bihar Cricket Association formed. The third tour by All India to England (captain, the Maharaj-kumar of Vizianagram): two Tests were lost and the other drawn. V. M. Merchant performed the feat of carrying his bat (135* and 77*) in each innings *v.* Lancashire at Aigburth (Liverpool), the first Indian ever to carry his bat in first-class cricket

1937 Third tour by New Zealand to England (captain, M. L. Page): New Zealand drew two and lost one of the Tests. In making 546 *v.* Sussex at Hove, New Zealand made their highest score so far in England

1937–8 In Auckland's innings of 590 *v.* Canterbury at Eden Park, four centuries were made, equalling the New Zealand record. First visit by a New Zealand women's team to Australia

1937–8 The Bombay Tournament became Pentangular, with the admission of 'The Rest'. The tournament lasted until 1945–6 in communal form, and for two more seasons after, in non-communal form. Proposals for tours by South Africa, and by the West Indies, successively fell through, and a sixth tour by an English team took place, Lord Tennyson's, which won three and lost two of the unofficial Tests. The Brabourne Stadium was opened in Bombay

1938–9 Twelfth visit by an English team – Sir Julien Cahn's: one representative match drawn

1939 D. D. Beard made 107* and took 10 for 39 in one innings in a minor match at Palmerston North, the first time this feat had been performed in New Zealand

1939–40 Auckland made 693 for 9 wickets declared against Canterbury, the present record first-class score by a New Zealand team. The Centennial Cup instituted for competition between Auckland and Wellington. The first match, to decide ownership, was between Veterans of the two provinces and was a tie: of the thirty-one subsequent matches Auckland have won eighteen, Wellington seven: of the six drawn matches, Wellington led in the first innings on five occasions. Auckland won the Plunket Shield for the fourth successive time, the longest run by any New Zealand province

1938 The Rajputana C.C. (not connected with the Rajputana C.A. in any way) undertook an unofficial tour to the U.K.: badly planned, the tour was abandoned half-way through

1939 *Crickinia* – Indian Cricketer's Annual – made its debut, lasting six issues, until 1944–5. A tour by the MCC planned for 1939–40 was cancelled on the outbreak of war

1939–40 Maharashtra made 798 *v.* Northern India at Poona, a fresh Indian record. V. S. Hazare (316*) and N. D. Nagarwalla (98) established the record Indian ninth-wicket partnership of 245, for Maharashtra *v.* Baroda at Poona

1940–1 The second tour by All Ceylon (captain, S. S. Jayawickreme): lost one and drew the other unofficial Test. W.I.S.C.A. made their record score of 459 *v.* Maharashtra at Rajkot

Continued on next opening

1937 The third MCC tour to Canada (captain, G. C. Newman)

1937–8 Fourth English tour to South America, Sir Theodore Brinckman's team: won one, lost one and drew one *v.* Argentina: the team also visited Uruguay

1938 L. Bronee took 110 wickets in the Danish season, the first time one hundred had been exceeded

1939 The first U.K. schools tour to Canada, and also the first representative schools side to go overseas from the U.K. A girls' schools team also visited Canada

1939 D. Ayling made 256* for North *v.* South in Argentina, the highest score in that country. The Egyptian record match aggregate of 1,279 runs for 23 wickets made in the match between H. M. Martineau's XI and Gezira Sporting Club

1939–40 Cecil Ayling (226*) and Cyril Ayling (136) established the Argentine first-wicket record of 292. In the same season R. G. Henderson (77) and C. S. Campbell (144) established the Argentine fourth wicket record of 210

1940 In Fiji, Saisasi Vunisakiki took 8 wickets in an eight-ball over, the first time this had been done anywhere

1940–1 S. K. Coen, the South African cricketer, made what is believed to be the record seasonal aggregate of 1,651 runs in Kenya

Continued on next opening

1941 The first partnership in India of over 400: 479* for the fourth wicket by R. S. Modi (253*) and R. S. Cooper (255*) for Bombay University v. Osmania University – both batsmen retired

1941–2 Northern India made their record score of 613 for seven wickets declared v. N.W.F.P. at Lahore

1942 In April Indian-made cricket balls were sanctioned for use in the Ranji Trophy and in other first-class matches

1942–3 K. C. Ibrahim (250) and C. M. Rangnekar (138) established the Indian record seventh-wicket partnership of 274 for the Bijapur XI v. Bengal XI at Bombay

1943–4 V. M. Merchant (359*) and R. S. Modi (168) established the Indian record sixth-wicket partnership of 371 for Bombay v. Maharashtra at Bombay. In this season, V. S. Hazara became the first Indian known to have scored over 1,000 runs in an Indian first-class season

1944–5 The first tour by All India to Ceylon (captain, V. M. Merchant): drew the one unofficial Test. In the match between Bombay and Holkar 2,078 runs were made for 40 wickets, the first time in the world a match aggregate had exceeded 2,000 runs. In this match, Bombay's 764 was the Bombay record. C. S. Nayudu bowled 917 balls in the match, the world's record

1945–6 Ninth official tour by Australians to New Zealand (captain, W. A. Brown): the only official Test played between the two countries lost by New Zealand

1945–6 The Australian Services team toured India (second and again unofficial Australian tour (captain, A. L. Hassett): lost one and drew two unofficial Tests. Holkar, at Indore, made 912 for 8 wickets declared v. Mysore, the record innings total for any grade of cricket in India. It included six centuries, the world record, and also seven century-partnerships, again the world record. Mysore in the same match made her record score of 509 for 6 wickets declared. The match between Southern Punjab and Baroda ended in a tie, the only Indian first-class match to have done so. Southern Punjab made her record score of 658 for 8 wickets declared against Northern India at Patiala

1946 The fourth All India tour to England (captain, Nawab of Pataudi, sen.): lost one and drew two Tests. C. T. Sarwate (124*) and S. N. Bannerjee (121) batting at numbers ten and eleven each made centuries – a unique feat – and added 249 for the last wicket v. Surrey at the Oval, a record for that wicket in England as well as the Indian record. V. M. Merchant made 2,385 runs in first-class matches during

1941. Fiji Cricket Association formed. Cricket balls made in Holland for the first time.

1942–3 In a Services match in Egypt, A. D. Nourse, jun. hit nine sixes off successive balls, six in one over

'1941. Cricket balls made in Holland for the first time'

1944 H. Hansen took 18 wickets in a match for 102 runs, the Danish record, of which ten were for 40 runs in one innings (the first). Cricket bats first made in Denmark

1945 W. Hendy took 10 wickets for 12 runs and made 125* for Rowing Club *v.* Vancouver, the first time this feat had been performed in North America

1945–6 Second three-day match between Australians and Ceylon: Australian Services won

1946 G. Headley captained a Jamaican team to the U.S.A. and repeated the trip the following year

1946 A United Services team from Cairo became the first to tour East Africa. Stonyhurst became the first of many schools to tour Holland. B. Pockendahl made 996 runs in the Danish season, the record

For 1947 onwards, see under Other Countries, Column 8, page 357

M

1946–7 12th MCC tour (captain, W. R. Hammond), lost three and drew two Tests. The first known six-day fixtures. D. C. S. Compton and A. R. Morris each made a century in each innings for their respective countries in the Adelaide Test. The world record fifth-wicket first-class partnership of 405 made by S. G. Barnes (234) and D. G. Bradman (234) for Australia v. England at Sydney

1947 A major revision of the Laws of Cricket was approved. D. C. S. Compton set up a new record seasonal total of 3,816 runs, average 90·85, and a new seasonal record of centuries of eighteen. He scored 1,000 runs (1,187 in all) against the South Africans, the only occasion this feat has been performed against tourists in England. W. J. Edrich (189) and D. C. S. Compton (208) made 370 for the third wicket for England v. South Africa at Lord's, the world record Test third-wicket partnership

1947–8 First visit by an Indian team to Australia (captain, L. Amarnath): lost four Tests and drew the other. Matches played against all States. E. R. H. Toshack took 5 wickets for 2 runs in the Brisbane Test. First match between Queensland and Western Australia, at Brisbane. Western Australia won the Sheffield Shield in their first season competing for it. D. G. Bradman, in completing 1,000 runs in his last full first-class season in Australia, did it for the twelfth time and far outstripped any rival in such an accomplishment. He scored eight centuries in the season, the record for first-class cricket in Australia. For an Australian XI v. Indians at Sydney, he hit his hundredth century (172) in first-class cricket, the only Australian ever to do so. His final tally was 117 centuries, fifty ahead of his nearest Australian rival; in all cricket he made 211 centuries, the only Australian to top 200. M. Peryman took 7 wickets in seven balls in a minor match in Sydney, equalling the Australian record. The fourth Australian cricket magazine issued, the *Australian Cricketer*, lasted for six weekly issues only

1948 Five-day Tests first played in England. The Australians made 721 in a day against Essex at Southend, the world record for first-class cricket. The record match aggregate for a five-day match in England was established during the Headingley Test, of 1,723 runs for 31 wickets. *Playfair Cricket Annual* first published. English Schools Cricket Association formed, largely but not exclusively representative of secondary schools. The English first-class record third-wicket partnership of 424* made by W. J. Edrich (168*) and D. C. S. Compton (252*) for Middlesex v. Somerset

1948 D. G. Bradman, on his last tour to England, captaining the 20th Australians, completed 1,000 runs ahead of any Englishman for the third time. Australia won four Tests and drew one, the best performance in England by any Australian team

1948–9 The first tie in Australian domestic first-class cricket: A. L. Hassett's XI, 406 and 430, v. D. G. Bradman's XI, 434 and 402–9. Second tour by English women: lost one and drew two Tests

1949 The English record first-class second-wicket partnership of 429* made by J. G. Dewes (204*) and G. H. G. Doggart (219*) for Cambridge University v. Essex

1949 D. G. Bradman knighted – the first Australian cricketer so honoured

1946–7 B. Mitchell (159) and A. Melville (153) for Transvaal v. Griqualand West at Kimberley, made the South African seventh-wicket record of 299. Rhodesia took part in the Currie Cup permanently from now on. First matches by Rhodesia against North-East Transvaal, Western Province, and Natal, and also first match Border v. North-East Transvaal

1947 Ninth tour by South Africans to England (captain, A. Melville): South Africa lost three and drew two Tests. B. Mitchell made 2,014 runs in the season, the only South African to exceed 2,000 runs on a tour to England. First score of over 400 by a non-white team in South Africa, 415 by Transvaal Indians v. Natal Indians at Johannesburg (a higher score had been made in multi-racial cricket in S. Rhodesia)

1947–8 First match Natal v. North-East Transvaal

1947 J. B. Stollmeyer (324) and G. E. Gomez (190) made 434 for Trinidad v. Guyana, the record third-wicket partnership in the West Indies. Trinidad made their highest score in this match, 750 for 8 wickets declared, and J. B. Stollmeyer made 324, the highest for Trinidad. A turf wicket established at Guaracara Park, Pointe-à-Pierre: in 1960 Trinidad played MCC here, the first colony game played outside Queen's Park. First match Jamaica v. Barbados, in Jamaica

1948 The MCC in their sixth tour to the West Indies (captain, G. O. B. Allen) set up the unique record of winning none of their matches – they lost two and drew two Tests. A. G. Ganteaume made a century in his first Test for West Indies and was never again chosen

1948–9 Eighth tour by MCC to South Africa (captain, F. G. Mann): South Africa lost two and drew three Tests. The record third-wicket partnership in South Africa of 399 made by R. T. Simpson (130*) and D. C. S. Compton (300) for MCC v. North-East Transvaal at Benoni

1948–9 The first tour by West Indies to India and Pakistan. (q.v. those countries). E. D. Weekes completed his fifth Test century in successive innings at Eden Gardens, Calcutta, being run out in his next Test innings for 90

the tour, the only Indian tourist to have exceeded 2,000. V. Mankad (1,120 runs and 129 wickets) did the double, the only tourist to have done so since 1928. In making 533 for 3 wickets declared against Sussex at Hove, India made the highest score by any Indian touring team in any class of cricket. A team from the Indian Military Academy toured England

1946–7 Seventh tour by MCC to New Zealand (captain, W. R. Hammond): New Zealand drew one Test. In a minor match, B. Neale took all 10 wickets, the wicket-keeper M. Wigmore assisting in 7 of them, stumping 6 and catching 1. The record New Zealand fourth-wicket partnership of 391 made by T. P. Reaney (299) and H. Hawthorne (162) for Hawke's Bay v. Wairarapa at Nelson Park, Napier

1946–7 The world record fourth-wicket partnership of 577 (unbroken) was made by V. S. Hazare (288*) and Gul Mohammed (319*) for Baroda v. Holkar at Baroda – the first partnership in India of over 500 and the Indian record for any wicket. In this match Baroda established her record score of 784. The annual *Indian Cricket* instituted, now the second oldest commercially produced cricket annual in the world. The record Indian third-wicket partnership of 410 was set up by L. Amarnath (262) and R. S. Modi (156*) for the Indian 1946 Touring team v. the Rest at Eden Gardens, Calcutta beating the 1898 record

1947–8 Second tour by a Fiji team to New Zealand (captain, P. A. Snow) (not first-class). First visit by Australian women to New Zealand: Australia won the only Test
1948 Establishment by A. H. Carman of the *Cricket Almanack of New Zealand*, annually since then

1947–8 First tour to Australia by India. Despite partition, the team represented undivided India (q.v. also Australia). V. S. Hazare made a century in each innings of the Adelaide Test (116 and 145), the only Indian batsman ever to have done so in Test cricket. V. S. Hazare (1,056) runs and L. Amarnath (1,162 runs) each made over 1,000 runs in the Australian season, following K. S. Ranjitsinhji's example of 1897–8. U. M. Merchant (217) and M. N. Raiji (170) established the record Indian fifth-wicket partnership of 360 for Bombay v. Hyderabad at Bombay

1948–9 B. Sutcliffe (141 and 135) and D. D. Taylor (99 and 143) in together making 220 and 286 for the first wicket in each innings of the match for Auckland v. Canterbury established a world first-class record. Second tour by English women to New Zealand: England won the only Test

1948–9 First tour by West Indies to India (captain, J. D. C. Goddard): won one and drew four Tests. First Tests played on the Brabourne Stadium in Bombay and on the Feroz Shah Kotla ground (formerly the Willingdon ground) in New Delhi. B. B. Nimbalkar in making the record Indian first-class score of 443* for Maharashtra v. Kathiawar at Poona was assisted by K. V. Bhandarkar (205) in establishing the world record partnership in first-class cricket for the second wicket of 455. In this match Maharashtra made their record score of 826 for 4 wickets. Bombay scored 1,365 runs for 18 wickets v. Maharashtra at Poona, the world record aggregate for a team in one match, and the match itself produced the world record aggregate of 2,376 runs for 37 wickets

1949 Fourth tour by New Zealand to England and also to the B.A.O.R. (captain, W. A. Hadlee): four Tests, all drawn. B. Sutcliffe made 243 and 100 v. Essex at Southend, and thus joined a very select band of batsmen: he had previously made two centuries in a match three times, and few have made so many as the four he now completed. His 243 is the highest first-class score by a New Zealander outside New Zealand. B. Sutcliffe and M. P. Donnelly each made 2,000 runs in first-class cricket, the only New Zealand tourists to do so. Of tourists' aggregates, Sutcliffe's 2,627 was second only to Bradman's aggregate in 1930

1949 Orissa Cricket Association formed. The East Punjab C.A. formed out of the remnant within India of N.I.C.A.: the name changed to Northern Punjab C.A. from 1960

7b. PAKISTAN

1947 Pakistan came into existence. At that time the following cricket associations existed from before Partition: Northern India Cricket Association, which now became the Punjab Cricket Association (it lasted as such until 1958 when it was superseded by Divisional Cricket Associations for Lahore, Multan and Rawalpindi and, in 1960, for Sargodha); Sind Cricket Association which, in 1948, became the Sind-Karachi Cricket Association and in 1950 reverted to the name of Karachi Cricket Association under which it had started life in 1924; and the North-West Frontier Province Cricket Association which became the Peshawar Divisional Cricket Association in 1956. A further Divisional Association was formed out of this area for Dera Ismail Khan in 1964

1948 Baluchistan Cricket Association formed which became the Quetta Cricket Association in 1956. Bahawalpur Cricket Association also formed

1948–9 First tour to Pakistan by West Indies (captain, J. D. C. Goddard): one unofficial test was drawn. During this tour, G. A. Carew made the first first-class century in Pakistan and Imtiaz Ahmed the first by a Pakistani. First tour by Pakistan to Ceylon (captain, Mohammed Saeed): won both unofficial tests. Nazar Mohammed (170) and Murrawat Hussain (164) made 269 for the second wicket v. Ceylon in Colombo, the highest for that wicket by Pakistani batsmen

1949 Board of Control for Cricket in Pakistan formed on May 1. *Cricket in Pakistan Annual* first issued – two more issues in 1951 and 1954. First tour by Ceylon to Pakistan (captain, S. S. Jayawickreme): both unofficial Tests lost by Ceylon

1947 H. Haislund scored two centuries (119 and 112) in the same match, the first of only two occasions on which this has been done in Denmark. The Hiram Walker Trophy presented for senior inter-provincial competition in Canada

1948 Malayan Cricket Association formed, also the Singapore Cricket Association (then a constituent part of the Malayan Cricket Association but now representing an independent country). The record Danish wicket partnership made by S. Eliasen and M. Worm – 307 unbroken for the third wicket. The same season saw the record Danish fourth-wicket partnership established of 247 unbroken by P. Poulsen and H. Gade. The last match took place between Hong Kong and Shanghai. In the North v. South match in Argentina, 1,495 runs were made for 31 wickets, the record match aggregate there (only four times exceeded in England, and *never* in a match in which *two* English teams took part. The thousand-run aggregate has altogether been exceeded in these North v. South matches fifteen times)

1949 The record Danish first- and second-wicket partnerships established: 294 by K. B. Rieck and E. Knudsen, and 257 by H. Buus and E. Larsen. The record Dutch last-wicket partnership of 99 made by A. Harmsen (83) and W. Honnebier (28*)

357

1949–50 Fifth tour to South Africa (q.v.). In a minor match by an Australian 'B' team against Wairarapa in New Zealand, A. K. Davidson took all ten wickets in the first innings and then made 157*, thus becoming only the third Australian to perform this very rare feat

1950–1 13th MCC tour (captain, F. R. Brown), won one and lost four Tests. This was the last series in which the final Test could have been played to a finish in certain circumstances which, however, did not arise.

1951 An Egyptian team toured England. Publication of the first comprehensive *Book of Cricket Records* by Roy Webber. Glamorgan made their record score of 587 for 8 wickets declared against Derbyshire at Cardiff (Arms Park)

1951–2 The MCC team to India and Ceylon (captain, N. D. Howard) became the first English team to visit Pakistan since the country came into existence

1951 Second tour by Australian women to England: won one, lost one, drew one Test

1951–2 First match Western Australia *v.* West Indians. West Indians' second tour (captain, J. D. C. Goddard), won one and lost four Tests

1952 Pakistan was admitted to the Imperial Cricket Conference. The first tour to England by a Pakistan team – the Pakistan Eaglets (not first-class)

1953 Imperial Cricket War Memorial Gallery opened at Lord's by H.R.H. the Duke of Edinburgh. First tour from West Africa – the Nigerian Cricket Association (not first-class)

1954 First New Zealand women's tour to England. The only first-class tour so far to England by Canada (captain, H. B. Robinson). The first first-class Pakistan tour to England (captain A. H. Kardar), and the first Tests between Pakistan and England: the series was drawn

1952–3 M. Hockney hit eight sixes off an eight-ball over for Clare Blues *v.* Mintaro in Adelaide. Oddly, he failed to score off a no-ball. His feat was eclipsed in 1968–9. Third tour by South Africa (captain, J. E. Cheetham), won two, lost two and drew one Test

1953 First visit by official Australian team (21st) to Holland. A. L. Hassett was captain: they lost one Test to England and drew four

1953–4 First match Western Australia *v.* New Zealand

1954 First visit by team of Australian club cricketers to Great Britain: C. E. Skitch's South Australian touring team. They also visited Germany, the first Australian team to do so

1954–5 Declaration henceforth permitted at any time. 14th MCC tour (captain, L. Hutton), won three Tests, lost one and drew one

1949–50 *South African Cricket Almanack* issued – one year only. Fifth tour of South Africa by Australians (captain, A. L. Hassett): South Africans lost four Tests and drew one. The Australians met North-East Transvaal for the first time. D. M. Seedat made 1,117 runs and took 135 wickets in the season, the first non-white cricketer to do the double

1950 South African Cricket Board of Control formed, covering all non-white cricket

1950–1 E. A. B. Rowan made 277* in the course of a day's play for Transvaal *v.* Griqualand West, the record for one day in South African first-class cricket. P. S. Heine made 123* in twenty-two minutes in senior club cricket in Pretoria, probably the fastest century on record in South Africa. J. E. Pothecary, aged sixteen, playing in a club match in Cape Town, took all 20 wickets in the match, the only time this has been recorded in Southern Africa

1951 First tour to East Africa by a team from Rhodesia. Tenth tour by South Africans to England (captain, A. D. Nourse (jun.)): South Africa won one, drew one and lost three Tests

1951–2 *South African Cricket Annual* issued (editor, G. Chettle): issued regularly since then. First score of over 500 by South African provincial coloured team, 519 for 8 wickets declared by Western Province *v.* Griqualand West at Cape Town. First women's interprovincial tournament at Johannesburg

1952 First tour to East Africa by a team from Natal: also tour by Kenya Kongonis to Southern Rhodesia. South Africa and Rhodesia Women's Cricket Association formed (white only)

1952–3 Third tour to Australia and New Zealand (q.v. both countries). The record fourth-wicket partnership in South African first-class cricket of 342 made by E. A. B. Rowan (195) and P. J. M. Gibb (203) for Transvaal *v.* North-East Transvaal at Johannesburg

1953–4 First tour by New Zealand to South Africa (captain, G. O. Rabone): South Africa won four Tests and drew the other. New Zealand met each of the Currie Cup contenders for the first time. *South African Non-European Cricket Almanack* issued (editors S. J. Reddy and D. N. Bansda) first of three issues. B. L. d'Oliveira for St Augustine's *v.* Trafalgar scored 46 in an eight-ball over, the South African record; for Croxley *v.* Mariedahl, he scored 225 out of 236 in sixty-five minutes, hitting twenty-eight sixes and ten fours. He hit each of his first five balls for six

1950 The 7th West Indians won the Test rubber in England for the first time – won three Tests and lost one. The captain was J. D. Goddard and the triumph was largely due to 'those little pals of mine Ramahdin and Valentine' as the calypso, composed almost on the spot, had it. The West Indians made their record score in England of 730 for three wickets declared *v.* Cambridge University at Fenner's. In this match E. D. Weekes made 304, the highest first-class score by a West Indian outside the West Indies. Weekes became the second West Indian tourist to score 2,000 runs in a season in making 2,310 runs

1951 First match Jamaica *v.* Guyana in Jamaica

1951–2 First West Indies tour to New Zealand (q.v.) after the Australian tour (q.v.) (a match had been played against Wellington in 1930–1, however). Barbados made 753 *v.* Kensington, their highest score. L. Wight (262*) and G. L. Gibbs (216) scored 390 for the first wicket for Guyana *v.* Barbados, the record for that wicket in West Indian first-class cricket: Guyana made 692 for 9 wickets declared, the highest ever by Guyana. The first match between Windward Islands and Leeward Islands.

1952 N. L. Bonitto (207) and A. P. Binns (157) made the record fifth-wicket partnership in the West Indies by West Indians of 283 for Jamaica *v.* Guyana at Bourda

1953 First visit by India to West Indies (captain, V. S. Hazare): they lost the only Test finished of five. The first match between Windward Islands and Guyana

1954 Seventh tour by MCC to West Indies (captain, L. Hutton): the series was drawn, two Tests each with one draw. The tour was marked by unpleasantness and especially during the Third Test at Bourda in Guyana. This tour also saw the first MCC visit to Bermuda. Turf wicket reintroduced at Queen's Park, coconut matting having been introduced there in 1900 for inter-colonial matches: jute fibre matting replaced it in 1935. The grounds in the other West Indian territories have always had turf wickets

359

1949–50 Tenth official tour by Australia to New Zealand (captain, W. A. Brown): one unofficial Test drawn

1950–1 Eighth tour by MCC to New Zealand (captain, F. R. Brown): New Zealand lost one and drew one Test. Central Districts Cricket Association formed, including Hawke's Bay, Nelson, Marlborough and most of the minor associations in the Wellington province. B. Sutcliffe (275) and L. A. Watt (96) made the New Zealand record first-class partnership for the first wicket of 373 for Otago v. Auckland at Eden Park

1951–2 Second tour by West Indies to New Zealand (captain, J. D. C. Goddard): New Zealand lost one and drew one Test. Miss Ana Tini became the first Maori to make a century in women's cricket, playing for Canterbury v. Wellington. The record New Zealand fifth-wicket partnership of 335 by R. T. Barber (254) and K. L. Parkin (120*) in a club match in Wellington

1952–3 Second tour by South Africa to New Zealand (captain, J. E. Cheetham): New Zealand lost one and drew one Test. D. J. McGlew's 255 in the Wellington Test is the highest first-class score made by a South African outside South Africa. B. Sutcliffe again established a New Zealand record in scoring 385 for Otago v. Canterbury at Lancaster Park. H. B. Cave (118) and I. B. Leggat (142*) made the record New Zealand ninth wicket partnership of 239 for Central Districts v. Otago at Carisbrook

1953 Northern Districts Cricket Association formed from Taranaki and most of the minor associations in the Auckland province

1953–4 First tour by New Zealand to South Africa and Australia (q.v. South Africa). J. R. Reid became the first tourist to South Africa to score 1,000 runs and take 50 wickets. At Newlands, New Zealand made her record Test score of 505. Third tour by Fiji to New Zealand (captain, P. T. Raddock): four first-class matches played. First tour by a Colts side from New South Wales to New Zealand. Central Districts made 547 for five wickets declared v. Wellington at Basin Reserve, their record

1954 First tour by New Zealand women to England: they lost one and drew two Tests

1954–5 Ninth tour by MCC to New Zealand (captain, L. Hutton): New Zealand lost both Tests. Plunket Shield matches henceforth limited to three days of 6½ hours playing-time

1949–50 First Commonwealth tour to India: won one, lost two and drew two unofficial Tests. C. T. Sarwate (235) and R. P. Singh (88) established the Indian record eighth-wicket partnership of 236 for Holkar v. Delhi at Delhi. Delhi made her record score of 544 v. Southern Punjab at Delhi

1950–1 Second Commonwealth tour to India: won two and drew three unofficial Tests. Ghulam Ahmed bowled 555 balls in one innings for Hyderabad v. Holkar at Indore, the record in Indian first-class cricket, and the world's second highest total. Bihar made her record score of 443 v. Orissa at Cuttack. Uttar Pradesh made their record score of 451 for 5 wickets declared v. Assam at Dehra Dun

1951 Travancore-Cochin C.A. formed: name changed to Kerala C.A. from 1957

1951–2 Third MCC tour to India (captain, N. D. Howard): won one, lost one and drew three Tests. First Test played at Kanpur, on the Green Park ground. India's first victory in an official Test was at Chepauk in Madras. Bengal made her record score of 760 v. Assam at Eden Gardens. Gujarat made her record score of 629 v. Maharashtra at Kolhapur

1952 First tour to the U.K. by post-partition India (fifth in all) (captain, V. S. Hazare): lost three Tests and drew one

1952–3 First tour by Pakistan to India (captain, A. H. Kardar): won one, lost two and drew two Tests. First Test played at Lucknow, on the University ground. B. C. Khanna and R. Balasundaram put on a century for the first wicket in each innings (166 and 108) for U.P. v. Madhya Pradesh at Nagpur, the only time this feat has been performed in Indian first-class cricket

1953 First tour to West Indies by India (q.v. West Indies)

1953–4 Third Commonwealth tour to India: won one, lost two and drew two unofficial tests. The Gopalan Trophy instituted for matches between Madras and Ceylon – Ceylon has won seven matches, Madras two and there have been four draws. S. V. Patker scored 431* in an inter-school match at Bombay, including 83 fours, believed to be the world record

1954–5 First tour to Pakistan by India (q.v. Pakistan), S. P. Gupte, 10 for 78, became the first Indian bowler to take all 10 wickets in an innings in a first-class match for Bombay C.A. Presidents XI v. Combined Pakistan Services-Bahawalpur XI at Bombay

1949-50 First tour to Pakistan by Commonwealth: one unofficial Test won. In a twelve-a-side match, Imtiaz Ahmed made 200*, the first double century in Pakistan

1950-1 Pentangular Cricket Tournament revived in Karachi

1951 East Pakistan Sports Control Board set up – various names have existed for it. In 1958 it was superseded by a Divisional Cricket Association for Dacca, and in 1962 for the Khulna, Rajshahi and Chittagong Divisions also. In a school match in Karachi, Hanif Mohammed made 305*, the first treble century in Pakistan

1951-2 First MCC tour to Pakistan (captain, N. D. Howard): drew one and lost the other unofficial Test

1952 Pakistan admitted to the Imperial Cricket Conference: the first of eight tours to the U.K. by the Pakistan Eaglets, teams of young Pakistani cricketers sent on tour for experience

1952-3 First tour to India by Pakistan (q.v. India): the team afterwards visited Burma. Hanif Mohammed became the first Pakistani cricketer to score a century in each innings in first-class cricket (121 and 109*), for Pakistan v. North Zone at Amritsar

1953 A new Sind Cricket Association formed to cover the area *outside* Karachi: from 1958 it became the Hyderabad Cricket Association. From part of the area, a Khairpur Cricket Association was formed in the same year

1953-4 Pakistan Services team (captain, A. H. Kardar), visited Ceylon. Qaid-i-Azam trophy instituted, the first winners Bahawalpur (owing to the many changes of name and boundary it is not helpful to summarize subsequent winners). Waqar Hassan made 201* for Air Vice-Marshal Cannon's XI v. Hassan Mahmood's XI at Karachi, the first double century made in Pakistan first-class cricket

1954 First tour to U.K. by Pakistan (captain, A. H. Kardar): won one, lost one, and drew two Tests. The first match between Pakistan and Canada was played at Lord's.

1954-5 First tour by India to Pakistan (captain, V. Mankad): all five Tests drawn. First Tests played at Lahore on the Lawrence Gardens (now Bagh-i-Jinnah) ground, Bahawalpur (Dring Stadium), Dacca (Stadium), Karachi (National Stadium) and Peshawar (Gymkhana). First appearance of a team from East Pakistan in the Qaid-i-Azam trophy. Playing for Karachi v. Services at Karachi, Abdul Wahab did the hat-trick for the first time in Pakistani first-class cricket

1950 The Hague C.C. Youth team became the first Dutch youth team to tour England. Sv. Morild took 128 wickets in the season, the highest in Denmark

1951 First inter-colonial match in East Africa: Kenya v. Tanganyika. The East African Cricket Conference formed. Ove Jensen made 252*, the Danish record. The fourth MCC tour to Canada (captain, R. W. V. Robins): beat Canada in a three-day first-class match. The record partnership in first-class or any other grade of cricket in Ceylon for the fifth wicket of 301 made by F. M. M. Worrell (285) and W. H. H. Sutcliffe (95) for Commonwealth v. Ceylon

1952 Uganda Cricket Association formed. *Canadian Cricket*, monthly magazine started; lasted till 1964. First match Kenya v. Uganda. The record Ceylon first-wicket partnership of 351 established by M. Salih (237) and H. C. Felsinger (114*)

1953 Kenya Cricket Association formed. The twenty-first Australian team to England visited Holland: the twenty-fourth in 1964 also did so, and were beaten in a one-day match by All Holland. The record Dutch fifth-wicket partnership of 232 established by L. C. de Villeneuve (170) and R. Colthoff (103*). The first Ugandan cricket annual appeared, *The Uganda Cricketer*: nine issues in all. First match Uganda v. Tanganyika. Dr A. B. Lang in making 111 and 107 for Ottawa v. Niagara Peninsula became the first cricketer to make two centuries in a match in North America

1954 W. J. Bennette stumped 6 and caught 4 in one innings in a school match in Ceylon, believed to be the world record. The fifth Canadian tour to the U.K. (captain, H. B. Robinson), and the first to play first-class matches in England – they met and lost to Pakistan at Lord's

M*

1955 First Australian team to visit the West Indies (captain, I. W. Johnson) won three and drew two Tests. Record Australian Test score of 758 for 8 wickets declared made in fifth Test at Sabina Park, Kingston. It included five centuries, the first time so many had been scored in one Test innings

1955–6 St Kilda Cricket Ground used in Melbourne for all first-class matches during this and the following season whilst the Melbourne Cricket Ground was prepared and used for the Olympic Games: like other grounds (S. Yarra, E. Melbourne, S. Melbourne, Fitzroy, Richmond and Carlton) in Melbourne St Kilda had occasionally been used before for first-class matches. South Australia made 27 against New South Wales at Sydney, the lowest score in Sheffield Shield matches

1956 J. C. Laker took 19 wickets in the Test against Australia at Old Trafford: the record number of wickets taken in any first-class match in the world, though 20 have several times been taken in minor cricket. County club formed in Cardiganshire – ended in 1961

1956 22nd Australians to England (captain, I. W. Johnson) won one, lost two and drew two Tests. It later paid the first visit by an official Australian team to India and Pakistan (q.v. those countries)

1957 M. J. Stewart caught seven in one innings, for Surrey v. Northamptonshire at Northampton – the first-class record. P. B. H. May (285*) and M. C. Cowdrey (154) made 411 for the fourth wicket for England v. West Indies at Edgbaston, the world record Test fourth-wicket partnership

1956–7 Television first used in Australia: Victoria v. New South Wales at St Kilda. Several other matches were televised. The first tie in the Sheffield Shield competition: Victoria, 244 and 197, v. New South Wales 281 and 160

1957–8 First MCC tour to East Africa (captain, F. R. Brown)

1957–8 R. Benaud, by taking 106 wickets during the Australian tour of South Africa (q.v.), became the only other Australian to take 100 wickets in an overseas first-class season, C. T. B. Turner having done so in 1887–8. For the first time, and henceforth, the Victorian Cricket Association was represented on the Board of Trustees of the Melbourne Cricket Ground. Third tour by English women: drew three Tests

1958 H. L. Jackson of Derbyshire obtained the best bowling average since 1894 of 10·99 (bowlers playing in only a few matches excluded) when conditions of pitch and batsmanship were very different. Surrey won the County Championship for the seventh successive time, the longest run by any county

1958–9 15th MCC tour (captain, P. B. H. May), lost four Tests and drew one

1954–5 O. C. Dawson and K. N. Kirton, in making 255 for the third wicket for Border *v.* Rhodesia, each made centuries before lunch, believed to be a unique record. First match North-East Transvaal *v.* Eastern Province

1955 Eleventh tour by South Africa to England (captain, J. E. Cheetham): South Africa won two and lost three Tests. First book on a South African tour in Afrikaans – *Amper Krieketkampioene* (Almost Cricket Champions) by Werner Barnard. Tour by Kenya Kongonis to Natal

1955–6 Natal made 714 for 9 wickets in a two-day friendly match against Rhodesia, the record South African score, and the only score in South Africa over 700. P. R. Carlstein (213) for St Andrews *v.* Gray College, OFS, made the highest recorded score in inter-school cricket in South Africa. North-East Transvaal made 552 for 8 wickets declared *v.* Orange Free State at Bloemfontein the North-East Transvaal record; Rhodesia also made its record this season of 570 for 6 wickets declared *v.* Griqualand West at Bulawayo

1956 Tour by Kenya Asians to South Africa. South Africa (non-white) won two and one Test. *South African Cricket Review*, first South African cricket magazine, issued – lasted till November 1958

1956–7 Ninth MCC tour to South Africa (captain, P. B. H. May): South Africa won two, lost two and drew one Test. W. R. Endean was given out, 'handled ball' in second Test at Newlands, the only such occasion in Test cricket. New 'Wanderers' ground at Kent Park taken into use

1957 First and only issue of *Rhodesian Cricket and Tennis Annual*

1957–8 Sixth tour by Australians (captain, I. D. Craig): South Africa lost three and drew two Tests, R. Benaud took 106 wickets, the record for a South African season, and only the second time it had been done. On this tour the Australians played for the first time in what is now Zambia, against a Northern Rhodesian Invitation XI at Kitwe (not first-class). Jan Smuts Oval brought into use at Maritzburg, supplanting the old Alexandra Park Oval, which is still, however, used for club cricket

1958 South African non-white team undertook first tour abroad, to East Africa: beat Combined East Africa. The record non-white third wicket partnership of 225 set up on this tour by S. Solomons and C. Abrahams *v.* Rhodesian Indian XI at Salisbury

1955 First Australian team to the West Indies (captain, I. W. Johnson) and also the first touring team to win a Test series in the West Indies, winning three of the five Tests, and drawing two. D. Atkinson (219) and C. C. Depeiza (122) made 347 for the seventh wicket for West Indies *v.* Australia at Kensington, the world record for that wicket in first-class cricket. C. L. Walcott established the unique record in that series of scoring a century in each innings of two Tests in one series. In making 758 for 8 wickets declared *v.* West Indies at Sabina Park, Australia compiled their highest Test total

1955–6 E. D. Weekes missed by 60 runs the accomplishment of making 1,000 runs in first-class cricket in a New Zealand season, during the first West Indian full-length tour of New Zealand (q.v.): in doing so he also made three centuries in consecutive innings in the series for the second time in his career, a unique record

1956 First knock-out Regional Tournament, involving the four major territories: Guyana won. The first of two matches lasted five days and the final six, but in later tournaments they were four days each of 5½ hours playing-time. Formation of Trinidad Cricket Council to organize and control cricket in Trinidad and Tobago, under the Queen's Park Cricket Club so far as regional and international cricket is concerned

1957 Eighth West Indian tour to England (captain J. D. C. Goddard): England won the three Tests finished of five. The Jones Cup donated for competition between the three counties of Guyana – Demarara, Berbice and Essequibo

1958 First visit by Pakistan to West Indies (captain, A. H. Kardar): West Indies won three Tests, drew one and lost one. G. S. Sobers in scoring 365* against Pakistan established not only a Test record, but also the record individual score in the West Indies. In making 1,007 runs in the first-class season, he became the first West Indian to do so in the West Indies. C. C. Hunte (260) and G. S. Sobers (365*) made 446 for the second wicket for West Indies *v.* Pakistan at Sabina Park, Kingston. West Indies made 790 for three wickets declared, the highest total ever by a West Indian team. First match Jamaica *v.* Leeward Islands

1958–9 Second tour by West Indies to India, Pakistan and Ceylon (q.v. those countries)

each. This season saw the first Test at Caris-brook, Dunedin

1955–6 First tour by New Zealand to India and Pakistan (q.v. those countries). First tour by a New Zealand Colts team to New South Wales. Third tour by West Indies (captain, D. Atkinson): New Zealand lost three and won one of the Tests, the first Test victory by New Zealand.

1956–7 Eleventh official tour by Australia to New Zealand (captain, I. D. Craig): New Zealand drew two of the unofficial tests and lost one. Second visit by New Zealand women's team to Australia: they lost the only Test

1957–8 Third tour by English women to New Zealand: both Tests drawn
1958 Fifth tour by New Zealand to England (captain, J. R. Reid): New Zealand lost four and drew one of the Tests

1958–9 Tenth tour by MCC to New Zealand (captain, P. B. H. May): New Zealand lost one and drew one Test. First tour by a New Zealand University team to Australia. Only once before had an overseas university gone on tour: Pennsylvania to England in 1907

1955–6 First tour by New Zealand to India (captain, H. B. Cave): lost two and drew three Tests. First Tests played at Hyderabad, on the Fateh Maidan and at Madras on the Corporation (or Nehru) Stadium. V. Mankad made the record Indian Test score of 231 on the Corporation ground in Madras, and with P. Roy (173) made the Test and Indian first-class first-wicket record of 413. Andhra made their record score of 462 for 9 wickets declared v. Kerala at Trivandrum
1956 First official tour by Australians (third in all) (captain, I. W. Johnson): won two and drew one Test
1956–7 Second tour by India to Ceylon (captain P. R. Umrigar): drew two unofficial tests. C. L. Malhotra made 502* for Mahendra College v. Government College, Rupar at Patiala – the highest in Indian school cricket

In his next two innings he made 360 and 144, thus completing 1,006 runs in three consecutive innings, a feat unequalled in any class of cricket in the world.
1957 Jammu and Kashmir C.A. formed. The Sunder Cricket Club of Bombay (a strong combination with many first-class players, not to be confused with the Sounder C.C. of Madras) toured East Africa and defeated Combined East Africa
1957–8 *Indian Cricket Field Annual* first appeared: eight issues, last in 1964–5. An Indian schools team toured Ceylon, the first representative schools team to leave India. Rajasthan made her record score of 615 v. Vidharba at Udaipur. Assam made her record score of 411 for 7 wickets declared v. Orissa at Cuttack

1958–9 Second West Indies tour to India (captain, F. C. M. Alexander): won three and drew two Tests. A. L. Wadekar made 324* for Bombay University v. Delhi University, the record individual score in Indian University cricket. Calcutta University made the record Indian inter-University score of 817 v. Bihar University

1955–6 Second tour by MCC – an 'A' team (captain, D. B. Carr): won one, lost two and drew one unofficial Test. (In this tour occurred the water-squirting incident in which a Pakistani umpire was drenched by MCC players.) First tour by New Zealand to Pakistan (captain, H. B. Cave): lost two and drew one Test. Waqar Hassan (189) and Imtiaz Ahmed (209) made 308 for the seventh wicket v. New Zealand at Lahore (Bagh-i-Jinnah ground – the former Lawrence Gardens): the first partnership of over 300 in Pakistan. In this match, Pakistan made her highest home Test score of 561

1956 A strong Pakistan team toured East Africa under the name 'Pakistan Cricket Writers': it included Test and other first-class players and beat Combined East Africa. First Australian tour to Pakistan (captain, I. W. Johnson): lost the only Test

1956–7 Karachi Whites made 762 v. Karachi Blues at Karachi, the first time even 600 had been exceeded in Pakistan. For Punjab v. Services at Lahore, Fazal Mahmood took 15 for 76, the greatest number of wickets in a first-class match by a Pakistani bowler

1957–8 Hanif Mohammed (146★) and Alimuddin (131★) made 277★ for the first wicket for Karachi 'A' v. Sind 'A', the record for that wicket in Pakistani first-class cricket

1958 First tour by Pakistan to the West Indies (q.v. West Indies). The team also visited Bermuda, Canada and the U.S.A. Pakistan made her record Test score of 657 for 8 wickets declared in the first Test at Kensington, Barbados, and it is also the world's largest Test second-innings score. In the match Hanif Mohammed made 337, the highest Pakistani Test score, and also the world's longest, lasting 16 hours 39 minutes

It is also the highest score made by a Pakistani batsman outside Pakistan

1958–9 Second tour by West Indies to Pakistan (captain, F. C. M. Alexander): won one and lost two Tests. The world first-class individual record score made by Hanif Mohammed of 499 for Karachi v. Bahawalpur. Punjab University made 702 v. Sind University at Karachi, the total including four centuries, the most in a Pakistani first-class match, but equalled by Railways v. Dera Ismail Khan in 1964–5

1955 A *Tanganyika Cricket Annual* appeared: one other issue in 1958. First match Holland v. Denmark

1956 First touring team to play first-class matches in East Africa, the Pakistan Cricket Writers (q.v. Pakistan). The Kenya Asians toured South Africa and drew one and lost two representative matches against South African non-Whites

1957 The West Indians who had toured England also paid a visit to Holland. F. Pereira made the record score in Ceylon of 352★. The record Ceylon second-wicket partnership of 301 established by R. Azzam and B. Aliman (226)

1957–8 The first MCC tour to East Africa (captain, F. R. Brown)

1958 Tanganyika Cricket Association formed. *Kenya Cricket Almanack* produced, only one issue. A representative South African non-white team toured East Africa and beat Combined East Africa. A West Indian team toured the U.S.A. Pakistan toured the U.S.A., Canada, and Bermuda: beat Canada in Canada. The record Ceylon seventh-wicket partnership of 243 established by Lionel Fernando (185) and Lasantha Fernando (113)

1958–9 The fifth English, and third MCC tour to South America (captain, G. H. G. Doggart): won two v. Argentina, and visited Brazil against whom they also won two

1959 Establishment of first-class counties Second Eleven competition. Kent have won three times, Worcestershire and Surrey have each twice

1960 J. G. Binks, of Yorkshire, took 97 catches in the season, the record by a wicket-keeper. *Playfair Cricket Monthly* established. First tour by Bermuda to England
1960–1 On its way to New Zealand, the MCC team played in Malaysia, the first MCC team to do so. The first English women's tour to South Africa

1961 On becoming a republic and leaving the Commonwealth, South Africa automatically ceased to be a member of the Imperial Cricket Conference as a result of rules of her own choosing

1962 The follow-on established at 200 runs for matches exceeding three days' duration
1963 The distinction between amateur and professional in English first-class, and some other grades of cricket, abolished. The Gillette Cup Knock-out competition inaugurated: at first for first-class counties only, it was extended the following season to include the five leading minor counties. Warwickshire, Yorkshire and Sussex have each won twice. *Cricket Quarterly* established: the only scholarly, literary, artistic, historical and statistical magazine on any sport or game, save chess: lasted eight years

1959 First visit by (unofficial) Australian team to France (Australian Old Collegians)
1959–60 A. T. W. Grout established a world first-class record by catching eight batsmen in the match between Queensland and Western Australia at Brisbane. Second tour to India and Pakistan (q.v. those countries)

1960 First visit by (unofficial) Australian team to Denmark and to Indonesia (Australian Old Collegians)
1960–1 Third tour by West Indies to Australia (captain, F. M. M. Worrell). The first Test at Brisbane between the West Indies and Australia ended in a tie – the only tied game in the history of Test matches. 90,800 attended the second day of the Fifth Test at Melbourne, a world record. Australia won two, lost one and drew the other of the five Tests
1961 23rd Australians to England (captain, R. Benaud) won two, lost one and drew two Tests. First visit by (unofficial) Australian team (Emus of New South Wales) to Hong Kong
1961–2 A first-class match played outside Melbourne, in Victoria, for the first time: Victoria v. Tasmania at Kardinia Park, Geelong. New South Wales won the Sheffield Shield for the ninth successive time, the longest run by any State. T. Nilsson hit nine sixes from successive balls, including eight from an 8-ball over, without no-balls being involved, in Brisbane minor cricket

1962–3 16th MCC tour (captain, E. R. Dexter) won one, lost one and drew three Tests. M. C. Cowdrey made 307 against South Australia: the highest score in Australia by any Englishman, or indeed any non-Australian. R. B. Simpson completed 1,000 runs in first-class cricket by December 22, the earliest date by which such a feat had been accomplished. Geelong College sent a team to New Zealand, the first Australian school to do so
1963 Third tour by Australian women to England: lost one and drew two Tests

1959–60 N. Kirsten playing for Border *v.* Rhodesia, caught six and stumped one while M. S. Smith, for Natal *v.* Border, caught seven, stumped 0 – the joint South African first-class records. Border made 16 and 18 *v.* Natal in the same match, the two lowest South African first-class totals, and the world record lowest match aggregate in first-class cricket. First and only issue of the *South African Cricketer* (covering non-white cricket). Surrey toured to Rhodesia. C. Richardson (258) and D. J. Schonegeval (115) made 280 for the third wicket for Orange Free State *v.* Transvaal 'B' at Wanderers, the highest third-wicket partnership by South Africans in South Africa

1960 Twelfth tour by South Africans to England (captain, D. J. McGlew): South Africa lost three and drew two Tests

1960–1 First tour by English women to South Africa: South Africa lost one and drew three Tests

1961 In accordance with the Rules of the Imperial Cricket Conference, of which she was a founder member, South Africa left the Conference on becoming a Republic and has not rejoined the International Cricket Conference. Unofficial South African team (Fezelas) toured England, playing some first-class matches

1961–2 First non-racial provincial tournament: winners Transvaal. (Though no distinction of race was made, white cricketers did not take part.) The record non-white first-wicket partnership of 283 made by I. d'Oliveira (145) and G. Jardine (142) for Western Province *v.* Griqualand West. Second New Zealand tour to South Africa (captain, J. R. Reid) New Zealand and South Africa each won two Tests, and one was drawn. J. R. Reid made 1,915 runs in the season in first-class matches, the record South African aggregate. An international team toured Rhodesia, thus giving B. L. d'Oliveira his first opportunity of playing unarguably first-class cricket in Southern Africa. This team also played the first match of first-class status in what is now Zambia: Rhodesian XI *v.* Commonwealth XI at Nkana. (From now on, references to Zambia occur under 'Other Countries' (below) as its cricket is henceforth concerned with the East African scene)

1962 A team of Rhodesian schoolboys toured England

1962–3 J. T. Partridge took 64 wickets in the first-class season, the record by a South African. Eastern Province made its record total of 594 for 6 wickets declared *v.* Western Province at Newlands. L. Irvine, playing for Durban High School made 1,310 runs in the season, the record for schools cricket in South Africa

1959 Playing in a Worsley Cup match (knockout between Lancashire League teams) O. G. Smith made 306* for Burnley *v.* Lowerhouse, the record score by a West Indian outside the West Indies

1960 Eighth tour by MCC to West Indies (captain, P. B. H. May). There was a riot on the Queen's Park ground in Port-of-Spain during the Second Test – the only one finished of five. The MCC played two matches in British Honduras, never before visited by any first-class side

1960–1 The first Test of the third West Indian team to Australia ended as a tie, at Brisbane, the only Test to have such a result (q.v. Australia)

1961 The first knock-out Regional Tournament involving also a combined team from the smaller islands, won by Guyana. In Jamaica in a commercial house competition match, G. Anderson took 6 wickets in six balls, the West Indian record

1962 The second tour by an Indian team to West Indies – they lost all five Tests. The captain was N. J. Contractor

1962–3 By making 1,006 runs in the Australian season, G. S. Sobers (playing for South Australia) became the first cricketer ever to make 1,000 first-class runs or more in each of four different countries, having made 1,162 during the West Indian tour of India in 1958–9 and 1,644 during his first tour of England in 1957. He also became the first cricketer ever to make 1,000 runs and take 50 wickets in an Australian season (1,006 runs average 62·87, 51 wickets average 26·56)

1963 Ninth tour by West Indies to England (captain, F. M. M. Worrell): West Indies won three Tests, lost one and drew the other. First match Windward Islands *v.* Trinidad

1959 Sixth tour to the U. K. by India (captain, D. K. Gaekwad): lost all five Tests. For the first time India was allotted five days for each Test in England

P. R. Umrigar made 252* *v.* Cambridge University at Fenner's, the highest by an Indian outside his own country, if K. S. Duleepsinhji's 333 for Sussex *v.* Northamptonshire at Hove in 1930 is excluded, Duleepsinhij having learnt his cricket in England. The same applies to K. S. Ranjitsinhji in respect of his 285* for Sussex *v.* Somerset at Taunton in 1901

1959–60 Twelfth official tour by Australia (captain, I. D. Craig): New Zealand drew three and lost one unofficial Test. Northern Districts made 384 *v.* Wellington at Seddon Park, Hamilton, their record

1960–1 Eleventh tour by MCC (captain, D. R. W. Silk): New Zealand drew two and won one of the unofficial Tests. Second tour by Australian women to New Zealand: the only Test drawn

1961–2 Second tour by New Zealand to South Africa and Australia (q.v. South Africa). J. R. Reid scored 2,083 runs in all first-class matches on the tour. Fourth tour by Fiji to New Zealand (captain, S. Snowsill): not first-class. Rothmans inter-provincial tournament (same boundaries as Plunket Shield) for under twenty-three teams inaugurated

1959–60 Second official tour by Australians (fourth in all) to India (captain, R. Benaud): won two, lost one and drew two Tests. First tour by Indian Starlets to Pakistan, a team of young cricketers sent for experience. Kerala made their record score of 555 for 5 wickets declared *v.* Andhra at Palghat

1960 Second tour by an Indian team to East Africa – Gujarat C.A. (a Ranji Trophy competitor) who won one and drew two matches *v.* Combined East Africa

1960–1 Second tour by Pakistan to India (captain, Fazal Mahmood): all five Tests drawn. Jammu and Kashmir made 51 in two innings *v.* Delhi, the lowest match aggregate by any team in Indian first-class cricket. Rajinder Pal (9 for 20) and P. Sitaram (11 for 30) bowled unchanged in the match, only the second time this has happened in India. A Ceylon schools team toured India

1961–2 A cricket annual appeared in Gujarati. The Duleep Zonal Tournament instituted, won so far by West Zone six times and once shared and South Zone three times. Fourth MCC tour to India (captain, E. R. Dexter): lost two and drew three Tests

1962 Second tour by India to the West Indies (q.v. West Indies)

1962–3 Twelfth tour by MCC to New Zealand (captain, E. R. Dexter): New Zealand lost three Tests. First visit by an Australian schools team to New Zealand, Geelong College. J. R. Reid scored the world's first-class record of sixes when he hit 15 in his 296 for Wellington against Northern Districts at Basin Reserve

1962–3 Eight-ball overs used this season in all Indian first-class matches. S. Saleem performed the remarkable and unique feat of scoring 210 and 301 in an inter-school match in Hyderabad

1963 V. Mankad completed a total of 776 wickets taken in his first-class career, the most by any Indian bowler

1959 Fifth MCC tour to Canada (captain, D. R. W. Silk): beat Canada in a three-day match. The first issue of a cricket annual by the Canadian Cricket Association – it has appeared in most years since then. The record total in Ceylon of 925 made in a minor club match. L. Fernando made 204 runs in one innings, and took all 10 wickets in an innings for 24 in a school match in Ceylon, a remarkable feat. I. L. Bula made the Fijian record of 246: Bula is an abbreviation for Talebulamaineiilikenamainavaleniveivakabulaimakulalakeba, thought at one time to the longest [surname in the world

1959–60 Second tour by Australia to Pakistan (captain, R. Benaud): won two Tests and drew the other. Matting wickets henceforth prohibited in Qaid-i-Azam matches. From now on Tests at Lahore were played on the Stadium ground. Asif Ahmad made 334 in an inter-collegiate match at Karachi University, the highest in a University match in Pakistan

1960–1 Second tour by Pakistan to India (q.v. India). Pakistan Eaglets (captain Shujaud-Din) toured Ceylon and Malaysia. Ayub Zonal Trophy instituted, first winners Railways-Quetta (as with the Qaid-i-Azam trophy, a summary of winners is not helpful)

1961–2 Third tour by MCC to Pakistan (captain, E. R. Dexter): won one and drew two Tests. Hanif Mohammed, Imtiaz Ahmed, Alimuddin and Mushtaq Mohammed each made 1,000 runs in the Pakistani first-class season. It had not been done before, nor has it been done since, and they achieved the total in the order shown, Hanif Mohammed first on March 10. The only tied match in Pakistani first-class cricket – Bahawalpur v. Lahore 'B' at Bahawalpur. The record number of first-class centuries was scored this season – 49

1962 Second tour by Pakistan to the U.K. (captain, Javed Burki): lost four Tests and drew one. Khalid Ibadulla, playing for Warwickshire, made 2,098 runs in the English season – the first Pakistani cricketer to do so

1962–3 Wallis Mathias (129) and Nasim-ul-Ghani (117) made 216 for the fifth wicket for Karachi 'A' v. East Pakistan at Karachi, the record for that wicket in Pakistani first-class cricket. Wallis Mathias (144*) and Afaq Hussain (87) made 134 for the last wicket for Karachi 'A' v. Karachi 'B' at Karachi: the first time a century partnership had been made for the last wicket in first-class cricket in Pakistan

1960 Harvard University toured Bermuda. The record Ceylon wicket partnership in any grade of cricket of 389 unbroken established for the third wicket by D. G. D. Edwards (220*) and W. Ranchigoda (165*)

1961 Second English tour to East Africa (captain, F. R. Brown). *Cricket and Rugger Times,* a monthly newspaper started in Montreal, lasted until 1966. Stockholm C.C. first toured to Denmark

1962 The first team from the U.K. to visit Corfu where cricket had been played for over a hundred years by the Corfiotes since the time of the British occupation of the Ionian Islands

1963 Third English, and second MCC tour to East Africa (captain, M. J. K. Smith): drew one and won one v. an Invitation XI (virtually a Combined East African XI). The Danish last-wicket partnership record of 129 established by Th. Provis and J. Ward

'1963–4. The Australian Board of Control issued stringent instructions to umpires regarding throwing'

1965 The Imperial Cricket Conference became the International Cricket Conference with Associate members: the first of these were Ceylon, Fiji and the U.S.A.

1963–4 Fourth South African team to Australia (captain, T. L. Goddard) won one, lost one and drew three Tests. Before the season began, the Australian Board of Control issued stringent instructions to umpires regarding throwing, in an effort, which proved successful so far as Australia was concerned, to remove this canker. The highest score by a Queenslander in Queensland: 283 by P. J. Burge for Queensland v. New South Wales at Brisbane. The record total of eighty-four centuries was scored in the season. R. B. Simpson completed 1,000 runs by the end of December for the second time running, a distinction shared with no one else. R. Benaud became the first player to make 2,000 runs and take 200 wickets in Tests. The Northern Territory Cricket Association sent a team of schoolboys to Adelaide, the first team to tour outside the Territory

1964 24th Australians (captain, R. B. Simpson) won one and drew four Tests. R. B. Simpson, in making 311 at Manchester, beat the previous highest Test score made by an Australian captain in England (W. L. Murdoch's 211 in 1884): it is also the record for an Australian captain in England v. Australia Tests in either country. The Australians beaten in a one-day match by Holland. They also visited Pakistan and India (q.v. these countries)

1964–5 First visit by a Pakistan team to Australia (captain, Hanif Mohammed): one Test, drawn. States met were Queensland, New South Wales, and South Australia. For the first time in first-class cricket play took place on a Sunday during the two matches between Western Australia and Queensland: the experiment was a financial success, and was continued in subsequent seasons, and by the 1968–9 season had spread to all State capitals, for Tests as well as inter-state matches

1965 Australia lost a Test Series in the West Indies (q.v.). The record first-wicket Test partnership of 382 was established by W. M. Lawry (210) and R. B. Simpson (201) in fourth Test at Kensington (Barbados): it is the second highest first-wicket partnership in any series of Tests. Although two batsmen have twice before each made a double century in the same innings in Tests, it was unprecedented in Tests for the two opening batsmen to do so

1963 First tour to England by South African schoolboys team

1963–4 Fourth South African tour to Australia and New Zealand (q.v. both countries). The record South African third-wicket partnership of 341 made by E. J. Barlow (201) and R. G. Pollock (175) v. Australia at Adelaide. In this match South Africa made her record score in Australia of 595

1963–4 G. S. Sobers again did the Australian double (1,128 runs average 80·57 and 51 wickets average 28·25). First Regional Tournament between major territories in which each played each other: won by Guyana. R. Roopnarine (aged eighteen) made 327* for Queen's College v. Berbice High School, at Queen's College, the Guyana record

1964 First issue of *Trinidad Cricket Council Year Book*, annually since then. Sir Frank Worrell received his knighthood this year

1964–5 Tenth MCC tour to South Africa (captain, M. J. K. Smith): South Africa lost one and drew four Tests. K. C. Bland made 1,048 runs in the season, the first South African to top 1,000 runs in first-class cricket in a South African season. Worcestershire toured Rhodesia during the course of a world tour

1965 Thirteenth (half-length) tour by South Africans to England (captain, P. L. van der Merwe): South Africa won one and drew two of the three Tests

1965 The second Australian team to West Indies (captain, R. B. Simpson): West Indies won two Tests and Australia one; two Tests were drawn. First match Leeward Islands v. Windward Islands

1963–4 First tour by a club team from New Zealand to Samoa – not first-class. Third tour by South Africa to New Zealand (captain, T. L. Goddard): the three Tests drawn. S. W. Kohlhase, playing for Northern Districts, became the first Samoan in the world to play first-class cricket

1964 First round-the-world tour by an officially sponsored New Zealand team – visited U.S.A., Canada, Bermuda, U.K., B.A.O.R., Kuwait, Hong Kong and Malaya

1964–5 First tour by Pakistan to New Zealand (captain, Hanif Mohammed): three Tests drawn. R. M. Schofield caught 9 in the match and 7 in one innings for Central Districts v. Wellington at Basin Reserve, both being the New Zealand first-class record: in this match Central Districts made 485 for 7 declared, their highest total. Nelson gave up the Hawke Cup on being defeated on the first innings by Manawatu in February 1965, having held it since December 1958

1965 Sixth tour by New Zealand to England (captain, J. R. Reid): lost three Tests against England; also visited India and Pakistan (q.v. those countries), Holland, Bermuda and U.S.A.

1963–4 Fifth tour by the MCC (captain, M. J. K. Smith): all five Tests drawn. The record number of first-class centuries in a season was scored – 84

1964 Third official tour by Australians (captain, R. B. Simpson): won one, lost one and drew one Test. Air-India undertook a short cricket tour to Fiji. All India schools toured Ceylon

1964–5 Third tour by All Ceylon to India (captain, M. H. Tissera): won one and lost two unofficial Tests. C. G. Borde made 1,604 runs in the first-class season, the record seasonal aggregate in India. Hyderabad made her record score of 635 for 6 wickets declared v. Bengal at Hyderabad

1965 Second tour by New Zealand to India (captain, J. R. Reid): lost one and drew three Tests

1963–4 Second tour by Commonwealth to Pakistan: drew all three unofficial Tests; the match between Pakistan and Commonwealth at Lahore resulted in the highest first-class match aggregate in Pakistan of 1,460 runs for 21 wickets

1964 Third tour by Australia to Pakistan (captain, R. B. Simpson): drew the only Test. A Pakistan International Airways team (captain, Hanif Mohammed), consisting solely of Test and other first-class players, toured East Africa and beat an Invitation XI (virtually a combined East African XI) at Mombasa

1964–5 The record Pakistan score of 910 for 6 wickets declared made by Railways Dera Ismail Khan at Lahore: they won by an innings and 851 runs, the world's most decisive victory. The Dera Ismail Khan total of 59 was the lowest team match aggregate and their second innings of 27 the lowest for an innings in Pakistani first-class cricket. The first tour by Pakistan to Australia and New Zealand (q.v. those countries). Pakistani 'A' team (captain, Imtiaz Ahmed), visited Ceylon and lost the only unofficial Test. Salah-ud-Din (169) and Wallis Mathias (228) made 388 for the third wicket for Karachi Blues v. Hyderabad at Karachi, the record first-class partnership for Pakistan for any wicket (*but see* 1969–70)

1965 Second tour to Pakistan by New Zealand (captain, J. R. Reid): lost two and drew the other Test. First Test played at Rawalpindi, on the Club ground

1964 The record Danish fifth-wicket partnership established of 228 unbroken by B. L. Petersen and E. Nielsen. A New Zealand team (not first-class) made a round-the-world trip visiting among the 'Other Countries', Canada, the U.S.A., Bermuda, B.A.O.R., Kuwait, Hong Kong and Malaysia. First matches Nigeria v. Gambia and Nigeria v. Sierra Leone

1964–5 Sixth English and fourth MCC tour to South America (captain, A. C. Smith: won one and drew one v. Brazil, won two v. Argentina and won three v. Chile

1965 *The American Cricketer* revived, an occasional publication by the U.S.C.A. The New Zealand team which had toured the U.K. visited Holland, Bermuda and California

1965–6 A London schools team toured India, the first such tour to India from England. The first representative English schools team, selected by MCC, to South Africa. On its way back from Australia and New Zealand, the MCC Test team visited Hong Kong, the first MCC team to do so

1966 Bermuda, Denmark, East Africa and the Netherlands admitted as Associate Members of the International Cricket Conference. All Ireland League (of a semi-provincial character) inaugurated. Sunday first-class cricket inaugurated in England

1967 Malaysia admitted as an Associate Member of the International Cricket Conference. Up to the end of that season, J. P. F. Misso had scored 284 centuries in minor cricket, the record. The first tour from Zambia: Zambian schoolboys

1967–8 First visit by an English team to West Africa – four matches played by J. Lister's XI of first-class cricketers in Sierra Leone

1965–6 17th MCC tour (captain, M. J. K. Smith) won one, lost one and drew three Tests. Decision made to take new ball in Australia only after 65 (eight-ball) overs: applicable to all grades of Australian cricket. R. M. Cowper's 307 in fifth Test at Melbourne is the highest Test innings in Australia and also the highest against an English team in Australia. R. B. Simpson (225) and W. M. Lawry (119), in making 244 for the first wicket v. England at Adelaide, made the highest opening stand by Australians in Tests in Australia and by Australians in Tests v. England. P. J. Allen, in taking 10 wickets for 61 runs for Queensland in the first innings of Victoria at Melbourne, was the second bowler to do so in Sheffield Shield cricket and only the third in all first-class cricket in Australia. H. Gunstone (334) and H. Bourke (201) in scoring 521 for the first wicket for St Andrews v. Methodist at Ararat in Victorian country cricket established the record first-wicket partnership in Australia: it is also the world record in minor cricket for that wicket. The tour by a team of schoolboys from Sydney (N.S.W.) to India and East Africa provided the first occasion on which tourists have played cricket in Ethiopia and also the first matches in India between Indian and Australian schoolboys

1966 The first visit by an (unofficial) Australian team (the Emus) to Bahrain

1966–7 Transvaal became the first South African side to beat the Australians outside Test matches. The Australians (seventh to South Africa) lost their first Test series in South Africa. For the first time a representative team of Australian schoolboys toured India. In reaching 620 v. Griqualand West, the Australians made the highest score by an Australian team in South Africa. R. B. Simpson (243) v. North East Transvaal made the highest score by an Australian in South Africa. Sydney Cricket Ground No. 2 used for the first time for a first-class match. New South Wales v. Western Australia

1967–8 Second visit by Indian team to Australia (captain, Nawab of Pataudi) – lost all four Tests. The season also saw a short tour from New Zealand but with no Tests. L. J. Brayshaw took all in 10 wickets for 44 runs, for Western Australia v. Victoria, only the fourth time this had been done in Australian first-class cricket. A representative team from Singapore paid a first visit to Australia (Western Australia only). Two representative Australian schoolboy teams toured South Africa and New Zealand respectively. A Melbourne University team visited Hong Kong and Malaysia

1965-6 The MCC sent a team of schoolboys to tour South Africa. The record non-white second-wicket partnership of 201 made by S. Conrad (194) and N. Lakay (84) at Durban. The record South African last-wicket partnership of 174 made by H. R. Lance (168) and D. Mackay-Coghill (58*) for Transvaal v. Natal at Johannesburg

1965-6 First Regional Tournament for Shell Shield: Barbados won. This was the first time each side had played each other in a tournament involving a combined team from the smaller islands. Worcestershire visited Jamaica, drawing the only first-class match v. Jamaica

1966 D. A. J. Holford made his second century (105*) in first-class cricket in a Test match at Lord's (he assisted Sobers (163*) in establishing the West Indian sixth-wicket Test record of 274 unbroken). In the fourth Test at Headingley S. M. Nurse (137) and G. S. Sobers (174) made 265 for the fifth wicket – also a West Indian Test record. West Indies won three Tests (two by an innings), drew one but lost the last by an innings. This was the tenth tour by the West Indies to England (captain, G. S. Sobers). First regional schoolboys' tournament played on same lines as Shell Shield: three-day matches, the tournament won by Barbados

1966-7 Seventh tour by Australians to South Africa (captain, R. B. Simpson): South Africa won three, lost one and drew one Test, and thus won a series against Australia for the first time. Transvaal became the first South African team in South Africa to beat the Australians. D. Lindsay made 606 runs in the series, the world record for a Test wicket-keeper. R. B. Simpson (243) and R. M. Cowper (171) established the South African first-class second-wicket record partnership of 374 for Australians v. North-East Transvaal at Pretoria. The record number of first-class centuries in a season was scored – 54

1966-7 Third tour by West Indies to India and Ceylon (q.v. India). Second Tournament for Shell Shield: won by Barbados. This time the Windward Islands and the Leeward Islands competed separately but not for points. First match Leeward Islands v. Jamaica

1967 South African Universities team toured England – played a few first-class matches
1967-8 First tour to South Africa by a representative team of Australian schoolboys. Natal won the Currie Cup for the seventh successive time (the fifth shared, however), the longest run by any province. J. Govendor made 117* and 120* for Royals C.C. v. Kismet C.C. in Durban, believed to be the first occasion a non-white cricketer has made two centuries in a match in South Africa.

1967-8 Ninth tour by MCC to West Indies (captain, M. C. Cowdrey): England won the only Test brought to a conclusion out of five. A riot interrupted play in the second Test at Sabina Park. Riots had now taken place at three of the four West Indian Test match venues, significantly only when an English team was touring, and the significant exception being Kensington in Barbados

1965–6 Thirteenth tour by MCC (captain, M. J. K. Smith): three Tests drawn

1966 Second tour by New Zealand women to England: all three Tests drawn

1966–7 Thirteenth official tour by Australia to New Zealand (captain, L. E. Favell): New Zealand won one and drew three of the four unofficial Tests. Canterbury had become, earlier, the first team from New Zealand to beat a representative Australian team in an eleven-a-side match.

1967–8 Fourth official tour by a New Zealand team to Australia (captain, B. W. Sinclair): no Tests played. Establishment of the monthly *New Zealand Cricketer*, edited by R. T. Brittenden, the first magazine on cricket ever to appear in New Zealand. First tour by India to New Zealand, and the first five-day Tests played in New Zealand (captain, Nawab of Pataudi): India won three, New Zealand one. G. T. Dowling made 968 runs in the first-class season, the record New Zealand first-class seasonal aggregate. He made the highest Test score by a New Zealander, 239 at Hagley Park. S. Fleming, aged fourteen, playing for Marlborough College against Bohally Intermediate School at Blenheim took nine wickets in nine balls. He dismissed Bohally's last batsman in the first innings, and with each ball of his first over in the second innings, took a wicket. His feat equalled the world record by P. Hugo in South Africa in 1930–1. (*See also* under 1940 in Fiji for 8 wickets in one eight-ball over.) First visit to New Zealand by a representative Australian Schools team. Fifth tour by Fiji (captain, N. Uluiviti): not first-class

1965–6 First tour by English schoolboys to India, members of the London Schools Cricket Association. They drew four matches and lost the fifth against representative Indian schools teams. S. N. Mohol took 4 wickets in four balls for Board President's XI v. Combined XI, the only time this feat has been performed in Indian first-class cricket. The record first-wicket partnership in any class of Indian cricket of 421 set up by S. M. Gavaskar (246*) and A. Quereshi (203), in 215 minutes, for West Zone Schools v. Central Zone Schools at Bombay (Islam Gymkhana ground)

1966 V. S. Hazare completed 17,972 runs in his first-class career, second only to K. S. Ranjitsinhji amongst Indians, and fifth of all overseas players

1966–7 Third tour by West Indies to India (captain, G. S. Sobers): won two Tests, and drew the other. From now on the Madras Chepauk ground was resumed for Tests. An Australian schoolboys' team visited India, the first representative schools team to do so from Australia. They won one, lost one, drew two of the five representative matches against All India schools, and the fifth had to be abandoned. The Vizzy Zonal Trophy instituted for inter-zonal University competition. B. S. Chandrasekhar took 85 wickets in the season, the record 'bag' in indisputably first-class cricket in India. The Cricket Club of India sent a team to tour Thailand, Hong Kong, Malaysia, Singapore and Australia, all being new ground for an Indian club tour, and the first four countries new to any Indian team

1967 Seventh tour to the U.K. by India (captain Nawab of Pataudi, jun.): lost all three Tests. The team made the record Test score for India in England of 510 at Headingley. It also visited East Africa, the third Indian team to do so, and the first official one, and beat Combined East Africa. A representative Indian schools team toured the U.K. for the first time

1967–8 The second Indian tour to Australia – it went on to New Zealand and was the first to go there (q.v. those countries). The Hyderabad Blues visited Hong Kong, Malaysia and Ceylon

1965–6 Zafar Altaf (268) and Majid Jehangir (241) made 346 runs for the fourth wicket for Lahore Greens *v.* Bahawalpur at Lahore, while Shakoor Ahmed (150*) and Pervez Sajjad (35) made 144 for the last wicket for Lahore Greens *v.* Karachi Blues at Karachi, both records for those wickets in Pakistani first-class cricket. Matting wickets forbidden in Ayub Trophy matches from now on

1966 First official *Cricket Annual* issued by the Board of Control for Cricket in Pakistan

1966–7 Second tour by Ceylon to Pakistan (captain, M. H. Tissera): lost all three unofficial Tests. Fourth MCC tour – 'Under 25' (captain, J. M. Brearley): drew three unofficial Tests. Punjab University made 906 *v.* Sind University, the record University score in Pakistan but not first-class

1967 Third tour to U.K. by Pakistan (captain, Hanif Mohammed): lost two and drew one Test. Asif Iqbal (146) and Intikhab Alam (51) put on 190 for the ninth wicket in the third Test at the Oval, the record partnership for that wicket in Test and Pakistani first-class cricket. Majid Jehangir hit thirteen sixes in his innings of 147 against Glamorgan at Swansea, the record number of sixes in an innings in Pakistani first-class cricket. Pakistan made 456 for 6 wickets *v.* Somerset at Taunton, the record by Pakistan in England

1966 The first schoolboy tour to East Africa (and the first by any team to Ethiopia and the Sudan) undertaken by a team of Australian schoolboys, led by W. A. Oldfield. Seventh English team to Argentina, the Druids (made up of former English public-school-boys)

1967 The sixth MCC tour to Canada (captain, D. R. W. Silk): beat Canada in a three-day match. In South Slesvig, the Husum C.C. formed amongst the Danish minority to encourage schoolboy cricket. This led to an indoor cricket tournament in a large sports hall in Flensborg, also in South Slesvig, in the winter of 1968–9, possibly the first organized indoor cricket matches in the world

1967–8 The Lima Cricket and Football Club became the first team from Peru to tour Argentina

1968 The Canadian Shield inaugurated for Canadian inter-provincial competition along Australian Sheffield Shield lines. Stockholm C.C. toured to Holland. The first representative U.S.A. team toured the U.K. Zambia now entered the East African international tournament: in the series in Nairobi, A. Lakhani made 102 and 161* for Kenya *v.* Tanzania, believed to be the first time this feat had been performed in any class of cricket in East Africa. Though not beating the Danish record of 252*, the seventeen-year-old Lars Hansen made a remarkable performance when scoring 236* and followed it up by taking 5–20 and 8–16 (including the hat-trick) in the same match, in a junior game for Svanholm *v.* Ringsted

1968 Canada admitted as an Associate Member of the International Cricket Conference. MCC tour to South Africa cancelled. A representative U.S.A. team toured England – not first-class. Welsh Cricket Association formed

1969 The first meeting of the Cricket Council, the new controlling body for all cricket in England. Inauguration of a limited-over Sunday afternoon county league – the Players County League, so-called because it was sponsored by the tobacco firm of John Player: first winners, Lancashire. Australian pattern short white coats adopted by umpires in England. In some respects this was the worst season for very many years; for example the leading wicket-taker captured only 109 wickets, the lowest such figure for a century, and the highest team total was 451 for 8 wickets declared, the lowest such total since 1878. Hong Kong and Gibraltar admitted as Associate Members of the International Cricket Conference

1969–70 First English women's cricket team to the West Indies (Jamaica)

1970 In an attempt to dissuade the English cricket authorities from proceeding with the proposed South African tour, the month of January saw fourteen first-class cricket grounds the objects of attention by demonstrators. As a result the tour was curtailed from twenty-eight to twelve matches, to be played on a maximum of seven different grounds. The tour was in the end cancelled. The Tests were replaced by a series of five unofficial representative games between England and The Rest of the World (captain, G. S. Sobers) who won the series 4–1

1968 25th Australians to England (captain, W. M. Lawry), won one, lost one and drew three Tests

1968–9 World record for runs in an over set up by H. Morley when he scored 62, including nine sixes and two fours (there were four no-balls) off R. Grubb in a Queensland country match. Fourth tour by West Indies to Australia (captain, G. S. Sobers), won one, drew one and lost three Tests. During this tour West Indies made 616 *v.* Australia at Adelaide, the record by a West Indian team in Australia. K. D. Walters performed the feat of scoring a double century and a century in the same Test, 242 and 103 at Sydney. Western Australia made her record score of 615 for 5 wickets declared *v.* Queensland at Brisbane. A representative team of All-India schoolboys toured Australia. Fifth cricket magazine started in Australia – *Australian Cricket*, monthly in the season, editor, Eric Beecher. H. B. Taber caught nine and stumped three for New South Wales *v.* South Australia adding his name to that of D. Tallon (1938–9) in equalling the 1868 world first-class record. Fourth tour by English women to Australia: drew three Tests

1969–70 First inter-State knock-out competition

1970–1 For the first time six Tests have been scheduled for one series. First Test match ever to be played at Perth, on the W.A.C.A. ground, is in the itinerary. The first issue of a fully comprehensive annual edited by Eric Beecher, *Australian Cricket Yearbook*

'*1969. Australian pattern short white coats adopted by umpires in England*'

1968 K. C. Bland was refused entry to Great Britain for a series of cricket matches as he is a Rhodesian. The MCC refused to play in Rhodesia on Government advice. The MCC tour to South Africa was later cancelled owing to the refusal by the South African Government to allow B. L. d'Oliveira to come with the team – he being by then a British subject though Cape coloured by origin

1968–9 R. G. Pollock playing for Eastern Province became the first South African cricketer to make 1,000 runs in the first-class season in purely domestic cricket. Playing in eight matches he made 1,043 runs for an average of 86·92. His highest score was 196 and he had only two innings under 40. Border made its record score of 470 *v.* Transvaal 'B'. A visit by an English women's team *en route* to Australia was cancelled at the insistence of the British government owing to the D'Oliveira affair.

1969 Unofficial white-only South African side, organized by W. Isaacs, toured British Isles and encountered many demonstrations (in Ireland as well as England) which included damage to pitches and 'sit-downs'

1969–70 Eighth Australian tour to South Africa (captain, W. M. Lawry). South Africa won all four Tests, the first time Australia had ever lost four Tests when on tour. South Africa made 622 for 9 wickets declared in the second Test at Kingsmead, Durban, the record South African Test score. R. G. Pollock made 274, the record South African individual Test score and the record South African individual score against a touring team. B. A. Richards made 1,103 runs, the record aggregate for a season by a South African in South Africa.

1968 G. S. Sobers became the first professional West Indian cricketer to captain an English county – Nottinghamshire. The record first-wicket partnership in the West Indies of 398 by B. A. Davis (189) and M. C. Carew (201*) in a senior club match in Trinidad, at Queen's Park *v.* Maple

1968–9 Fourth tour to Australia and New Zealand (q.v.). Third Shell Shield tournament – won by Jamaica. First matches Barbados *v.* Leeward Islands, Leeward Islands *v.* Guyana and Windward Islands *v.* Jamaica. Sir Learie Constantine created a life peer

1969 Eleventh tour by West Indies to England (captain, G. S. Sobers): West Indies lost two Tests and drew the third. B. F. Butcher (151) and C. H. Lloyd (201*) made 335 for the fifth wicket *v.* Glamorgan at Swansea, the record for that wicket by West Indians. Barbados (captain, S. M. Nurse) made a short tour to England, with some first-class matches. With this tour, South Africa is now the only first-class country from which a domestic competing team has *not* toured abroad

1969–70 Australian schoolboys toured the West Indies. An English women's team toured Jamaica. Fourth Shell Shield won by Trinidad **1970** The first issue of a fully comprehensive annual, edited by Tony Cozier, *The West Indian Cricket Annual*. A West Indian Youth team, and also Jamaica toured England. Jamaica also did so, with some first-class matches

1968–9 Fourth tour by West Indies (captain, G. S. Sobers): New Zealand won the second Test, to draw the series, having lost the first: the third was drawn. Sunday first-class cricket inaugurated. Fourth tour by English women who won two Tests and drew one. The record number of first-class centuries in a season was scored – twenty-seven

1968–9 A proposed MCC tour to India fell through as the Indian Government would not permit the remittance of the £20,000 guarantee demanded. The Indian schoolboys who visited Australia also visited Singapore

1969 Seventh tour by New Zealand to England and drew one; also visited Pakistan and India (q.v. those countries). New Zealand won a Test series v. Pakistan for the first time

1969–70 Fifth official tour by New Zealand to Australia (captain, G. T. Dowling): no Tests played but first-class matches. New Zealand took part with the Australian States in a knock-out competition and won easily. Fourteenth official tour by Australians (captain, S. C. Trimble): no official Test played. The three unofficial Tests were drawn. The final Hawke Cup challenge match this season was between Southland and Northland, the first time teams from these minor associations at the extreme opposite ends of the country had met: Southland won

1970 Unofficial New Zealand tour to Chile, Argentina, Brazil, Peru, Colombia, Venezuela, lesser West Indian islands, Lisbon, Gibraltar, U.K., Bermuda and U.S.A. In Colombia, they played at what must be the highest altitude ever to have seen international cricket – Bogota, over 8,500 feet

1969–70 After touring England, New Zealand paid her third visit to India (captain, G. T. Dowling): the series was left drawn, each country winning one Test and the third left unfinished owing to rain and riots. Two new Test venues were scheduled, one at Ahmedabad on the Vallabhai Patel ground had to be moved to Bombay owing to civil disturbances, but the other took place at Nagpur on the Vidharba C.A. ground. Fourth official tour by Australia (captain, W. M. Lawry): won three Tests, lost one and drew one. Bombay won the Ranji Trophy for the twelfth successive time, the longest winning run in any first-class competition. A proposed visit by an MCC team was turned down on instructions from the Indian Government owing to the MCC's intention, at that time, to proceed with the tour by South Africa in 1970

1968–9 Fifth MCC tour to Pakistan (captain, M. C. Cowdrey): two Tests drawn and the last abandoned and therewith the tour, owing to political riots on the Karachi ground. First English schools visit to Pakistan – a Surrey and Middlesex schools team who lost two and drew one of the representative matches against Pakistan under-19 teams. Projected tours by West Indies and Australia to Pakistan at the end of 1969 turned down as each country demanded too high a guarantee. Salahuddin (256) and Zaheer Abbas (197) made the Pakistani sixth-wicket partnership record of 353 for Karachi *v.* East Pakistan Sports Federation at Karachi. Aftab Alam (154) and Wasim Bari (92) made the Pakistani eighth-wicket partnership record of 205 for Karachi *v.* Khairpur at Karachi

1969 A P.I.A. team toured Ireland (captain, Hanif Mohammed)

1969–70 After touring the U.K., New Zealand made her third tour to Pakistan (captain, G. T. Dowling): New Zealand won the only completed match of the series, the other two being left drawn. In each case they had been interfered with by riots which may have prevented a result being reached. In the Qaid-i-Azam trophy, Shahid Mahmood, playing for Karachi Whites *v.* Khairpur at Karachi National Stadium, took all 10 wickets for 58 in the innings, the first time this had been performed in first-class cricket in Pakistan. Ahad Khan took 16 wickets for 57 runs in a club match in West Pakistan, the greatest number of wickets in a match by a Pakistani bowler (he took 10 for 45 in the first innings). Arshad Parvez (396*) and Usman (236*) playing for Government College, Sargodha against Islamia College, Chiniot added 599 unbroken for the third wicket, the record Pakistani partnership for any wicket and the fourth highest partnership in the world

1970 Pakistan cancelled a tour to England by a Pakistan Under 25 team on account of the MCC's then attitude to the intended tour by South Africa

1968–9 The match between MCC and Ceylon was left drawn, the first of six three-day games between Ceylon and English teams not to have been lost by Ceylon

1969 Bermuda made a brief tour to Holland and Denmark. A London schools team toured East Africa. An official British Columbia Cricket Association team toured the U.K., playing club teams for the most part. Canada thus joined the list of countries from which competitors in the top level domestic competition have toured abroad. First three-day match between official Australian team and Ceylon: drawn

1969–70 In the first four-day unofficial Test played by Ceylon against MCC, Ceylon lost. The MCC team (captain, A. R. Lewis) was touring Ceylon, Thailand, Malaysia, Singapore and Hong Kong: the earlier part of the tour to Kenya, Uganda and Zambia was cancelled, partly for political reasons (by the Kenya and Uganda authorities) arising out of the projected tour by South Africa to England in 1970

1970 First matches Holland *v.* Ireland and Ireland *v.* Denmark (the latter was Denmark's first three-day match). Tour of East Africa by Cricket Club of India (captain, Hanumant Singh) programme included six three-day matches

Appendix III

DATES OF FIRST MATCHES BY ENGLISH COUNTIES

The map on p. 30 shows the spread of cricket out of the south-east by means of the dates when cricket is first known to have been played *in* each county. Appendices I and II show when the first known county cricket club or similar organization was set up in each county, and also the date of formation of the present club (the Index shows on which page each county will be found).

The table below shows the earliest known date *for a match by* each county: these dates are generally years before a county club was set up, often generations before, and in nine cases, over a century before.

Bedfordshire	1741	Huntingdonshire	1813
Berkshire	1769	Kent	1709§
Buckinghamshire	1741	Lancashire	1849
Cambridgeshire	1813	Leicestershire	1791
Cheshire	1818	Lincolnshire	1828
Cornwall	1813†	Middlesex	1730
Cumberland	1853	Norfolk	1764
Derbyshire	1870	Northamptonshire	1741
Devon	1824†	Northumberland	1834†
Dorset	1845	Nottinghamshire	1798
Durham	1853	Oxfordshire	1779
Essex	1737	Rutland	1814
Gloucestershire	1839	Shropshire	1818
Hampshire	1766	Somerset	1798
Herefordshire	1836†	Staffordshire	1846
Hertfordshire	1749	Suffolk	1764

Surrey	1709§	Wiltshire	1798
Sussex	1728	Worcestershire	1844
Warwickshire	1826‡§	Yorkshire	1798§
Westmorland	1835		

Of the Welsh counties which have played in the first-class or Minor counties championships, cricket was first played by each as follows:

| Carmarthenshire | 1852† | Glamorganshire | 1861‡ |
| Denbighshire | 1864 | Monmouthshire | 1823† |

† In these cases the date is inferred from the date of formation of a county cricket club: the first known date of a match being a few years later.

‡ Possibly 1860.

§ There is dispute about the status of the teams in these cases.

Books Consulted

This is not a bibliography of cricket: not a catalogue of the author's own books; nor a list of recommended literature on the game; nor is it exhaustive. Any history of this nature must be the result of the unconscious distillation in an author's mind of hundreds or even thousands of publications on the game of vastly differing types. To list all would be impossible: what is here presented is a summary of those works which have had the greatest influence on the author.

Readers of *The Cricket Quarterly* will perceive that it has been heavily drawn upon not only for the author's own contributions therein, but also for those of JOHN GOULSTONE, PETER WYNNE-THOMAS and KEITH WARSOP to name only a few.

Other works have been R. S. RAIT KERR'S *The Laws of Cricket* (1950), a seminal and important work not yet enough appreciated by those who study and write on the game's history; the same may be said about G. B. BUCKLEY'S *Fresh Light on 18th-century Cricket* (1935) and *Fresh Light on Pre-Victorian Cricket* (1937), though published over thirty years ago, as well as his unpublished 'Cricket Notices', which have been vital. P. F. THOMAS ('H.P.-T.') with his six pamphlets collectively entitled *Old English Cricket* (1923–9) was next in importance. F. S. ASHLEY-COOPER wrote much, and many items are referred to in the text: most important have been his *Lord's and the MCC*, written with LORD HARRIS, and his *Cricket 1742–1751* which appeared serially in the excellent magazine *Cricket* in 1900 (much else has been dug out of its thirty-three volumes). M. J. LUCKINS'S *History of South African Cricket* down to 1914 has been valuable: so also J. A. LESTER'S *Century of Philadelphian Cricket* (1951), and both volumes of T. W. REESE'S *New Zealand Cricket* (1927, 1936). Amongst other periodicals *The American Cricketer* has been drawn upon and also many issues of *The Cricketer* to 1962. Countless long runs of county cricket annuals, and overseas cricket association annuals, as well as copies of old overseas annuals, *Wisden* and the three series of Lillywhite annuals, have also gone towards the mash here distilled: and, too, countless other works of biography or contemporary comment, on tours or other matters. And HAYGARTH'S *Scores & Biographies* (1862) has also played its part, but not without the invaluable amendments supplied by Buckley (1925), who also supplied similar amendments to the two important works by H. T. WAGHORN, *Cricket Scores* (1899) and *The Dawn of Cricket* (1906). Other works are noted in the text.

Anyone else, with the same material, could have written the same work: provided he was free from prejudice as to what the game is about, as well as from prejudices about what has been written, by way of history, or myth, in the past. It is, however, necessary to say that very little that has been published in the last ten years, other than in *The Cricket Quarterly* or on current events, has been used in the text or appendices of this book.

Index

BY JOHN McILWAINE

NOTE ON THE INDEX

Abbreviations used are as follows:

C.A. – Cricket Association
C.C. – Cricket Club
C.U. – Cricket Union
f.c. – first-class; in first-class cricket

For references to dates of formation of clubs and other organizations, see FORMATION OF ...; for references to competitions, tournaments, etc., see COMPETITIONS; for references to cricket grounds, see GROUNDS. A few organizations and competitions also receive an individual entry.

A performance recorded in the Appendices has normally been indexed under the feat as such, rather than under the player or team performing it. Major entries will be found under:

ALL-ROUND CRICKET	TEN WICKETS IN INNINGS
AGGREGATES, INDIVIDUAL	TOTALS, TEAM
CENTURY; CENTURIES	WICKET PARTNERSHIPS
INNINGS, HIGHEST INDIVIDUAL	WICKETS IN MATCH
MATCH AGGREGATES	WICKETS WITH CONSECUTIVE BALLS

See also references given under 'Batting' and 'Bowling' to further headings.

When the first performance of a feat occurred at a high level, for example, the first recorded total over 400 being in fact over 500, it has normally been entered at the higher level only, and not duplicated at all the lower levels.

First matches played by English counties have not been included in the Index, since they are all set out in Appendix III, 382–3.

Personal names occurring in the Appendices have been indexed very selectively. Only the better known figures, thought likely to be sought for by name, have been included.

Abel, R., 297, 306, 310

Admission charges: 51; first recorded, 264; first levied in Australia, 276

Afghanistan: first reference to cricket, 98, 272

Aggregates, individual (batting)

in career: probable record by any player in all cricket (W. G. Grace), 110–11

in consecutive innings: over 1000 runs in 3 innings, 364; in 4 innings in f.c. cricket, 336; in first 8 innings of f.c. career, 332; other notable performances, 284, 326

in month: 1000 runs or over, first recorded, 284; outside England, 336; probable record aggregate for calendar month outside Australia and England, 341

in season: 1000 runs or over, first recorded, 280; in Australia, 286; in Australia f.c., 306; in Australian domestic f.c., 332

in England, 280; by Australian, 129, 290; by West Indian, 329

in Holland, 343

in India f.c., 334; by Indian in India f.c., 352

in Kenya, 339

in New Zealand, 308

in North America (and U.S.A.), 291

in Canada, 295

in Pakistan, 369

in South Africa, 293; in South Africa f.c., 321; by South African in South Africa f.c., 371; in South African domestic f.c., 379

in West Indies, 293; in West Indies f.c., 341; by West Indian in West Indies f.c., 363

in Barbados, 325

in Guyana, 293

in Jamaica, 349

1000 runs or over, against touring team, first and only record in England, 354

before end of May in England, first recorded, 302; by non-Englishman, 340

before end of December in Australia, first recorded, 336; by non-Australian, 344; in two successive seasons, 370

earliest date for reaching total, in England, 348; in Australia, 366; overseas players reaching total in England before English players, 290, 324, 340, 348, 354

in each of four different countries, first recorded, 367

in six successive seasons in Australia f.c., 344

in South Africa f.c., only batsmen to perform feat twice, 321

most in career in Australia f.c., 354

without dismissal, 332

2000 runs or over, first recorded, 284

in Australia, 306

in England f.c., 284; by Australian, 310; by Indian, 356; by New Zealander, 356; by Pakistani, 369; by West Indian, 345

3000 runs or over, first recorded f.c., 306

in Australia, all matches, 336

4000 runs or over: in England, 324, 344

Record: in Argentina, 305

in Australia f.c., 336; by Englishman and any tourist, 336; by South African, 320; in Tasmania, 344

in Ceylon, 327

in Denmark, 353

in England, f.c., 354; progressive record, 267, 271, 278, 280, 284, 306, 310, 316, 354

in Fiji, 335

in Holland, 347

in India, f.c., 372

in Ireland, 292

in Kenya, 351

in New Zealand, f.c., 376

in North America (and U.S.A.), 305; in Canada, 331

in South Africa f.c., 367; by South African in South Africa f.c., 379

in West Indies f.c., 341; by West Indian in West Indies f.c., 363

in club cricket, 344

by schoolboy in South Africa, 367

in Test series: record, 340; by wicket-keeper, 375

in twelve months' play: notable instances, 340

Aggregates, individual (bowling)

in season: 100 or over, first recorded, 271 (and see 82)

in Australia, 278; in Australia f.c., 292

in Denmark, 351

in England, 271 (and see 82)

in Holland, 315

in Kenya, 339

in North America (and Canada), 289

in U.S.A., 291

in South Africa f.c., 325; by Australian, 363

in West Indies, 307

200 or over, first recorded, 272

in Ceylon, 309

in England, 272; by Australian, 290

300 or over, first recorded, f.c., 336

400 or over, in England, 276

Highest: in Australia, 292; other notable aggregates, 292

in Ceylon, 323

in Denmark, 361

in England f.c., 336; progressive record, 268, 271, 272, 282, 288, 292, 302, 336; by touring player, 292; by Australian, 292; by South African, 325

in India f.c., 334, 376

in New Zealand f.c., 314; by New Zealander in New Zealand f.c., 314; in Christchurch senior club cricket, 338; in Wellington senior club cricket, 330

in North America (and U.S.A.), 319

in Canada, 305

in South Africa f.c., 363; by South African in South Africa f.c., 367

in West Indies f.c., 311; by West Indian in

Aggregates, Highest – *contd.*
 West Indies f.c., 307
 other notable aggregates, 297, 307, 311
Alberta: first reference to cricket, 291
Alcock, C. W., 119
Aleppo: site of first certain reference to Englishmen playing cricket abroad, 47, 50, 72, 262
Alexander, F. C. M., 364, 365
Alimuddin, 365, 369
All England XI; formation, history and derivatives, 111, 273
All-round cricket
 in career: 10,000 runs and 1,000 wickets in f.c. cricket; first recorded by Australian, 129
  2,000 runs and 200 wickets in Tests; first recorded, 370
 in match: century and hat-trick in same match; first and only record by Australian, f.c., 290
  by West Indian f.c., 337
  other notable occurrences, 320, 377
 century and ten wickets in innings in same match, first recorded, 278
  in Australia, 300
  in England, 278
  in India, 330
  in New Zealand, 350
  in North America, 353
  in South Africa, 303
 200 and ten wickets in innings in Ceylon, 369
  other notable occurrences, 358
 other notable all-round performances in match, 129, 296, 320, 377
 in season: 1,000 runs and 50 wickets
  in Australia f.c., only instances, 367, 371
  in South Africa f.c., first recorded by touring player, 360
 1,000 runs and 100 wickets
  first recorded in f.c. cricket, 284
  in Australian first grade cricket, 332
  in Ceylon, 319
  in England f.c., 284; by West Indian (in all matches), 317; (in f.c. matches), 337
  in Kenya, 339
  in North America (Philadelphia cricket), 299
  in Canada, 309
  in South Africa, by non-white cricketer, 359
  by schoolboy cricketer in England, 336
  by wicket-keeper, 336
  by woman player, 336
  four consecutive seasons in Australian schools cricket, 316
  other notable occurrences, 309, 322, 326
 2,000 runs and 200 wickets: first and only record in f.c. cricket, 316
 two successive seasons in Ireland, 302
 3,000 runs and 200 wickets, 342
 3,000 runs and 300 wickets, 280
 4,000 runs and 200 wickets, 316
Allen, G. O. B., 340, 344, 346, 355

Altham, H. S., 190
Amarnath, L., 354, 356
Amateurs: effects of the 'amateur approach' to the game, 168–170; 'shamateurism', 112; status of amateurs defined by M.C.C., 112, 286; distinction between amateur and professional abolished, 116, 366; social changes restrict opportunities of amateur in f.c. cricket, 144, 207; proposals to enable amateurs to return to f.c. cricket, 254
 in Australia, 219; in South Africa, 195, 215; in U.S.A., effect of American concept of cricket as 'amateur' game, 120–1, 160
 see also Country house cricket; Professionals; Social factors and cricket
Amateur touring clubs: formation of most notable examples, 93, 273
American Cricketer, 121, 159, 183, 287
Ames, L. E. G., 245, 246, 336, 340
Antigua: formation of first C.C., 272
Anville Bourguignon, H. F. d' *dit* Gravelot, *see* Gravelot
Apartheid and cricket, *see* Colour prejudice and cricket; South Africa: non-white cricket
Archives de France, 30
Argentina, 85, 97–8, 123–4, 156, 184–5, 232, plate 72
 first reference, 268; formation of Buenos Aires C.C., 98, 271, of Argentine Cricket Championship Committee (later Argentina C.A.), 156, 309; establishment of competitive cricket in Buenos Aires, 156
 first representative match *v.* South American state, 283; *v.* overseas touring team, 327; first match *v.* Brazil, 331; *v.* Chile, 331; *v.* Uruguay, 283; results of matches *v.* South American states, 331
 first tour by team from Argentina to England, 335
 first tour to Argentina by team from Brazil, 295; by M.C.C., 156, 327; by team from New Zealand, 380; by team from Peru, 377
Armed services: and role in spreading cricket abroad, 72, 73, 202; War Office decision to provide cricket grounds for all barracks in U.K., 87; abandonment of cricket by Pakistan services, 227; decline in Forces cricket in England, 208
Armstrong, W. W., 310, 312, 318, 322, 328, 334
'Ashes': tradition established, 125, 288; position regarding in 1882–3 series, 126, 290; later attitudes towards, 126–7
Ashley-Cooper, F. S., 52, 59, 63, 66, 159, 299
Asif Iqbal, 227, 377
Atkinson, D., 363, 364
Attewell, E., 305
Auckland, 154, 221; first reference to cricket, 273; formation of C.A., 291
 first match *v.* Canterbury, 285; *v.* Otago, 285; *v.* Wellington, 279
Austin, H. B. G., 307, 317, 329
Australia: 73, 74, 75, 85, 98–9, 118, 125–32, 138, 144, 152–4, 173, 175, 186–90, 203, 217–20, 239,

o*

Grounds – *contd.*
  in West Indies
    Bourda Ground, Georgetown; occupied by Georgetown C.C., 291; first Test, 341
    Guaracara Park, Pointe-à-Pierre, Trinidad; first used for game by Trinidad *v.* touring team, 355
    Kensington Oval, Bridgetown; occupied by Pickwick C.C., 289; first Test, 341; plate 65
    Sabina Park, Kingston, plate 64; occupied by Kingston C.C., 289; first Test, 341
    St Clair (Queen's Park) Oval, Port-of-Spain; occupied by Queen's Park C.C., 307; first Test, 341
  in other countries
    Germantown C.C. Ground, Manheim, plate 34
    Martindale, Argentina, plate 72
    Merion C.C. Ground, Haverford, plates 18, 33
Grout, A. T. W., 366
Guildford: first definite reference to cricket in England, 29, 36, 45, 261, plate 2
Gunasekara, C. H., 346
Gupte, S. P., 360
Guyana, 123, 157, 184, 228; first reference to cricket, 272; first match *v.* Barbados, 281, (return, 281); *v.* Jamaica, 307, (return, 359); *v.* Leeward Islands, 379; *v.* Trinidad, 283, (return, 287); *v.* Windward Islands, 359

Hadlee, W. A., 356
Haigh, S., 333
Halifax Cup (Philadelphia); inauguration and details of winners, 285
Hall, W. W., 73, 228
Halliwell, A. E., 301
Hambledon C.C.: formation, 55, 265; history, 57–64; no evidence for having law-giving authority, 57–8
Hammond, W. R., 48, 179, 243–4, 245, 321, 336, 349, 354, 356
Hampshire, 95, 113, 114; first reference to a cricket match, 264; formation of first county club, 274; of present county club, 274; recognized as f.c., 140, 300
Handled ball: dismissal first recorded, 268; only occurrence in Tests, 363
Hanif Mohammed, 226, 361, 365, 369, 370, 372, 373, 377, 381
Harris, D., 76–7, 78
Harris, G. R. C. *4th Baron*, 66, 130, 131, 133, 169, 199, 286, 287
Harrow School: depiction of cricket at, 265; first match *v.* Eton, 268; significance of declining attendance at Eton *v.* Harrow match, 247–9
Harvey, R. N., 243
Hassett, A. L., 352, 354, 358, 359
Hat-trick, *see* Wickets with consecutive balls
Haverford College, 85, 97, 121, 159, 183; cricket introduced, 271; first tour to England, 309

Hawaii, 156, 223; first reference to cricket, 277
Hawke, M. B. *7th Baron*, 133, 156, 157, 299, 303, 304, 305, 306, 307, 312, 314, 315, 320, 327
Hawke Cup (New Zealand): inauguration and details of winners, 154, 322; longest tenure of trophy, 372
Hawkes Bay, 154; formation of C.A., 291; member of Central Districts C.A., 360
Haygarth, A., 66, 73, 82, 88, 117, 140, 278
Hayman, F., 263
Hayward, T., 142, 278, 282, 306, 310, 316
Hazare, V. S., 225, 350, 352, 356, 359, 360, 376
Headley, G. A., 184, 228, 341, 345, 353
Hearne, J. T., 151
Heathcote Williams Shield (New Zealand Schools): inauguration and details of winners, 155, 185, 322
Heine, P. S., 359
Hendren, E., 184, 310, 336, 341
Hendricks, T., 149, 301
Herefordshire: first reference to cricket, 270; formation of county club, 271
Hertfordshire, first reference to cricket, 263; formation of first county club, 271; of present county club, 271
Hill, C., 128, 152, 153, 187, 302, 306, 310, 320
Hindus (Bombay): first match *v.* Europeans, 318; *v.* Parsis, 318
Hirst, G. H., 129, 167, 316
Hit: longest known, 276; in Australia, 340; in England, 276; in New Zealand, 291
Hoad, E. L. G., 345
Hobbs, *Sir* J. B., 48, 141–2, 171, 186, 189, 310, 321, 332, plates 35 to 44
Hofmeyr, J. H., 303
Holland, 37, 120, 148, 195, 211, plates 19, 57; first reference to cricket, 273; formation of first known C.C., 277; of Dutch C.A., 291; joins I.C.C., 374
  first representative match by Dutch team, 299; first match *v.* Belgium, 319; *v.* Denmark, 365; *v.* Ireland, 381
  first tour by team from Holland to England, 120, 305, (first by Dutch Youth team, 361)
  first tour to Holland by team from Australia, 358; from Bermuda, 381; from England, 289, (first by M.C.C., 148, 310); from New Zealand, 372; from South Africa, 195, 347; by Stockholm C.C., 377; by team from West Indies, 365
Holmes, P., 333, 340
Hong Kong, 98, 132, 152, 191, 203, 223, 242, 376; first reference to cricket, 272; formation of Hong Kong C.C., 277; joins I.C.C., 378
  matches *v.* Shanghai, Singapore and Malaysia, 132, 281, 357
  first tour to Hong Kong by team from Australia, 366; from India, 376; by M.C.C., 374; by team from New Zealand, 372
Hope, – (of Amsterdam), 71–2, 267, plate 10
Hordern, H. V., 319, 321
Hornby, A. H., 310

Massie, H. H., 290
Match aggregates
BY ONE TEAM
highest in world, 356
lowest in world f.c., 367; in important match,
268
in India f.c., 368
in Pakistan f.c., 373
in South Africa f.c., 367
BY BOTH TEAMS
1000 runs or over; first recorded, 82, 269
in Australia, 284; in Australia f.c., 288
in England, 82, 269
in West Indies f.c., 303
2000 runs or over; first recorded, 352
highest recorded; in world, 356; progressive
record, 302, 306, 320, 332, 349, 352, 356
in Argentina, 357
in Australia, 332
in Ceylon, 327
in Egypt, 351
in England, 5 day match, 354; 4 day match,
340; 3 day match, 334; progressive
record, 269, 280, 282, 286, 296, 302, 310,
312, 334
in India, 356
in New Zealand, 330, 334
in Pakistan, 373
in South Africa, 349; in Currie Cup, 333
in West Indies, 329; in West Indies f.c.,
341; in West Indies domestic f.c., 333
in Tests, 349
other notable occurrences, 285, 297, 323, 349,
357
lowest recorded; in f.c. cricket, 286
in England f.c., 286
in New Zealand f.c., 281
other notable occurrences, 286, 345
Match attendances, 110, 177; in 18th century, 265;
at single wicket matches, 92; at Eton v. Harrow,
248; in Australia, 218; in Philadelphia, 159
world record for day's play, 366
see also Admission charges
Match duration: in 18th century, 74; first recorded
2 day fixture, 263; first match known to last 2
days, 263; 2 day matches prevail, 265; first
recorded 3 day fixture, 265; first match known to
last 5 days (with rain), 265; first match known
to last 4 days (without interruption), 265; 3 day
matches prevail, 266; first recorded 4 day fixture,
266; first match known to last 5 days (without
interruption), 266; first match known to last 6 days,
267; first known 5 day fixture, 267; first known
6 day fixture, 354; first f.c. match to last more than
5 days, 297; first f.c. match to last 7 days, 297, (in
South Africa, 297; in West Indies, 329; in West
Indies f.c., 337); first f.c. match to last 8 days,
332; to last 9 days, 333; to last 10 days, 349
experiments with 2 day county championship
matches, 175, 328; 2 day f.c. fixtures in South
Africa, 329; in New Zealand, 346

regulations for Currie Cup matches, 329; for
Plunket Shield matches, 338, 360; for Ranji
Trophy matches, 346; for Regional Tournament (West Indies) matches, 363; for Sheffield
Shield matches, 300, 336, 340
'play-to-a-finish' matches, 74, 186, 242; in
Sheffield Shield, 300; in Tests, 292, 316, 324
see also Fixtures; Hours of play
Match involving odds: first match, eleven v.
twenty-two, 265; only recorded instance of
county giving odds to England, 267
Match played on two different grounds: only
known fixture in f.c. cricket, 304
Matches: unusual locations; at over 8,500 feet
altitude, 380; in cathedral, plate 12; on ice, 75
see also Indoor cricket
Matting pitches: in Australia, 234; in Denmark,
234; in East Africa, 233; in Holland, 234; in
India, 233–4; in North America, 233; in
Pakistan, 233–4, 369, 377; in South Africa, 195,
233; in West Indies, 158, 233, 359
May, P. B. H., 168, 243, 362, 363, 364, 367
Melbourne C.C., 132; formation, 99, 271; estab-
lished on Richmond Paddock, 276; organizes
Australian tour to England, 292; first tour to
New Zealand, 310
Melville, A., 355
Merchant, V. M., 225, 308, 350, 352
Merritt, W. E., 185, 223, 338
Metrication and cricket, 256
Mexico: formation of first known C.C., 98, 271
Middlesex, 95, 114, 117; first reference to cricket,
262; formation of county club, 280
Midwinter, W. E., 130, 282, 286, 288
Milburn, C., 219
Miller, K. R., 243
Minor Counties Championship, 140; inauguration
and details of leading winners, 302; most con-
secutive wins, 306
Minshull, J., 56, 57, 62, 67, 265
Mistri, K. M., 151, 308, 318
Mitcham Green, plate 25; 17th century reference to
cricket, 262
Mitchell, B., 355
Mitchell, F., 305, 313, 325
Modi, R. S., 225, 352, 356
Moody, C. P., 118, 126
Morild, Sv., 361
Morris, A. R., 348, 354
Mowing machines: introduced on cricket grounds,
276
Murdoch, W. L., 126, 131, 286, 288, 290, 296, 310,
370
Mushtaq Mohammed, 369
Mynn, A., 90–2, 96, 103, 274

Natal: first reference to cricket, 272; formation of
C.U., 297
first match v. Border, 307; v. Eastern Province,
297; v. Griqualand West, 297; v. North-East
Transvaal, 355; v. Orange Free State, 317; v.

Natal — *contd.*
Rhodesia, 355; *v.* Transvaal, 301; *v.* Western Province, 297
first tour by team from Natal to East Africa, 359
Nayudu, C. K., 334, 340, 342
Nayudu, C. S., 352
Nazir Ali, S., 342
Nelson (New Zealand), 154; formation of C.A., 285; member of Central Districts C.A., 360
Netherlands, *see* Holland
Nets: practice nets established at Eton, 271-2; at Lords, 280
New-ball legislation: one ball used throughout match, 268; new ball at start of each innings, 69, 268; after 200 runs, 163, 316; after stated number of overs, 237, 316; in Australia, 374
New Caledonia, 223
New South Wales, 127, 131, 153, 186-8; first reference to cricket, 268; first known C.C., 270; formation of C.A., 276-7
first match *v.* Queensland, 280; *v.* South Australia, 296; *v.* Tasmania, 306; *v.* Victoria, 276; *v.* Western Australia, 316
first tour by team from New South Wales to New Zealand, 298, (first official tour, 302); to Tasmania, 284
New York: possible first reference to cricket, 262, plate 3; first certain reference, 264; other 18th century references 264, 266, 267, plate 9
New Zealand, 73, 74, 75, 85, 100, 124-5, 154-5, 173, 175, 185, 203, 220-3, 243, plate 73
first reference to cricket, 73, 85, 271; first fully recorded match, 272; other references to 1850, 272, 273, 274; (for references 1851–1970, *see* Appendix II, column 5, 277 ff); formation of New Zealand Cricket Council, 125, 154, 304; joins I.C.C., 334
first representative match, 304; first Test, 336
first tour by team from New Zealand to Australia, 287, (first by official New Zealand team, 308; by New Zealand Colts, 364); to B.A.O.R., 356; to Bermuda, 372, (first by official New Zealand team, 372); to Canada, 372; to Ceylon, 334; to England, 334; to Holland, 372; to Hong Kong, 372; to India, 364; to Kuwait, 372; to Malaysia, 372; to Samoa, 372; to South Africa, 359, 360; to South America, 380; to U.S.A., 372, (first by official New Zealand team, 372); to West Indies, 380
first tour to New Zealand by team from Australia, 287; from England, 281, (first by M.C.C., 318); from Fiji, 155, 304, (earlier proposal abandoned, 304); from India, 376; by Melbourne C.C., 308; by team from New South Wales, 298, (by official New South Wales team, 304; by New South Wales Colts, 360); from Pakistan, 372; from Queensland, 308; from South Africa, 342; from Tasmania, 291; by Victoria, 334; by team from West Indies, (visit), 342; (tour), 360

Newenden, Kent: site of first probable reference to cricket in England, 29, 261
Newfoundland: last references to cricket, 161
Newman, L. W., 344
Nigeria, 149, 194, 212; formation of Nigerian C.A.s (African and European), 343
first match *v.* Gambia, 373; *v.* Ghana (Gold Coast), 315; *v.* Sierra Leone, 373
first tour by team from Nigeria to England, 358
No-ball: introduced, 269; first penalized, 269
Noble, M. A., 310, 312, 316, 320
Norfolk, 143; first reference to cricket, 264; formation of first county club, 270; of present county club, 270
North *v.* South matches (England): first match, 271; last match, 282
North America, 47-8, 69-70, 75, 85, 96-7, 120-3, 158-61, 173, 182-3, 202, 230-2; first possible reference to cricket, 47, 262, plate 3; first definite reference, in Virginia, 47, 263; in New England, 263; in Georgia, 263; in New York, 264; in Maryland, 264; in Connecticut, 265; *for other references before 1850, see* U.S.A. *(after 1776) and* Canada *(first reference, 1785)*
early versions of cricket in North America, 42, 43, 69-70, 72, 85, 161, 264, 269, plate 4
North-East Transvaal: formation of C.U., 349
first match *v.* Border, 355; *v.* Eastern Province, 363; *v.* Griqualand West, 349; *v.* Natal, 355; *v.* Orange Free State, 349; *v.* Rhodesia, 355; *v.* Transvaal, 249; *v.* Western Province, 349
North Island (New Zealand): first match *v.* South Island, and summarized results of series, 314
Northamptonshire, 95; first reference to cricket, 263; formation of first county club, 270; of present county club, 270; admitted to county championship, 143, 164, 316
Northumberland: first reference to cricket, 265; formation of first county club, 271; of present county club, 271
Nottingham: first match *v.* Sheffield, 265; lacemakers from Nottingham play cricket in France, 83; tour by team from Nottingham to France, 280
Nottinghamshire, 95, 114, 117; first reference to cricket, 265; formation of county club, 272
Nourse, A. D. *Sr*, 329, 345
Nourse, A. D. *Jr.*, 349, 353, 359
Nunes, R. K., 336, 337
Nupen, E. P., 341
Nurse, S. M., 375, 379
Nyren, J., 58, 61 76, 77, 167, 181, 250, 271

Oldest cricketers: playing in f.c. match in South Africa, 345; team of players all over seventy, 263
Oldfield, W. A., 213, 377
O'Neill, N. C., 243
Ontario, 97, 122, 161, 183, 231; first reference to cricket, 270
Orange Free State: formation of C.U., 297
first match *v.* Border, 321; *v.* Eastern Province